Criminal Law

Criminal Law

Alan Birbeck

LLB (LSBU), MSc (Oxon), Barrister, SFHEA
Senior Lecturer in Law, London South Bank
University Barrister
and
Academic Associate Tenant,
Drystone Chambers

Cameron Giles

MLaw PhD (Northumbria), LLM (York),
Barrister, FRSA
Senior Lecturer in Law,
London South Bank University

CILEX | Education

Disclaimer

ISBN: 978-1-911698-53-1
E-ISBN: 978-1-911698-54-8

First paperback edition 2025

Layout by codemantra U.S. LLC

British Library Cataloguing in Publications Data
A catalogue record for this book is available from the British Library

Printed by CILEX Education in the United Kingdom.
CILEX Education
2nd Floor,
The Pinnacle,
Midsummer Boulevard,
Milton Keynes,
MK9 1BP
Cover image: Julian Gazzard/iStock

www.cilex.org.uk

Printed and bound by Mimeo, who are very proud to be a part of the Woodland Trust's Woodland Carbon Capture Scheme via Premier Paper. Mimeo partner with Woodland Carbon because 100% of the money they give is spent on planting deciduous trees in the UK. Papers are from sustainable sources and waste is recycled. Mimeo continue to use only Forest Stewardship Council accredited paper in their printed items.

About the Authors

Alan Birbeck is the Deputy Head of the School of Law and Education and a Senior Lecturer in Law at London South Bank University. He is also Course Leader for Undergraduate Law and Criminology programmes. He is module lead for Undergraduate and Postgraduate Criminal Law and Criminal Advocacy & Evidence. Alan has significant practice experience initially for six years defending suspects in the police station and then over 10 years experience as a practicing criminal barrister defending in London and the South East, and is currently an Academic Associate Tennant at Drystone Chambers.

Alan is a contributing editor of *Archbold Criminal Practice*, the leading criminal practice text used by all Crown Courts in England and Wales. Alan is the sole editor for the chapter on Joint Participation (formerly known as Joint Enterprise). Alan holds an LLB from London South Bank University and an MSc in Criminal Justice and Criminology from the University of Oxford. He is a Senior Fellow of the Higher Education Academy.

Dr Cameron Giles is a Senior Lecturer in Law at London South Bank University, where he is module lead for Sentencing, Crime and Punishment and Tort Law. Cameron has been published in a range of academic books and journals, including the *Journal of Criminal Law* and *Information & Communications Technology Law*, with his research focusing on sexual offending, digital technology and sentencing law. He is the author of the *Tort Law* textbook, published by CILEX.

Cameron is a member of the executive committee of the Association of Law Teachers and an editorial board member of *The Law Teacher: The International Journal of Legal Education*. Cameron holds an MLaw and a PhD from Northumbria University, an LLM in Legal and Political Theory from the University of York, is a barrister (unregistered) and is a Fellow of the Royal Society of Arts.

Guide to the Book

This course book contains a range of features which have been developed to help support your learning and reinforce your understanding. The guided tour below explains how to use these features to get the most from your study.

Aims of this chapter

By the end of this chapter, you will:

- Be able to identify and discuss the categorisation of a range of *actus reus* elements you encounter when looking at various criminal offences.
- Understand how to apply the law of causation in a problem scenario, including understanding the distinction between causation in fact and causation in law.
- Be able to critically evaluate aspects of criminal liability for omissions and the development of the law on causation, including through comparisons with other jurisdictions.

Chapter Aims

At the beginning of each chapter learning objectives are clearly defined so that you understand what it is you are expected to learn before engaging with the chapter content.

Reflective question

One day whilst truanting from school, Ari attempted to climb onto the roof of a public library in his hometown. A large section of the roof consisted of glass panels, which were fragile, and as Ari stepped onto one of these it cracked. Several shards of glass fell and injured Sam, a librarian working in the building below, causing minor wounds to her arm. Ari is charged with assault occasioning actual bodily harm, which can be committed with intent or recklessly. Ari maintains that he did not realise that the glass panels would break and risk injuring anybody below.

Consider whether Ari is likely to be liable for the offence charged.

Reflective Questions

All textbooks contain reflective questions, positioned at key points throughout the text. These allow you to take time to reflect on what you have learnt, ensure that you have understood the concepts, and contextualise your learning.

Activity

Criminal conduct

The offences we discuss in subsequent chapters provide a good foundation for research into your own areas of particular interest. As you begin to explore the scope of criminal law, make a note of offences you have heard about in the past and are interested in. Is there a particular reason why you are interested in these crimes? Ask yourself, do they address particular problematic behaviours, or are the offences themselves open to critique? Do they relate to other areas of law you are familiar with, such as contract or tort law?

Activities

In each chapter you are presented with activities which engage you with the content and help you to develop research skills, explore topics in more depth and consolidate your knowledge.

1.5 Summary

This chapter has introduced criminal law, generally, as well as the criminal law topics explored in this book. We have discussed how to go about beginning to study criminal law and introduced some of the ways in which you will apply your legal knowledge and skills when doing so. The key points to take away from this chapter are:

- Criminal offences are a **public** wrong, which the state responds to through arrest, prosecution and sentencing.

Chapter Summaries

At the end of each chapter the key points are summarised, allowing you to reinforce your understanding before moving on to study the next topic. The summaries can also be used for quick revision.

Terminology alert!

Rebuttable and irrebuttable presumptions

The key difference between the presumptions found in **s75** and **s76** is that where either of the circumstances set out in **s76** are found to apply "it is to be conclusively presumed" that the complainant did not consent and the defendant did not reasonably belief that the complainant was consenting. This means that the presumption is **irrebuttable**, the defendant cannot bring forward evidence to counter the presumption. This contrasts with the rebuttable presumption made when the circumstances found in **s75** apply, where a defendant can challenge the presumption with evidence to the contrary.

Terminology Alerts

Terminology alerts introduce you to commonly used legal terminology.

In the News

A duty to rescue?

There have been repeated calls from members of the public for a duty to rescue to be introduced into UK law. In recent years, there have been several petitions to Parliament on this matter, although these have not yet attracted the level of support necessary for a parliamentary debate.[21] These proposals have been highlighted in articles such as: Asha Patel, "Matthew Schofield: Mum of son who died after attack calls for new law" *BBC News* (21 May 2024).

In the News

News articles which help to illustrate the topics under discussion and provide some real-world context.

Further reading

Cath Crosby, "Gross Negligence Manslaughter by Omission: The Emergence of a Good Samaritan Law?" (2018) *82(2) Journal of Criminal Law 127*

Grant Firkins, "Rethinking Causation in English Criminal Law" (2023) *87(1) Journal of Criminal Law 18*

Andrew Ashworth, "A new generation of omissions offences?" [2018] *Criminal Law Review 354*

Andrew Simester, "Causation in (Criminal) Law" (2017)113(3) *Law Quarterly Review 416*

JJ Child, "Defence of a Basic Voluntary Act Requirement in Criminal Law from Philosophies of Action" (2020) *23(4) New Criminal Law Review 437*

Further reading

Options for further development are highlighted throughout the book.

Preface

Criminal law is a fascinating and central aspect of legal education and training in England and Wales. It sets out a foundation on which many other subjects, including sentencing and penal law, criminal advocacy, evidence and litigation, and international criminal law, build upon. It is also an area which is frequently subject to significant developments, through legislation passed in Parliament and in appellate decisions. Recent years have seen the passage of the **Police, Crime, Sentencing and Courts Act 2022** and the introduction of the **Criminal Justice Bill 2023–24**, which fell at the dissolution of Parliament prior to the 2024 general election.

This text was initially being written during the pre-election period, as well as briefly following the election. Where we discuss proposed reforms and debates, we have attempted to identify issues of longstanding concern, in addition to issues which are likely to arise over the coming years. We have taken the opportunity to incorporate reflective questions on law reform into several key chapters – we hope you find these useful and thought provoking.

This text is intended to provide a grounding both in the application and the evaluation of key aspects of criminal law in England and Wales. We have enjoyed working together on this task, bringing together our respective backgrounds as a criminal barrister and criminal law focused researcher, respectively, as well as our experiences as legal educators at London South Bank University. You will find that each chapter will display our individual idiosyncrasies dependent upon who primarily drafted the chapter (AGB: Chapters 2; 5-7; 9-10; 13-15. CG: Chapters 1; 3-4; 8; 11-12 and 16), demonstrating the different perspectives that can be brought to the study of criminal law.

We have used the neutral citation other than where there is no neutral citation. If students wish to venture further, we recommend either Lexis and Westlaw (search by citation) and to use where available the best available report. In a few specific instances we have referenced individual reports where these would advance a student's understanding.

We aspire to state the law as of Wednesday 01/01/2025. We would welcome constructive comments, feedback or other suggestions from readers and can be contacted by email at birbeca2@lsbu.ac.uk and gilesc4@lsbu.ac.uk.

We are grateful to Edward Stone and colleagues at CILEX for inviting us to write this text and for the copy-editing and production support. We gratefully acknowledge Victoria Weaver and Dr Michael Rodney for proofreading some early draft chapters and their contribution to teaching Criminal Law and Advocacy at LSBU. We would like to thank Margaret Clay and Robert Hodgson of the Inner Temple Library and Rebecca Fong of the LSBU Library. We would also like to thank our colleagues and students at London South Bank University, past and present, as well as our respective families, who have inspired and supported us in our work.

Alan Birbeck (AGB) and Cameron Giles (CG)
April 2025

For Mike Birbeck and Ann Birbeck
Alan Birbeck

For James
Cameron Giles

Contents

Table of Secondary Legislation

Section

Table of Cases

Table of Statutes

Bills

Germany

European Union

International Convention

CHAPTER 1

Introduction to Criminal Law

1.1 Introduction

> The criminal law is not the state's primary tool for the reduction of harms generally. At the most, it shares this useful function with public health agencies, safety inspectors, equipment maintenance and repair departments, regulatory commissions, and like agencies. But the criminal law system is the primary instrumentality for preventing people from intentionally or recklessly harming one another. Acts of *harming* then are the direct objects of the criminal law, not simply states of harm as such.[1]

Criminal law plays a dominant role in our understanding of legal systems, particularly in England and Wales and other comparable jurisdictions. If we hear of somebody "breaking the law" it is likely that we picture somebody who has committed a criminal offence, in contrast to somebody who has failed to follow principles or requirements of contract or business law. The consequences of criminal behaviours can be significant for both those accused of offending – who we will refer to as the

---

1 Joel Feinberg, *Harm to Others: The Moral Limits of the Criminal Law* (OUP 1984) 31 (emphasis in original).

defendant – and those who are directly impacted by their behaviours – who we will refer to as the complainant. The defendant risks, if convicted, being deprived of their liberty through a sentence which may range from a discharge, likely with conditions the defendant would need to follow, through to a sentence of imprisonment, potentially for life.

Criminal law does not exist in isolation and many of the behaviours which can constitute criminal offences may also give rise to other forms of liability. There is an important distinction between criminal law and areas of law such as contract and business: criminal law addresses public, rather than private, wrongs. There is a growing recognition of the role of victims within the criminal justice system, through legislation such as the **Domestic Violence, Crime and Victims Act 2004, Part 3** and the recently enacted **Victims and Prisoners Act 2024, Part 1**. However. unlike areas of civil law – where individuals who are wronged bring cases against the wrongdoer – it is the state which brings criminal cases against those who are accused.[2] Whilst remedies in civil law often focus on compensating those who have been wronged; the objectives pursued through criminal law often focus on condemnation and censure of criminal behaviour and the imposition of sanctions through sentencing.

This book explores some of the more common forms of criminal liability in England and Wales, as well as some offences which demonstrate the complexity of the law. It will also introduce you to some of the ways in which the law is evaluated, debated, and reformed. This chapter begins by discussing the challenges of defining criminal law, before then going on to discuss how criminal laws are developed and reformed. It then discusses how to approach your study of criminal law, including offering some initial advice on how to approach particular types of question you may encounter. It concludes by introducing some of the sources of information which you might wish to consider when exploring the subject.

1.2 The scope of criminal law

The focus of this text is on a range of criminal offences in England and Wales and what elements need to be proven in order for a defendant to be found guilty of these offences. Criminal offences may be statutory offences, created by Parliament through legislation, or common law offences which have developed over time through case law. You may already be familiar with a range of criminal offences, some of which you will encounter in this text, including murder, theft and possession of a controlled substance.

Other offences you may be familiar with conceptually, without knowing specifically how relevant offences criminalise behaviour or the consequences of how they do so.

---

2 Although private prosecutions can be brought by individuals, these are rare and the state may take over such cases at any stage of proceedings, highlighting the dominance of the state in this area.

Take, for instance, the range of non-fatal, non-sexual offences against the person, many of which are set out in the **Offences Against the Person Act 1861**. Whilst it is common to speak of someone who is attacked as having been "assaulted",[3] the specific offence a defendant would be charged with will depend upon several factors, including whether the harm is more or less serious and the culpability or blameworthiness of the defendant.

More serious injury could amount to an offence of grievous bodily harm, an offence under **s20** or **s18 Offences Against the Person Act 1861**, whereas if no or little injury was sustained this could constitute battery or common assault, a common law offence. Which end of this "ladder" of offences a specific attack is categorised as is consequential. A defendant charged with common assault will see their case tried in a Magistrates' Court, either by a professional District Judge (Magistrates' Court) or by a bench composed of three "lay" magistrates (volunteers who receive guidance from a Magistrates' Court adviser). A defendant charged with grievous bodily harm with intent will see their case being sent to the Crown Court to be heard by a jury, if not entering a guilty plea, with a Crown Court Judge ruling on points of law.

Before an offence is prosecuted, it must be investigated by the police (or another relevant body such as the Serious Crime Agency) and a decision to prosecute taken. Whilst this book does not focus on criminal evidence and litigation, we discuss the pre-charge process in **Chapter 2**, highlighting practical and policy considerations which shape the decision-making process undertaken by the Crown Prosecution Service. Decisions to prosecute frequently require prosecutors to weigh up available evidence and to consider the range of possible offences the defendant could be charged with.

The range of criminal offences in England and Wales is vast – and growing with some regularity – so it is not possible for us to discuss every possible offence in this text. Instead, we focus on offences which provide a good introduction to criminal liability and establish a foundation which you can build on through independent research and further study. **Chapters 3–4** introduce the key concepts of *actus reus* and *mens rea,* which underpin criminal liability and the discussion of later chapters. We then move on to discuss substantive criminal offences.

Whilst the exact hierarchy of offence "seriousness" is debatable, we start in **Chapter 5–6** with homicide offences including murder and manslaughter. **Chapter 7** also addresses offences of violence, considering non-fatal offences against the person. **Chapter 8** considers offences of sexual violence created by the **Sexual Offences Act 2003**, whilst **Chapter 9** and **Chapter 10** consider theft and fraud related offences, respectively, with reference to the **Theft Act 1968** and **Fraud Act 2006**. **Chapter 11** considers offences related to the possession, creation and supply of controlled drugs. The final chapter focusing on a specific category of offences, **Chapter 12**, considers a range of offences connected with the protection of the environment.

---

3 Including the nature of the harm, on which see Chapter 7 and cases including Collins v Wilcock [1984]

Understanding criminal law inherently involves an awareness of offences defendants are commonly charged with; however, it also necessitates knowledge of the different ways in which a defendant can go about committing a crime or establishing a defence. In the later parts of this book, we consider defences – those involving an absence of fault in **Chapter 13** and those involving justification of the defendant's actions in **Chapter 14**. Finally we review more complex forms of involvement in crime, including participation in offences with others in **Chapter 15** and inchoate (incomplete) offences, such as attempt, in **Chapter 16**.

Activity

Criminal conduct

The offences we discuss in subsequent chapters provide a good foundation for research into your own areas of particular interest. As you begin to explore the scope of criminal law, make a note of offences you have heard about in the past and are interested in. Is there a particular reason why you are interested in these crimes? Ask yourself, do they address particular problematic behaviours, or are the offences themselves open to critique? Do they relate to other areas of law you are familiar with, such as contract or tort law?

1.3 Criminal law, politics and society

Criminal law, as with law generally, is inherently connected to politics. A substantial quantity of the criminal law is created by Parliament, i.e. with the involvement of elected MPs in the House of Commons, dependent upon the policy positions of the government of the day. Criminal cases and common law principles applied in them are frequently discussed by politicians, political commentators and in public debate. This results in a system of criminal law which is consistently being (re-)developed and reformed.

Activity

Drafting a new offence

Suppose that you are a civil servant. You have been asked by the Deputy Prime Minister, who has just been appointed to the post, to identify an area of criminal law to be reformed, with an announcement to be incorporated into an upcoming King's Speech. What areas of law might you consider suitable subjects for reform and why?

As you progress through this book, return to the area you have identified and try to identify some initial proposals for reform. Once you are familiar with the current law, or lack thereof, draft an outline of your proposed new (or reformed) offence.

Parliament and the courts do not make the law in isolation. Campaigning organisations, such as the Howard League for Penal Reform,[4] professional groups, such as the National Police Chief's Council,[5] and statutory bodies, such as the Law Commission,[6] all influence criminal justice policy and, consequently, the offences we discuss in this book. Many organisations, as well as political parties, seek to reform the law in response to developing public opinion.

On the one hand, it seems entirely appropriate that experts and public opinion play a role in shaping the law in a democracy. On the other hand, in some circumstances, there is also a risk of too quickly turning to legal reform as the solution to more complex issues. Criminal activity is rightly an issue of significant concern to many in society, particularly when new, serious and complex forms of offending emerge. However, as we will see throughout this book, the balance between under- and over- criminalisation is often difficult to achieve.

In the News

Deaths involving dangerous dogs

In recent years there has been an increase in media attention given to deaths resulting from people being attacked by breeds of large dog. The "XL Bully", in particular, has gained notoriety for being involved in these kinds of attacks, resulting in calls for the government to use powers under the **Dangerous Dogs Act 1991** to designate the breed as dangerous. The government responded to these calls, passing secondary legislation – the **Dangerous Dogs (Designated Types) (England and Wales) Order 2023 (SI 2023/1164)** – making it a criminal offence to own an unregistered XL Bully.

To see a discussion of an early prosecution taking place under these provisions, consider reading: Josh Salisbury, 'XL bully owner first in UK known to be prosecuted for breaching ban' *The Standard* (2 April 2024).

To see concerns about the practicality of enforcing these provisions, consider reading: Jeremy Culley, *XL bully ban: Police chief warns of challenges in enforcing law BBC News* (1 February 2024).

4 See, https://howardleague.org/
5 See, https://www.npcc.police.uk/
6 See, https://lawcom.gov.uk/

1.4 Studying criminal law

Criminal law is a nuanced and diverse subject area, whatever stage of your legal studies you are currently undertaking. Without prejudice as to any other legal subject areas, many of which share common features – and, in some instances, common heritage – with criminal law, this subject is a particularly rewarding area of law to explore. It may be a topic which you are interested in because you aspire to practice at as a barrister, solicitor or legal executive in the area, however, even if it is not, criminal law informs many other areas of law. For example, if your interests are more directed towards civil areas of law such as contract or tort, an understanding of criminal law is essential given the role of illegality as a defence to claims in those areas.

Studying criminal law will require you to synthesise together information from a variety of sources. As we discuss in **Chapter 2**, criminal law is located throughout Acts of Parliament, other legislation, case law and more specific sources. The majority of cases you will encounter during your studies will be appellate cases, heard in the Court of Appeal (Criminal Division) or the Supreme Court.[7] These are best accessed through a reputable legal database, such as Lexis or Westlaw, which has the advantage of telling you if the case is still current or if it has been superseded, using formal court reports such as the *All England Law Reports* and specialist reports such as the *Criminal Appeal Reports*. It is important that you become familiar with reading and understanding judgments, particularly the principles they establish: whilst the facts of cases can provide a useful example of when and how principles are applied, the *ratio decidendi* of a case should be the key takeaway whenever you encounter case law.

In this text, you will encounter activities, reflective questions and problem scenarios which encourage you to apply the knowledge you will develop. Activities will often situate the issues we are exploring in a broader context, encouraging you to explore the role of criminal law and criminal justice policy more broadly. Problem scenarios require you to apply your knowledge to a problem, as if you were advising a client (or preparing a prosecution against a defendant). These are a useful way of checking your understanding of key concepts. It is often easier to identify where you need to focus by checking a draft answer and a good answer is often more effective than abstract notes when first becoming familiar with new topics.

There are numerous ways to approach answering problem questions. Our advice is to develop a consistent style: first, break the offence or defence you are considering into the elements which need to be proven for it to apply. Some of these elements may need to be further broken down into individual points which need to be addressed sequentially (e.g. when considering causation, whether there is causation in fact, causation in law, and any new intervening acts: see **Chapter 3**).

7 Prior to 2009, the role of the Supreme Court was carried out by its predecessor, the Appellate Committee of the House of Lords.

Second, for each point which needs to be addressed, write a separate paragraph which explains the **issue**, discusses the relevant legal **rules** and provisions (citing statute, case law or commentaries as necessary), **applies** these to the scenario you are discussing, before coming to a **conclusion** on the point in question. Finally, draw together each of these paragraphs in an overall conclusion which answers the original question.

You will sometimes see this approach referred to as the "IRAC" method – other approaches employ different acronyms, but the fundamental approach is similar – focusing on examining each element separately to build up an overall answer. We discuss this approach further when considering problem questions in **Chapter 3**.

Studying criminal law is not, however, exclusively about applying the law as it currently stands. Throughout this text, we will explore critical analysis and evaluation of the law, how the law has developed and further reforms which have been proposed. Being able to engage with these debates is an essential skill to develop as a law student and builds the foundations for a strong graduate career, inside or outside the legal professions. You will often encounter evaluative questions during your studies, these should be approached in a logical, evidence-based way, focusing on a systematic analysis of the law. In **Chapter 2**, we set out a suggested framework for evaluative questions, which we apply to the topics we discuss in **Chapters 3-15**.

As we stated at the beginning of this chapter, criminal law does not exist in isolation. The issues which criminal law addresses and responds to are issues in other fields and areas of study, both legal and non-legal. In particular, as well as areas of law such as tort and public law, criminal behaviour is examined by psychologists, criminologists and other social scientists. Responses to criminal behaviour are the subject of penologists as well as political scientists, historians and others. These perspectives are important: we would encourage you to maintain an awareness of the broader context of the criminal justice system, alongside developing a detailed understanding of why and how criminal liability arises.

1.5 Summary

This chapter has introduced criminal law, generally, as well as the criminal law topics explored in this book. We have discussed how to go about beginning to study criminal law and introduced some of the ways in which you will apply your legal knowledge and skills when doing so. The key points to take away from this chapter are:

- Criminal offences are a **public** wrong, which the state responds to through arrest, prosecution and sentencing.

- Criminal liability exists alongside other forms of liability, such as liability in contract, which may address the same or similar behaviour but with a different fundamental aim.
- Criminal offences are located in a mix of primary and secondary legislation, case law and other sources of common law.
- Criminal law is frequently the subject of **political** and **public** debate, resulting in developments of the law.
- Criminal cases are initially heard in the **Magistrates' Court** or the **Crown Court** and can be appealed to the **High Court, Court of Appeal** and **Supreme Court**.
- As you study criminal law, you will encounter questions which require you to **apply** your knowledge and advise on the application of the law to problem scenarios and questions which require you to **evaluate** the law and potential reforms.
- Perspectives from other fields and disciplines, such as criminology, are useful for maintaining a broader awareness of the context in which criminal law operates – although this should not be to the detriment of your study of criminal law itself.

Further reading

Nicola Lacey, "Historicising Criminalisation: Conceptual and Empirical Issues" (2009) 72(6) *Modern Law Review 936*

R A Duff and S E Marshall, "Is Criminal Law 'Exceptional'?" (2023) 17 *Criminal Law and Philosophy 39*

John Gardner, "Crime: In Proportion and in Perspective" in John Gardner, *Offences and Defences: Selected Essays in the Philosophy of Criminal Law (OUP 2007)*

Louise Ellison and Vanessa E Munro, "Taking trauma seriously: Critical reflections on the criminal justice process" (2017) 21 *International Journal of Evidence & Proof 183*

Lindsay Farmer, "Criminal law as an institution: rethinking theoretical approaches to criminalisation" in R A Duff et al (eds) *Criminalisatization: The Political Morality of the Criminal Law (OUP 2014)*

CHAPTER 2

Principles of criminal law and example offence

2.1 Introduction

Criminal law is a core aspect of any law studies. It is a fascinating area of law. It is often complex and contested in terms of theory. Where there is a modern era statute most offences usually clearly elucidate the harm, fault and any justifications. Unfortunately some of the most serious crimes such as murder and manslaughter are defined by the case law and most offences against the person by an archaic statute. There is sometimes a lack of clarity. This chapter will focus on introducing criminal law; the principles of criminal law and conclude with an example statutory offence.

Aims of this chapter

By the end of this chapter, you can be expected to know and have tools to evaluate criminal law:

- **Nature of criminal law**: This will help you to pin down what is criminal law.
- **Criminal censure: process and proof**: This will help you to understand how criminal law fits within broader criminal procedure.
- **The trinity**: This section explores the three aspects which are normally necessary to prove a crime: harm, fault and no justification.
- **Evaluation**: This section introduces evaluation as a learning outcome and how students can confidently approach evaluation when writing a coursework or answering an essay style question in an exam.
- **Evaluation and reform framework for criminal law**: This important section sets an evaluation framework which will be utilised throughout most of the book in relation to evaluating the quality of English criminal law. The framework includes the following value criteria:
    - Legal certainty and legal clarity;
    - Equality before the law;
    - Fair warning; fair labelling and sufficient breadth principles;
    - Human rights compliance: autonomy and welfare principles;
    - International comparators and reform: practicality, principle and politics.
- **Criminal law sources**: This is a brief exploration of the sources of criminal law including statute law and case law.
- **Example offence**: Using the statutory offence of criminal damage we will explore how to analyse a specific criminal offence using the trinity method to systematically identify harm, fault and justification issues.

2.2 Nature of criminal law

2.2.1 Criminal law is a public law wrong not a private law wrong

Criminal law is a species of public law where the variables are:

- Who? State v Individual
- What? Substantive criminal law
- Burden? Burden on the State (normally)
- Standard? To prove beyond reasonable doubt i.e. so that you are sure
- Stakes? Includes individual liberty

Criminal law is NOT a private law wrong where the variables are:

- Who? Individual v Individual
- What? Substantive civil law e.g. contract law
- Burden? On the claimant
- Standard? Balance of probabilities
- Stakes? Usually money

2.2.2 Contrasting criminal and civil law

There is a significant contrast between criminal law and civil law

	Criminal	Civil
• **Substantive law**	Criminal law	e.g. Contract law
• **Procedural law**	Criminal procedure	Civil procedure
• **Adjectival law**	Restrictive rules of evidence	Free rules of evidence
• **Enforcement**	Law of sentencing	Damages
• **Ancillary Orders**	Numerous restrictive	Additional orders
• **Litigation funding**	Legal aid and private	Mostly private

2.2.3 How do you define what is a crime?

To define a crime is strangely very difficult. Sometimes we know it when we see it e.g., murder, rape, robbery, theft. Sometimes we are surprised it is a crime e.g., minor disorderly behaviour or regulatory offences relating to food safety. As with other areas of law there are numerous definitions of what criminal law is. It is a vexed question and one we will only explore briefly. There are two schools of thought:

a) Defining crime as a social wrong

> "Crime is crime because it consists in wrongdoing which directly and in serious degree threatens the security or well-being of society, and because it is not safe to leave it redressable only by compensation of the party injured."[1,2]

b) Defining crime by process

> "[Crime is] an act that is capable of being followed by criminal proceedings having one of the types of outcome (e.g., punishment) known to follow these proceedings."[3]

In this course book we ascribe to school b) i.e. defining by process as the more accurate if not particularly descriptive route. We also note the debate is circular. We will know crimes when we see them!

2.2.4 Are we talking about moral wrongs or the harm caused?

Historically there has been a significant debate in relation to whether criminal law should focus on morality or harm. Historically the major focus was moral wrongs. This often-followed religious approaches to the natural law. This school of thought still has a significant influence on the legal principles that exist. In the modern era the focus has shifted in part to looking at the level of harm caused (or which could be caused) by the actions of the defendant.

a) Moral wrongs

The very significant *Report of the Committee on Homosexual Offenses and Prostitution* (commonly known as the *Wolfenden Report*) stated:

> "[the] function [of criminal law], as we see it, is to preserve public order and decency, to protect the citizen from what is offensive or injurious, and to provide

1 Carlton Kemp Allen, 'The Nature of a Crime' (1931) Journal of Society of Comparative Legislation, Feb, reprinted in Legal Duties 221 at 233–234

2 Grant Lamond 'What is crime?'; [2007] 27 OJLS 609, 610, 631

3 Glanville Williams 'The Definition of Crime' (1955) Current Legal Problems 8: 107 at 108

> sufficient safeguards against exploitation and corruption of others, particularly those who are especially vulnerable because they are young, weak in body or mind, inexperienced, or in a state of special physical, official or economic dependence."[4]

In the modern era this has been endorsed by Lord Hobhouse:

> "An essential function of the criminal law is to define the boundary between what conduct is criminal and what merely immoral... objective and transparent certainty [is required]." [5]

b) Harm caused

John Stuart Mill placed harm caused as the core justification for criminal law. He stated:

> "The ***only purpose for which power can be rightfully exercised*** over any member of a civilized community ***against his will is to prevent harm to others***. His own good, either physical or moral, is not sufficient warrant. He cannot rightfully be compelled to do or forbear ... because in the opinion of others to do so would be wise or even right...If anyone does an act hurtful to others, there is a prima facie case for punishing him by law or, where legal penalties are not safely applicable, by general disapprobation...".[6]

In the modern era the significant legal philosopher Herbert Hart endorses the harm principle. In the current era Professor Denis Baker states harm is a constitutional bedrock principle for criminal law:

> "Wrongful harm to others provides the only moral and constitutional justification for sending people to jail. .... the sufficient conditions for sending [D] to jail are:
>
> (1) that ***[Ds] actions have (or risk) bad consequences*** that are ***sufficiently harmful*** to make [D] commensurately deserving of penal detention; and
>
> (2) that **[D] culpably** (that is, with a state of mind somewhere along the intentional/reckless/gross negligence continuum) **chose** (aimed or attempted) **to bring about those bad consequences ...**"

4 Home Office, *Report of the Committee on Homosexual Offences and Prostitution* (Cmnd 247, 1957) para 13

5 Hinks [2000] 4 ALL ER 833, 853 (Lord Hobhouse)

6 John Stuart Mill, *On Liberty* (John W Parker and Son, 1859)

Baker then states:

> "[The] Harm Principle should be recognized as a constitutional principle of justice to prevent the government from depriving offenders of their liberty for engaging in harmless wrongdoing."[7]

There is also significant debate about the scale of harm. For example, tickling somebody with a feather has a very different scale of harm to hitting someone on the head with a hammer yet both could be criminal offences against the person!

2.2.5 How does criminal law relate to other areas of law?

It is important to note common law principles often overlap between the criminal law and the civil law. The Supreme Court (and its predecessor the House of Lords) as the apex judicial body consists of the same judges dealing with public law and private law cases.

For example common law tortious (civil wrongs) principles often overlap with criminal law principles. There are commonalities between the civil law and the criminal law in relation to the law on assaults; false imprisonment and harassment. All of these are civil wrongs and also criminal offences.

Unfortunately, the law does not always smoothly or directly accord between the civil position and the criminal position. We will see later in **Chapter 9** particularly in relation to theft offences there can be a differential approach to the term "appropriation of property" between the civil law and the criminal law.

2.2.6 Are we interested in why people commit crimes?

It is undoubtedly interesting to know why people commit crimes. This is why in popular fiction and films often the most popular genres include crime fact and crime fiction. For our studies we are not directly interested in why people commit crimes. The study of 'Why?' is a different field of study namely Criminology. We will not ignore the context, but this book is not a criminological or sociological study.

---

7 Dennis J Baker, 'Constitutionalizing the Harm Principle' (2008) 27(2) Criminal Justice Ethics 3

2.2.7 Are we interested in the police and their powers?

Again it's undoubtedly interesting to look at police powers. It is also important. Detection, detention, questioning, court process (a separate body of law) are the separate but linked discipline of criminal procedure or criminal justice.

2.2.8 Are we interested in the rules of advocacy and evidence?

Yes, again advocacy and evidence are undoubtedly important and interesting but not our area of study. The rules about evidence of character (usually previous conviction or previous good character), confessions, improperly obtained evidence, inferences from silence, hearsay, opinion evidence are important to the trial process. Advocacy has a very important role to play in presenting a case (the prosecution role) or persuading a jury (the defence role). They are not the immediate concerns of the study of criminal law and are part of the separate body of law on criminal procedure and criminal justice.

2.2.9 Are we interested in sentencing?

Yes, sentencing is undoubtedly interesting but the study of sentencing (formerly known as penology) is a separate discipline. That said some issues such as the life sentences have an indirect influence on the development of the law in relation to areas such as homicide.

2.2.10 So, what are we studying?

We are studying substantive criminal law. i.e.:

- The general principles relating to all offences including harm (*actus reus*); culpability (*mens rea*), justifications (defences general fault; general justification and specific defences); participation in crime and preparatory offences (inchoates).
- The specific offences against the person (homicide voluntary; homicide involuntary; offences against the person; sexual offences).
- The specific offences against property (criminal damage, theft and theft related and fraud).

The elements of offences are the building blocks of crime. We are thus taking a forensic approach to the elements of crime. We are studying the rules of law, not the mechanism of proving facts which is the rules of evidence and procedure.

2.3 Criminal censure: Process and proof

2.3.1 Outline of criminal procedure

In chronological steps criminal procedure can be summarised as:

- Investigation
- Detection
- Searches
- Arrest
- Police station powers (detention, samples, interview, charge)
- For low/medium level crime e.g. common assault – Magistrates Court (plea, trial, sentence)
- For higher seriousness crime e.g. murder – Crown Court (plea, trial, sentence)
- Appeal.

In terms of role:

- State v Individual
- Police investigate
- Crown Prosecution Service (CPS) charge and prosecute
- Judge is in charge of the law (for the Crown Court)
- Jury is in charge of the facts (for Crown Court).

2.3.2 Criminal process censure and sanction

The Criminal process has two parts:

- **Censure: Censuring proven wrongdoing which is contrary to law.**

This is most commonly shown through the trial. In the Crown Court this is where the jury make a finding of guilt. In the Magistrates Court this is where the magistrate(s) make a finding of guilt.

- **Sanction: Punishing the individual proportionately for the harm caused whilst considering their culpability.**

This is most commonly shown where after the trial and the person having been found guilty is sentenced for their criminal offending. It also gives the court access to ancillary orders (such as compensation; confiscation and restraining orders).

2.3.3 Police powers

Police powers are governed in large part by a very important statute called the **Police and Criminal Evidence Act 1984**.

2.3.4 The decision to prosecute

The Crown Prosecution Service (CPS) have the power to bring proceedings (under **Prosecution of Offences Act 1985**). Under the *Code for Crown Prosecutors*, latest edition 2018[8] two stages apply:

(1) **Evidential test** – Whether there is sufficient evidence to provide a realistic prospect of conviction? Considering whether the evidence is reliable, credible and sufficient.

(2) **Public interest test** – Is it in the public interest to prosecute the offender? Considering whether the public interest factors tending in favour or prosecution outweigh those against prosecution. Factors will include: harm; culpability; circumstances; D's age and maturity at the time of the offence; the impact on the community; whether a prosecution is a proportionate response and whether sources of information require protecting.

2.3.5 Private prosecutions

Private prosecutions are relatively rare. The private prosecutor would lay an information before a magistrate so that a summons can be issued. Legal aid is not available to the prosecutor. The CPS can intervene and adopt or discontinue a private prosecution.

2.3.6 The classification of offences: Summary, triable either way (hybrid) and indictable

Name	Court	Example
• **Summary**	Magistrates Court ONLY	Common assault
• **Either way**	Magistrates Court or Crown Court	Burglary
• **Indictable ONLY**	Crown Court ONLY	Murder

8 Crown Prosecution Service, 'The Code for Crown Prosecutors' (CPS 2018) <https://www.cps.gov.uk/publication/code-crown-prosecutors> accessed 06 April 2025

2.3.7 Magistrates court summary trial process

- Prosecution case
- Defence case
- District Judge or magistrates decisions of law and fact.

2.3.8 Crown court trial on indictment

- Prosecution case
- Defence case
- Judge rules on the law (both substantive criminal law; rules of evidence and rules of procedure) and guides the jury on the law and summarises the salient evidence heard.
- Jury makes the decisions on the facts.

2.3.9 Appeals

Cases referred to the Court of Appeal (CA).

- Defence appeal to the CA:

  (1) Appeal conviction where there have been errors on points of law (usually) or errors on the facts (rarer and very difficult to pursue) where the conviction is rendered unsafe.[9]

  (2) Appeal sentence where the sentence is either wrong in principle or manifestly excessive.

- Prosecution appeal to the CA:

  (1) Point of law (***Attorney-General's Reference*** – **s36 Criminal Justice Act 1972**).

  (2) Sentencing unduly lenient sentences (***Attorney-General's Reference*** – **s36 Criminal Justice Act 1988**).

- Interlocutory appeal:

  During the Crown Court proceedings a pause, an appeal and a ruling by the CA and then proceedings revert to the Crown Court.

9 Criminal Appeals Act 1968

- Appeals to the Supreme Court (pre 2009 the House of Lords Judicial body): Point of law of public importance e.g. as we will see in **Chapter 4** *mens rea* on the definition of recklessness: ***G* [2004]**.

2.3.10 What case decisions are we interested in?

It is important to contrast decisions at first instance and the appellate jurisdiction. At first assistance the Magistrates Court hears 95% of criminal cases and the Crown Court hears less than 5% of cases by volume. However the Crown Court is trying the more serious crimes. The reality is that most first instance cases turn on the evidence/interpretation of the factual scenario and the decisions of the judges are not binding but can be of persuasive value.

Appeals are exceptional. At the appellate jurisdiction, cases usually turn on errors of law that are appealed to the higher court where the conviction may be deemed unsafe by the error of law. By the stage of an appeal it is important to remember normally that the defendant has been convicted and is appealing. Public policy factors may limit the remit of the appeal court to review as to whether the decision is within the band of legal principles and reasonable responses. Public policy can play a significant limiting factor on the ability of the defendant to appeal successfully.

2.4 The trinity: Harm; culpability and no justification

In order to prove a criminal offence there must be proof of a trinity of three aspects:

- Harm
- Culpability
- No justification.

2.4.1 The harm principle: Proof of actus reus

Explained in **Chapter 3** the proof of Harm (or potential harm) to the

• Individual	Homicide Offences; assault; and sexual offences
• Property	Criminal damage; theft; fraud
• State	Official secrets; terrorism

2.4.2 The culpability principle: Proof of mens rea

Explained in **Chapter 4** the attribution of blame/fault.

If we scale it from highest to lowest:

- **Intention**

  Direct intention, i.e. aim or purpose

  Indirect intent, i.e. foresight of a virtual certainty

- **Recklessness**

  Advertent subjective recklessness, i.e. knowingly taking an unjustified risk

- **Gross negligence** – explained **Chapter 6**
- **Strict liability** – explained in **Chapter 4**
- **No fault** – explained in **Chapter 4**
- **Dishonesty** – explained in **Chapter 9**.

2.4.3 The no justification principle: The proof of the absence of a defence

If there is a legally good reason for the illegal action (which often reflect moral position of D) then D can justify his actions. In this situation usually the prosecution are obliged to prove there was no such good justification, e.g., self-defence – necessary reasonable force. The defence evidentially raises the defence and the prosecution must prove beyond reasonable doubt the defence does not exist.

2.5 Evaluation

2.5.1 Learning outcomes

At undergraduate level there are numerous learning outcomes. These can include:

- knowledge of the law and procedure;
- practical problem solving skills (including application of the law to the facts using the IRAC method);
- critical analysis and evaluation of the law;
- professional and academic skills (including advocacy, research and referencing);

- awareness of theory, principles and values (including professional ethics);
- intellectual independence.

2.5.2 Criminal law modules often focuses on three of these

- Knowledge of the law and procedure.
- Practical problem solving skills (including application of the law to the facts using the IRAC method).
- Critical analysis and evaluation of the law.

2.5.3 What is evaluation?

Let's start with what evaluation is not. Evaluation is not pure description of the law. You will need for any evaluation style questions to briefly describe what the law is.

Evaluation goes beyond description. Evaluation is a crucially important skill for undergraduate and postgraduate study but also for life as a practising lawyer.

Evaluation is in simple terms placing defined criteria of value (i.e. your measuring stick) and using each criteria of value to measure a specific dispute within an area of law (i.e. your legal issue).

You should explore what value both good and bad the theme you are discussing has – i.e. look at the issue from all angles.

Two well-known artists and their songs may assist:

- From Joni Mitchell: Both Sides Now
  i.e. Argue both sides using authoritative sources: produce an argument not a polemic.
- Aretha Franklin: Respect
  i.e. comply and respect the rules on ethical referencing and research to evidence your arguments by citation.

2.5.4 How to secure learning outcomes and the best results?

One word "practice". The more you practice the better you will get. Learning is long in getting, i.e. it takes time and practice. It is crucial that you attend your taught sessions (which may include lectures – usually a provocation and outline, workshops – usually knowledge and skills building and seminars – usually applying or evaluating the law. Even more importantly it is crucial you engage with independent study outside of the classroom. It is also crucial when you are in the classroom where possible you engage with your fellow students and academics to analyse practical problems and critically evaluate the law.

2.5.5 Do you have any tips for evaluation assessments?

- Read the question carefully and repeatedly to ensure you know what is the aim of the assessment.
- Read and engage with any revision guidance.
- Check the operator word: e.g. analyse, evaluate, critically evaluate.
- Do a Plan and breakdown the answer into headings.
- Answer the question set: DO NOT answer the one you want it to be!
- Structure your answer using headings.
- Space out your thinking and work into different headings.
- Quotes should be brief and only used if essential.
- Think principle – what is the legal principle?
- Referencing is easy.

Golden rule: Reference your sources.

Silver rule: Use footnotes and bibliography if a coursework.

Bronze rule: Use the Oxford Standard of Citation of Legal Authorities.[10]

2.5.6 How to structure your answer using headings

This is an example of how you might structure an answer to coursework involving evaluation.

Introduction

Give a road map to help the reader know how your work is structured and provoke thought (approx 5% of the word count).

10 Faculty of Law, 'OSCOLA: Oxford University Standard for the Citation of Legal Authorities' (4th edn, University of Oxford 2012) <https://www.law.ox.ac.uk/sites/default/files/migrated/oscola_4th_edn_hart_2012.pdf> accessed 05 April 2025

Law

Lay out briefly the context and legal position (approx 15% of the word count).

Evaluation

Critically evaluate the law according to defined criteria of value which can be used to measure the law (approx 60% of the Word Count).

Example criteria below:

Criteria 1: Legal certainty and legal clarity – define & apply.

Criteria 2: Equality before the law – define & apply.

Criteria 3: Fair warning; fair labelling and sufficient breadth – define & apply.

Criteria 4: Human rights compliance: autonomy and welfare – define & apply.

International comparator and reform: practicality; principle and politics

Explain an international comparator law briefly and "bring it home", i.e. how could it be used or adapted in England and Wales?

Explain any reform proposals (e.g. Law Commission) and look at the practical issues, the certainty of the principles involved and the political impact (approx 10% of the word count).

Conclusion

Draw together the strands and answer the question(s) set (Approx 10% of the word count).

2.6 Evaluation and reform framework for criminal law

In this section we will lay out an evaluation framework which can be utilised to critically evaluate the criminal law. Throughout this course book we will return to some of these headings and use them to introduce the critical evaluation of the criminal law by Chapter. The frame is based on a rule of law model. Others have stressed some or all of the criteria[11].

11 Andrew Ashworth 'Is the Criminal Law a Lost Cause?' [2000] 116 Law Quarterly Review 225

2.6.1 Legal certainty and Legal clarity

Legal certainty

In public law the rule of law indicates (in most models) that legal certainty and legal clarity are bedrock principles and a fundamental starting point for a substantive model of the rule of law. Legal certainty provides the law must be sufficiently available, certain and enable the individual to know the legal boundaries of their actions and potential consequences of breach[12]. Legal certainty reflects a principal of justice: you need to know the law in order to avoid doing something or make a rational choice to do it anyway! Legal certainty allows people to plan their lives. Buxton describes reasons why legal certainty is desirable in criminal law namely

> "[i.] human rights interests: the citizen is entitled to know what he can do and what he cannot, and in particular is entitled to be protected from the arbitrariness of state action that must attend punishment for breaches of a law that is erratic in its operation.
>
> [ii.] uncertainty in, or difficulty of access to, the criminal law makes criminal trials not only unpredictable in their outcome but also unduly lengthy and expensive."[13]

Legal clarity

Legal clarity provides that the law must be accessible, clear, intelligible, and predictable[14]. As Lord Bingham has said

> "No one should be punished under a law unless it is sufficiently clear ...to enable him to know what conduct is forbidden before he does it."[15]

In the most serious criminal cases the jury is the tribunal of fact governed by the directions on the law given by the judge. The research shows juries need clear and cogent guidance[16]. It is axiomatic that certain and separately clear law is prerequisite

---

12 Richard Buxton, 'The Human Rights Act and the Substantive Criminal Law' (2000) Criminal Law Review 331, 332

13 Richard Buxton, 'The Human Rights Act and the Substantive Criminal Law' (2000) Criminal Law Review 331, 332

14 Rimmington; Goldstein [2005]

15 Rimmington; Goldstein [2005]

16 Alan Travis, 'The verdict on juries: fair, effective and efficient' *The Guardian* (London, 17 February 2010) <https://www.theguardian.com/uk/2010/feb/17/juries-fairness-research> accessed 06 April 2025, Cheryl Thomas, 'Are juries fair?' (Ministry of Justice Research Series 1/10, February 2010) <https://www.ucl.ac.uk/judicial-institute/sites/judicial-institute/files/are_juries_fair.pdf> accessed 06 April 2025, Cheryl Thomas, 'Ethnicity and the fairness of jury trials in England and Wales 2006-2014' [2017] Crim Law Review 860

of clear guidance. Post 2010 there have been strong movements for clearer jury directions gathering pace culminating in continuing and improving guidance for judges within the Crown Court compendium. This superb guide assists judges in framing their legal directions with legal clarity for a lay jury.[17] It also indirectly helps the jury to make properly reasoned decisions.[18]

2.6.2 Equality before the law: Protected characteristics and socio-economic barriers

The impact of unequal power relationships in society has a significant impact on the criminal justice system.

Equality before the law is an important value.

Its scope includes a prohibition on discrimination based on protected characteristics under the **Equality Act 2010** such as:

- disability
- gender
- gender identity
- race[19]
- sexual orientation.

Its scope arguably should also include socio-economic status which is highly relevant and impacts on the unequal power relationships in society that have a significant impact on the system.

Particular but not exclusive examples could include

- Policing "working class" easy to detect community crime vigorously v Light touch deferred prosecution arrangements in fraud.
- Policing stop and search v Policing financial organisations.
- Prosecuting domestic violence offences and sexual offences particularly (but not exclusively) against women v Defences such as "the guardsman's defence" (alleging the homosexual approach of the victim); "the rough sex defence" (alleging the victim asked for rough sex which went wrong).

17 Judicial College, 'The Crown Court Compendium-Part 1' (Judicial College, July 2024) <https://www.judiciary.uk/wp-content/uploads/2024/09/Crown-Court-Compendium-Part-I-July-2024.pdf> accessed 11 April 2025
18 Which accords with the ECHR Article 6 Right to a fair trial
19 See particularly David Ormerod, 'Racism in the Criminal Justice System' [2020] Crim LR 659

"The Lammy Review: An independent review into the treatment of, and outcomes for, Black, Asian, and Minority Ethnic individuals in the Criminal Justice System"[20] is a crucial report. Although its full scope is beyond this book it is particularly notable that trust is the bedrock of good relationships and good policing.

s149 Equality Act 2010 creates the public sector equality duty:

> *(1) A public authority must, in the exercise of its functions, have due regard to the need to—*
>
> *(a) eliminate discrimination, harassment, victimisation and any other conduct that is prohibited by or under this Act;*
>
> *(b) advance equality of opportunity between persons who share a relevant protected characteristic and persons who do not share it;*
>
> *(c) foster good relations between persons who share a relevant protected characteristic and persons who do not share it.*

2.6.3 Fair warning; Fair labelling and sufficient breadth principles

Fair warning

The law should give fair warning to the community of the consequences of law. The public for example needs fair warning of a change in the law. This will involve communication of changes in the law.

Fair labelling

Fair labelling involves labelling criminal offences at a macro scale to indicate categorisation, indicative punishment scales and specialist ancillary orders[21].

---

20 David Lammy, 'The Lammy Review: An independent review into the treatment of, and outcomes for, Black, Asian and Minority Ethnic individuals in the Criminal Justice System' (2017) <https://www.gov.uk/government/uploads/system/uploads/attachment_data/file/643001/lammy-review-final-report.pdf> accessed 06 April 2025

21 James Chalmers and Fiona Leverick, 'Fair Labelling in Criminal Law' (2008) 71 Modern Law Review 217, 221-222

Fair labelling also involves labelling at a micro scale. It helps with categorising the wrongdoing with a public label which has a communicative value to wider society[22].

The correct labelling of offences and offenders is an important aspect of censure.

A label apportions the category to the offence and the offender.

e.g.

Offence	**Label for the offender**
Murder	Murderer
Burglary	Burglar
Rape	Rapist

There are strong arguments that in prosecuting a crime the correct label is "the person has been convicted of murder" rather than the simplistic label "he is a murderer". There are strong arguments that conviction of the crime, even murder, does not simply render a person with a single point label. It fails to acknowledge the complexity of the situation.

Sufficient breadth

Equally the state should strive to strike a balance between the principle of minimum criminalisation (i.e., no more than is strictly necessary for society to function fairly and effectively) and social defence of offences of sufficient breadth to capture wrongdoing.

The courts have stated:

> "The rule of law is not well served if a crime is defined in terms wide enough to cover conduct which is not regarded as criminal and it is then left to the prosecuting authorities to exercise a blanket discretion not to prosecute to avoid injustice."[23]

Most offences are drafted sufficiently widely to capture within their ambit the mischief of offending.

22 James Chalmers and Fiona Leverick, 'Fair Labelling in Criminal Law' (2008) 71 Modern Law Review 217, 221-222

23 K [2002] 1 AC 462

Activity

You work in Tesco's on the Old Kent Rd in London.

There is a problem with shoplifting. So you want to propose an offence but starting from a "blank slate".

What are your options?

(1) Narrow option: You could create an offence of theft specifically from the Old Kent Road branch of Tesco's.

(2) Wider option: You have a slightly wider option of creating an offence of theft from a shop.

(3) Widest option: You have an even wider option of just creating an offence of theft of which theft from a shop is a specific form that the police could measure and collate statistics on.

Unsurprisingly it is the third category which is the normal breadth of offending. However it is notable that the government is constantly seeking more and more specificity in relation to offences, e.g. having a separate offence of assault on a shop worker rather than using the normal offences against the person legislation.

Practicality, cost, and expense

Firstly, practicality: the law must be sufficiently practical and enforceable to achieve its goals. For example you could ban alcohol. Its harms may meet the criteria for criminalisation but it would be practically problematic to the police to enforce. There are those who argue in relation to the maintenance of a ban on Class B cannabis is not practical or a good use of taxpayers money.

Secondly, parsimony or the avoidance of undue cost and expense. It is obvious, particularly in this time of austerity, that the government (and indirectly the taxpayer) would not want to invest undue expense if it was not proportionate to the harm caused.

Finally, never rule out political expediency. This is the so called "knee jerk reaction". There is sometimes public or media clamour (or perceived clamour) to change the law. The power of the media and social media is significant. Whilst many campaigns may have good motivations, it is submitted that it is important the government does not simply react spontaneously without due consideration for good law making. There are numerous examples of quick reactions resulting in poor law making, e.g. the **Dangerous Dogs Act 1991**.

2.6.4 Human rights compliance: Autonomy and welfare principles

Autonomy: Assumes capacity and then allows choice

Autonomy assumes:

- free will, i.e. it allows a freedom of choice;
- free capacity; and
- a fair opportunity to obey the law.[24]

Autonomy protects the individual's liberty to choose their actions. It is linked to the principle of minimal criminalisation.

Welfare: Protecting society

Welfare is the principle of the desire to protect society as a whole from harm by creating some duties on persons to look after their "neighbour".

The balancing autonomy and welfare is a core concern in criminal law

The balance is particularly engaged in criminal law. For example, seatbelts in cars, mobile phones in cars, drink-driving, and smoking in confined spaces all engage issues of the autonomy of the individual to make their own choice. However, they also engage the welfare of society to prevent against harm to others.

European Convention on Human Rights relevance to English substantive criminal law

The **European Convention on Human Rights** (**ECHR**) provides a crucial framework for the protection of human rights for those who are members of the European Council.

This text will provide only a summary of some of the key issues arising in relation to the context of criminal law. For further information please see the public law textbooks and the specialist textbooks on **ECHR**.

24 R A Duff, 'Choice, Character and Criminal Liability'(1993) 12(4) Law and Philosophy 345

A	Provision	Relevance to english criminal law
2	**Right to life**	-Euthanasia, the protection/sanctity of life -Investigation of death, the police and the coroner -Legitimacy of self defence Justifiable force in the prevention of crime -Justification for abortion
3	**Right not to be subjected to torture or inhuman or degrading treatment**	-The defence of parental chastisement -The prevention and investigation of torture of victims -Prisoners' rights
5.1	**Right to liberty and security of the person "...Arrested shall be informed promptly..." "...brought before the court promptly..."**	The defence of insanity
6.1	**Fair and public hearing of criminal charges "within a reasonable time by an independent and impartial tribunal established by law.**	Inferences from silence
6.2	**Presumption of innocence**	Reverse burdens
7	**(1) No one shall be held guilty of any criminal offence on account of any act or omission which did not constitute a criminal offence under national or international law at the time when it was committed. Nor shall a heavier penalty be imposed than the one that was applicable at the time the criminal offence was committed.**	*"Article 7 is not confined to prohibiting the retrospective application of the criminal law to an accused's disadvantage: ...it also embodies, more generally, the principle that only the law can define a crime and prescribe a penalty .... [and] the principle that the criminal law must not be extensively construed to an accused's detriment, for instance by analogy ... it follows that an offence must be clearly defined in the law. ... Article 7 cannot be read as outlawing the gradual clarification of the rule of criminal liability through judicial interpretation from case to case provided that the resultant development is consistent with the essence of the offence and could be reasonably foreseen"* (***SW v UK (1996)***). An example of such clarification can be seen in abolishing the so-called "Marital exemption" in rape cases. (***R v R [1992]***).

A	Provision	Relevance to english criminal law
8	**Right to respect for private life**	Sexual offences (particularly homosexual offences generally and in respect of private premises).
9	**Freedom of religion**	Blasphemy
10	**Freedom of expression**	-Contempt of court -Obscenity -Public order -Racial hatred offences
...		
14	**Prohibition on discrimination**	Not freestanding

The Human Rights Act 1998

The Human Rights Act 1998 provides a framework to give further effect the European Convention of Human Rights through convention rights which are given effect at a domestic level. This text provides an outline of some of the key sections of the statute.

For further information please see the public law textbooks and the specialist textbooks on the European Convention on Human Rights.

S	Provision
	Long Title: "An act to give ***further effect*** to rights and freedoms guaranteed under the European Convention on human rights,"
1	**The Convention rights** **(1) "The convention rights"** **IS Article.2-12 & 14,Protocol.1 Article.1-3, Protocol 13 Article.1** **NOT Article 1 & 13 & 15, and other Protocols** **(2) "Those articles have effect...subject to any designated derogation or reservation"** **(3) "The Articles are set out in Schedule 1"**
2	**Jurisprudence clause** **Interpretation of convention rights** (1) "A court ... determining a question which has arisen in connection with a Convention right_**must *take into account any judgment*** ...of the ECtHR ...whenever made or given, ***so far as,*** in the opinion of the court...***it is relevant to the proceedings in which that question has arisen***."

S	Provision
3	**Construction clause** **Interpretation of [DOMESTIC] legislation** **(1) "So far as it is possible to do so** Primary and [Secondary] legislation **must** be read and given effect in a way which is compatible with the convention rights." (2) [Does not affect the validity ...of incompatible ... legislation i.e., upholding parliamentary Supremacy].
4	**Declarations of Incompatibility (DOI)** (2) If [the Superior Courts i.e., SC/HL, CA, HC are] satisfied primary or secondary legislation is incompatible with a convention right it **may** make a declaration of incompatibility. (6) [A DOI] ".... does not affect the validity, continuing operation or enforcement of the provision...; and is not binding on the parties to the proceedings..."
6	**Public authorities [duty to act compatibly]** **(1) It is unlawful for a public authority to act in a way which is** incompatible with a Convention right. [Except where required to do so by primary legislation].
7	**Victim of an unlawful act** (1) A person can bring proceedings "only if he is (or would be) a victim of the unlawful act." ***(7)* [Victim has the same meaning** as ECHR **Art 34].**

2.6.5 International comparators and reform

Comparators

It is often very useful to look at international comparators. In particular other common law jurisdictions which have retained jury trial can provide some excellent inspiration for reform. For example, looking at the law in Australia, Canada, South Africa and New Zealand can provide some really interesting examples of legislation or common law where they face familiar problems in fresh ways.

Although based on the Roman system (as opposed to the common law system) it can be useful to look at the Scottish examples as well.

Other jurisdictions can provide great value but require careful contextual analysis of their individual legal system.

Law Commission and reform bodies

The Law Commission[25]

The Law Commission is an excellent repository of learning and thought about law reform. For a recent example see **Chapter 10** and the origins of the **Fraud Act 2006**.

Criminal Law Revision Committee

The Criminal Law Revision Committee was historically a very influential body of the top expert academic and practitioner lawyers. Its reports preceded for example the **Theft Act 1968** and **Criminal Damage Act 1971**. Its August membership included Professor Glanville Williams QC, Professor Rupert Cross; Professor Edward Griew; and finally Professor John Smith QC.

Draft Criminal Code

The Draft Criminal Code (DCC) was a very carefully thought-out systematic attempt to synthesise all of the core general principles and many of the most important offences into one codified document. The work included August members including Professor John Smith QC and Professor Ian Dennis.

Such codification, we would submit, bring about amongst other virtues:

- Certainty, clarity and accessibility
- Coherence and internal consistency
- Efficiency
- Systematic approach to updating.

2.6.6 Academics and practitioners

There are many august academics and practitioners who have had a significant influence on the criminal law who have also had a significant impact on law reform.

2.7 Criminal law sources: Statute law and case law

2.7.1 Statute law

Statute law is the main source of law in criminal law.

25 See, https://lawcom.gov.uk/

Important examples include

- **Offences against the Person Act 1861**
- **Theft Act 1968**
- **Criminal Damage Act 1971**
- **Fraud Act 2006.**

2.7.2 Case law and presumptions

Case law (also known as common law) is an important legal source for some of the most serious common law offences. Important examples include:

- murder
- manslaughter.

Case law also provides presumptions:

- The presumption in favour of *mens rea* ***B*** **[2000]**
- The presumption that *mens rea* will be subjective ***G*** **[2004]**

Case law also provides important interpretations of statutes.

There are contrasting views regarding whether the courts can create new offences, exemplified by two judgments in ***Shaw*** **[1962]**:

Firstly Viscount Simonds:

> *"Need I say my Lords, that I am no advocate of the right of judges to create new criminal offences ...But....in the sphere of criminal law, I entertain no doubt that there remains in the courts of law a residual power to enforce the supreme and* ***fundamental purpose of the law****, to* ***conserve*** *not only the safety and order* ***but also the moral welfare of the state,*** *and that it is their duty to guard it against attacks which may be the more insidious because they are novel and unprepared for."*[26]

Secondly, contrastingly is the very persuasive heavyweight view of Lord Reid:

> *"I think, or at least I hope, that* ***it is now established that the courts cannot create new offences by individuals****.... when there is sufficient support from*

26 Shaw [1962]

public opinion, ***Parliament does not hesitate to intervene****. Where Parliament fears to tread it is not for the courts to rush in....."*[27]

Finally, it clear to any modern audience that only Parliament should be creating new offences.

2.7.3 Conflict between statute and case law

Where there is a conflict between statute and case law the presumption is statute should prevail.

2.8 Example offence: Criminal damage

2.8.1 The statute

s1 Criminal Damage Act 1971

(1) A person who without lawful excuse destroys or damages any property belonging to another intending to destroy or damage any such property or being reckless as to whether any such property would be destroyed or damaged shall be guilty of an offence.

2.8.2 The elements

Ask yourself, what are the elements of this criminal offence?

2.8.3 The trinity

Align those elements using the trinity approach to establish:

- Harm: *Actus reus*
- Culpability: *Mens rea*
- No justification: Defences (whether specific to the offence or general).

---

27 Shaw [1962]

2.8.4 Break down the elements to have systematic analysis

Harm: ***Actus reus***

1) Destroys or damages
2) Property
3) Belonging to another.

Culpability: *Mens rea*

4) Intentionally or recklessly

No justification defences

5) General or specific defences are captured by the term "without lawful excuse" which incorporates general and specific defences.

2.8.5 Analysis

(1) Destroys or damages

(a) Destroy appears to mean "(1) put out of existence by severe damage; or (2) completely ruin or spoil."[28]

(b) Damage appears to mean "physical harm reducing the value, operation or usefulness of something."[29]

(c) Principle: D does not have to permanently damage the fabric of the property.

Examples:

- Water-soluble paints which would have washed away did amount to damage because the local authority had incurred the expense by jet washing it off. (***Hardman v Chief Constable of Avon and Somerset*** [1986]).
- Removal of machine part (***Tacey* (1821)**).

---

28 Catherin Soanes (Ed.), *Compact Oxford English Dictionary*, (2nd edn, Oxford University Press 2002)

29 Catherin Soanes (Ed.), *Compact Oxford English Dictionary*, (2nd edn, Oxford University Press 2002)

- The "*temporary functional derangement*" of a police officer's cap by being stamped on constituted damage even though the hat itself could simply be pushed back into shape. (***Samuels v Stubbs* [1972]**).

(d) Principle: "*'What constitutes criminal damage is a matter of fact and degree and it is for the justices, applying their common sense, to decide whether what occurred was damage or not."* (***Roe v Kingerlee***).

Example: Smearing mud on the walls of a police cell is damage (***Roe v Kingerlee* [1986]**).

Example: Adulterating milk with water (***Roper v Knott* [1898]**).

(e) Principle: Damage need not be visible and the cost of restoration is relevant

Example: Plastic circuit card for controlling a saw had been damaged by erasing the programme written on it especially as restoration needed "*'time, labour and expense*". (***Cox v Riley* (1986)**).

(f) Principle: "Damage...should be widely interpreted so as to include not only permanent or temporary physical harm but also permanent or temporary impairment of value or usefulness."

Example: Damaging the usefulness of a computer disk (now covered by **s3 Computer Misuse Act 1990**) was damage (***Whiteley* (1991)**).

(g) Principle: Damage includes temporary physical harm

Example: D flooding a police cell and soaking a police blanket clearly damage. (***Fiak* [2005]**).

(2) Any Property

s10 Criminal Damage Act 1971:

(1) In this Act "property" means property of a tangible nature, whether real or personal, including money and—

(a) including wild creatures which have been tamed or are ordinarily kept in captivity...; but

(b) not including mushrooms growing wild on any land or flowers, fruit or foliage or a plant growing wild on any land.

Commentary

1. Broad definition includes tamed creatures such as your pet cat or dog. This is a wider definition than under the **Theft Act 1968**.
2. Property does not include wild mushrooms, flowers, fruit or foliage.
3. Land can be damaged, e.g. by dumping on it (***Cox v Riley*** **(1986)**).
4. Copyright cannot be damaged (N.B. **s107 Copyright, Designs and Patents Act 1988**).

(3) Belonging to another

s10 Criminal Damage Act 1971

> *(2) Property shall be treated for the purposes of this Act as belonging to any person—*
>
> (a) having the custody or control of it;
>
> *(b) having in it any proprietary right or interest (not being an equitable interest arising only from an agreement to transfer or grant an interest); or*
>
> *(c) having a charge on it.*

Commentary

1. Custody or control; right or charge.
2. D can be guilty of criminal damage to his or her own property if jointly owned.
3. D can be guilty if he has a mistaken belief of owning the property if he also believes another person has a propriety interest (***Seray-Wurie v DPP*** **[2012]**).
4. However, a genuine belief in that the others consent may be a defence – see below **s5(2)**.

(4) With intention or recklessness as to destroying or damaging property

Intention as to destroying or damaging property; or

Synonymous with:

- Direct intent, i.e. aim or purpose (we will explore in **Chapter 4**); or
- Indirect intent, i.e. foresight of a consequence as a virtual certainty being evidence of intention: ***Woollin*** **[1999]**.

Recklessness as to destroying or damaging property

Synonymous with advertent risk taking (We will explore in **Chapter 4**): ***G* [2004]**.

(5) Without a justification – general or specific defences

- For general defences – see **Chapters 13** and **14**.
- For specific defences – see **s5**.

s5 Criminal Damage Act 1971:

(2) A person charged with an offence to which this section applies shall, whether or not he would be treated for the purposes of this Act as having a lawful excuse apart from this subsection, be treated for those purposes as having a lawful excuse—

(a) if at the time of the act or acts alleged to constitute the offence, ***he believed*** *that the person or* ***persons*** *whom he believed to be entitled to consent to the destruction of or damage to the property in question had* ***so consented, or would have*** *so* ***consented to it if he or they had known of the destruction or damage and its circumstances****; or*

(b) if he destroyed or damaged or threatened to destroy or damage the property in question or, in the case of a charge of an offence under section 3 above, intended to use or cause or permit the use of something to destroy or damage it, ***in order to protect property belonging to himself or another or a right or interest in property which was or which he believed to be*** *vested in himself or another, and at the time of the act or acts alleged to constitute the offence he believed—*

(i) that the property, right or interest was in immediate need of protection; and

(ii) that the ***means of protection adopted or proposed to be adopted*** *were or would be* ***reasonable*** *having regard to all the circumstances.*

(3) For the purposes of this section it is ***immaterial whether a belief is justified or not if it is honestly held.***

(4) For the purposes of subsection (2) above a right or interest in property includes any right or privilege in or over land, whether created by grant, licence or otherwise.

(5) This section shall not be construed as casting doubt on any defence recognised by law as a defence to criminal charges.

Commentary

1. **s5(2)** lawful excuse opens up general defences and specific defences.
2. Subjective nature of belief confirmed by **s5(3)**

Principle
Mustill J,

"the court is required by section 5(3) to focus on the existence of the belief, not its intellectual soundness; and a belief can be just as much honestly held if it is induced by intoxication, as if it stems from stupidity, forgetfulness or inattention."

3. Two specific defences under **s5(2)**: *Lawful excuse:*
   (a) Consent; and
   (b) Protection.

a) Belief in consent

An example is where D is intoxicated and mistakenly believes they have a neighbour's consent to break a window to gain access and D then breaks into the wrong house. The High Court quashed the conviction (***Jaggard v Dickinson* [1981]**).

***Attorney-General's Reference (No.1 of 2023)* [2024]**

In this case D's were charged with conspiracy to commit criminal damage in the context of climate change protests. D's were all acquitted. The Attorney-General referred a point of law (under **s36 Criminal Justice Act 1972**).

Question: What were "circumstances" under **s5(2)(a)** consent that could be left to the jury?

The Court of Appeal held that:

"[1] *The Words of the statute have primacy and should be interpreted in the way that best reflected the ordinary and natural meaning of the legislative intention.*

[2] *in this case that meant*

i. The belief in consent at the time of the Commission of the offence.

ii. It could not be based on seeking to persuade the owner of the climate crisis.

iii. The belief must be genuinely and honestly held.

iv. This required a certainty in the belief that the owner would have consented.

v. There must be evidence that the defendant believed the owner would have consented.

[3] *Circumstances can include: time, place and extent of damage caused. The circumstances did not include the political or philosophical beliefs of the person causing the damage. The circumstances must belong to the damage not the defendant.*

[4] *Circumstances does not include the urgency or merits in relation to the climate action* taken.

[5] *A judge may withdraw the defence from the jury if no properly directed jury could reach such a conclusion. The judge must exercise considerable caution before so doing."*

b) Belief in the immediate need to protect property

The question is whether D believed it to be reasonable "in order to protect property" may have some objective aspect.

Example: D sets fire to bedding to point out a faulty fire alarm in the old persons' home. No defence (***Hunt* (1977)**).

In the ***Attorney-General's Reference No. 1 of 2022* [2022]**; (*The Colstons Statue Case* – see ***In the News***, below, for the facts) the issues were under the **ECHR Art 9**, Freedom **of Thought and Conscience**; **Art 10**, **Freedom of Expression**; and **Art 11**, the **Right to Protest.**

The **Human Rights Act 1998** (**HRA 1998**), **s3** construction clause required the court to interpret **CDA 1971**, **s5** so far as possibly compliant **ECHR Arts 9**; **10** and **11**.

The court held firstly, **ECHR** did not provide protection for those who caused criminal damage during a protest that was violent or not peaceful. Secondly, when the damage was inflicted violently and not peacefully **Arts 9**, **10** and **11** were not engaged and no question of proportionality arose.

Burnett LCJ commented:

> *"We have concluded that prosecution and conviction for causing significant damage to property during protest would fall outside the protection of the convention, either because the conduct in question was violent or not peaceful, alternatively (even if theoretically peaceful) prosecution and conviction would clearly be proportionate."*

In the News

The Colston statue

On 23 March 2020 the country was locked down due to a global pandemic.

On 25 May 2020, in the United States, a man by the name of George Floyd was killed by a police officer in the city of Minneapolis. This killing gave rise to huge public concern in relation to racism in society generally and in particular in relation to policing. In the United States and the UK the "Black Lives Matter" movement was a movement giving voice to the significant concerns about racism in society.

On 7 June 2020, in Bristol, as part of the black lives matter movement an infamous statue was toppled. The man on the statue plinth was Edward Colston. Edward Colston was a significant slave trader. He lived much of his life away from Bristol. He did however donate significant quantities of money and became a notorious philanthropist in Bristol. In Bristol numerous public buildings were named after him and a statue of him was stood in the City Centre appearing to "celebrate" his life. There was a significant history of public protest against the memorialisation of Colston dating back decades in the Bristol area.

Please now read these two articles

1. Martin Farrer, "Who was Edward Colston and why was his Bristol statue toppled?" The Guardian (8 June 2020) <https://www.theguardian.com/uk-news/2020/jun/08/who-was-edward-colston-and-why-was-his-bristol-statue-toppled-slave-trader-black-lives-matter-protests> accessed 06 April 2025
2. Haroon Siddique and Damien Gayle, "Colston four: protesters cannot rely on 'human rights' defence, top judge rules" *The Guardian* (28 September 2022) <https://www.theguardian.com/law/2022/sep/28/colston-four-protesters-cannot-rely-on-human-rights-defence-top-judge-rules> accessed 06 April 2025

Firstly, it is obvious that Colston's behaviour during his life was appalling. He was an important part in a trade that reduced human virtue to property.

Secondly, it is submitted that it is an obvious anomaly that the man whose behaviour was so appalling in his life is celebrated with numerous memorials.

Finally, however in a society ruled by law there is an open question whether lawful protest against the statues or unlawful damage to the statue is the right route ahead.

What approach did the judge in Bristol take to the **s5** defences?

What did the jury do?

What approach did the Court of Appeal take?

Why do you think they took this approach?

2.9 Summary

- **Nature of criminal law**: we looked at the nature of criminal law and concluded that the best way to define it is by process. An offence is criminal if followed by a criminal process.
- **Criminal censure**: process and proof: we looked at the legal and moral opprobrium which follows someone being found guilty of a criminal offence. We introduced the criminal process.
- **The trinity**: we explored the trinity of harm, fault and the absence of justification.
- **Evaluation**: we reviewed learning outcomes and specifically evaluation. We looked at methods by which students can attain the best results in courseworks and essay by stating the criteria value, defining the criteria of value then utilising the criteria of value to measure the law from both sides.
- **Evaluation and reform framework for criminal law**: we then set the evaluation framework that will be utilised throughout this book to evaluate the quality of English criminal law.

  The framework we set included but is not limited to:

  1. Legal certainty and legal clarity
  2. Equality before the law: protected characteristics and socio-economic barriers
  3. Fair warning; fair labelling and sufficient breadth principles
  4. Human rights compliance: autonomy and welfare principles
  5. International comparators and reform: practicality, principle and politics.

- **Criminal law sources**: we looked at the two main sources. Statute law being very helpful when well drafted, identifying the elements of the offence and any specific defences. Common law although relatively certain in relation to serious offences has some failings on certainty and clarity.
- **Example offence: criminal damage**: using the offence of criminal damage we focused on how you can use a step-by-step elemental approach dealing with each aspect of the trinity reviewing the harm, culpability and justification factors.

Further reading

Andrew Ashworth, "Is the Criminal Law a Lost Cause?" (2000) *116 Law Quarterly Review 225*

Dennis Baker, "Constitutionalizing the Harm Principle" (2008) 27 *Criminal Justice Ethics 3*

Antony Duff, "Theorizing Criminal Law: A 25th Anniversary Essay" (2005) *25 Oxford Journal of Legal Studies 353*

Grant Lamond, "What is crime?", [2007] *27 Oxford Journal of Legal Studies 609*

Glanville Williams, "The Definition of Crime" (1955) *Current Legal Problems 8: 107*

CHAPTER 3

Actus reus: Harm, omissions and causation

3.1 Introduction

In England and Wales all criminal offences include at least one *actus reus* – or "guilty act" – element; although some offences – such as conspiracy (see **Chapter 16**) – include *actus reus* elements, such as reaching an agreement, which demonstrate that the *actus reus* element(s) of an offence need *not* be a physical act. Whilst the literal translation of *actus reus* refers to *acts*, in limited circumstances, it is also possible for the *actus reus* of an offence to consist of an omission, a failure to act, as well as including other forms of *actus reus* such as the bringing about of specific consequences by the defendant's actions. In this chapter, we will explore the foundational principles of *actus reus* elements of criminal offences, including the distinction between acts and omissions, which it is helpful to understand generally before we apply these principles to the specific offences discussed in **Chapters 5–12** and categories of offences discussed in **Chapters 15–16**.

Offences typically require the prosecution to establish more than one *actus reus* element. These elements can take different forms, focusing on things such as the defendant's conduct, surrounding circumstances which are required for the offence to arise, or on the consequences of the defendant's conduct. Whether a specific offence has *actus reus* elements from each of these categories has a significant impact on what the prosecution are required to prove. On the one hand, offences without consequence elements place a greater emphasis on the defendant's conduct. On the other hand, where an offence has one or more consequence elements, it is necessary to establish **causation**, in fact and in law, between the defendant's conduct and the eventual outcome.

Whilst many criticisms and proposed reforms address *actus reus* elements in the context of specific offences or forms of offending, towards the end of this chapter, we will consider some of the broader points of evaluation and critique which have been made by academics and bodies such as the Law Commission.[1] You will also find that these general principles provide an excellent opportunity to take a comparative approach to evaluation, looking at the distinctions between the law in England and Wales and other jurisdictions, or between criminal law and other legal disciplines.

Aims of this chapter

By the end of this chapter, you will:

- Be able to identify and discuss the categorisation of a range of *actus reus* elements you encounter when looking at various criminal offences.
- Understand how to apply the law of causation in a problem scenario, including understanding the distinction between causation in fact and causation in law.
- Be able to critically evaluate aspects of criminal liability for omissions and the development of the law on causation, including through comparisons with other jurisdictions.

3.2 Actus reus

As discussed in **Chapter 2**, the traditional justification of criminal liability consists of *harm*, *culpability*, and a lack of *justification*. Whilst the term *actus reus*, translated literally, means guilty act: the *actus reus* of most offences consists specifically of the harm caused – or, in relation to inchoate crimes, the potential harm caused, by the defendant, without making a judgment on the defendant's culpability or potential justifications for their actions. As a reminder, the burden of proof is on the

1 See, for example, The Law Commission, *Legislating the Criminal Code: Offences against the Person and General Principles* (Law Com No 218, 1993) Paras 11.1-11.6

prosecution to establish each individual element of the offence and where there is a reasonable doubt as to any of these, the defendant should be acquitted.[2]

Criminal offences can, generally, be separated into conduct offences and consequence offences. Crimes of conduct are criminal regardless of the eventual outcome of the defendant's actions, such as the offence of fraud by false representation contrary to **s2 Fraud Act 2006**, which does not require anyone to have been deceived by the defendant's false representation.[3] Consequence offences, also termed result crimes, require the defendant's actions to have brought about a specific outcome, such as the offence of recklessly causing grievous bodily harm contrary to **s20 Offences Against the Person Act 1861**, which requires the defendant to have caused really serious harm to the complainant.[4]

Similarly, it is possible to distinguish between different forms of *actus reus* offence elements. Conduct offences will typically include:

- Conduct elements, such as making a demand (a requirement of blackmail) or appropriating (a requirement of theft);
- Circumstance elements, such as the absence of consent (a requirement of various sexual offences).

Result offences will also require one or more:

- Result elements, such as damage (a requirement of criminal damage offences) or death (a requirement of homicide offences).

It is also important to note a less common category of offences which require a particular state of affairs to exist, without the need for specific conduct or result elements to have been voluntarily committed by the defendant. For example, in ***Winzar v Chief Constable of Kent* (1983)** the defendant, who was drunk, was detained by the police and placed in a police car to be taken to a police station. At the police station he was charged with being found drunk in the highway contrary to **s12 Licensing Act 1872**. Despite his presence on the highway (the circumstance element of the offence) whilst in the police car being involuntary, the offence was concerned with a particular state of affairs (defendants being in a state of intoxication in the highway) and the defendant was liable.

3.2.1 Conduct as actus reus

Many offences will require the defendant to have conducted themselves in a specific way. Whilst it is common to think of actions which immediately and directly

2 See, Woolmington v DPP [1935]
3 See, Chapter 10
4 See, Chapter 7

impact the complainant, such as a punch, conduct also includes elements such as the making of a false representation, which may not necessarily impact anybody at all. As this example also demonstrates, conduct includes the saying (or writing) of words—which might amount to an assault where they do go on to cause a complainant to fear immediate violence.

Similarly, silence, which we might ordinarily think of as being an example of inaction, can suffice as conduct. In ***Ireland and Burstow* [1998]** the defendant was convicted of assault occasioning actual bodily harm after repeatedly silent calling three women who went on to develop psychological conditions as a result. The House of Lords upheld the conviction on the basis that silence can amount to an assault where the context of the silence is such that it gives rise to fear of immediate violence.

More generally, allegations that the defendant has committed an offence through inaction require analysis using principles of liability for omissions, which are discussed further at **3.3** below.

3.2.2 Consequences as actus reus

Where an offence requires a specific consequence, the defendant will not be liable for that offence unless the specific consequence occurs. Of course, there might be other, less serious offences, which the defendant commits if certain consequences do not come about. For example, a defendant who recklessly injures another may be liable for grievous bodily harm (**s20 Offences Against the Person Act 1861**) if the injury is sufficiently serious (a consequence) but can be liable for actual bodily harm (**s47 Offences Against the Person Act 1861**) if the injury is not so serious. Defendants may also be liable for inchoate offences, such as attempted murder, where they do not succeed in bringing about an intended consequence.

Where an offence has a consequence element, it is necessary to consider the issue of causation. Liability requires the prosecution to establish that the defendant was the factual and legal cause of the outcome, using the principles discussed at **3.4-3.6** below.

3.2.3 Circumstances as actus reus

Where an offence requires – as part of the *actus reus* – for a particular circumstance or state of affairs to exist, such a requirement does not also require the defendant to be aware of the existence of this circumstance or state of affairs, unless there is a corresponding *mens rea* element of knowledge of these circumstances. As an example, the offence of murder requires the killing to have taken place under the King's peace. As you will see in **Chapter 5**, this addresses whether the death occurred as part of a war or other official conflict. It is an *actus reus* element and does not require the defendant to appreciate that the killing takes place outside of the King's peace in order to be liable.

Activity

Actus reus elements

Categorise the following *actus reus* elements according to whether they are conduct elements, consequence elements, or circumstance elements of their respective offences:

- Supplying – An element of offences relating to controlled drugs: see **Ch 11**.
- The absence of consent – An element of several sexual offences: see **Ch 8**.
- Encouragement – An element of participatory offences: see **Ch 14**.
- Belonging to another – An element of theft: see **Ch 9**.

3.2.4 Coincidence of actus reus and mens rea elements

In order for the defendant to be liable, each element of the *actus reus* must be satisfied *and* at the point the defendant commits the *actus reus* they must also have the necessary *mens rea*. As you might expect, it is not necessary for any result elements to instantly occur, these may follow later provided that causation can be established.

As an example, where a defendant throws a punch at the complainant, causing a minor injury (actual bodily harm), the defendant must intend or be reckless as to applying force to the complainant (the *mens rea* of actual bodily harm) at the same time that they apply force to the complainant (a conduct element of actual bodily harm). In this scenario, the defendant's actions instantaneously cause some injury (a required consequence element of actual bodily harm), however, this element could arise later – such as where a punch causes bruising – provided that causation could be established.

However, the courts have had to address situations where a gap in time appears to exist between the defendant's actions and the necessary *mens rea*. In order to enable liability, the courts have developed the "continuing act" theory of liability.

The leading authority on this point is the case of ***Fagan v Metropolitan Police Commissioner* [1969]**. In ***Fagan*** the defendant inadvertently drove his car onto the foot of a police officer when following instructions to park at the side of the road. Upon becoming aware that he had done this, he left his car parked on the police officer's foot, refusing to move it when asked to do so.

Fagan was charged with assaulting a police officer in execution of his duty. The issue before the court was that the defendant's actions appear to have occurred before he had the necessary *mens rea* to commit the offence. But, the Court of Appeal held that the initial act of battery was an ongoing act, beginning when Fagan drove onto the officer's foot and continuing whilst the car was parked there up to and including the point at which the *mens rea* was formed through Fagan's decision to leave the car there. The *actus reus* and *mens rea* therefore coincided at that point and the offence was committed.

Although ***Fagan*** involved the *actus reus* being committed prior to the *mens rea*, it is also possible for a continuum to arise where *mens rea* precedes the *actus reus*. ***Meli v The Queen* [1954]** provides a potential example of this situation. In that case, the defendants had severely injured the complainant and had left the complainant believing him to be dead. In fact, the complainant was not dead at that time and subsequently died from exposure to the elements instead. The defendants' argument that they did not have the necessary intent to kill when leaving the body in the open – on the basis they believed the complainant to already be dead – did not succeed. The defendants' intent applied to the continuum of events beginning with the initial attack and continuing up to and including the disposal of the "body".

3.3 Omissions

Criminal offences are usually proven through the defendant's positive actions, as there is no general liability in English criminal law for merely failing to act. However, liability can arise where there is a specific legal duty to act which applies to the defendant. In an oft given example, there would be no general duty to save a drowning child, even if rescuing them would be comparatively easy, unless the defendant had a special relationship with the child – such as being their parent or guardian.

In order to establish liability for an omission, it is first necessary to note that some offences cannot be committed via an omission. For instance, the offence constructive act manslaughter, discussed in **Chapter 6**, can only be committed through positive acts (***Lowe* [1973]**). Some offences appear to only be capable of being committed via an omission, such as the offence of failing to prevent fraud contrary to **s199 Economic Crime and Corporate Transparency Act 2023**, although these are comparatively rare.

Further reading

Acts and omissions

The distinction between positive acts and omissions is complex. In many instances it is not exceptionally difficult to reconceive of what at first seems to be inaction, an omission, as something closer to a positive act, as seen in ***Speck* (1977)** – where a defendant's inaction, allowing a child's hand to remain on his trousers, was construed as a positive act for the purpose of a gross indecency offence. For a critique of the reliance on the distinction between acts and omissions as the basis for criminalisation, consider reading: Mark Dsouza, "Beyond acts and omissions: remarkable criminal conduct" (2021) 41(1) Legal Studies 1.

In order to establish liability for an omission, it is necessary to demonstrate that the defendant was under a duty to act. Duties may arise from statute, through a special relationship between the defendant and complainant, where the defendant has created a dangerous situation, or where the defendant is employed, holds an office or is contractually obligated to act. In such situations, a defendant will be liable for a failure to act, unless they have been absolved of the duty to do so, such as when consent to medical treatment is withdrawn or treatment is no longer in the best interest of a patient who is unlikely to ever regain consciousness (***Airedale NHS Trust v Bland* [1993]**).

3.3.1 A Statutory duty to act

Arguably, the most straightforward situation in which a duty to act may arise is where the statute creating an offence sets out such a duty. For example, **s170(2) Road Traffic Act 1988** states that, where a driver's vehicle is involved in an accident which causes damage or injury:

> *The driver of the mechanically propelled vehicle must stop and, if required to do so by any person having reasonable grounds for so requiring, give his name and address and also the name and address of the owner and the identification marks of the vehicle.*

In this instance, the offence of failing to stop and give details, or otherwise to report the accident in accordance with other sub-sections of the act, is *only* capable of being committed by an omission – it is the very failure to act which constitutes the offence.

Other offences are capable of being committed by a positive act or an omission. The offence of causing or allowing the death of a child or vulnerable adult, contrary to **s5 Domestic Violence, Crime and Victims Act 2004**, provides an example of this. **sub-s5(6)** states that for the purposes of the offence, an act *includes a course of conduct and also includes omission*. Further examples of offences capable of being committed via an act or omission can be seen in the offence of cruelty to children contrary to **s1 Children and Young Persons Act 1933** and false accounting, contrary to **s17 Theft Act 1968**, where a required accounting document is not completed (***Shama* (1990)**).

3.3.2 A duty which arises from a special relationship

Although statute creates duties which apply to certain categories of relationship between defendant and complainant, such as parent and child, the courts have also found that "special" relationships can arise in situations involving other relationships. In ***Instan* [1893]** the defendant failed to call for medical assistance or provide food for her bedridden aunt, who subsequently died of gangrene. The Court for Crown Cases Reserved held that a duty did exist, and the defendant was liable for manslaughter, with Lord Coledridge CJ stating that:

> *"It would not be correct to say that every moral obligation involves a legal duty; but every legal duty is founded on a moral obligation. A legal common law duty is nothing else than the enforcing by law of that which is a moral obligation without legal enforcement. There can be no question in this case that it was the clear duty of the prisoner to impart to the deceased so much as was necessary to sustain life of the food which she from time to time took in, and which was paid for by the deceased's own money for the purpose of the maintenance of herself and the prisoner; it was only through the instrumentality of the prisoner that the deceased could get the food. There was, therefore, a common law duty imposed upon the prisoner which she did not discharge."*[5]

Failure to provide care or summon medical attention for vulnerable complainants has given rise to liability for omissions in cases involving children and parents/guardians (***Gibbins and Proctor* (1918)**) and spouses (***Hood* [2004]**). Similar to the duty of care principles you may be familiar with from the law of torts, these and other categories of relationship – such as doctor and patient or between road users – are broadly accepted due to the nature of the relationship.

However, where there is not a pre-existing close relationship between defendant and complainant, it may be necessary to demonstrate that the defendant voluntarily assumed responsibility for the complainant's wellfare in order for a special relationship to exist. In ***Stone and Dobinson* [1977]**, the complainant was the sister

5 Instan [1893], 453-454

of the first defendant and came to live with him and his partner, the second defendant. The complainant had several serious medical conditions which deteriorated, and she became bedridden and subsequently died. Both defendants were convicted of manslaughter on the basis that they had assumed responsibility for the complainant. In Dobinson's case, the fact she was not a blood relative of the complainant did not prevent liability, as she had knowledge that the complainant was relying on her for food and care and was therefore under a duty to act.

3.3.3 A duty where a defendant creates a dangerous situation

It is also possible for a duty to arise in situations where the defendant has created a danger or harm, has knowledge that this has happened, and fails to act. The main authority on this point is ***Miller* [1983]**. The defendant was homeless and sleeping in an unoccupied house. The defendant fell asleep on a mattress whilst smoking and the lit cigarette set the mattress on fire. Upon waking up and noticing the fire, the defendant did not attempt to extinguish the fire or seek help, instead moving to another room. The defendant was convicted of criminal damage by arson, whilst he may not have been culpable at the time he was asleep, upon waking and becoming aware that he had created a fire, he was under a duty to act to limit the harm.

A further example of duties arising from the creation of a dangerous situation can be seen in ***DPP v Santa-Bermudez* [2003]**. In that case, the defendant was subject to a full body search by a police officer. The defendant failed to warn the officer that there were needles in the pocket of his jacket and the officer suffered a needlestick injury when carrying out the search. The defendant's conviction for actual bodily harm was upheld on the basis that the defendant not only failed to warn of the danger he had created by placing the needles there, but also dishonestly represented that there was no danger at all.

3.3.4 A Duty arising from employment, office or a contractual relationship

Duties have also been found to exist in situations where the defendant is employed, or holds an office, which requires them to act.

In ***Pitwood* (1902)**, the defendant was employed by a railway company to open and close the gates at a level crossing. The defendant had opened the gates, gone for lunch, and therefore omitted to close them ahead of a train passing through. The train struck a cart which was crossing over the trainlines at the time, killing the one of the people on the cart. The defendant was convicted of manslaughter on the basis that he had been under a contractual duty to shut the gates, had failed to do so, and was therefore criminally negligent.

A further example of this kind of duty to act can be seen in ***Dytham* [1979]**. The defendant was a police officer and failed to summon assistance after witnessing an attack on a man outside a nightclub. The officer was guilty of misconduct in public office for his "*deliberate failure and wilful neglect*" of the duties required of his office.[6]

Reflective question

Andrew and Rashid are a co-habiting couple. Without Rashid's knowledge, Andrew arranges for his elderly mother, Margaret, to move into the attic bedroom of their house. Andrew initially brings food and medicine for Margaret, who is bedridden, but over time does this less and less. Rashid discovers that Margaret has moved in but objects to Andrew not telling him and does nothing to help care for Margaret. Subsequently, Margaret develops a chest infection and dies due to lack of medical attention.

Consider whether Andrew or Rashid may be liable for failing to act. Use the IRAC approach mentioned in ***Chapter 1****, breaking the problem down into individual elements and writing a paragraph for each element which explains:*

a. *The issue: explaining the relevant facts in issue from the scenario.*
b. *Relevant rules: the applicable rules/law/legal principles, supported by citing statute, case law or relevant commentaries.*
c. *Application of the law: applying the rules to the facts of the scenario.*
d. *The conclusion: reaching a conclusion on the individual issue.*

3.4 Causation

Causation between the defendant's culpable act or omission and the injury, loss or other harm experienced by the complainant is an essential element of crimes with one or more consequence elements to the *actus reus*. The law on causation has developed through case law, particularly homicide cases, but the principles discussed below are applicable to any offence with a consequence element.

In order to establish causation, the prosecution will need to demonstrate that both **causation in fact** and **causation in law** can be identified in the case. Causation in fact is generally more readily established than causation in law, which can be impacted by **new intervening acts**. Both are necessary if the defendant is to be liable and you should resist any temptation not to discuss causation in fact simply because it is obviously present in a given set of facts.

---

6 Dytham [1979]

3.4.1 Causation in fact

The first step in establishing causation is to determine whether the defendant is factually causative of the outcome, which is assessed using the **"*but for*"** test. This test examines whether the outcome would have occurred without the defendant's negligent act or omission and is best demonstrated in the case of ***White* [1910]**.

In ***White* [1910]** the defendant intended to poison his mother. He placed two grains of potassium cyanide in her bedtime drink. The defendant's mother consumed a small quantity of this drink and died overnight. The defendant was charged with her murder; however, medical evidence demonstrated that the complainant had died of natural causes rather than through cyanide poisoning. The defendant was not liable for murder – as but for his action the outcome would have been the same, his mother would be dead – but was liable for attempted murder.

Causation in fact can be established even if there are other, later, events which are necessary for the outcome to be the same, provided that the defendant's actions are also necessary for this outcome. In ***Pagett* (1983)**, the defendant used the complainant as a human shield and shot at police officers. The police officers returned fire, killing the complainant. The defendant was guilty of unlawful act manslaughter, as the death of the complainant (the consequence element of the offence) would not have occurred if he had not used them as a shield.

3.4.2 Causation in law

The second step in establishing causation is to determine whether the defendant's act or omission was also the legal cause of the outcome detailed in the offence. Whilst causation in fact is, for the most part, easy to assess; causation in law is often more complex, because public policy plays a key role in determining the limits of the defendant's responsibility. Unlike causation in fact, there is one single test for causation in law, instead:

> *"[T]he meaning of causation is heavily context-specific and … Parliament (or in some cases the courts) may apply different legal rules of causation in different situations. Accordingly it is not always safe to suppose that there is a settled or "stable" concept of causation which can be applied in every case. That said, there are well recognised considerations which repeatedly arise in cases turning on causation."*[7]

The recognised considerations which provide general guidance include a requirement that the outcome be a reasonably foreseeable consequence of the defendant's act or omission and the *de minimis* principle, which suggests that a defendant's conduct should make more than a minimal contribution to the prohibited outcome.

---

7 Hughes [2013], [20]

Pagett* (1983)** provides a good example of this. The defendant was not the only cause of the complainant's death – the police also made a significant contribution – but the defendant taking the complainant as a human shield clearly accelerated the complainant's death and made a more than minimal contribution to this outcome. Another way of discussing this point has been to suggest that the defendant must be the **operating and substantial** cause of the outcome (Smith* [1959]**).

Another consideration which may be relevant when assessing causation in law is the **egg shell skull** rule, which states that the defendant must take their victim "*as they find them*" which includes existing vulnerabilities (such as a thin skull) or an unusual reaction to events. In ***Blaue* (1975)**, the defendant stabbed the complainant, a Jehovah's witness, who subsequently refused a life-saving blood transfusion on religious grounds. The defendant was found liable, on the basis that they had to "*take their victim as they find them*", which included not only physical attributes but also factors such as religious beliefs.

The blameworthiness of the defendant's conduct is also a relevant factor when assessing causation in law. In ***Hughes* [2013]**, the defendant was charged with causing a death whilst driving without a licence or insurance. The defendant was not in possession of a full licence, nor did he have insurance, and had he not been committing the offence of driving without these the complainant would not have died (i.e. causation in fact was established). However, the defendant's driving was "faultless" and fault for the crash rested entirely with the complainant who died. The Supreme Court held that a defendant could not be held liable for causing a death unless some aspect of their conduct in causing the death was open to criticism, displaying fault or attracting blame in the eyes of the jury.

3.5 New intervening acts

Of course, in many real-life situations, the defendant is not the only person involved in bringing about an outcome, the acts and omissions of another party may also make a contribution to the eventual consequences. Where the acts or omissions of others, or natural events, ocour after the defendant's conduct, a defendant will not be liable if these new intervening acts – often referred to by the Latin *novus actus interveniens* – break the chain of causation.

New intervening acts are relevant to the question of whether there is causation in law. Case law has explored various archetypal examples of new intervening acts, which we discuss below, however, it is important to start with the general principles of legal causation discussed above, particularly if addressing a situation in which more than one new intervening act occurs.

3.5.1 Third party acts

Third party actions can readily break the chain of causation where these actions are voluntary, on the basis of "free, deliberate, and informed" choices. ***Pagett* (1983)**, discussed above, demonstrates a situation where the third party's actions were not a free choice, but instead an act of self-defence, and therefore there was no break in the chain of causation.

When the third party's actions were reasonably foreseeable is also relevant when determining whether they break the chain of causation. In **A [2020]**, the defendant was charged with causing death and serious injury by dangerous driving. The defendant pulled her car onto the hard shoulder of a motorway in the early morning and not placed her hazard warning lights on. A truck subsequently struck the back of the car, likely due to the driver falling asleep, killing a passenger. In ordering a re-trial, the Court of Appeal held that the actions of the truck driver did not necessarily break the chain of causation, in part because it was reasonably foreseeable that parking on the hard shoulder without warning lights in the early morning could result in another vehicle crashing into it leading to death or serious injury.

As **A [2020]** demonstrates, a third party's actions may not break the chain even where they do constitute a criminal offence by the third party. However, where a third party goes on to commit a fundamentally different crime, which the defendant has no involvement in, there will be a break in the chain in relation to any later consequences the defendant has no part in causing (***Rafferty* [2007]**).

3.5.2 Medical treatment

Medical treatment can be considered a specialist category of third party actions and, like other third party acts, can break the chain of causation, albeit in very limited circumstances. Several cases have explored the impact of discontinuing medical treatment, such as the withdrawal of life support or discontinuation of CPR. Where medics stop attempting to save the complainant's life and the injury caused by the defendant then results in death, it is clear that the chain of causation remains unbroken: ***Malcherek and Steel* [1981]**. However, the situation is more complex in situations involving potential medical negligence.

In ***Cheshire* (1991)** the defendant shot the complainant in the stomach during a fight. Later, when recovering in hospital, the defendant required a tracheotomy and during this procedure he died. The Court of Appeal held that although medical negligence may have contributed to the complainant's death, unless it "*was so independent*" of the defendant's actions and "*in itself so potent in causing death*" that it made the defendant's actions "*insignificant*", it did not break the chain of causation.[8]

A rare example of where medical negligence has broken the chain of causation can be seen in ***Jordan* (1956)**. In that case the complainant had almost completely recovered from the injuries caused by the defendant when he was given antibiotics to which he was allergic. The Court of Appeal held that the medical negligence in

8 R v Cheshire (1991)

the case did break the chain of causation. However, ***Jordan*** has had limited application in subsequent cases with the courts emphasising that medical negligence must be extraordinary in order to constitute an intervening act. Even in cases where medical negligence is significant, such as ***Smith* [1959]** where the defendant was dropped twice whilst being taken to receive treatment, this has not proved sufficient to break the chain.

3.5.3 The complainant's own actions

As well as third parties, it is also possible for the reaction of the complainant to amount to an intervening event. The leading authority on this point is ***Roberts* (1972)** in which the complainant jumped out of a moving car whilst resisting the defendant's steps towards committing a sexual assault on her. The Court of Appeal held the defendant liable for the actual bodily harm suffered by the complainant. The complainant's actions were a reasonably foreseeable consequence of the defendant's improper conduct and therefore did not break the chain of causation.

Where, however, a complainant "*does something so "daft" ... or so unexpected*" that it is not reasonably foreseeable, the chain will be broken.[9] This is quite a high threshold to meet, as it is recognised that complainants may react hastily in the moment (***Williams* [1992]**). The standard is an objective one, so it is important to ask what are the range of reactions that we might expect from a reasonable person in response to defendant's conduct (***Marjoram* [2000]**). As seen in ***Blaue* (1975)**, discussed above, and ***Holland* (1841)**, refusing medical treatment is unlikely to constitute an intervening act of the complainant.

Reflective question

Many complex causation cases may involve multiple prospective defendants and several possible breaks in the chain(s) of causation between the defendants' actions and complaints injuries. Identify any potential causes of injury in this scenario and consider whether new intervening acts break the chain between these causes and the outcome:

Debbie is driving her motorcycle along a country lane when, suddenly, she swerves to avoid being hit by a car driven by Jonathan. As she swerves, Sean, a young child, runs from behind a hedge in order to cross the road and Debbie is unable to avoid hitting him. Sean is knocked down and an ambulance has to be called to take him to hospital. On the way to the hospital, the ambulance drives over a bumpy road and a small fracture in Sean's arm is worsened as he is jostled.

9 R v Roberts (1972)

Drug use by the complainant

The use of illegal drugs by the complainant has been a significant issue in a number of recent cases, including ***Kennedy (No 2)* [2007]** and ***Gemma Evans* [2009]**. Before discussing these cases, it is important to note that here we are speaking about voluntary drug use, where the complainant self-administers the drug. Involuntary drug use, such as where the defendant injects the complaint without their agreement, are unambiguously criminal offences and raise no particular issues of legal causation (see, e.g., ***Cato* [1976]**).

In ***Kennedy (No 2)* [2007]**, the defendant prepared a syringe of heroin and supplied this to the complainant. The complainant self-administered the heroin and returned the syringe to the defendant, who then left the room. The complainant then died as a result of injecting the heroin. The defendant was initially convicted of manslaughter, however this was quashed on appeal, in part because:

> *"The criminal law generally assumes the existence of free will. The law recognises certain exceptions, in the case of the young, ... and it acknowledges situations of duress and necessity .... But, generally speaking, informed adults of sound mind are treated as autonomous beings able to make their own decisions ... Thus D is not to be treated as causing V to act in a certain way if V makes a voluntary and informed decision to act in that way rather than another."*[10]

Key to his judgment was the fact that the complainant had self-administered the heroin and, therefore, it was difficult to demonstrate that the defendant's actions were the cause of the death. By way of contrast, in ***Gemma Evans* [2009]**, the defendant – who was the complainant's half-sister – supplied the heroin to the complainant but also became aware that she had overdosed after the heroin had been injected. The Court of Appeal upheld the defendant's conviction for gross negligence manslaughter (see **Chapter 6**) on the basis that the defendant had assumed responsibility and was therefore liable for the omission of failing to get medical assistance, drawing on the principles of omissions liability discussed above.

For a further example of the application of ***Kennedy (No 2)* [2007]**, see ***Field* [2021]**. In that case, over a three-year period, the defendant had been in a coercive relationship with the complainant. The defendant had begun lacing the complainant's food with drugs and was "gaslighting" him, whilst stating to others that the complainant had developed a problem with alcohol and was suicidal. The complainant died after consuming a combination of drugs and alcohol, the latter of which had been left out to tempt the complainant. The defendant's conviction for murder was upheld by the Court of Appeal. The complainant's actions were not the free and informed choice required by ***Kennedy (No 2)* [2007]** in order to break the chain of causation. The judgment emphasises that questions of causation are a matter for

---

10 Kennedy (No 2) [2007], [14]

the jury,[11] following the judge's directions on the law: a point also made in ***Clarke and Morabir* [2013]**.

Self-harm by the complainant

Self-harm, including death by suicide, is a particularly distressing example of a complainant's own action. In some earlier cases, it has been suggested that a complainant's refusal to seek medical treatment as a form of suicide constituted a new intervening action, however, these suggestions were rejected and, as with other cases of refused medical treatment, the chain of causation was unbroken (***Dear* [1996]**). The leading contemporary authorities on the impact of self-harm by complainants are the cases of ***Dhaliwal* [2006]** and ***Wallace* [2018]**.

In ***Dhaliwal* [2006]** the defendant had, over a protracted period, domestically abused his wife. This included multiple physical assaults including, on the evening of the complainant's death, striking the complainant on the head. After the complainant's death by suicide, the defendant was charged with GBH contrary to **s18 Offences Against the Person Act 1861** and manslaughter. The defendant was ultimately acquitted on the basis that the prosecution could not establish that he had caused a recognised psychiatric illness. However, the Court of Appeal stated in *obiter* comments that where a defendant's actions cause a recognised psychiatric illness, such as post traumatic stress disorder, and this then leads to the complainant's suicide, the defendant can be liable for manslaughter:

> *"We should however record that, subject to evidence and argument on the critical issue of causation, unlawful violence on an individual with a fragile and vulnerable personality, which is proved to be a material cause of death (even if the result of suicide) would at least arguably, be capable of amounting to manslaughter."*[12]

Although this excerpt speaks of complainants who are "fragile and vulnerable", there is no need for a complainant to have a pre-existing mental health condition. Instead, the judgment in ***Dhaliwal* [2006]** simply suggests that where a defendant's actions bring about a mental health condition, these actions are capable of being a substantial cause for later self-harm by the complainant. Such an approach was adopted in the more recent case of ***Wallace* [2018]**.

The defendant in ***Wallace* [2018]** threw sulphuric acid over the complainant, causing severe and life limiting injuries. The complainant was nearly blinded by the attack and suffered from constant pain as a result of his injuries. After moving to Belgium to be closer to his family whilst still hospitalised, the complainant chose to undergo voluntary euthanasia, which is legal in Belgium. The Court of Appeal was required to consider whether the victim's own actions in choosing to undergo

11 Or, in a summary trial, for the Magistrate(s) acting as the tribunal of fact.
12 Dhaliwal [2006], [8]

voluntary euthanasia and/or the actions of the medics who performed the procedure was sufficient to break the chain of causation.

The Court of Appeal held that the complainant's decision to undergo voluntary euthanasia was not a free choice, separate from the defendant's attack on him, but instead a direct consequence of the defendant's actions. The fact that the complainant had sought and received lawful euthanasia "*as a response to horrific injuries does not preclude the jury finding that the defendant's conduct made a significant contribution to [the complainant's] death.*"[13] The Court of Appeal ordered a re-trial, where the defendant was acquitted of murder and manslaughter, but convicted of a lesser offence relating to the acid attack itself.

3.5.4 Natural events

Natural events, or what are sometimes termed "acts of God", may break the chain of causation where the events "*were of so powerful nature that the conduct of the defendant was not a cause at all, but was merely part of the surrounding circumstances*".[14] It is also important to keep in mind the general principles, discussed above, particularly the principle of reasonable foreseeability. A natural event which is an ordinary part of everyday life – such as rainfall – is reasonably foreseeable and won't break the chain of causation; whereas a natural event which is extraordinary – such as an earthquake in London – would likely constitute a new intervening event (***Southern Water Authority v Pegrum* [1989]**). In ***Environment Agency v Empress Car Co Ltd* [1999]**, Lord Hoffman explained:

> "*The true common sense distinction is, in my view, between acts and events which, although not necessarily foreseeable in the particular case, are in the generality a normal and familiar fact of life, and acts or events which are abnormal and extraordinary. Of course an act or event which is in general terms a normal fact of life may also have been foreseeable in the circumstances of the particular case, but the latter is not necessary for the purposes of liability.*"[15]

3.6 Evaluation and reform

Unlike the offences discussed in subsequent chapters, it is difficult to locate the principles of *actus reus* discussed in this chapter in a single statute, case or individual legal development. Similarly, the development of these principles has taken place gradually across different sources of law and, consequently, critical evaluation of the law often focuses on these principles in the context of specific offences,

13 Wallace [2018], [85]
14 Southern Water Authority v Pegrum [1989]
15 Environment Agency v Empress Car Co Ltd [1999]

which you will encounter in later chapters, or on issues such as liability for omissions and causation, which are discussed here.

3.6.1 Omissions

There is longstanding debate over the appropriateness of criminalising a defendant for failing to act, with most agreeing that liability for omissions should be reserved for offences which are particularly serious or which are, at a minimum, non-trivial.[16] The need for a defendant to be under a duty to act in order to attract liability goes some way to providing **fair warning** to individuals, however, it can also be suggested that some of the ways in which the law goes about imposing these duties do not satisfy the need for **legal clarity and certainty**.[17]

Whilst duties to act created by statute are, generally, relatively clear and unambiguous, as may be duties arising from a contractual obligation; the scope of liability arising from a special relationship and/or the creation of a danger is less so. It has been suggested that the development of the law in ***Evans* [2009]**, where the defendant was held to have assumed responsibility after the complainant had self-administered drugs, has made the limits of liability less clear.[18] Concerns about broadening the scope of liability too wide often raise concerns about **fair labelling** and whether it is appropriate to label, as well as punish,[19] those who fail to act as if they have positively brought about the result.

Imposing liability for a failure to act clearly raises questions concerning the extent to which the law can impose on individual autonomy. The limited circumstances in which liability can arise for an omission, in circumstances where it would not be particularly onerous for a defendant to intervene and assist, have been a particular point of contention in academic analysis. On the one hand, some have suggested that liability should be extended where the defendant could intervene at limited/no cost or risk to themselves, a so-called "easy rescue".

On the other hand, opponents of easy rescue provisions often argue that once liability can arise for situations that we are not directly involved with or responsible for creating, it is difficult to decide on where our responsibility to help should end. Some have addressed this point by arguing that we are inherently involved in some

---

16 See, The Law Commission, *Legislating the Criminal Code: Offences against the Person and General Principles* (Law Com No 218, 1993) 11.2-11.3

17 See, for example, J C Smith, 'Liability for omissions in the criminal law' (1984) 4(1) Legal Studies 88

18 Mohammed Subhan Hussain, '"Failure to Act"' (2017) 181 Criminal Law and Justice Weekly 872

19 Dennis J Baker, 'Omissions Liability for Homicide Offences: Reconciling R v Kennedy with R v Evans' (2010) 74 Journal of Criminal Law 310, 316-317

situations, without a prior connection to those involved, where – as Greasley puts it – we are "singled out, by fate, as the only person capable of assisting".[20]

In the News

A duty to rescue?

There have been repeated calls from members of the public for a duty to rescue to be introduced into UK law. In recent years, there have been several petitions to Parliament on this matter, although these have not yet attracted the level of support necessary for a parliamentary debate.[21] These proposals have been highlighted in articles such as: Asha Patel, "Matthew Schofield: Mum of son who died after attack calls for new law" *BBC News* (21 May 2024).

Internationally, there are a wide variety of international comparisons to compare England and Wales with. For example, **s323c(a) German Criminal Code** criminalises failure to provide help, where safe to do so, in emergency situations. When looking at examples from other jurisdictions, it is important to distinguish provisions which impose criminal penalties for a failure to help and provisions which provide a level of protection from civil liability where rescue attempts do not succeed or make the situation worse. Whilst England and Wales does not currently have the former, it does offer some protection to those who voluntarily go to the rescue of others via the **Social Action, Responsibility and Heroism Act 2015** against claims in the tort of negligence.

Activity

Suppose that you are a Member of Parliament and are preparing to take place in a debate on legislation which would establish an offence of failure to rescue in English law. What potential arguments and counterarguments would you address in your speech? Make a list of these points and consider which way you would vote on the proposals.

20 Kate Greasley, 'How Omissions Aren't Special' [2023] Criminal Law and Philosophy, 14

21 See, for example, 'Introduce a Duty to Rescue Law in England and Wales' (*Petitions: UK Government and Parliament*) <ttps://petition.parliament.uk/petitions/654757#:~:text=There%20is%20currently%20no%20statutory,a%20duty%20to%20rescue%20others.> accessed 11 July 2024

3.6.2 Causation

As with liability for omissions, the principles of causation play an important role in limiting liability in criminal law. The law should only impose liability where a defendant can be said to be the cause of a prohibited outcome: which English law attempts to achieve by requiring both **factual causation**, to establish that the defendant was a necessary condition for the prohibited outcome, and **legal causation**, to establish that the defendant's contribution was significant enough to attract censure and sanction.

Of course, criminal liability is not the only way in which a defendant can be held responsible for their actions. As Turton and Kyd discuss, causation in criminal law shares many similarities, but also key differences, with the principles of causation applied in tort law.[22] They highlight that the higher standard of proof in criminal law – beyond reasonable doubt as opposed to civil law's balance of probabilities standard – creates a need for **legal clarity** around factual causation so that jurors (or magistrates) can readily determine whether a defendant is liable.[23] The "but for" test for factual causation may help to achieve this clarity, but it is also liable to critique. Williams points out that the breadth of factual causation is, perhaps overly, broad: any precondition of the defendant's actions is factually causative, going back as far as "primeval slime".[24]

Legal causation offers some protection to defendants – or Williams' primeval slime – against being held liable for events far removed from their actions. Simester discusses this in terms of causation "petering out", highlighting that we would not hold a grandmother causative of a crime committed by a grandson, simply because giving birth to his father was a necessary precondition for the crime.[25] Cases such as ***Kennedy* (No 2) [2007]** and ***Wallace* [2018]** demonstrate that new intervening acts, such as the complainant's own acts, can break the chain of causation but only where the complainant makes a "*voluntary and informed decision*".[26] However, many have highlighted the difficulties in ascertaining whether a complainant's choice was "free, deliberate and informed".[27]

Some have questioned whether, rather than looking at whether a complainant (or third party's) actions are free and informed, it would be more appropriate to look at whether an intervening act was "expectable" as a result of the defendant's

22 Gemma Turton and Sally Kyd, 'Causing controversy: interpreting the requirements of causation in criminal and tort law' (2019) 70(4) Northern Ireland Legal Quarterly 425

23 Ibid 430

24 Glanville Williams, 'Causation in the Law' (1961) 19 Cambridge Law Journal 62, 64

25 Andrew Simester, 'Causation in (Criminal) Law' (2017)113(3) Law Quarterly Review 416, 421

26 Kennedy (No 2) [2007], [14]

27 G R Sullivan and A P Simester, 'Omissions, duties, causation and time' (2021) 137 Law Quarterly Review 358

conduct.[28] Du Bois-Pedain discusses ***Field* [2021]** and queries whether rather than trying to frame the complainant's choice to drink alcohol as an uninformed choice in order for it not to break the chain of causation, it might be preferable to ask whether the complainant's response was an expectable consequence of the defendant's coercion and gaslighting.[29] This would potentially expand the scope of criminal liability, arguably bringing it closer to the approach taken in civil law. However, in civil law, principles such as contributory negligence can temper the liability in claims where a claimant makes a significant contribution to their own injury.[30]

3.7 Summary

This chapter explored the *actus reus* principles which you will encounter when looking at offences in subsequent chapters. The key points to take away from this chapter are:

- The ***actus reus*** of a criminal offence consists of the defendant's acts and omissions, the consequences of those actions, and/or the surrounding circumstances which must be present in order for the defendant to commit the offence.
- Where an offence involves a conduct element, this will typically be demonstrated through the defendant's positive act. However, it is also possible for inaction to amount to conduct where the circumstances contextually make it so (***Ireland and Burstow* [1998]**).
- Liability for **omissions** is limited to situations in which the defendant is under a duty to act, such as where the defendant has created a danger or is in a special relationship with the complainant.
- Offences which require a specific consequence, often termed results offences, require the prosecution to prove **causation in fact** and **causation in law** in order for the defendant to be liable.
- **Causation in fact** asks whether the defendant's actions were a necessary condition for the outcome, applying the "but for" test seen in ***White* [1910]**.
- **Causation in law** asks whether the defendant's actions made a sufficient contribution to the outcome for the defendant to be liable. The defendant's actions need not be the only cause, or even the major cause, but must make a substantial contribution (***Padgett* (1983)**; ***Smith* [1959]**).

---

28 Antje De Bois-Pedain, '*Novus Actus* and Beyond: Attributing causal responsibility in the criminal courts' (2021) 80 Cambridge Law Journal s61, s75

29 Ibid s75-s76

30 Turton and Kyd (n 22) 431

- Where **new intervening events** occur following the defendant's actions, these may break the **chain of causation** and prevent liability, but only where they are so serious that they supplant the defendant's actions.
- Common new intervening events include the **victim's** own **acts** and the **acts of a third party**, including **medical negligence**, as well as **natural events**.
- Although each has established case law demonstrating specific approaches, it is always best to keep general principles, including the need for reasonable foresight, in mind when considering whether the chain of causation is broken.

Further reading

Cath Crosby, "Gross Negligence Manslaughter by Omission: The Emergence of a Good Samaritan Law?" (2018) *82(2) Journal of Criminal Law 127*

Grant Firkins, "Rethinking Causation in English Criminal Law" (2023) *87(1) Journal of Criminal Law 18*

Andrew Ashworth, "A new generation of omissions offences?" [2018] *Criminal Law Review 354*

Andrew Simester, "Causation in (Criminal) Law" (2017)113(3) *Law Quarterly Review 416*

JJ Child, "Defence of a Basic Voluntary Act Requirement in Criminal Law from Philosophies of Action" (2020) *23(4) New Criminal Law Review 437*

CHAPTER 4

Mens rea: Culpability and responsibility

4.1 Introduction

In the previous chapter, we explored principles of *actus reus*: the consequences, circumstances and conduct elements of an offence, which serve to highlight the harm caused (or, in the case of inchoate offences, at risk of being caused) by an offence. In this chapter, we discuss *mens rea*, the mental elements of offences, which relate to the defendant's fault. With limited exceptions, we are not typically concerned with proving **why** a defendant has committed a criminal offence, i.e. their motive, however, offences will often require the prosecution to prove that a defendant has acted with **intent** or **recklessness** in respect of their actions. Other forms of *mens rea*, such as **dishonesty**, also arise in relation to specific offences, such as some of those discussed in **Chapters 5–12** and **15–16**.

Although a commonly expressed maxim of English criminal law – "*Actus non facit reum nisi mens sit rea*": "An act does not make one guilty unless the mind is guilty" – suggests that all offences require fault on the part of the defendant, this is not always the case. Some offences, termed offences of **strict liability**, do not require the prosecution to establish the defendant's fault. These offences are often, although not always, regulatory offences and have become increasingly common in contemporary law. We will consider a number of these offences later in this chapter and discuss their role within the legal system.

As in **Chapter 3**, evaluation and reform of the law on *mens rea* is often focused on the elements of individual offences, which we will consider in subsequent chapters. Towards the end of this chapter, we apply some of the evaluative principles discussed in **Chapter 2** to concepts such as oblique intent and recklessness. As you will see throughout this chapter, establishing *mens rea* in the context of a criminal trial presents particular challenges. Unlike the physical elements of an offence, it is impossible to fully evidence what is going on in a defendant's mind at the time of an offence. The law, therefore, makes some assumptions and draws inferences from the defendant's conduct and the surrounding circumstances, both of which may expose the law to some criticism.

Aims of this chapter

By the end of this chapter, you will:

- Develop an awareness of common forms of *mens rea* seen in English criminal law and be able to identify these elements when looking at various offences.
- Be able to apply the principles of *mens rea* in the context of problem scenarios, including being able to distinguish between forms of intent and recklessness.
- Be able to critically evaluate the development of the law on intent and recklessness, drawing on your understanding of relevant case law.

4.2 Intention

When we think of a criminal offence, a scenario involving a criminal who sets out to commit the offence – be it a murder, robbery, or something similar – might be the first to come to mind. However, intention is conceptually complex, and the courts have often struggled to establish a workable definition for it. What is clear is that intention is not the same as, or directly related to, motive. This point was highlighted by the Court of Appeal in ***Mohan* (1974)**, which stated:

> *"[W]hat is the meaning of "intention" when that word is used to describe the mens rea in attempt? It is to be distinguished from "motive" in the sense of an emotion leading to action: it has never been suggested that such a meaning is appropriate to "intention" in this context."*

Similarly, a defendant may have a motivation that some would consider good or worthy, but still have the intent to carry out an offence (***Chandler* v DPP [1964]**). By contrast, a limited number of offences require the defendant to have a reprehensible motive, which is part of the definition of the offence, such as where an offence is committed due to racial hostility, discussed at **4.4** below.

English law employs two forms of intention: **direct** intent and **indirect**, or "oblique", intent. It is important to understand both and the distinction between them. However, it should be noted that, in the majority of cases, it is direct intent which will be argued by the prosecution. The relationship between the two concepts and recklessness has seen significant academic, judicial and professional commentary as well as proposed reforms.

4.2.1 Direct intent

Direct intent has been defined in a number of cases. In ***Mohan* (1974)** at 276**,** the court states that "**"***specific intent*" can be defined as *"a decision to bring about a certain consequence"* or as the *"aim"*." Similarly, in ***Hyam* [1974]**, the court explains that:

> *"Now in the ordinary use of language the word "intent" (or the commoner word "intention") has the meaning of "purpose" or "aim"."*[1]

This ordinary use of language is important because it has been determined that, generally, it should not be necessary for judges to give juries directions on the meaning of intention (***Moloney* [1985]**). Instead, juries should apply their common sense understanding of the term.

Of course, in many situations the defendant may deny that they held a specific intention or may not give evidence on the point. Since juries cannot read a defendant's mind or memory, in many cases it is necessary to draw on the circumstances of the case and to infer the defendant's state of mind. This will often be quite simple: a defendant who shoots a complainant at point-blank range clearly has the aim of causing severe harm or death (the *mens rea* of murder) or, as an example given in ***Moloney* [1985]** at 926 states:

> *"A man who at London Airport, boards a plane which he knows to be bound for Manchester, clearly intends to travel to Manchester, even though Manchester is the last place he wants to be and his motive for boarding the plane is simply to escape pursuit. The possibility that the plane may have engine trouble and be diverted to Luton does not affect the matter. By boarding the Manchester plane, the man conclusively demonstrates his intention to go there, because it is a moral certainty that that is where he will arrive."*

1 Hyam [1974]

As juries are instructed to do, it is important to draw upon your common sense to evaluate whether a given set of facts supports a finding of intent.

4.2.2 Indirect ("oblique") intent

In some cases, a defendant may attempt to argue that the outcome of their actions was secondary to their actual intended consequence. In many of these cases, the jury will reject this argument and find, as a matter of fact, that the defendant did intend the eventual outcome. However, where they do not, it is open to the court to find that there was intent, on the basis that the defendant had foresight that the outcome was virtually certain as a consequence of their actions.

Activity

Oblique intentions

An everyday example of an oblique intention might be as follows: when you switch the kettle on to make a cup of coffee, it is not your aim or purpose to cause your electricity bill to rise – you may, indeed, desire it does not – however it is a consequence of your actions.

Make a list of some other everyday situations which demonstrate oblique intentions.

This ***virtual certainty*** approach was developed in ***Nedrick* [1986]** and refined in ***Woollin* [1999]**. In ***Woollin***, the defendant lost his temper with his three month old son and, whilst the baby was choking on food, picked him up and threw him across the room toward a pram. The baby did not hit the pram but instead landed on the floor, suffered a fractured skull, and died. The defendant was charged with murder but argued that he did not intend to cause death or serious injury (the necessary *mens rea*) and that the purpose of his actions was to place the baby in the pram.

Confirming the approach from ***Nedrick***, the House of Lords held that the jury should have been directed that they could not find intent unless "*they feel sure that death or serious bodily harm was a virtual certainty (barring some unforeseen intervention) as a result of the defendant's actions and that the defendant appreciated that such was the case.*"[2]

The House of Lords quashed Woollin's conviction for murder, on the basis that whilst there was a significant risk of death or serious injury, it was not conclusive that a jury would have found these to be virtually certain. As murder is a crime of intention

2 Woollin [1999], 96. The necessary direction is that developed in **Nedrick,** except that Nedrick speaks of a jury's entitlement to "infer" rather than to "find" intent.

only, as we discuss in **Chapter 5**, the defendant's conviction was substituted for an offence which could be committed recklessly: manslaughter.

Reflective question

The history of the law on intention is long and complex. In ***DPP v Smith* [1961]**, the House of Lords took an approach which involved presuming that a defendant intended all "natural and probable consequences" of their actions. This **objective** approach was rejected by Parliament in **s8 Criminal Justice Act 1967** which requires juries to consider the defendant's actual foresight and intent when looking for proof of criminal intent. Further appellate cases enabled intent where defendants **subjectively** knew that outcomes were "*highly probable*" (***Hyam* [1974]**) or, later, "*natural*" consequences (***Moloney* [1985]**) of their actions.

Write a short essay comparing and contrasting the contemporary approach to indirect intent with these historic comparators, drawing on the cases discussed below.

The virtual certainty approach from ***Nedrick*** and ***Woollin*** has been applied across a number of later cases. Three of these cases provide useful examples of the role of the virtual certainty test and the limitations on its use.

First, in ***Matthews and Alleyne* [2003]**, the defendants were charged with the murder of the complainant, who they had pushed off a bridge with the knowledge that he could not swim. The defendants maintained that they had not intended to kill the complainant. The Court of Appeal held that the jury were entitled to find that the complainant's death was a virtual certainty, barring assistance from the defendants, and that the defendants appreciated this. Consequently, the defendants' convictions for murder were upheld. The court did, however, emphasise that the virtual certainty approach is an evidentiary principle, rather than a point of substantive law. This means that where there is (i) virtual certainty and (ii) the defendant(s) appreciates this, a jury **can** find intent but is not **required** to do so.

Second, **R (*on the application of Charles*) *v Criminal Cases Review Commission* [2017]** examines a case where the defendant had struck the complainant with a bottle, causing serious wounds from which the complainant later died. The defendant argued that he never intended to cause death or serious injury and that the ***Woollin*** direction should have been given to the jury. The defendant brought a judicial review against the Criminal Cases Review Commission for their decision not to refer the case for review. The High Court held that the situations in which a ***Woollin*** direction will be necessary are exceptional. In a case where the evidence clearly supports a finding of direct intent, it is unnecessary to give a direction, particularly as it carries a risk of confusing the jury.

Third, in ***Thacker and Others* [2021]**, the 15 defendants were involved in a protest at London Stansted Airport which aimed to prevent the departure of a deportation flight. The defendants were charged with offences under the **Aviation and Maritime Security Act 1990** relating to endangering safe operation at the airport. The defendants appealed on multiple grounds, which included the argument that they did not have a direct intent to disrupt services in a way which would endanger others. Within the judgment, the Court of Appeal highlights that whilst there is "*some debate as to whether foresight of "virtual certainty" as opposed to "a very high degree of probability" is required ... "virtual certainty" ... probably still represents the law.*"[3] Applying this principle, the court held that it was necessary to prove that endangerment of safe operations was a virtual certainty of the defendants' (intentional) efforts to disrupt the specific flight being used to carry out deportations. As this was not established, the defendants' convictions were quashed.

In the News

A news article on the initial conviction of the defendants in ***Thacker* [2021]** shows that whilst motive is generally not relevant to the question of intent (and therefore liability) it often has an impact during sentencing. Of course, this report should now be read with the knowledge that the appeal mentioned toward the end of the article was successful.

Damien Gayle, "Stansted 15: no jail for activists convicted of terror-related offences" *The Guardian* (9 February 2019).

4.3 Recklessness

Of course, in many cases a defendant may not have set out to carry out a particular act or bring about a particular consequence which is prohibited by law. Recklessness is a less culpable form of *mens rea* than intention, which makes the defendant liable for taking an unjustified risk. Generally, the lower culpability involved in committing an offence recklessly does not prevent liability (other than for offences, such as murder, which can only be committed with intent) but, instead, impacts the sentence a defendant will receive.

For a significant period, debate existed about whether a **subjective** or an **objective** approach to recklessness should be taken by the law. Both involve the defendant taking an unjustified risk. A subjective approach looks at the defendant's mental state, including whether they foresaw the risk of the consequence occurring; whereas, an objective approach involves the jury or magistrates considering

3 R v Edward Thacker and Others [2021]

whether a reasonable person would have foreseen risk of the consequence instead. This debate was resolved by the House of Lords in **G [2004]**.

4.3.1 Contemporary recklessness

In ***G***, the House of Lords held that only subjective recklessness should be considered when examining whether a defendant satisfies the *mens rea* of an offence. The defendants were two boys, aged 11 and 12, charged with an offence under the **Criminal Damage Act 1971**. Whilst on a camping trip, without their parents' permission, the two boys set fire to some newspaper outside a supermarket and threw this under a plastic wheelie bin. The lit newspaper caused a fire, which spread to nearby buildings, causing approximately £1 m in damage. The boys denied intending the damage and thought that the newspapers would burn out rather than causing a fire. In quashing the defendants' convictions, the House of Lords adopted the approach to recklessness taken by the Law Commission,[4] and stated that:

> "A person acts recklessly …with respect to –
>
> (i) a circumstance when he is aware of a risk that it exists or will exist;
>
> (ii) a result when he is aware of a risk that it will occur;
>
> and it is, in the circumstances known to him, unreasonable to take the risk."[5]

This subjective approach to recklessness has been confirmed in a number of subsequent cases, including ***Foster v Crown Prosecution Service* [2013]** and ***Westlake v Crown Prosecution Service* [2016]**. This approach does not require the risk to be "obvious" or "significant" but, instead, simply requires the defendant to have foreseen it (***Brady* [2006]**).

Reflective question

One day whilst truanting from school, Ari attempted to climb onto the roof of a public library in his hometown. A large section of the roof consisted of glass panels, which were fragile, and as Ari stepped onto one of these it cracked. Several shards of glass fell and injured Sam, a librarian working in the building below, causing minor wounds to her arm. Ari is charged with assault occasioning actual bodily harm, which can be committed with intent or recklessly. Ari maintains that he did not realise that the glass panels would break and risk injuring anybody below.

Consider whether Ari is likely to be liable for the offence charged.

---

4 See, The Law Commission, *A Criminal Code for England and Wales, Volume 1: Report and Draft Criminal Code Bill* (Law Com No 177, 1989) 51-52

5 R v G [2004]

4.3.2 Development of the law

In order to understand the significance of ***G* [2004]** and how it developed the law, it is useful to consider how the law developed before 2003. During the 20th century, a number of cases considered what was necessary where it was alleged that a defendant had been reckless. Subjective recklessness, sometimes referred to as "*Cunningham* recklessness" after the case which developed the principle, was initially the only recognised form of recklessness. This changed with the development of "*Caldwell* recklessness", an objective form of recklessness, which was applied to offences under the **Criminal Damage Act 1971**. However, as we will see, *Caldwell* recklessness presented several significant problems, contributing to the decision in ***G* [2004]** to abolish it.

In ***Cunningham* [1957]**, the defendant was charged with an offence under **s23 Offences Against the Person Act 1861**. The defendant had tampered with a gas meter in order to steal money from it and this caused gas to escape into a neighbouring house, endangering the life of the complainant. The *mens rea* for the offence required malice, which the Court of Appeal held required:

> (1) An actual intention to do the particular kind of harm that in fact was done; or (2) recklessness as to whether such harm should occur or not (i.e., the accused **has foreseen that the particular kind of harm** might be done **and** yet has **gone on to take the risk of it**).[6]

Cunningham recklessness formed the basis of a successful appeal in ***Stephenson* [1979]**. In that case, the defendant had been rough sleeping in a stack of straw and had created a fire in order to keep warm. The straw stack caught on fire and caused significant damage. At trial, the defendant brought forward medical evidence of schizophrenia and an expert witness testified that there was a possibility that the defendant did not appreciate the risk in the manner of a neurotypical person. The defendant's conviction was overturned, with the court emphasising that it was the evidence that the defendant did not appreciate the risk, rather than just the fact he was schizophrenic, which demonstrated the absence of *mens rea*.

***Caldwell* [1982]** was a case involving criminal damage by arson. The defendant, whilst drunk and holding a grudge against the owner for whom he had previously worked, set fire to a hotel. The defendant denied a charge of recklessly endangering life by arson, on the basis that he was so drunk that he had not considered the people in the hotel and therefore had not foreseen the risk to their lives. The House of Lords held that self-induced intoxication was a form of recklessness in itself and therefore did not provide a defence. But, it also developed an alternative approach to recklessness, stating that a defendant could be reckless in two distinct ways:

> *"(1) [The defendant] does an act which in fact creates an **obvious risk** that property will be destroyed or damaged and (2) when he does the act he either*

6 R v Cunningham [1957] (emphasis added)

> *has* ***not given any thought to the possibility*** *of there being such risk* ***or*** *has* ***recognised that there was some risk involved and has nonetheless gone on to do it****."*[7]

This approach did not replace the subjective approach from **Cunningham [1957]** but supplemented it. This meant that a defendant could be subjectively reckless or, if that could not be established, could be found guilty on the basis of objective recklessness.

There were a number of problems with the objective approach to recklessness in ***Caldwell***. These included a risk of potential injustices when defendants were not comparable to the "reasonable person" and what came to be termed the "*Caldwell* lacuna". The problem with comparing a defendant with a reasonable person becomes apparent when looking at cases such as ***Elliott v C* (1983)**. C was a 14-year-old girl, with learning difficulties, who set fire to a neighbour's shed with white spirit and matches. At trial it was held that C did not appreciate how flammable white spirt is and had given no thought to the possibility of the shed catching on fire, putting her own life at risk. Despite this, applying ***Caldwell***, the defendant was liable because a reasonable adult would have appreciated the risk involved in lighting the white spirit.

The "*Caldwell* lacuna" was a possible loophole in the law where a defendant could attempt to argue that they were not reckless objectively or subjectively, because the risk was a less obvious/minimal one and they had considered it and decided there was no risk. As such if a defendant would fall outside both conceptualisations of recklessness set out in ***Caldwell* [1982]**, seen in the quotation above, a defendant might avoid liability. This point was unsuccessfully argued by the defendant in ***Shimmen* (1987)**, where a defendant professed to be a Taekwondo expert and believed he could kick at a shop window in a controlled manner and not strike it. The court accepted that a defendant who genuinely believed there was no risk, after consideration of it, would be not guilty but held that on the evidence the defendant in this particular case had recognised a risk. Similarly, in ***Reid* (1992)**, the House of Lords appeared to accept that:

> *"if the defendant is addressing his mind to the possibility of risk and suffers from a bona fide mistake as to the specific fact which if true would have excluded the risk, he cannot be described as reckless[.]"*[8]

The abolition of "*Caldwell*" recklessness in **G [2004]** resolves both of these issues. Subsequent cases have demonstrated that defendants are no longer to be compared with the objective "reasonable" person, instead the defendant "*must*" have a subjective awareness of the risk and go on to take that risk (***Pinkney v DPP* [2017]**). Evidence such as psychiatrists' reports may support a defendant's argument that

---

7 Caldwell [1982] (emphasis added)

8 R v Reid (1992).

they did not have the necessary foresight of risk, however, where such evidence is inconclusive, it is open to magistrates or a jury to conclude that a defendant did in fact foresee the risk (***D v DPP* [2006]**). The return to a single approach to recklessness, overturning the approach taken by Lord Diplock in ***Caldwell* [1982]**, means that there is no longer a lacuna in the law.

4.4 Other forms of *mens rea*

Intent and recklessness are common elements of the *mens rea* across many offences, including several of the offences discussed in this text, however, they are not the only requirements which can be placed on the defendant's state of mind. Other forms of *mens rea*, such as **knowledge** and **belief**, are relevant to specific offences or categories of offence.[9] Some of these forms of *mens rea* are discussed in subsequent chapters, however, there are a number of forms of *mens rea* it is useful to be aware of as you begin to become familiar with criminal law.

4.4.1 Negligence and gross negligence

It could be argued that objective recklessness, where the defendant is not also subjectively reckless, is closer to the concept of negligence. Negligence employs an objective standard: a defendant is negligence if they fall below the standard of a reasonable person in relation to a duty of care owed to another. However, where a defendant is carrying out some specialist task, such as surgery, they will be held to a higher standard of a reasonable professional in that field. A defendant is negligent whether or not they are aware of the risk they are taking, although a defendant who is knowingly negligence may well demonstrate intent, or recklessness, as well.

Negligence is an uncommon concept in criminal law, finding much more application in areas of law such as tort. However, it arises in some strict liability regulatory offences and gross negligence is important in the context of **involuntary homicide** offences. In contrast to recklessness, which is a binary concept, there are degrees or levels of negligence. For example, several statutory offences under the **Road Traffic Act 1988** employ the concept of negligence: dangerous driving offences (**ss1–2**) involve a defendant falling far below the standard of a reasonable driver, whilst driving without due care and attention (**s3**) involves a defendant falling below what would be expected, but not *far* below.

Similarly, the involuntary homicide offence of **gross negligence manslaughter** requires the defendant to not only have been negligent but, also, for their breach to be sufficiently serious. In ***Adomako* [1995]**, the House of Lords confirmed the continued existence of gross negligence manslaughter in a case involving an anaesthesiologist, however, the offence can arise from duties owed by non-professionals as well. We discuss this offence in more detail in **Chapter 6**.

9 We discuss these in the context of specific offences in later chapters.

Further reading

Culpability and criminal liability

Labelling somebody a criminal seems very different to finding someone liable for negligence in tort law. The requirement for gross negligence indicates that a particularly heinous breach of duty is required for liability. Robson et al highlight that contemporary criminal law also focuses, particularly, on gross negligence which results in death (arguably among the most heinous consequences of criminal conduct). They argue that both of these limitations require reform and that a wider range of culpable negligence, resulting in severe but perhaps not fatal consequences, should be criminalised. Consider reading: Michelle Robson, Jon Maskill and Warren Brookbanks, "Doctors Are Aggrieved—Should They Be? Gross Negligence Manslaughter and the Culpable Doctor" (2020) 84 *Journal of Criminal Law 312.*

4.4.2 Dishonesty

Dishonesty is a common element in offences under the **Theft Act 1968** and **Fraud Act 2006**. It has seen significant developments in recent years, particularly in the case of ***Ivey v Genting Casinos* [2018]**, a civil case which was confirmed to apply in criminal law in ***Barton* [2021]**. The law as it now stands involves ascertaining what the defendant subjectively understood the facts of the situation to be and then asking whether the defendant was honest or dishonest from an objective standpoint. We look at this common law definition, as well as related statutory provisions, in more detail in **Chapter 9** and **Chapter 10**.

4.4.3 Hostility

In recent decades, the law has sought to acknowledge the particular problem of offences which are motivated on the grounds of hostility towards individuals on the basis of vulnerabilities or personal characteristics. Whilst some of these situations are addressed at the sentencing stage, with hostility treated as an aggravating feature by **s66 Sentencing Act 2020**, hostility based on race or religion is also addressed as an aggravated form of offending by **Part 2 Crime and Disorder Act 1998** (**CDA 1998**).

CDA 1998 identifies 11 offences which can become racially aggravated, many of these are offences against the person, which we discuss in **Chapter 7**. To be liable for these offences, the prosecution must establish either that the defendant demonstrated hostility on the basis of membership or presumed membership of a racial or religious group or that the offence was motivated, in whole or in part, by the victim's membership of a racial or religious group (**s28 CDA 1998**). In the latter case, the prosecution has the burden of proving that the defendant's motivations included hostility on one of the grounds specified (***DPP v Dykes* [2008]**).

4.5 Principles of *mens rea*

In addition to the various *mens rea* elements which you may encounter when exploring different forms of criminal liability, there are a number of principles which may be relevant when considering how different *mens rea* elements are applied.

4.5.1 Basic and specific intent

You may sometimes encounter a crime which is described as an offence of specific intent. Confusingly, some of these offences may have a *mens rea* element which on first inspection does not appear entirely specific: for example, **murder** is a specific intent crime, despite the fact it can be committed where there is an intent to kill **or** an intent to cause grievous bodily harm.

The distinction between **basic intent** and **specific intent** can generally be approached by considering the availability of recklessness as a form of *mens rea* (***DPP v Majewski* [1977]**). Crimes of specific intent can only be committed intentionally whereas crimes of basic intent can be established with other forms of *mens rea*. As well as murder, other specific intent offences include theft, burglary and wounding or causing grievous bodily harm with intent.

Whether an offence is a basic intent or a specific intent offence is relevant to the availability of certain defences, specifically **self-induced automatism** and **intoxication** (see **Chapter 13**). For basic intent offences, such as rape, assault occasioning actual bodily harm, and criminal damage, these defences cannot succeed – because the defendant's actions in drinking or causing automatism are themselves reckless.

For specific intent offences, these defences can establish that a defendant did not possess the necessary *mens rea* to be convicted of the offence. However, defendants who succeed in arguing these defences will often be found guilty of a less serious basic intent offence. For example, a defendant who is found not guilty of the specific intent offence of grievous bodily harm (**s18 Offences Against the Person Act 1861**) with intent may be found guilty of recklessly causing grievous bodily harm (**s20**) instead.

4.5.2 Ulterior intent

Offences of ulterior intent require proof of the defendant's intention to carry out a further offence, going beyond intentionally or recklessly committing the *actus reus* of the offence itself. Burglary, contrary to **s9(1)(a) Theft Act 1968** is the main example of this category of offence you should be aware of. To be guilty of a burglary under **s9(1)(a)** the defendant must enter a building or part of a building as a trespasser, intending or being reckless to do so, but must **also** have an ulterior intent to:

- steal;
- inflict grievous bodily harm; or
- cause criminal damage.

We discuss burglary in greater detail in **Chapter 9**, however, for present purposes you should note that a defendant does not need to actually go on to commit the intended ulterior offence: a defendant would have an ulterior intent to steal even if they went on to discover there was nothing worth stealing, for example (***Walkington* (1979)**). It should be emphasised that a defendant must **intend** the ulterior offence: recklessness as to the commission of the ulterior offence will not suffice.

Other offences which can require an ulterior intent include possession with intent to supply (**s5(4) Misuse of Drugs Act 1971**, discussed in **Chapter 11**) and committing an offence with intent to commit a sexual offence (**s62(1) Sexual Offences Act 2003**).

4.5.3 Transferred mens rea

The doctrine of transferred malice applies when the defendant has the necessary *mens rea* for commiting an offence, in one way, but goes on to commit the offence in a way which was unintended. When successfully relied upon, the defendant's *mens rea* for the intended offence satisfies the requirements of the offence which has been committed. Although the doctrine is termed transferred **malice**, it applies in cases involving recklessness as well, although such cases can often be resolved through the application of recklessness alone.

The most straightforward example of this is where the defendant intends to commit an offence against Person A but goes on to commit it against Person B. For those of you familiar with the Shakespeare play *Hamlet:* in Act 3, Scene 4, Hamlet believes that Claudius is hiding behind a curtain and stabs through the curtain intending to kill him. In fact, it is not Claudius but Polonius, who consequently dies. In this example, were Hamlet to be subject to English criminal law, Hamlet's intent to kill Claudius would transfer to his actions against Polonius and he would be liable for murder. A real-world example of this type of case can be seen in ***Gnango* [2012]**.

An example of transferred malice being applied can be seen in ***Latimer* (1886)**. The defendant got into a fight with a man, Chapple, in a pub. The defendant took off his belt and attempted to hit Chapple but, as he did, also struck a woman, Rolston, in the face. As the intended offence against Chapple and the offence committed against Rolston were the same, malicious wounding, the defendant's intent to commit the offence against the former could be transferred to the offence against the latter.

Reflective question

Hannah is a member at a local golf club and has a longstanding feud with Simon, another golfer at the club. Simon recently beat Hannah in the club's annual tournament and has been bragging about this in the club's coffee shop since. Hannah decides to "accidentally" strike a golf ball into Simon's car in retaliation. Hannah goes to the driving range and lines up a shot into the club car park aiming at Simon's car. However, when she strikes the ball a freak gust of wind blows it to one side and it hits the office window of John, the club president. Hannah is charged with criminal damage.

Consider whether Hannah has the necessary mens rea, intent or recklessness, for the criminal damage caused to the office window. Is the principle of transferred malice applicable in this situation?

In order for the doctrine of transferred malice to apply, the *mens rea* of the defendant's intended offence must be the same as the *mens rea* of the offence the defendant is charged with. Consequently, in ***Pembliton* (1872-75)**, the principle could not be used to make a defendant liable for criminal damage when he threw a stone intending to hit another person. The *mens rea* for the two offences were distinct, an intent to harm and an intent to damage, and therefore the principle did not apply. In such circumstances, it may be appropriate to consider whether a defendant's actions are reckless.

Transferred malice applies even where the defendant succeeds in committing the intended offence, provided that the *actus reus* of the unintended offence can be demonstrated and there is causation between the defendant's acts and the outcome. In ***Mitchell* [1983]**, the defendant hit a man, Smith, during an argument in a Post Office. Smith fell backwards and into a woman, Crafts, who suffered a broken thighbone. Whilst receiving treatment, Crafts developed a blood clot as a result of her injuries and suddenly died. Mitchell was convicted of constructive act manslaughter. It did not matter that Mitchell's intended unlawful act was directed against Smith, provided causation was established between the intended act and the victim's death. A similar approach was taken in the more recent case of ***Grant* [2014]**.

4.6 Strict liability

Strict liability is defined by the absence of a *mens rea* or fault requirement: a defendant is liable for a strict liability offence when they commit the *actus reus*, irrespective of their mental state. Strict liability often arises in the context of regulatory offences and in many situations, the behaviour it addresses might not be considered serious criminal conduct but instead "quasi-criminal".

An early example of strict liability can be seen in the case of ***Larsonneur* (1934)**. The defendant was a French national and had been permitted entry into the UK subject to conditions which included departing by a particular date. The defendant then travelled to the Free Irish State only to be deported back to the UK. The defendant did not choose to travel back to the UK, however, on her arrival she was detained and found to have committed an immigration offence. It did not matter that the defendant had not made the decision to return; the *actus reus* of being present after the departure date on her passport was the only requirement of the offence.

Although many of the offences you will encounter throughout your legal studies will be well drafted and clear, this is not always the case. Generally, there is a presumption that offences require fault from the defendant and when an offence does not explicitly state a *mens rea* requirement,[10] the courts will often imply a requirement based on the offence (***Tolson* (1889)**).

In ***Gammon (Hong Kong) Ltd v Attorney-General of Hong Kong* (1985)**, the Privy Council stressed that this presumption is particularly strong "*where the offence is "truly criminal" in character*" and should only be disregarded where doing so will support policy aims of "*social concern*" being pursued by the legislation creating the offence. Many cases regarding strict liability have been concerned with public safety related offences, such as offences related to the provision of prescription medicines (***Pharmaceutical Society of Great Britain v Storkwain* [1986]**) or possession of firearms (***R v Zahid* [2010]**).

Activity

Strict liability

Case law on strict liability often has to grapple with complexities in the law, where Parliament's intention is unclear and public safety is concerned. However, there are many more commonplace offences – such as failure to pay for a television licence – which are undisputedly strict liability offences. These offences raise questions about **fair labelling**, **politics** and criminal justice **policy**.

Suppose you are a Civil Servant advising a new Minister who is considering creating a strict liability offence. What issues might they need to be aware of before coming to a decision and what would your advice be about the advantages and disadvantages of such a law?

10 There is a presumption that offences possess a mental element. For statutory offences, the statute merely being silent to the mental element may not be sufficient: see, CPS v M [2009].

4.7 Evaluation and reform

Throughout this chapter, there have been several examples of the significant reforms seen around the mental element of criminal offences in recent decades. These include the evolution of the approach taken to reckless offending, leading up to **G [2004]**, and changes to the definition of dishonesty following ***Ivey v Genting Casinos* [2018]**. Many proposed reforms focus on the *mens rea* of particular offences, which you will encounter in subsequent chapters; however, there are a number of more general points which you may wish to consider when exploring criminal law on a macro level.

Several scholars have argued that the law on intention is insufficiently clear and that it fails to properly address the moral culpability of offenders with sufficient breadth. At present, the law allows a jury to find intent where they are satisfied that the defendant's **aim or purpose** demonstrates that intent, or where the defendant foresaw that an outcome was **virtually certain** as a result of their actions. Pedain, however, argues that virtual certainty is sometimes an inappropriately high fault requirement. Giving the example of a terrorist, who plants a bomb but is not virtually certain it will go off and injure people, Pedain argues that some defendants demonstrate sufficient approval of a "possible", but not "virtually certain", outcome that intent is the appropriate label for their culpability.[11]

Similar arguments are advanced by Leigh, who argues that **virtual certainty** is likely to be confusing to juries. Drawing on the approach taken in South Africa, Leigh suggests that the *mens rea* of murder should be satisfied when "defendants knew the likelihood of death or GBH might logically contribute to their purpose".[12] This would be a significant reform, not only in the context of murder, but also having consequences when looking at the mental element of other offences, including constructive act manslaughter.

International comparators provide a useful source of analysis for many of the *mens rea* concepts discussed in this chapter, especially when English legal concepts have equivalents in other legal jurisdictions.[13] Beyond academic analysis, there are numerous examples of international comparisons being made by judges as they consider developments to the law. For example. in ***Reid* (1992)**, Lord Goff draws on the German equivalent of recklessness in his analysis:

> *"[I]t is of interest that in Germany a similar controversy has arisen whether Leichtfertigkeit (recklessness in German criminal law) always requires the*

---

11 Anyje Pedain, 'Intention and the terrorist example' (2003) Criminal Law Review 579

12 Gavin Leigh, 'Murderous intent—The attitude of a murderer?' (2022) 86 Journal of Criminal Law 18, 28

13 See, for example, Pasquale Mastrolia, 'Transferred Malice: Hsitorical Underpinnings of the Rule and Legal Arguments for Its Abrogation' (2023) 87 Journal of Criminal Law 344

conscious causing of a danger; and I understand that the prevailing opinion is that it does not, so that it does not matter if, because of his thoughtlessness, the defendant did not recognise the danger, provided that there was a considerable possibility of a negative outcome which the defendant could have recognised with a minimum of attention."

Lord Goff's discussion also serves to highlight that whether the law should apply an **objective** standard or look at the defendant's **subjective** state of mind is an issue of significant debate when looking at mental culpability for offending. For a significant proportion of the 20th century, there was insufficient **legal certainty** around this point in the context of recklessness, until the House of Lord decision in ***G* [2004]** settled the position. However, this is not the only example of such uncertainty.

In ***DPP v Heard* [2007]**, the Court of Appeal considered the appeal of a defendant convicted of a charge of sexual assault contrary to **s3 Sexual Offences Act 2003**. This offence requires the defendant to have intentionally touched another person in a sexual manner, without their consent and without a reasonable belief in consent (see **Chapter 8**). The defendant argued that his self-induced intoxication provided a defence because it prevented him forming the necessary *mens rea*. However, the court rejected this argument, finding that the offence was not easily categorised as either **basic** or **specific** intent.

Fitzpatrick argues that the decision in ***Heard*** is problematic, but also that it demonstrates the challenges of achieving legal clarity whilst also achieving the need for the law to meet policy objectives and practical concerns:

"The policy dimension reflects the acknowledgement that this whole body of law is informed by questions beyond the confines of pure legal rules–the significant proportion of crime which is committed by persons in a condition of intoxication is taken to demand a response that criminal law doctrine cannot necessarily provide. Hence, we see deployed arguments to the effect that the voluntary consumption of an intoxicant can in some way "count' as the relevant mens rea for certain offences, even if, in orthodox terms, a defendant was actually lacking mens rea because of his or her intoxication. This is not to suggest that this approach is necessarily deficient."[14]

As we saw in this chapter, policy objectives play a key role in justifying the imposition of **strict liability**, where a defendant can be liable without the need for a particular mental state to be established. Whether this provides sufficient justification for liability in situations where the defendant has taken every possible precaution has been subject to debate, with some suggesting that defendants should be able

14 Ben Fitzpatrick, 'Sexual assault: intoxication' (2008) 72 Journal of Criminal Law 16, 18

to argue a defence of acting with "due diligence".[15] Furthermore, whilst historically arguments that strict liability conflicts with human rights have been unsuccessful,[16] a more recent case has seen arguments that strict liability conflicts with some rights under the **European Convention on Human Rights**, in particular the right to freedom of expression, succeed (***PWR v Director of Public Prosecution* [2022]**).

Arguably, although strict liability may be problematic from a human rights and moral culpability standpoint, it also avoids the issue inherent with all other forms of *mens rea*: that determining the defendant's actual mental state is perhaps an impossible task. Juries and magistrates in criminal cases are asked to infer a defendant's mental state from the evidence, following judicial guidance on the law based on the principles discussed in this chapter and their "common sense". In many circumstances, the defendant's mental state might be apparent from the facts; however, as you will encounter throughout your studies, this is not always the case.

4.8 Summary

This chapter examined the mental element of offending, *mens rea,* including many of the more common forms of *mens rea* you are likely to encounter when looking at criminal offences during your legal studies. The key points to take away from this chapter are:

- ***Mens rea*** elements of criminal offences examine the defendant's fault/culpability in committing the offence, which is assessed independently of any ***actus reus*** elements which must be satisfied.
- Various offences require different forms of *mens rea*, although common *mens rea* requirements include **intention** and **recklessness**.
- A defendant's **intention** can either be **direct,** where an action or outcome is the defendant's **aim or purpose,** or **indirect**, where the defendant foresees a consequence as **virtually certain** of their actions.
- **Recklessness** is assessed **subjectively** by asking if the defendant foresaw that there was a risk and yet went on to take that risk, unreasonably.
- Many offences can be committed with intent, recklessness or another form of *mens rea* such as **negligence**. Where a defendant is charged with one of these **basic intent** offences, they cannot claim some defences such as **voluntary intoxication**.

15 Alan Reed, 'Strict Liability Crimes: The Contours of Liability and Crimogenic Impact' in Alan Reed et al (eds) *Fault in Criminal Law: A Research Companion* (Routledge 2022)

16 Ibid, 52.

- Some offences, such as burglary, require the defendant to have an **ulterior intent** to commit a further offence, such as theft, in order to be liable.
- A defendant who intends to commit an offence against one person (or object) but who goes on to commit that offence against a different person (or object) will still be deemed to have intended the offence, due to the principle of **transferred malice**.
- Offences of **strict liability** do not require the prosecution to establish *mens rea*. A defendant is liable for strict liability offences whenever they commit the necessary *actus reus*.
- *Mens rea* is a complex area of law. Some have suggested that there are issues of **legal certainty** and **sufficient breadth**, however, potential reforms also raise important questions about the **fair labelling** of offenders based on their moral culpability.

Further reading

Findlay Stark, "It's Only Words: On Meaning and Mens Rea" (2013) *72 Cambridge Law Journal 155*

Cath Crosby, "Recklessness:The Continuing Search for a Definition" (2008) *72 Journal of Criminal Law 313*

Alan Reed, "Strict Liability Crimes: The Contours of Liability and Crimogenic Impact" in Alan Reed et al (eds) *Fault in Criminal Law: A Research Companion* (Routledge 2022)

Dennis J Baker, "Rethinking the Mental Element in Involuntary Manslaughter" (2021) *85 Journal of Criminal Law 280*

Anyje Pedain, "Intention and the terrorist example" (2003) *Criminal Law Review 579*

CHAPTER 5

Homicide: Voluntary

5.1 Introduction

Homicide involves the death a human being or human beings. It is unsurprisingly seen as the most serious form of offending.

It can be divided into two categories.

(1) **Voluntary homicide**

Where death is the desired result and there is intent to kill or do GBH this is termed voluntary homicide and discussed in this **Chapter 5**.

The common elements are:

- unlawful
- killing of a human being

- caused by D
- with intention to kill or do grievous bodily harm.

The specific partial defences which can reduce Ds crime from murder to voluntary manslaughter are where:

- D has lost all self-control; or
- Ds responsibility is diminished by mental ill health.

(2) **Involuntary homicide**

Where death is not the desired result and there is no intent to kill or do GBH, but death is caused then this is termed as involuntary homicide and we will explore this at **Chapter 6** specifically focusing on the two most common forms prosecuted namely:

- Constructive act manslaughter; and
- Gross negligence manslaughter.

Aims of this chapter

By the end of this chapter you can be expected to know and be able to evaluate the law on voluntary homicide.

- **Murder**

  1. Unlawful
  2. Killing of a human being
  3. Caused by D
  4. With intention to kill or do grievous bodily harm.

- **Loss of control**

  Where D kills with the *mens rea* for murder but at the time of the killing can show

  1. Lost self-control [LSC]; caused by a
  2. Qualifying trigger [QT]; and
  3. A person of the normal degree of tolerance [NDT] would also have lost self-control.

Burden of proof: Evidentially D raises and the P must legally disprove [BOP]

Standard of proof: beyond reasonable doubt [SOP].

- **Diminished responsibility**

  Where D kills with the *mens rea* for murder but at the time of the killing can show:

  1. D has an abnormality of mental functioning [AMF];
  2. Which substantially impaired [SI] Ds ability to do one or more of the following:
     i) Understand their conduct;
     ii) Form rational judgment;
     iii) Exercise self-control.
  3. The AMF provides an explanation for D's acts or omissions [E].

  Burden of proof: Legally D raises [BOP]

  Standard of proof: D must show on a balance of probabilities [SOP].

- **Suicide pact**

  Where D kills in pursuance of a suicide pact.

- **Infanticide**

  Where a woman kills her child, who is under the age of 12 months, by any wilful act or omission and, at the time, the balance of her mind was disturbed due to the birth.

5.1.1 Homicide in context

The context in which homicide offences exist is important to your understanding of how the laws have historically approached homicide.

(1) Death penalty

The death penalty for murder in England and Wales was abolished in the middle of the 20th century. Prior to that point partial defences to murder were originally often used as a method to deal with "less culpable/partially justified" killings and could be used to avoid the death penalty.

(2) Life sentences

The exchange principle was that the death penalty was exchanged for a mandatory life sentences for murder (albeit with varying tariff lengths).

Today the partial defences enable D to avoid the mandatory life sentence for murder and diminish the label "murderer" to the less used term "the person who committed the manslaughter".

(3) The sanctity of life

The sanctity of life is a fundamental feature of most world religions. It has a profound impact on life and death decisions in England and Wales. The leading case of ***Nicklinson* [2014]** allowed the Supreme Court to elucidate on the principles relating to sanctity of life where the court held:

> *"[1] The sanctity of life is a fundamental principle of common law, reflected in the unqualified right to life found in the European Convention on Human Rights Article 2 (ECHR A2). There was no self-evident reason it should give way to the values of autonomy or dignity, and there were cogent reasons why sensible people might think that it should not.*
>
> *[2] There was no right to commit suicide, the **Suicide Act 1961 s1** merely conferred immunity from the criminal process for those who actually committed suicide. If there was no right to kill yourself, there could be no right to require the state to allow others to kill you or assist you to die.*
>
> *[3] A "blanket ban" on assisting suicide was not outside the margin of appreciation afforded to Convention states on that issue. The **Suicide Act 1961, s2** did not impose what the European Court of Human Rights would regard as an impermissible "blanket ban" on assisted suicide, which would take it outside the margin of appreciation."*

It is submitted these principles on the sanctity of life inform all criminal and civil law cases relating to death.

5.1.2 Elements common to all forms of homicide

(1) General defences

General defences unless excluded by statute or common law apply to murder and some of them can completely exculpate D. For example, self defence would exonerate the defendant totally from responsibility for the causation of death.

(2) **Causation of death**
Causation includes the three steps, discussed at **Chapter 3**, of *actus reus* namely:

1) Causation in fact (CIF)
2) Causation in law (CIL)
3) No new intervening act (NIA).

For every homicide scenario a student should go through each of these steps of causation.

(3) **The victim must be a live human being**

***Attorney-General's Reference (No 3 of 1994)* [1998]**

In this case D stabbed V1 (his pregnant girlfriend). V1 was pregnant with V2 (the child *in utero*). V2 was born prematurely and died as a consequence of their premature birth.

The House of Lords decided:

- The foetus was not in law a person at the time of the stabbing.
- To refuse to extend the doctrine of transferred mens rea (explained in **Chapter 4**) from the mother to the child in utero.
- The court stated the doctrine of transferred malice could be used to convict D of manslaughter of V2 (the child in utero).

The decision was based on the transferred *mens rea* for murder reasoning being seen as false due to being based on double transfer of intent – from V1 (mother) to V2 (child *in utero*) and this would have "*overstrained the* idea *of transferred malice to make it fit the case*" (Lord Mustill).

Per Lord Mustill:

> *"The effect of transferred malice, as I understand it, is that the intended victim and the actual victim are treated as if they were one, so that what was intended to happen to the first person (but did not happen) is added to what actually did happen to the second person (but was not intended to happen), with the result that what was intended and what happened are married to make a notionally intended and actually consummated crime.*
>
> *"The cases are treated as if the actual victim had been the intended victim from the start. To make any sense of this process there must, as it seems to me, be*

some compatibility between the original intention and the actual occurrence, and this is, indeed, what one finds in the cases."

It is submitted this decision is open to a rigorous critique and should be re-visited. There is an argument it does not make sense in terms of the moral journey or the base logic of transferred *mens rea*. Surely there is a transfer?

(4) ***Jurisdiction: "Under the King's Peace"***

Under the King's Peace is usually a straightforward issue of jurisdiction which is beyond the scope of this book.

However to pick one example **s72 Domestic Abuse Act 2021 states**:

(1) If—

(a) a person who is a United Kingdom national or is habitually resident in England and Wales does an act in a country outside the United Kingdom,

(b) the act constitutes an offence under the law in force in that country, and

(c) the act, if done in England and Wales, would constitute an offence to which this subsection applies, the person is guilty in England and Wales of that offence.

(2) The offences to which subsection (1) applies are—

(a) murder;

(b) manslaughter;

(c) an offence under section 18, 20 or 47 of the Offences Against the Person Act 1861 (offences relating to bodily harm or injury);

(d) an offence under section 23 or 24 of that Act (administering poison);

(e) an offence under section 1 of the Infant Life (Preservation) Act 1929 (child destruction).

(5) **Lapse of time between D's act and V's death**

The **Law Reform (Year and a Day Rule) Act 1996** applies to any offence committed after 17 June 1996. **s1** it states there is no longer any requirement of death within a year and a day of the act or omission. In **s2** it states the Attorney-General's consent is required before proceedings can be instituted for a *fatal offence* if:

i) The injury said to have caused the death was more than three years before the death; or ii) D has previously been convicted of an offence committed *in relation to the death.*

NB The three years runs from the date the injury is sustained.

5.2 Murder

(1) **Definition**

Archbold Criminal Practice 2025; at para 19.1 states according to *Coke's Institutes (Co. Inst. Pt III (1797 ed.), ch 7, p47*), modified to conform with changes made by statute and decisions of the courts:

> "Subject to three exceptions, the crime of murder is committed where
>
> a person of sound mind and discretion
>
> —unlawfully
>
> —kills
>
> —any reasonable creature in being
>
> —under the [King's] peace
>
> —with intent to kill or cause grievous bodily harm"

(2) **Note of caution**

The so called "high drama" of a criminal trial where someone has died often relates to the factual *nexus* and the human interest.

The reality is many homicides are utterly tragic but often utterly mundane. The high volume of crime frequently relates to domestic killings, killing of children and gang related killings.

The common issues within a trial may include:

- **Identification**: Who did it?
- **Causation**: Did they cause the death? (see **Chapter 3**)

- **Culpability**: Was there intention? (see **Chapter 4**)
- **Justification**: Was there a general defence of general applicability (see **Chapters 13–14**) e.g. self defence.
- **Partial justification**: Was there a specific partial defence (See below **Chapter 5 Loss of self control and diminished responsibility**).
- **Participation**: Where there is more than one participant. Who played what role? (See **Chapter 15** on participation).

Factored into most crimes and particularly homicide may include motives such as: anger, envy, greed, jealousy, lust, and revenge

The "high drama" is not usually based on the legal *nexus* where the law is usually certain, clear and not in issue. The appellate authorities have settled definitions.

All of the offences and defences are controversial but well established.

(3) **Defence: unlawful**

See **Chapters 13** and **14** Defences – particularly self-defence [other defences may be restricted by Public Policy factors e.g. Duress excluded].

(4) **Actus reus: causation of death**

See **Chapter 3**.

(5) **Actus reus: human Being**

See above re: **5.1.4**.

(6) **Actus reus: under the King's Peace**

See **5.1.4**.

(7) **Mens rea: with malice aforethought - intention to kill or intention to do GBH**

See **Chapter 4** *Mens rea* both direct and indirect intention.

5.2.1 Abolition of the offence of constructive murder

Where a person kills another in the course or furtherance of some other offence, the killing shall not amount to murder unless done with the same ***malice aforethought*** *(express or implied) as is required for the killing to amount to murder when not done in the course or furtherance of another offence.* (**s1 Homicide Act 1957**).

***Mens rea* "malice aforethought"**
Malice aforethought means in the modern era an intention to kill or cause grievous bodily harm to the victim (***Cunningham* [1982]**).

The scope of intention has been widely criticised
"One could expect a developed system to embody a law of murder clear enough to yield an unequivocal result on a given set of facts, a result which conforms with apparent justice and has a sound intellectual base. This is not so in England, where the law of homicide is permeated by anomaly, fiction, misnomer, and obsolete reasoning…"

(***Attorney-General's Reference (No 3 of 1994)* [1998] per Lord Mustill**)

"In English law a defendant may be convicted of murder who is in no ordinary sense a murderer....A person is liable to conviction for a more serious crime than he foresaw or contemplated... Lord Windlesham, writing with great Home Office experience, has said that a minority of defendants convicted of murder have been convicted on the basis that they had an intent to kill…

"The present definition of the mental element of murder results in defendants being classified as murderers who are not in truth murderers…It results in the imposition of mandatory life sentences when neither justice nor the needs of society require the classification of the case as murder and the imposition of a mandatory life sentence."

(***Powell; English* [1997] per Lord Steyn**)

5.2.2 Breadth of the offence of murder

"Murder, as every practitioner of the law knows, though often described as one of the utmost heinousness, is not in fact necessarily so, but consists in a whole bundle of offences of vastly differing degrees of culpability, ranging [#] From brutal, cynical, and repeated offences like the so-called Moors murders (**Brady and Hindley, 6 May 1966, unreported**) *[#] To the almost venial ([i.e. worthy of forgiveness], if objectively immoral, 'mercy killing' of a beloved partner."* (***Howe* [1987]** per Lord Hailsham).

5.3 Voluntary manslaughter – Loss of control

5.3.1 Context

Provocation: The old law
(1) Flawed concept?

"My Lords, it is impossible to read even a selection of the extensive modern literature on provocation without coming to the conclusion that the concept has serious logical and moral flaws...the doctrine of provocation has always been described as a concession to human frailty and the law illustrates Kant's dictum that, from the crooked timber of humanity, nothing completely straight can be made... [the] jury shall take into account everything both done and said according to the effect which, in their opinion, it would have on a reasonable man."

(***Smith* [2000]**, per Lord Hoffman)

(2) The common law recognised a defence of provocation for centuries.

(3) The common law was modified by the Homicide Act 1957, s3 which stated that murder could be reduced to manslaughter if:

(i) when D killed, things said or done provoked him; and

(ii) he suffered a sudden and temporary loss of self-control; and

(iii) the provocation was enough to make a reasonable man do as D did (with the reasonable man sharing those of D's characteristics which would affect the gravity of the provocation but not those which affected his ability to exercise self-control).

(4) The defence was controversial and courts, including the House of Lords and Privy Council, struggled with its application.

Common examples noted historically and currently the equality disparity.

(1) Men

- Husband becomes aware of his wife's alleged infidelity and kills his wife.
- Male states the so called "Guardsman's defence" i.e. an alleged unwanted homosexual advance rebuffed by killing the supposed flirt.

Both defendants are likely to state "I had a short fuse, fast burn loss of control". Historically (and arguably presently) men in this situation had a relatively good opportunity at running the partial defence of loss of self-control.

(2) Women

- Wife states she is the victim of sustained domestic violence and eventually bursts out in anger and kills the husband. She may state: "I had no chance. I paused I reflected. I had a long fuse, slow burn anger and then lost control."

Historically (and arguably presently) women in this situation have had a very difficult run at running the partial defence of self-defence as there is a time delay between the trigger and the killing.

5.3.2 Loss of self-control: The new law

(1) Abolition of provocation

The defence of provocation has been abolished and replaced by a partial defence to murder involving loss of control, defined in **ss 54–56 Coroners and Justice Act 2009**.

(2) Burden

The legal burden of proof is on the prosecution. If sufficient evidence is adduced to raise an issue with respect to the defence, the prosecution must prove beyond reasonable doubt that the elements of loss of control are not satisfied.

(3) Basis

The defence covers loss of control arising from both anger and fear.

Someone who has "lost it", e.g:

> "I completely lost it when he told me he was leaving and taking the children…"
>
> "It blew my mind they had abused our son. I lost my mind and control…"
>
> "I was so enveloped in the situation finally I broke. I lost all rational control…"

(4) Statute

s54 Coroners and Justice Act 2009

(1) *Where a person ("D") kills or is a party to the killing of another ("V"), D is not to be convicted of murder if—*

- (a) D's acts and omissions in doing or being a party to the killing resulted from D's loss of self-control.
- (b) *the loss of self-*control *had a qualifying trigger, and*

(c) a person of D's sex and age, with a normal degree of tolerance and self-restraint and in the circumstances *of D, might have reacted in the same or in a similar way to D.*

(5) How to approach

***Mustafa Gurpinar* [2015]**

"The three principal elements of the defence .... had to be analysed sequentially and separately; if a component was absent, the defence failed."

(6) Structure for analysis

1. LSC Did D lose self-control?
2. QT Was the LSC as a result of a qualifying trigger?
3. NDT Might a person of a normal degree of tolerance have LSC?

5.3.3 LSC: Did D lose self-control?

(1) This is subjectively assessed: did D lose self-control?

(2) It is not defined in the Act. In ***Jewell* [2014]** the Court of Appeal approved the meaning submitted by Professor Ormerod in *Smith and Hogan's Criminal Law* (13th edn, 2011):

"*...whether D has lost his ability to maintain his actions in* accordance *with considered* judgement ***or*** whether he had lost normal powers of reasoning,"

(3) D's failure to positively assert a loss of control is not necessarily fatal to his case.

(4) The loss of control need not be sudden **s54(2):** "the last straw" cases.

"*It was in regard to his obsession with his property and this dispute that the [threatened demolition of D's bungalow] was "the last straw" in the build-up of* stress *upon the appellant.*"

Lord Taylor CJ in ***Dryden* [1995]**.

(5) D must not have acted from a considered desire for revenge **s54(4).**

- Did D deliberate and reflect on the events?
- If so – there is no loss of control: ***Evans* [2012]**.

(6) Fast burn anger v slow burn anger.

5.3.4 Was the LSC as a result of a qualifying trigger? (s55 CJA 2009)

(1) Two triggers

(a) The **fear** trigger – D's fear of serious violence from V: **s55(3) CJA 2009**.

i.e. "I was in fear of serious violence, and I lost it" – similarities to self-defence.

(b) The **anger** trigger – circumstances of an extremely grave character that caused D to have a justifiable sense of being seriously wronged: **s55(4)**.

i.e. "I was triggered by something, and I lost it."

(2) The qualifying trigger(s) may be a combination of the matters mentioned in s55(4)-(5) CJA 2009 (s55(5)).

(3) The existence of a qualifying trigger requires an objective assessment by the judge at the end of the evidence and, if the defence is left to the jury, by the jury considering their verdict.

Whether a defendant's sense of being seriously wronged is justifiable will be an ***objective question*** *for a jury to determine ...Subsection (4) therefore sets a very high threshold ...The effect is to substantially narrow the potential availability of a partial defence.*

(Explanatory notes)

(4) D must not have incited the violence he feared, or the circumstances which caused him to lose control:

"Neither qualifying trigger in s.55(6)(a) and s.55(6)(b) was available to a defendant who had deliberately sought to provide himself with an excuse to use violence by inciting or encouraging or manufacturing a situation for that purpose."

Carlos Dawes, Mark John Hatter, Barry Francis Bowyer **[2013]**

e.g. Gang membership

The fear trigger: fear of serious violence s55(3) CJA 2009

If the full defence of self defence is not available then consider the following.

(1) Partial defence applies if D's loss of self-control was attributable to D's fear of serious violence from V against D or another identified person (**s55 (3)**).

(2) D's fear is subjectively assessed: he must have a genuine fear of serious violence, but his fear need not be reasonable.

(3) D's fear of serious violence is to be disregarded if it was caused by a thing which D did or said for the purpose of providing an excuse to use violence (**s55(6)(a)**) e.g. where D incited a fight.

(4) The fear trigger is in practice rarely used as D's rely on the total defence of self-defence.

The anger trigger: thing said or done giving rise to justifiable sense of being seriously wronged **s55(4) CJA 2009.**

(1) Applies if D's loss of self-control was attributable to a thing said or done (or both), which:

    (a) constituted circumstances of an extremely grave character; and

    (b) caused D to have a justifiable sense of being seriously wronged (**s55(4)**).

(2) A sense of being seriously wronged by a thing said or done is not justifiable if D incited the thing done or said for the purpose of providing an excuse to use violence (**s55(6)(b)**).

(3) Whether D's sense of being seriously wronged was "justifiable" will be determined objectively.

The sources do not always have to be the victim (e.g. victim's new partner X in ***Davies* [1975]**).

(4) **CJA 2009** does not define "extremely grave character" or "justifiable sense of being seriously wronged". They are issues to be determined by the jury: ***Carlos Dawes, Mark John Hatter, Barry Francis Bowyer* [2013]**.

(5) Something said or done constituting sexual infidelity will not amount to a "qualifying trigger" (**s55(6)(c)**).

Basis from Lord Hoffman and a strong feminist critique of provocation:

> *"Male possessiveness and jealousy should not today be an acceptable reason for loss of self-control leading to homicide, whether inflicted upon the woman herself or her new lover."* ***Smith (Morgan) [2000].***

This was examined in the Court of Appeal in the case of ***Clinton; Parker; Evans* [2012]**.

The effect of the court's decision in this case is that sexual infidelity may be considered as part of the contextual background to a case where there is another potential qualifying trigger, but it may not be considered as a potential qualifying trigger in itself [on its own].

5.3.5 NDT: Might a person of a normal degree of tolerance have LSC?

(1) A person of *D's sex and age, with a* normal *degree of tolerance and self-restraint and in the* circumstances of D, might have reacted in the same or in a similar way to D: (**s54(1)(c)**).

(2) This follows the "reasonable person" approach taken in ***DPP v Camplin*** [1978] and ***Attorney-General for Jersey v Holley* [2005]** before implementation of **CJA 2009**.

"The public policy that underlay the adoption of the "reasonable man" test in the common law doctrine of provocation was to reduce the incidence of fatal violence by preventing a person relying upon his own exceptional pugnacity [(pugnacity meaning = argumentative and wanting to start a fight)] or excitability as an excuse for loss of self-control.... for the purposes of the law of provocation the "reasonable man" has never been confined to the adult male. It means an ordinary person of either sex, not exceptionally excitable or pugnacious, but possessed of such powers of self-control as everyone is entitled to expect that his fellow citizens will exercise in society as it is today." (***DPP v Campling* [1978]** (Lord Diplock)).

(3) Reference to the "circumstances of D" is a reference to all of D's circumstances other than those whose relevance to D's conduct is that they bear on D's general capacity for tolerance or self-restraint (**s54(3)**).

(4) If D was suffering from a mental disorder at the time of the killing, the potential relevance of this will be fact-specific: it depends on the nature of D's disorder, the effect it had on D and the facts of the case.

(5) **s54(1)(c) CJA 2009** makes it clear that *the defendant is to be judged against the standard of a person with a normal degree, and not an* abnormal *degree, of tolerance and self-restraint.*

(6) If, and in so far as, a personality disorder reduced the defendant's general capacity for tolerance or self-restraint, that would not be a relevant consideration. Moreover, it would not be a relevant consideration even if the personality disorder was one of the "circumstances" of the defendant because it was relevant to the gravity of the trigger.

(7) Expert evidence about the impact of the disorder would be irrelevant and inadmissible on the issue of whether it would have reduced the capacity for tolerance and self-restraint of the hypothetical "*person of D's sex and age, with a normal degree of tolerance and self-restraint*". (***Rejmanski* [2017]**).

(8) The "circumstances of D" can include the impact of sexual infidelity on D provided combined with another QT (***Clinton, Parker & Evans* [2012]**).

(9) **Battered person syndrome**

Supportive

"Thus, a defendant's history of abuse at the hands of the victim could be taken into account in deciding whether an ordinary person might have acted as the

defendant did, whereas the defendant's generally short temper could not. Consequently, when applying the test in subsection (1)(c) the jury will consider whether a person of the defendant's sex and age with an ordinary level of tolerance and self-restraint and in the defendant's specific circumstances ...might have acted as the defendant did."[1]

This is likely to be of relevance in cases of long-term domestic abuse, for example.

(10) **Voluntary intoxication**

Judge as if D were sober

In ***Dawit Asmelash* [2013]** the Court of Appeal held:

"*1. Voluntary intoxication is **not** a factor to be taken into account in determining whether a person of the D's age and sex, with a normal degree of tolerance and self-restraint and in the circumstances of D, might have reacted in the same or in a similar way to D.*

2. A drunk defendant can plead loss of control but will be assessed against a sober person in D's circumstances, with normal levels of tolerance and self-restraint.

3. Where D suffered from alcoholism or a drug addiction and he was taunted about that condition to the extent that it constituted a qualifying trigger, then the alcoholism or drug addiction would form part of the circumstances for consideration."

5.4 Voluntary manslaughter – diminished responsibility

5.4.1 Diminished responsibility: The old law

(1) Under the old law in the **Homicide Act 1957 s2**, the defence of diminished responsibility was available on a charge of murder where D could prove that:

he was suffering from such abnormality of mind (whether arising from a condition of arrested or retarded development of mind or any inherent causes or induced by disease or injury) as substantially impaired his mental responsibility for his acts and omissions in doing or being a party to the killing.

(2) The law was regarded as chaotic and lacking in precision. There were numerous calls for reform.

---

1 Explanatory Notes to the Coroners and Justice Act 2009, para 228

5.4.2 Diminished responsibility: The new law

(1) Statute

s2 Homicide Act 1957, (as amended by s52 Coroners and Justice Act 2009)

Persons suffering from diminished responsibility

(1) *A person ('D') who kills or is a party to the killing of another is not to be convicted of murder if D was suffering from an* ***abnormality of mental functioning*** *which–*

(a) *arose from a recognised medical condition, substantially* ***impaired D's ability*** *to do* <u>*one or*</u> <u>*more*</u> *of the things mentioned in subsection (1A), and*

(b) ***provides an explanation*** for D's acts and omissions *in doing or /being a party to the killing.*

(1A) *Those things are –*

(a) *to* ***understand the nature of D's conduct;***

(b) *to* ***form a rational judgment****;*

(c) *to* ***exercise self-control.***

(1B) *For the purposes of subsection (1)(c), an abnormality of mental functioning provides an explanation for D's conduct if it causes, or is a significant contributory factor in causing, D to carry out that conduct.*

(2) *On a charge of murder, it shall be for the defence to prove that the person charged is by virtue of this section not liable to be convicted of murder.*

(3) *A person who but for this section would be liable, whether as principal or as accessory, to be convicted of murder shall be liable instead to be convicted of manslaughter.*

(4) *The fact that one party to a killing is by virtue of this section not liable to be convicted of murder shall not affect the question whether the killing amounted to murder in the case of any other party to it.*

(2) Burden of proof: The burden of proof is on D

(3) Standard of proof: D must prove all of the elements of diminished responsibility on the balance of probabilities

***Lee Robert Foye* [2013]**

There was no justification for departing from the decision in ***Lambert (Steven)*** **[2002]** that the reverse burden of proof applicable to the partial defence of diminished responsibility was not incompatible with the presumption of innocence in the **European Convention on Human Rights 1950 Art 6(2).**

(4) Elements

(a)	AMF	Abnormality of mental functioning
(b)	SI	Substantial impairment of understanding, judgement or self control
(c)	E	Explanation

5.4.3 AMF: Abnormality of mental functioning

(1) Under the old law in **s2** (*abnormality of mind* test) the determination could be left entirely to the jury. In the leading authority of ***Byrne* [1960]**, Lord Parker CJ explained the meaning of abnormality of mind in wide terms as follows:

"a state of mind so different from that of ordinary human beings that the reasonable man would term it abnormal. It appears to us to be wide enough to cover the mind's activities in all its aspects, not only the perception of physical acts and matters, and the ability to form a rational judgment as to whether an act is right or wrong, but also the ability to exercise will power to control physical acts in accordance with that rational judgment."

(2) Terminology

The older term Abnormality of the Mind (AOM) was replaced with Abnormality of Mental Functioning (AMF).

(3) Experts

- It is usually absolutely crucial to have expert psychiatrists who give expert evidence.
- The courts, parties and jury heavily rely on the experts.

(4) The prosecution

- The prosecution has the right to assess the medical evidence and to challenge it.
- The prosecution does not have to accept the defence medical evidence.

(5) The defence

The defence medical evidence will often be crucial.

(6) The judge

The judge will rarely exercise the power to withdraw the case from the jury, even if the prosecution does not call evidence to contradict the psychiatric evidence adduced by the defence (***Blackman* [2017]**).

(7) Unchallenged medical evidence

Where there is unchallenged medical evidence of diminished responsibility and no other evidence which, looked at in the round, was at least capable of rebutting the defence, the trial judge should withdraw a charge of murder from the jury (***Michael Brennan* [2014]**).

(8) Jury

The jury ultimately determines the issue.

(9) Recognised medical condition

The recognised medical condition aspect will be determined on a case-by-case basis and diagnostic manuals will be indicative but not determinative of the matter.

In their submission to the Law Commission's report *Murder, Manslaughter and Infanticide*, the Royal College of Psychiatrists advocated for the recognised medical condition requirement suggesting that it's inclusion would:

"encourage reference within expert evidence to diagnosis in terms of one or two of the accepted internationally classificatory systems of mental conditions ([World Health Organisation: International Classification of Diseases (ICD-10); and the American Psychiatric Association: Diagnostic and Statistical Manual of Mental Disorders (DSM-1V)]) without explicitly writing those systems into the legislation."[2]

(10) Scope of the abnormality of mental function (AMF)

AMF does include

- Alcoholic dependency will qualify, regardless of whether it resulted in brain damage. (***Dowds* [2012]**)
- Autistic spectrum issues (***Conroy* [2017]**)
- Depression
- Paranoid personality disorder (***Squelch* [2017]**)
- Personality disorder (***Foye* [2013]**)
- Post traumatic stress disorder (***Brown* [2019]**)

---

2 Law Commission, *Murder, Manslaughter and Infanticide* (Law Com No 304, 2006) Para 5.114

- Psychosis
- Schizophrenia (***Kay* [2017]**).[3]

AMF does not include

- Acute intoxication which is voluntary cannot be relied upon as a recognised medical condition: (***Dowds* [2012]**)
- Morbid jealousy (***Vinagre* [1979]**).

(11) Medical evidence

Medical evidence is a practical necessity if the defence is to succeed (***Bunch* [2013]**).

(12) Alcohol and intoxication

The law does not require abnormality of mental functioning to be the **sole** cause.

Where intoxication is involved D should be "taken as if sober".

Therefore where D suffers from a recognised medical condition and is voluntarily intoxicated at the time of the killing, the defence will succeed if D can prove the elements required under **s52 CJA 2009** ignoring his voluntary intoxication.

(***Dietschmann* [2003]**).

Alcohol dependency syndrome can amount to abnormality of mental function (***Dowds* [2012]**).

Voluntary intoxication alone is **not** capable of founding diminished responsibility (***Dowds* [2012]**), (***Lindo* [2016]**).

Where schizophrenia coincides with alcohol intoxication with heroin, the courts will treat the defendant as a sober person with schizophrenia (***Kay* [2017]**).

Where there is psychosis with alcohol intoxication and heroint, the courts are reluctant to hear fresh evidence where diminished responsibility has already been considered. There appear to be some contrasts between schizophrenia with drugs as opposed to psychosis with drugs (***Foy* [2020]**).

---

3 Commentary by Ronnie Mackay and Barry Mitchell has suggested this is the most common AMF: see, Ronnie Mackay and Barry Mitchell, 'The New Diminished Responsibility Plea in Operation: Some Initial Findings' [2017] Criminal Law Review 18.

5.4.4 Substantial impairment (SI)

This is substantial impairment of the defendant's ability to do one or more of the following:

- understand the nature of his own conduct;
- form a rational judgment;
- exercise self-control.

(1) Substantial impairment is a question for the jury to determine and trial judges should not ordinarily attempt a gloss or re-definition of the term (***Golds* [2016]**).

(2) ***Golds* [2016]** per Lord Hughes:

*"[27] '... dictionary definition, '**substantial'** is capable of meaning either*

(1) 'present rather than illusory or fanciful, thus having some substance' or

(2) 'important or weighty', as in 'a substantial meal' or 'a substantial salary'.

[We interpret 'substantial' in the latter wider meaning' as] ***'important or weighty'.***

[43]

'(1) ***Ordinarily in a murder trial*** *where diminished responsibility is in issue the* ***judge need not direct the jury beyond the terms of the statute and should not attempt to define the meaning of 'substantially'***.

Experience has shown that the issue of its correct interpretation is unlikely to arise in many cases.

The jury should normally be given to understand that the expression is an ordinary English word, that it imports a question of degree, and that whether in the case before it the impairment can properly be described as substantial is for [the jury] to resolve.

(2) **If, however, the jury has been introduced to the question of whether any impairment beyond the merely trivial will suffice**, or if it has been introduced to the concept of a spectrum between the greater than trivial and the total, ***the judge should explain that whilst the impairment must indeed pass the merely trivial before it*** need ***be considered, it is not the law that any impairment beyond the trivial will suffice***.

The judge should likewise make this clear if a risk arises that the jury might misunderstand the import of the expression; whether this risk arises or not is a judgment to be arrived at by the trial judge who is charged with overseeing the dynamics of the trial ...

***Illustrative expressions of the sense of the word may be employed so long as the jury is given clearly to understand that no single synonym is to be substituted for the statutory word** ..."*

Confirmed no requirement for a "gloss" in ***Sargeant* [2019]**.

(3) Approved direction

*"'Substantially' is an **ordinary English word on which you will reach a conclusion in this case, based upon your own experience of ordinary life**.*

*It means **less than total and more than trivial.** Where you, the jury, draw the line is a matter for your collective judgment."*

The first instance judge confirmed partial is **not** substantial (***Squelch* [2017]**).

(4) Whether D has or does not have the ability to do these things is a matter for expert psychiatric evidence.

(5) The impairment must be such as to impair one or more of the list below:

(a) to understand the nature of his own conduct;

Similar to insanity, e.g. child with learning difficulties.

(b) to form a rational judgment;

Examples from the Law Commission: Victim of domestic abuse; child with learning difficulties overborne by another; depressed person killing a terminally ill spouse.

(c) to exercise self-control;

Example: *Blackman* [2017].

In this case a marine was serving in Helmand province, Afghanistan. Whilst on duty the marine was killed. The marine was charged with the murder of a wounded insurgent and convicted.

The Court of Appeal replaced the murder conviction with one for manslaughter by reason of diminished responsibility. This was based on new psychiatric evidence that the marine had been suffering from an adjustment disorder which substantially impaired his ability to form a rational judgment and exercise self-control.

5.4.5 Explanation

(1) The abnormality must "provide an explanation for D's acts and omissions in doing or being a party to the killing".

(2) **Law Commission phrase** was an **"appropriate connection"** between the abnormality and the killing (**Law Com No. 304, para. 5.124**)

(3) **Government wanted an "explicit causal requirement"** (see, *Blackstone's Criminal Practices 2023*)

(4) It appears this element is to rule out the random coincidence of AMF and killing and thus ensures a link between AMF and the killing

(5) **D need not give evidence at trial**

> *"...an evidential basis upon which the partial defence is mounted. Be that an account by the defendant in interview with police or psychiatrists or a contemporaneous narrative eyewitness account of the assault leading to death and which provides the context for a psychiatric opinion as to the impact of or link between the likely abnormality of mind and the assault."*

(***Curran* [2021]**, [39] per Macur LJ).

(6) **Judge need not accept the plea:** the fact that the prosecution accept the plea does not bind the judge. (**Sutcliffe ["The Yorkshire Ripper"] *The Times*, (23 May 1981)**).

(7) **Post 2010 evidence DR pleas not as readily accepted by the prosecution**

e.g. pre 2010 77% accepted, post 2010 44% accepted.[4]

5.5 Suicide pact

(1) Arises where two or more people agree to kill each other. If one party to the agreement survives s/he may be charged with murder and may plead this defence which, if successful, will reduce the conviction to manslaughter.

(2) **s4(1) Homicide Act 1957**

- *It shall be manslaughter, and shall not be murder,*
- *for a person acting in pursuance of a suicide pact*
- *between him and another*
- *to kill the other or be a party to the other...being killed by a third person.*

(3) **Burden**

The legal burden of proof is on the defendant to prove, on the balance of probabilities, that s/he was acting under a suicide pact with the victim.

4 Ronnie Mackay and Barry Mitchell, 'The New Diminished Responsibility Plea in Operation: Some Initial Findings' [2017] Criminal Law Review 18.

(4) "Suicide pact"

This is defined in **s4(3)** of the Act and requires that all persons who are party to the pact have a "common agreement" which has at its object the death of all parties to the pact. Acts committed while the defendant has a "settled intention of dying" may be treated as acts done in pursuance of the suicide pact.

5.6 Infanticide

(1) s1(1) Infanticide Act 1938 (as amended by **s57 Coroners and Justice Act 2009**)

- *Where a mother*
- *kills her child,*
- *the child is under the age of 12 months,*
- *the mother does not have a younger child*
- *by any wilful act or omission and, at the time, the balance of her mind was disturbed due to the birth.*

(2) Charge or defence

A woman may be tried for the offence of infanticide or may raise it as a defence under **s1(2)** of the Act. It is treated like a conviction for manslaughter and carries a maximum sentence of life imprisonment.

(3) Burden

The D bears an evidential burden, and the prosecution bears the legal burden of proving that infanticide does not apply.

(4) Purpose

In ***Tunstill (Rachel Julie)*** **[2018]** the Court of Appeal stated that the purpose of the Act is to "*ameliorate the potential harshness of the law of murder by recognising that in a period after birth a mother's balance of mind may be affected*". The Court stated that the intention of the legislation is "*to be merciful*".

5.7 Evaluation and reform

5.7.1 Legal certainty and legal clarity

Firstly the law in relation to murder although archaic in terms of common law terminology is relatively clear. Although the law would benefit from modernisation of terminology and clarification of the distinction between first degree homicide and second degree homicide. It is easy for the citizen to be certain as to what the law is and for a jury to be relatively clear. Sentencing tariffs also provide a judge with some flexibility.

Secondly in relation to diminished responsibility there are clearly some distinct positives about the law post 2009. It is certain and relatively clear what is meant by diminished responsibility. It does rely heavily on psychiatric evidence but this would seem to be a positive – it is drawing on a body of established expertise.

Finally post 2009 the law in relation to loss of self-control is arguably marginally clearer. However cases like ***Clinton*** do appear to ride a coach and horses through the sexual infidelity scenario laid out in the statute. It is also clear that in terms of the relative position of men and women the law seems to be no better than it was pre-2009. A woman seeking to run a partial defence will still face more difficulties than the equivalent male counterpart who acts at speed.

It is perhaps disappointing that the 2009 statute did not seize the opportunity to endorse a partial defence contextual to domestic violence victims. It seems clear on the statistics that women will find it more difficult to claim that they lost self-control than their male counterpart. The women would then be obliged to seek to state that they were mentally unwell under the partial defence of diminished responsibility as a safer road to avoid the monetary life sentence.

5.7.2 Equality before the law: protected characteristics and socio-economic barriers

Firstly see above in relation to legal certainty and clarity. The relative positions of men and women are clear. Men seemed to have a better run on the defence of loss of self-control than women do even under the new law.

Secondly it seems a surprising anomaly that given the frequency of the domestic violence situation arising that there is no specific partial defence in relation to the domestic violence. It is so often the context in which a domestic partner kills. This clearly militates against women who kill who would benefit from a specific defence.

Finally, it is submitted Wistrich accurately critiques LOSC stating "it was a law designed for men who kill in anger, not for women who kill out of fear".[5]

5.7.3 Fair warning; fair labelling and sufficient breadth principles

(1) Fair warning

The law does seem to give fair warning in relation to the primacy of the sanctity of life. The only area that is slightly opaque is the capacity to define what is meant

5 Harriet Wistrich, *Sister in Law: Fighting for Justice in a System Designed by Men* (Torva 2024)

by loss of self-control and the circumstances in which it can be used as a partial defence by victims of domestic violence.

(2) Fair labelling

The labelling of a defendant is a very controversial area.

Firstly if one takes a mercy killing where a domestic partner has killed their terminally ill partner at the request of the ill partner. In this scenario the law is very clear that this amounts to a murder. There is discussion of reform in relation to the law on euthanasia which may change under the New Labour Government.

Secondly, the term loss of self-control inherently has some ambiguity to it. There is an argument to say that actually not only is the concept outdated but the label is also.

Thirdly, the position in relation to diminished responsibility is largely that the labelling is left in the hands of psychiatrists. This is not to critique the professionals (as they are often the people best qualified to define mental health disorders and impact) however constitutionally if the jury has primacy does this anomaly accord for standard principles? However there are large number of scenarios in domestic violence cases where women are forced to rely on the defence of diminished responsibility (with the higher relative degree of certainty as to success) and "label" themselves under a mental health disorder rather than the reality. In these situations are we not able to recognise the reality of the situation? It may be thought to label this person mentally ill is not necessarily to apply an appropriate label.

(3) Sufficient breadth

There is certainly no issue that the law currently has sufficient breadth and not undue specificity.

(4) Practicality, cost, and expense

(a) Practicality – in relation to murder and diminished responsibility the law remains relatively clear, practicable and proportionate in terms of investment.

In relation to loss of self-control (as with its predecessor provocation) the law is complex. It is submitted that it would be beneficial for a full statutory reform of both loss of self-control and arguably a specific defence extended to a domestic violence victim who kills in specific partially explicable circumstances.

(b) Avoid undue cost and expense

It seems there is not undue cost in relation to murder and diminished responsibility. However a controversial area is the intersection of alcoholism and mental health.

It may be that the general principles on intoxication merit fresh consideration (see **Chapter 13**).

5.7.4 Human rights: Autonomy and welfare principles

The position for purposes of **ECHR Article 7**, legal certainty seems to have improved (see above **Legal Certainty**) namely the law post 2009 is relatively certain and clear.

The position in terms of equality (**ECHR Article 14**) does not seem to have improved (see above **Equality**). It seems to most commentators that women are in a weaker position in terms of claiming the partial defences than the male defendant.

5.7.5 International comparators and reform: practicality principle and politics

Comparators

There are some interesting international precedents which could be looked at in terms of how partial defences can be framed or whether there should be a tiering of the homicide offences. We will focus on the Law Commission who have taken account of the international norms.

Law Commission: Murder, Manslaughter and Infanticide (Law Com No 304, 2006)

The Law Commission has recommended a relatively straightforward 4-step categorisation

Category 1: First degree murder

This would have a mandatory life sentence. This would cover the very worst of deliberate killings including for example a hitman deliberately firing a gun at point blank range as part of a pre-planned hit with intention to kill. This would cover the scenario of a killing where the intention of the killer was done with an awareness that their conduct involved a serious risk of causing death.

Category 2: Second degree murder

This would have a discretionary life sentence. This would cover the scenario where there is an intention to do serious injury or D being aware there is a serious and obvious risk of causing death, or they successfully plead a partial defence such as loss of self-control, diminished responsibility or suicide pact.

Category 3: Manslaughter

This would have a flexibility in sentencing which would vary depending on the harm and culpability factors.

Category 4: Specific homicide offences

This would include assisting a suicide and infanticide.

This would have a flexibility in sentencing which would vary depending on the harm and culpability factors.

There is a recent Law Commission Background Paper: *Defences for victims of domestic abuse who kill their abusers*; 10 December 2024 (version updated 20 January 2025). This may prove fertile ground for a fresh debate on this fundamental issue.

In the News

Victims of domestic violence

Please read these the following sources:

1. Catherine Baksi, "Landmarks in law: the case that shone a spotlight on domestic violence" *The Guardian* (London, 18 June 2019)

   <https://www.theguardian.com/law/2019/jun/18/landmarks-in-law-the-case-that-shone-a-spotlight-on-domestic-violence> accessed 06 April 2025

2. Amelia Hill and Matthew Weaver, "Sally Challen walks free as court rules out retrial for killing abusive husband" *The Guardian* (London, 7 June 2019)

   <https://www.theguardian.com/uk-news/2019/jun/07/sally-challen-will-not-face-retrial-for-killing-husband> accessed 06 April 2025

3. ***Ahluwalia* [1992]** the facts were V threatened to injure D the next day. D overnight whilst V was asleep poured petrol onto V and set him on fire leading to his death. The reasoning of the courts is now historic but the example evocative of the potential need for a specific domestic violence defence.

4. ***Challen* [2019]** the facts were D was the subject of domestic violence by V. V was coercive, controlling and engaged in numerous extra marital affairs. D was his wife 57 year old married for 31 years with two adult children to V. V found out her husband had an affair and the couple separated.

V had then agreed to attempt a reconciliation. D had accessed Vs social media to see he was still engaging in affairs. D killed V by bringing a hammer to their family home and hitting V 20 times on the head. D then travelled to Beachy head to kill herself but was talked down by a Chaplain. D was charged with murder and her defence in her words was "I have gone off my rocker. I am just so very depressed". Essentially she had "flipped" and killed V. At trial D was convicted of murder. Some years later with fresh evidence D appealed stating she was suffering from an undiagnosed coercive control influenced bipolar affective disorder.

The Court of Appeal allowed the appeal and ordered a re-trial. At the re-trial prosecution accepted a plea to manslaughter. It should be noted coercive control was not a defence to murder but it was a relevant factor regarding loss of self-control and diminished responsibility. The new evidence was accepted. Karl Laird in the *Criminal Law Review* has noted:

> "The judgment in this case was welcomed, as it was assumed that it heralded a sea-change in how coercive control is recognised by the law. This is far from clear, however, as it remains to be seen whether evidence of the kind that led the Court of Appeal to quash the appellant's conviction would be relevant to a jury's consideration of loss of control. If it transpires that it is only relevant to diminished responsibility, then the law has not come very far despite the 2009 reforms." [6]

The question really is: has the 2009 statute and related case law improved the lot of women who are the victims of domestic coercion and violence? The answer seem to be a clear "no".

6 Karl Laird, 'Homicide: R v Challen (Georgina) Court of Appeal Criminal Division [2019]

5.8 Summary

- **Murder**
  1. Unlawful
  2. Killing of a human being
  3. Caused by D
  4. With intention to kill or do grievous bodily harm.

- **Loss of control**

  Where D kills with the *mens rea* for murder but at the time of the killing can show

  1. Lost self-control [LSC]; caused by a
  2. Qualifying trigger [QT]; and
  3. A person of the normal degree of tolerance [NDT] would also have lost self-control.

  Burden of proof: Evidentially D raises and the P must legally disprove [BOP].

  Standard of proof: beyond reasonable doubt [SOP].

- **Diminished responsibility**

  Where D kills with the *mens rea* for murder but at the time of the killing can show

  1. D has an abnormality of mental functioning [AMF]
  2. Which substantially impaired [SI] Ds ability to do one or more of the following:
     i) understand their conduct
     ii) form rational judgment
     iii) exercise self-control.
  3. The AMF provides an explanation for D's acts or omissions [E].

  Burden of proof: Legally D raises [BOP]

  Standard of proof: D must show on a balance of probabilities [SOP].

- **Suicide pact**

  Where D kills in pursuance of a suicide pact.

- **Infanticide**

  Where a woman kills her child, who is under the age of 12 months, by any wilful act or omission and, at the time, the balance of her mind was disturbed due to the birth.

Further reading

Andrew Ashworth "Principles pragmatism and the law commission's recommendation on homicide reform" [2007] *Criminal Law Review 333*

Hannah Bows and Jonathan Herring, "Getting Away with Murder: A Review of the 'Rough Sex Defence'" (2020) *Journal of Criminal Law 84: 525.*

Jeremy Horder and Kate Fitz-Gibbon "When Sexual Infidelity Triggers Murder: Examining The Impact Of Homicide Law Reform On Judicial Attitudes In Sentencing" (2015) *Cambridge Law Journal 74*

Law Commission Background Paper: *Defences for victims of domestic abuse who kill their abusers*; 10 December 2024 (version updated 20 January 2025)

Ronnie Mackay, "The Impairment Factors in the New Diminished Responsibility Plea" (2018) *Criminal Law Review 462.*

Eizabeth Stuart-Cole, "Substantially Confused? The Paradox of Golds" (2017) *Journal of Criminal Law 81: 99.*

CHAPTER 6

Homicide: Involuntary

6.1 Introduction

Our focus in **Chapter 6** is homicide involuntary. This is where causation of death is proven but the death is not "willed" by the defendant and culpability of the defendant is not as high as where a homicide is voluntarily caused. Two main examples are:

- **Constructive act manslaughter (CAM)**

  (1) Base offence:

  Intentional volitional criminal act with the *mens rea* for the underlying offence; with no defence to the underlying offence.

  (2) Objectively physically "dangerous" to the reasonable person.

  (3) Causing the death of the victim.

- **Gross negligence manslaughter (GNM)**

  (1) Duty of care-based on tortious principles.

(2) Gross breach, and reasonably foreseeable that the breach gives rise to a serious and obvious risk of death.

(3) Causing the death of the victim

- Common to both:
  - Causing the death of the victim.
- Differences:
  - Different underlying *mens rea* namely:
  - CAM the *mens rea* of the underlying offence;
  - GNM the *mens rea* gross negligence;
  - CAM usually involves a guilty act; and
  - GNM usually involves a guilty omission to act.

Examples

Constructive act manslaughter

"One punch manslaughter" – one punch which causes the victim's death

1. Intentional volitional criminal (common assault or ABH) with the intention or recklessness as to the assault; with no defence such as self defence.
2. Objectively physically dangerous in the sense that punching somebody is clearly to the reasonable person objectively physically dangerous.
3. Causing the death of the victim that in the normal way causation in fact, causation in law and no intervening act breaking the chain of causation.

Gross negligence manslaughter

Very bad hospital treatment by a qualified medic which causes the victim's death

1. Duty of care is axiomatic to the medic and patient relationship.
2. Gross breach for example a fundamental error, such as the removal of an oxygen tube during an operation. Reasonably foreseeable that such a serious breach would give rise to a serious and obvious risk of death.
3. And that this causes the death of the victim in the usual way, i.e. causation in fact, causation in law, and no known intervening act

Aims of this chapter

By the end of this chapter you can be expected to know and be able to evaluate the law on homicide voluntary in criminal offences

- **Constructive act manslaughter (CAM)**

  1. Background.
  2. Base offence: Intentional volitional criminal act with the *mens rea* for the underlying offence; with no defence to the underlying offence.
  3. Objectively physically "dangerous" to the reasonable person.
  4. Causing the death of the victim.

- **Gross negligence manslaughter (GNM)**

  1. Background.
  2. Duty of care – based on tortious principles.
  3. Gross breach and reasonably foreseeable that the breach gives rise to a serious and obvious risk of death.
  4. Causing the death of the victim.

- **Causing or allowing the death of or serious physical harm to a child or vulnerable adult (CAD)**

  1. Context.
  2. Unlawful Act: Offence.
  3. Relationship: Member of same household.
  4. *Mens rea.*

- **Corporate manslaughter (CM)**

  1. Context.
  2. Duty of care.
  3. Gross breach.
  4. Causation.

- **Evaluation framework**

6.2 Constructive act manslaughter (CAM)

6.2.1 Background

Lord Hope helps us to confidently say with certainty the requirements in relation to constructive act manslaughter (CAM) are

1) Base offence: Intentional volitional criminal act with the *mens rea* for the underlying offence; with no defence to the underlying offence.
2) Objectively physically "dangerous" to the reasonable person.
3) Causing the death of the victim.

(***Attorney-General's Reference (No. 3 of 1994)* [1998]**)

Example base offences include:

- Common assault or actual bodily harm (see **Chapter 7**).
- Criminal damage (see **Chapter 2**).
- Burglary (see **Chapter 9**).
- Robbery (see **Chapter 9**).

By far the most common underlying offence is that of assaults, specifically the "one punch manslaughter" which is based on an underlying assault occasioning actual bodily harm.

6.2.2 Base offence

This required an intentional volitional criminal act with the *mens rea* for the underlying offence; with no defence to the underlying offence.

This element requires breaking down:

a) Intentional volitional (i.e. voluntary not automatic or accidental)
b) Criminal
c) Act
d) With the *mens rea* for the underlying act required

e) With no defence to the underlying offence

f) No longer any need for the act to be "directed at the victim".

Intentional volitional (i.e. voluntary not automatic or accidental)

1. This "intentional act" requirement is open to being misleading.
2. It does not mean "intentional" in the **Chapter 4** "Intention" sense.
3. It does mean "Intentional" in the **Chapter 3** sense, i.e. it was voluntary not automatic or accidental act, e.g. bumping by accident is not an "intentional"/ volitional action. It is an accident.

Criminal

In ***Franklin*** **(1883)**, D who was on Brighton Pier threw a box from a stall into the water and it struck a swimmer. The prosecution case was that the civil tort of trespass against the shopkeeper would be a sufficient basis. The Court of Appeal held that the unlawful act manslaughter **must be based on Criminal Act**.

N.B. If the crime were prosecuted today it would properly be prosecuted on the basis that it is a gross negligence manslaughter killing.

Mr Justice Field stated:

> *"The mere fact of a civil wrong committed by one person against another ought not to be used as an incident which is a necessary step to a criminal case."*

The criminal nature was confirmed in ***Arobikie*** **[1988]**, D and V (also in Brighton) had some history of animosity. D saw V sat outside a swimming baths. V was nervous and walked away towards the railway station. V then tried to cross railway tracks and was electrocuted. A witness indicated D had followed V. The prosecution case was based on D's mere presence at the railway station had caused V, who was terrified of him, to attempt to escape across the tracks and was electrocuted.

The Court of Appeal allowed the appeal. Firstly, no criminal act by D as evidence did not show D had physically threatened or chased V. Secondly, the evidence could not amount to evidence of an assault by the D against V.

In the commentary by Professor Sir John Smith QC he made it clear *"A threat to cause even serious injury is not at present an offence unless it causes and is intended to cause apprehension of immediate unlawful violence."*

Act

Lowe **[1973]** confirms an omission by neglect of a child causing death under **s1(1) Children and Young Persons Act 1933** is not sufficient basis for constructive act manslaughter. The conviction was quashed.

Per Phillimore LJ:

> *"...If I strike a child in a manner likely to cause harm it is right that if the child dies, I may be charged with [constructive act] manslaughter.*
>
> *"**If**, however**, I omit to do something** with the result that it suffers injury to its health which results in its death, **we think that a charge of manslaughter should not be an inevitable consequence even if the omission is deliberate.**"*

In terms of commentary, it is important to note the case has a questionable status. Smith and Hogan amongst others are of the view an omission may be sufficient. However, the point is entirely moot as the omission can form the basis of gross negligence manslaughter and that is usually the most appropriate charge. Therefore this stage it might be a safe rule to say that where there is an act it is normally charged as constructive act manslaughter. Where there is an admission to act, that is normally charged with gross negligence manslaughter.

This position was confirmed in ***Khan (Rungzabe)* [1998]** which stated

> *"Manslaughter by omission was a type of manslaughter arising from a breach of duty coupled with gross negligence and, in order for a person to be criminally responsible for an omission, he had to have a relationship with the victim of such a nature that a duty to act arose.*
>
> *"Where the prosecution alleged manslaughter by omission, it was appropriate to leave the jury to consider whether a duty of care was owed by the accused to the victim, whether there had been a breach of that duty, whether the breach caused the death of the victim and whether the breach in question amounted to gross negligence and thus a criminal act."*

This was later confirmed in ***Gemma Evans* [2009]**; which is a case we will revisit below.

With the mens *rea* for the underlying act required

D can be guilty of manslaughter even if you do not foresee death. D needs to simply have the *mens rea* of the underlying crime. The case law is not consistent but this seems to be anything from recklessness and above (absolute, strict and negligent liability being insufficient for CAM).

In ***Lamb* [1967]** the charge was CAM. The facts are D as a "joke" pointed a gun at V (his best friend). V was also treating this as a "joke". D then pulled trigger. The gun fired a live bullet killing V. D had checked the chamber of the gun. The gun had two bullets in chambers neither being opposite the barrel. D mistakenly thought the striking pin could not hit the bullets. D had not known pulling the trigger rotated the cylinder bringing one bullet into the firing position.

Three experts agreed D's mistake was natural for someone unaware of gun mechanisms. The defence case was therefore a denial of *mens rea* and stating accident i.e. "I had no intention to kill or do GBH; I was not aware I was taking an unjustified risk; I was honestly subjectively mistaken in my belief that the pulling of the trigger would not discharge a bullet."

The trial judge ruled the mistake was irrelevant. He ruled the evidence of three experts that this mistake was natural for ordinary people and was inadmissible. He ruled that pointing the gun and pulling the trigger itself was sufficient to be unlawful. The judge did not direct the jury as to the defence of accident. The Direction given was:

> *"It is manslaughter if death results from an unlawful and dangerous act on the part of the accused. It is also manslaughter if death results from an extreme degree of carelessness, negligence, on the part of the accused. Those are both grounds on which manslaughter can be found; it is quite possible that to some extent they overlap."*

The case went to the Court of Appeal which asked the question: Was D's mistake obliged to be reasonable?

The Court of Appeal quashed the conviction.

1. *Mens rea* is an essential element of an offence. The prosecution were obliged to prove the intention to harm for the *mens rea* of the underlying assault.
2. The Direction was faulty as it covered both CAM & GNM.

If the prosecution could not prove the underlying intention, D was not guilty.

Sachs LJ:

> *"... it would, of course, have been fully open to a jury, if properly directed, to find the defendant guilty because they considered his view as to there being no danger was formed in a criminally negligent way [Ed. By way of Gross Negligence Manslaughter]. But* ***he was entitled to a direction that the jury should take into account the fact that he had undisputedly formed that view and that there was expert evidence as to this being an understandable view.****"*[1]

With no defence to the underlying offence

If D had a total defence to the underlying charge (e.g., self-defence) he would not be guilty (e.g. ***Scarlett* (1994)** where a one punch manslaughter self-defence argument was valid and the jury should have been directed they could only convict if the force used was excessive).

1 R v Lamb [1967]

No longer any need for the act to be "directed at the victim"

In ***Mitchell* [1983]** (also relevant to **Chapter 3** Causation); in this case D was inside a post office and ended up in a fight. D assaulted V1 a 72 year old man. This caused V1 fall over onto V2 an 82 year old woman. V2 was injured and subsequently died from her injuries in hospital.

The Court of Appeal upheld the conviction for manslaughter for the following reasons:

1. D committed the AR of the underlying offence with the MR of the underlying offence and had no defence.
2. D's actions were objectively dangerous.
3. D caused the death: It was sufficient for the jury to be satisfied that D's intentional act caused the death of V2. The actions of V1 were entirely foreseeable and did not break the chain of causation between D's assault and V2's death.

Per Staughton J:

> *"The Court [in Dalby] was there concerned with the* ***quality of the act rather than the identity of the person at whom it was aimed.*** *Again, we do not read Waller LJ as saying that the unlawful and dangerous act must be aimed at that very person whose death is caused. If, however, that was what the Court was saying, then we would, with the greatest respect, hold that it was not part of the ratio decidendi of the case."*

In ***Goodfellow* (1986)**, the facts were D was unhappy in his council house and petrol bombed it. Sadly his partner and children died. D was then charged with unlawful act manslaughter and convicted on the basis of:

1.	Unlawful intentional criminal act with *mens rea*	Criminal damage	YES
2.	Objectively dangerous to the reasonable person		YES
3.	Causing death of V.		YES

The Court of Appeal stated there was **NO requirement for the unlawful act to be directed at the person** – it was an offence against a person. Dalby was not to be construed as requiring proof of an intention on the part of D towards V's.

Per Lord Lane CJ: "… *there must be* ***no fresh intervening cause between the act and the death****' but the act need not be directed at the victim."*[2]

2 Goodfellow (1986)

6.2.3 Objectively physically "dangerous" to the reasonable person

a) Reasonable person test

In ***Church* [1965]** D had a fight with V. D knocked V unconscious. D believed V was dead. D then put V in the river. V in fact died as a result of being put in the river. The Court of Appeal stated D should be acquitted of murder but convicted of manslaughter. Of importance the court stated the test was an **objective test**.

Per Edmund Davies J:

1. Prove the unlawful intentional act.
2. Prove

   *"....the unlawful act must be such as all **sober and reasonable people would inevitably recognise** must subject the other person to, at least, **the risk of some harm resulting therefrom, albeit not serious harm**."*

3. Prove causation.

In ***Newbury and Jones* [1977]** D's were standing on a railway bridge and pushed a paving stone off the bridge which landed on the front of a train. D's actions killed the train guard. At trial, D was convicted of manslaughter. The House of Lords upheld the conviction for UAM but confirmed it is not necessary to prove D foresaw his act might cause harm to another. The test is objective i.e., whether a reasonable person would recognise the risk of harm to another.

Per Lord Salmon: " ......

[D] is guilty of manslaughter if it is proved that he

*[1] intentionally did **an act** which was **unlawful**; and*

*[2] [D]**angerous** and that*

Dangerous = *Would all sober and reasonable people recognise as dangerous?*

*It is **unnecessary to prove that D knew that the act was unlawful or dangerous.***

[3] [T]hat act caused the death."

More recently in ***JM and SM* [2012]**. D was outside of a nightclub. V (a doorman) in fact may not have been physically struck but did collapse and died from a renal artery aneurism. The Court of Appeal stated firstly, an affray (a type of public order offence which did not require physical contact) could constitute an unlawful and dangerous act whether by fear created or direct violence suffered. Secondly, what mattered was whether reasonable and sober people would recognise that the unlawful activities of the defendant inevitably subjected the victim to the risk of some harm resulting from them.

Lord Judge CJ [20]:

> *"certainly since Church and Newbury , it has never been a requirement that the defendant personally should foresee any specific harm at all, or that the reasonable bystander should recognise the precise form or "sort" of harm which did ensue. What matters is whether reasonable and sober people would recognise that the unlawful activities of the defendant inevitably subjected the deceased to the risk of some harm resulting from them."*

In ***JF and EN* [2015]**. JF was 14 but had an IQ equivalent of a six year old and EN was 16. Both were convicted of manslaughter after they had set alight a duvet on a pile of tyres before leaving. Both were unaware homeless men lived in the building. One of the homeless men died.

The Court of Appeal decided that the unlawful act was arson. The act was objectively dangerous to the reasonable person and it caused death. The convictions were upheld.

b) Physical harm not "mere" emotional disturbance

In ***Dawson* (1985)** the facts were that D attempted to rob a petrol station kiosk with a replica gun. Unknown to D, the V was a 60-year-old attendant with a weak heart. V suffered shock and died of a heart attack.

The question was: did harm include emotional disturbance or just physical disturbance?

The Court of Appeal quashed the conviction stating:

1. Physical disturbance could give rise to liability; but
2. Emotional disturbance alone cannot constitute harm.

Test: Would the reasonable person at the scene have foreseen the physical harm?

Answer: No as the reasonable person at the scene would not have been aware the V had a heart condition.

Analysis

1.	Unlawful intentional act with *mens rea*	Attempted robbery	YES
2.	Dangerous: RP foresee physical harm		NO
3.	Causing death of V		YES

Per Watkins LJ:

> *"[The* ***objective test for dangerousness****] …* ***can only be undertaken upon the basis of the knowledge gained by a sober and reasonable man as though he were present at the scene of and watched the unlawful act being performed*** *and who knows that, as in the present case, an unloaded replica gun was in use, but that the victim may have thought it was a loaded gun in working order. In other words,* ***he has the same knowledge as the man attempting to rob and no more. It was never suggested that any of these appellants knew that their victim had a bad heart****. They knew nothing about him."*[3]

Commentary

C.f. "Take your V as you find him or her" rule of causation (See **Chapter 3** and ***Blaue***).

In ***Watson* [1989]** D burglar who broke into V's house. D wanted to commit burglary. V householder was in fact at home and elderly (87). V disturbed burglar. D verbally abused V and then ran away. V dies of shock. D charged with manslaughter.

The Court Appeal quashed the conviction *on grounds of causation*. The conviction was overturned on other grounds because his barrister had been denied sufficient opportunity to address the jury on the issue of whether the excitement caused by the arrival of the police and the council workman could have taken over as the substantial and operating cause.

The court stated the test was: **"Would the reasonable person at the scene have foreseen the physical harm?** Answer: Yes.

Analysis

1.	Unlawful intentional act with *mens rea*	Burglary	YES
2.	Dangerous: RP foresee physical harm		NO
3.	Causing death of V		YES

Per Lord Lane CJ:

> *"When one is deciding whether* **the sober and reasonable person** *(the bystander) would realise the risk of some harm resulting to the victim, how much knowledge of the circumstances does one attribute to the bystander?...*
>
> ***'... the jury were entitled to ascribe to the bystander the knowledge which [D] gained during the whole of his stay in the house ...***

3 Dawson (1985)

> *The unlawful act in the present circumstances comprised the whole of the burglarious intrusion and did not come to an end on the [D's] foot crossing the threshold ...*
>
> *That being so, [D] (and therefore the bystander)* ***during the course of the unlawful act must have become aware of [V's] frailty and approximate age****......"*

In ***Ball* [1989]** neighbours in dispute about the storage of a Land Rover. D grabbed a handful of cartridges (live & blanks) and loaded them into a gun. D tried to claim his act was not dangerous because he thought that he had a loaded a blank.

The Court of Appeal dismissed the appeal. It was dangerous because the RP would have realised there was a risk of loading a mix of blank and live cartridges.

The Court refused to impute RP with D's mistake of fact.

Per Stuart-Smith LJ:

> '...the question whether the act is a dangerous one is to be ***judged <u>not</u> by the [D's] appreciation but by that of the sober and reasonable man,*** and it is impossible to impute into his appreciation the mistaken belief of [D] that what he was doing was not dangerous because he thought he had a blank cartridge in the chamber. At that stage the [D's] intention, foresight or knowledge is irrelevant.'[4]

1.	Unlawful Intentional criminal Act with *mens rea* Assault	YES
2.	Objectively dangerous to the reasonable person	YES
3.	Causing death of V	YES

In ***Bristow* [2013]**, six burglars entered a farm building. The Ds stole quad bikes, tyres, and a land rover. Ds then left at speed. V intervened whilst burglary was ongoing. V was killed by being run over by Ds.

The Court of Appeal dismissed the appeal.

1.	Unlawful Intentional criminal Act with *mens rea* burglary	YES
2.	Objectively dangerous to the reasonable person	YES
3.	Causing death of V	YES

4 Ball [1989]

The Court of Appeal made it clear the instant danger was obvious due to the nature of the vehicles and layout of the site. It was such that a reasonable bystander would have realised the risk of some physical harm being caused.

6.2.4 Causing the death of the victim

The defendant's act must have caused the death of the victim. This applies the same concepts of causation (**Chapter 3**) discussed in relation to murder (**Chapter 5**).

6.3 Gross negligence manslaughter (GNM)

6.3.1 Background

a) Why impose liability on D who does something lawfully but does it so badly it is criminal?

Firstly, in order to encourage high standards of care in the professions: doctors, pharmacists, opticians etc.

Secondly, do note the concept of the duty of care is wider and can be used against e.g., plumber and lay persons who owe a duty care to other under the neighbourhood principle of the moral duty to look after ones neighbour.

b) History

The history dates back to ***Bateman* [1927]**. In that case D operated on V who was pregnant. D had to turn the foetus in utero. D's actions caused significant internal injuries. D accidentally removed V's uterus and failed to refer V. V subsequently died.

The advocates were namely Norman Birkett KC and Sir Edward Marshall KC. The trial judge failed to distinguish between degree of negligence for civil cases and criminal cases.

The Court of Appeal, namely LJ Hewart stated to secure a conviction, prosecution must prove:

1. D owed V a ***duty of care***;
2. D had ***breached*** the duty of care;
3. Breach had ***caused the death*** of V;
4. D negligence was gross in that it ***went beyond a matter of compensation*** between subjects.

> *"... the facts must be such that, in the opinion of the jury, the negligence of [D] went beyond a mere matter of compensation between subjects and showed such disregard for the life and safety of others as to amount to a crime against the State and conduct deserving punishment."*

Similarly in ***Andrews v DPP* [1937]** D killed a pedestrian whilst driving a car. At trial D was convicted of GNM. The House of Lords confirmed ***Bateman*** i.e. manslaughter required a very high degree of negligence.

c) *Modern era*

Adomako [1995] was a case about four professionals

- S &K Death of a patient from Leukaemia. Two junior doctors inject into the spine rather than a muscle. Outcome conviction quashed.
- H Central heating engineer. Erroneously left wires loose which touched a metal sink causing electrocution. Outcome conviction quashed.
- A An anaesthetist supporting a routine eye operation. V died because the oxygen tube became detached for nine minutes (expert evidence indicated most competent anaesthetist would have noticed in 15 seconds). A did not notice V had gone blue. Outcome conviction upheld.

The House of Lords was set this certified question:

> *"In cases of manslaughter by [gross] negligence ...involving a breach of duty is it a sufficient direction to the jury to adopt the gross negligence test set out by the Court of Appeal in the present case following [**Bateman (1927)**] and [**Andrews (1937)**] without reference to the test for recklessness ...or as adapted to the circumstances of the case?"*[5]

The House of Lords Held **yes** – GNM could be the basis of the charge and dismissed A's appeal & upheld the conviction.

Per Lord Mackay LC (confirmed ***Andrews*** had not been overruled, and was thus still binding):

> *"... in my opinion the ordinary principles of the law of negligence apply to ascertain whether or not the defendant has been in breach of a duty of care towards the victim who has died. If such a breach of duty is established the next question is whether that breach of duty caused the death of the victim. If so, the jury must go on to consider whether that breach of duty should be characterised as gross negligence and therefore as a crime. This will depend*

5 Adomako [1995]

on the seriousness of the breach of duty committed by the defendant in all the circumstances in which the defendant was placed when it occurred ... ***The jury will have to consider whether [1] the extent to which the defendant's conduct departed from the proper standard of care incumbent upon him, [2] involving as it must have done a risk of death to the patient, [3] was such that it should be judged criminal.***

It is true that to a certain extent this involves an element of circularity, but in this branch of the law I do not believe that it is fatal to its being correct as a test of how far conduct must depart from accepted standards to be characterised as criminal. ... The essence of the matter which is supremely a jury question is whether, having regard to the risk of death involved, the conduct of the defendant was so bad in all the circumstances as to amount in their judgment to a criminal act or omission."[6]

d) Evolution?

The most recent leading authority is ***Broughton* [2021]**.

For the facts please see below under Causation.

The Court of Appeal with Lord Burnett CJ identified six elements that must be proved or admitted in any case of gross negligence manslaughter:

"i) DOC D owed an existing duty of care to V

ii) B *D* ***negligently breached that duty of care.***

iii) SORD At the time of the breach there was a ***serious and obvious risk of death****. ... An obvious risk is one that is present, clear, and unambiguous. It is immediately apparent, striking and glaring rather than something that might become apparent on further investigation.*

iv) RF It was ***reasonably foreseeable at the time of the breach of the duty that the breach gave rise to a serious and obvious risk of death****.*

v) C The breach of the duty **caused or made a significant** *(i.e. more than minimal) contribution to the death of the victim.*

vi) Gross In the view of the jury, the circumstances of the breach ***were truly exceptionally bad and so reprehensible as to justify the conclusion that it amounted to gross negligence and required criminal sanction."***

6 Adomako [1995]

e) Synthesis

For the purpose of clarity this text synthesises this test into three elements:

(1) Duty of care.

(2) Gross breach and reasonably foreseeable that the breach gives rise to a serious and obvious risk of death.

(3) Causing the death of the victim.

f) Examples

There are numerous examples of duty of care relationships that have given rise to potential liability in gross negligence manslaughter. These include but are not limited to:

- Medical treatment. It is axiomatic that a medic will have a duty towards a patient **_Adomako_ [1995]; _Rose_ [2017]**.
- People smuggling: **_Wacker_ [2002]**.
- Failure to heed food allergies: **_Kuddus_ [2019]**; **_Zaman_ [2017]**.
- Welfare support for those using or withdrawing from drug usage: **_Evans_ [2009]**.

6.3.2 Duty of care – based on tortious principles

a) Examples

There are numerous non-exhaustive examples of the relationships that give rise to the duty of care. These include but are not limited to:

- Medic and patient: **_Adomako_ [1995]**; **_Rose_ [2017]**.
- Food supplier and customer: **_Zaman_ [2017]**.
- Relationship duties such as carer and person cared for: **_Hood_ [2004]**; **Reeves [2012]**.
- Smuggler and the person smuggled: **_Wacker_ [2002]**.

b) Examples of what would now be gross negligence manslaughter based on special relationships

- **_Hood_ [2004]**
- **_Evans_ [2009]**
- **_Reeves_ [2012]**.

c) Modern examples post *Adomako*

In ***Wacker* [2002]**, D was the driver of a lorry with 58 dead illegal immigrants in the lorry. D was convicted of conspiracy to facilitate the entry into the United Kingdom of illegal immigrants and 58 offences of manslaughter on the basis of gross negligence. D had closed the one ventilation hatch for long periods of time.

The question was, could the principle that the law of negligence does not recognise the relationship between those involved in a criminal enterprise as giving rise to a duty of care owed by one participant to another (ex *turpi causa non oritur actio*) be applied?

The Court of Appeal dismissed the appeal. It held that a duty of care had been established and that it had been breached. The negligence was gross and gave rise to a reasonably foreseeable (RF) and serious and obvious risk of death (SORD). Causation was also established.

The court stated consent provided no defence and the civil tortious principle of *ex turpi causa* was not applicable in criminal cases.

> ***"The public policy considerations that underpinned criminal law were different and in contrast to those that led to the application in civil law of the principle of ex turpi causa;*** *accordingly, a person could be criminally responsible for the death of another notwithstanding that the two were engaged in some unlawful activity at the time or in circumstances where there was an acceptance of a degree of risk by the victim in order to further the joint unlawful enterprise."*

Wacker was recently confirmed in ***Bah* [2024]**. In this case D steered a small boat carrying 45 people across the Channel from France to the UK. Unfortunately mid-crossing the boat began to take on water. The vessel flooded and four of the passengers died whilst 41 were saved by a local fishing boat. D was convicted of four counts of GNM.

It held that a duty of care had been established and that it had been breached. The negligence was gross and gave rise to a reasonably foreseeable (RF) and serious and obvious risk of death (SORD).

> Causation was established. Ds duty to Vs was not obviated by the fact Vs voluntarily entered the boat. Vs free deliberate choices would not normally relieve D of legal liability. The calibration of legal causation should focus firmly on whether D was legally responsible (confirming Wallace **Chapter 3** Causation). It was not necessary to show joint participation. In this case there was no break in the chain of causation.

6.3.3 Gross breach and reasonably foreseeable that the breach gives rise to a serious and obvious risk of death

a) Early examples professionals

The case law after ***Adomako* [1995]** tended to focus on professionals, e.g.

- Medics ***Adomako* [1995]**
- Owner and master of the sailing ship ***Litchfield* [1998]**
- Gas fitter ***Singh (Gurpal)* [1999]**

b) Evolution to the lay person

In recent times the concept has evolved to include social justice principle scenarios such as ***Gemma Evans* [2009]**, where the layperson would owe a duty of care to those they can reasonably expect to care for such as family members or others within a proximate relationship in time. (See also **Chapter 3** *Actus reus*/Omissions).

c) No breach of the ECHR

In ***Amit Misra* [2004]**, the court was asked whether the ingredients of GNM were sufficiently certain for the purposes of **ECHR Art 7**.

The Court of Appeal ruled:

1) The need for the criminal law to be predictable and certain had long been understood at common law. The incorporation of **ECHR**, although providing a salutary reminder, had not affected a significant extension or change to that principle. The requirement was for sufficient, not absolute certainty, and there was a distinction between uncertainty about the necessary ingredients of a criminal offence, and uncertainty in the process by which it was decided whether the required ingredients of the offence had been established in an individual case.
2) The application of the principle might involve an element of uncertainty, but the offence itself was clearly defined. Accordingly, the offence neither contravened principles at common law nor was it incompatible with **ECHR**.

Judge LJ:

> *"The decision of the House of Lords in Adomako clearly identified the ingredients of manslaughter by gross negligence. In very brief summary, confirming*

Andrews v DPP [1937] AC 576, *the offence requires first, death resulting from a negligent breach of the duty of care owed by the defendant to the deceased, second, that in negligent breach of that duty, the victim was exposed by the defendant to the risk of death, and third, that the circumstances were so reprehensible as to amount to gross negligence....the law is clear. The ingredients of the offence have been clearly defined, and the principles decided in the House of Lords in Adomako. They involve no uncertainty. The hypothetical citizen, seeking to know his position, would be advised that, assuming he owed a duty of care to the deceased which he had negligently broken, and that death resulted, he would be liable to conviction for manslaughter if, on the available evidence, the jury was satisfied that his negligence was gross. A doctor would be told that grossly negligent treatment of a patient which exposed him or her to the risk of death, and caused it, would constitute manslaughter."*

d) The problem of defining "gross"

For a significant period of time the case law showed the difficulty of the court defining what was meant by the term gross.

- *"The essence of the matter ... is whether having regard to the risk of death involved, the conduct of the defendant was* ***so bad*** *in all the circumstances as to amount in their judgment to a criminal act or omission."* ***Adomako* [1995]**.
- "Mistakes, even very serious mistakes, and errors of judgment, even very serious errors of judgment, will not of themselves suffice. A proper direction to the jury on the issue of gross negligence was held in that case to be that they should be sure that the conduct in question was something '***truly exceptionally bad*** and which showed such indifference to an obviously serious risk to life and which showed such a departure from the standard to be expected' so as to constitute the very serious crime of manslaughter. The bar is thus set high: perhaps unsurprisingly so, given that such cases ordinarily involve no criminal intent." ***Misra* [2004]**, at [11]. This was confirmed in ***Oliver* [2016]** and ***Sellu* [2016]; *Bawa-Garba* [2016]**.

e) Reasonable foreseeability of a serious and obvious risk of death (RF SORD)

This new requirement that it is reasonably foreseeable that there is a serious and obvious risk of death was noted by the Law Commission and adopted by the Court of Appeal first in the case of ***Rudling* [2016]**.

The facts were D, a Doctor, spoke to V's mother by phone. V, a 12-year-old child was unwell. Mother explained V's symptoms which were consistent with a rare disease. D did not recommend a physical, in-person check-up. D should have gone to see V who was very unwell.

Noting V's symptoms as described by V's mother did not indicate a serious and obvious risk of death.

The Court of Appeal confirmed the trial judges ruling that there was no case to answer as there was a "*requirement it was reasonably foreseeable the breach gives rise to a serious and obvious risk of death*".

Sir Brian Leveson P at [39]:

> "...***At the time of the breach of duty, there must be a risk of death, not merely serious illness; the risk must be serious; and the risk must be obvious***. *A GP faced with an unusual presentation which is worrying and undiagnosed may need to ensure a face to face assessment urgently in order to investigate further. That may be in order to assess whether it is something serious, to use Dr Peter's expression, which may or may not be so serious as to be life-threatening. A recognisable risk of something serious is not the same as a recognisable risk of death.*
>
> [40] "*What does not follow is that if a reasonably competent GP requires an urgent assessment of a worrying and undiagnosed condition, it is necessarily reasonably foreseeable that there is a risk of death. Still less does it demonstrate a serious risk of death, which is not to be equated with an 'inability to eliminate a possibility'. There may be numerous remote possibilities of very rare conditions which cannot be eliminated but which do not present a serious risk of death. Further, and perhaps most importantly,* ***a mere possibility that an assessment might reveal something life-threatening is not the same as an obvious risk of death. An obvious risk is a present risk which is clear and unambiguous, not one which might become apparent on further investigation."***

This was confirmed in the notorious cases of ***Rose* [2017]**. In that case D, an optometrist. was charged with GNM. In law, D had duties under **s26(1) Opticians Act 1989**, and **reg 3(1) Sight Test (Examination and Prescription) (No. 2) Regulations 1989**; namely the duties were to examine the internal eye structure to detect disease and abnormality.

Unfortunately D had failed to spot a rare issue in a 7-year-old V. The V died five months later. D did not carry out a test which would, in rare cases, highlight the fatal condition (acute hydrocephalus). D did not know V was at risk and stated the child uncooperative and the optometrist may have been shown the wrong images of another patient.

At trial D, the optometrist, was convicted. The case went to the Court of Appeal with significant media interest. The Court of Appeal allowed the appeal and quashed the conviction. It stated:

"1. The question of whether there had been a serious and obvious risk of death had to be assessed with respect to knowledge at the time of the breach of duty;

2. A recognisable risk of something serious was not the same as a recognisable risk of death; that an obvious was a present risk which was clear and unambiguous, not one which might become apparent on further investigation

3. The question of available knowledge and risk was always to be judged objectively and prospectively at the moment of breach."

Sir Brian Leveson P [84]:

> *"The test of reasonable foreseeability is, of course, resolutely objective and there is no question of it being decided by reference to the subjective knowledge of the person whose conduct is under scrutiny.*
>
> ***"The test of reasonable foreseeability simply requires the notional objective exercise of putting a reasonably prudent professional in the shoes of the person whose conduct is under scrutiny and asking whether, at the moment of breach of the duty on which the prosecution rely, that person ought reasonably (i e objectively) to have foreseen an obvious and serious risk of death."***

Applying the principles

1. DOC	YES
2. Breach	YES
Gross?	NO
RF SORD	NO
3. Causation	YES

Examples of RF SORD

- Giving nuts in a restaurant meal having issued specific assurance no nuts were in the meal ***Zaman* [2017]**.
- Digging a trench where the trench was not built correctly and collapsed causing the victim's death: ***Winterton* [2018]**.

***Kuddus* [2019]** confirmed the new test. Sir Brian Leveson P commented:

> ***"the foreseeable risk for the purposes of gross negligence manslaughter is that, armed with notice that a particular customer or patient falls into***

> ***the category which the system*** *(or statute) was designed to deal with, a reasonable person in the position of the restaurateur or optometrist would, at the time of breach of duty, have foreseen an obvious and serious risk of death. It is in those circumstances that the jury would have to go on to consider whether the negligent breach of duty* ***was "gross" within the meaning of that term defined by the authorities."***

In ***Rebelo* [2021]** D ran an internet business selling the chemical, Dinitrophenol (DNP). DNP is a food supplement claimed to promote weight loss. The problem is DNP can be toxic to the liver and kidneys and cause cardiac arrest.

V, a young female suffering from depression, bulimia nervosa and emotionally unstable personality disorder had a history of overdosing on paracetamol and taking cocaine. V began to use DNP but was unable to control her use. V was aware that it was causing her harm and had warnings from her GP, social worker and friends of the dangers and potential consequences of taking DNP.

V consumed a grossly excessive volume, suffered a cardiac arrest, and died.

In this case the court ruled that the conviction stood and would not be quashed.

The judge was obliged and right to direct on focusing on the "*substantial and operative*" cause of death. The jury correctly had two options, either:

(1) This was a fully free voluntary and informed decision of V leading to acquittal; or

(2) This was not a fully free, voluntary, and informed decision of V and then GNM applied.

6.3.4 Causing the death of the victim

The defendant's act must have caused the death of the victim. This applies the same concepts of causation (**Chapter 3**) discussed in relation to murder (**Chapter 5**).

In ***Morby* (1882)**, D was convicted of manslaughter of his son V. D failed for certain religious reasons to seek out medical treatment. V had smallpox.

The evidence of the the expert medical evidence could only say death "**might** have been averted" had medical assistance been given. He could not say "would" have been averted. Thus no positive evidence that death was caused or accelerated by the neglect.

The Court of Appeal ruled causation was not proven on the medical evidence.

***Broughton* [2021]** is now the leading authority. The facts were that D supplied V (his girlfriend) with a cocktail of controlled Class A drugs. The Drugs included 2CP, ketamine and MDMA (ecstasy). V took the drugs in D's presence in woodland adjacent to a rock festival site. V experienced a violent reaction. D did not call for medical assistance (even after phoning members of V's family and V's family begged him to do so). Instead, D video-recorded V as her condition deteriorated.

Note here as V had voluntarily consumed the drugs, so this could not be advanced as a case of constructive manslaughter by unlawful administration.

At trial D was convicted of manslaughter by gross negligence (based on ***Gemma Evans*** style of reasoning).

The issue on appeal was:

> "*The prosecution must prove to the criminal standard that the gross negligence was at least a substantial contributory cause of death. That means that the prosecution must prove that the deceased would have lived in the sense that life would have been significantly prolonged.*"[7]

The only evidence indicated a 90% chance of survival if medical treatment had been provided more promptly. This left a "*a realistic possibility that [V] would not have lived*" (para [101]). Therefore there was a 10% chance V might have died anyway, even with no breach.

The Court of Appeal ruled the case should have been withdrawn from the jury as "*the evidence adduced by the prosecution was incapable of proving causation to the criminal standard*".

Why?

1. Causation was problematic: the evidence was problematic.
2. There was no clear evidence that V died because of D's neglect.
3. There was only evidence that this had "*drastically reduced her chances of survival*", but that alone cannot suffice.
4. Such has been the law at least since ***Morby* (1882)**, in which D failed to secure medical treatment for his child, who then died of smallpox. Medical experts testified that treatment would not necessarily have saved the child, but would merely have improved his chances of survival, and that was held to be fatal to the prosecution case.
5. In ***Broughton***, the exact cause of V's death could not be determined, and the only expert witness to address the causation issue concluded:

7 Broughton [2021]

> *"In view of the lack of previously documented deaths from 2CP, the combined effect of three stimulant drugs and the unknown mechanism that resulted in L's death, it is not possible to state beyond reasonable doubt that earlier medical intervention would have been able to save L's life once she had ingested the 2CP. At best, L might have had a 90% chance of survival if given prompt medical intervention, which still leaves ample room for reasonable doubt."*

Burnett LCJ ruled:

> *"The prosecution must prove to the criminal standard that the gross negligence was at least a substantial contributory cause of death. That means that the prosecution must prove that the deceased would have lived in the sense that life would have been significantly prolonged. It is well established that being 'sure' is not the same as scientific certainty. .... The jury must make judgements on 'realistic not fanciful possibilities'. To be sure that the gross negligence caused the death the prosecution must exclude realistic or plausible possibilities that the deceased would anyway have died."*

Similarly, in ***Wood Treatment Ltd* [2021]** where there was an explosion at a wood mill, the expert evidence did not rule out a credible potential cause of death not attributable to D's negligence. Experts stated four potential causes.

The Court of Appeal upheld the trial judge's ruling that there was no case to answer.

Edis LJ 38:

> *"The problem in this case was that at the conclusion of the prosecution case there was no evidence which would enable them rationally to say that [the expert's] evidence about scenario 3 was wrong, and no evidence which would enable them to say that the negligent acts or omissions of [D1 or D2] had caused the explosion if it had resulted from a scenario 3 event."*

6.4 Causing or allowing the death or serious physical harm to a child or vulnerable adult (CAD)

Domestic Violence, Crime and Victims Act 2004, s5

(1) A person ('D') is guilty of an offence if—

*(a) **a child or vulnerable adult ('V') dies or suffers serious physical harm** as a result of the unlawful act of a person who—*

(i) ***was a member of the same household as V,*** *and*

(ii) **had frequent contact with him,**

(b) ***D was such a person at the time of that act,***

(c) *at that time there was* ***a significant risk of serious physical harm being caused to V*** *by the unlawful act of such a person, and*

(d) ***either D was the person whose act caused the death or serious physical harm*** *or—*

(i) ***D was, or ought to have been, aware of the risk*** *mentioned in paragraph (c),*

(ii) ***D failed to take such steps*** *as he could reasonably have been expected to take to protect V from the risk, and*

(iii) ***the act occurred in circumstances of the kind that D foresaw or ought to have foreseen****.*

(2) The prosecution does not have to prove whether it is the first alternative in subsection (1)(d) or the second (sub-paragraphs (i) to (iii)) that applies.

. . .

(6), as 'a person aged 16 or over whose ability to protect himself from violence, abuse or neglect is significantly impaired through physical or mental disability or illness, through old age or otherwise'.

6.4.1 Context

1. V (child or vulnerable adult) dies at home, but it is unclear which of two carers caused the death.
2. Clear that one or both caused death.
3. Pre-2004 if not able to prove either D1 or D2 or both were acquitted.
4. Research

   Three children per week under 10 died or suffered serious injury each week.

   Only 27 per cent of cases led to a conviction.

5. Both can be charged on the basis either:

   - they caused; or
   - they failed to protect.

6. Historical examples and context

***Lane* (1986)**

Law Com No. 282, Children: Their Non-Accidental Death or Serious Injury **(Criminal Trials).**

6.4.2 Unlawful act: offence

See case of ***ATT* [2024]** for guidance on the elements of the **Domestic Violence, Crime and Victims Act 2004, s5:**

(5)

(a) constitutes an offence, or

(b) would constitute an offence but for being the act of—

(i) a person under the age of ten, or

(ii) a person entitled to rely on a defence of insanity.

Paragraph (b) does not apply to an act of D.

6.4.3 Relationship: member of same household

Domestic Violence, Crime and Victims Act 2004, s5:

(4) For the purposes of this section—

(a) a person is to be regarded as a 'member' of a particular household, even if he does not live in that household, if he visits it so often and for such periods of time that it is reasonable to regard him as a member of it;

(b) where V lived in different households at different times, 'the same household as V' refers to the household in which V was living at the time of the act that caused the death or serious physical harm.

6.4.4 *Mens rea*

This is negligence.

6.5 Corporate manslaughter (CM)

6.5.1 Context

Corporate Manslaughter and Corporate Homicide Act 2007, s1

(1) An organisation to which this section applies is guilty of an offence if the way in which its activities are managed or organised—

(a) causes a person's death, and

(b) amounts to a gross breach of a relevant duty of care owed by the organisation to the deceased.

(2) The organisations to which this section applies are—

(a) a corporation;

(b) a department or other body listed in Schedule 1;

(c) a police force;

(d) a partnership, or a trade union or employers' association, that is an employer.

(3) An organisation is guilty of an offence under this section only if the way in which its activities are managed or organised by its senior management is a substantial element in the breach referred to in subsection *(1).*

6.5.2 Duty of care

Corporate Manslaughter and Corporate Homicide Act 2007, s2

(1) A 'relevant duty of care', in relation to an organisation, means any of the following duties owed by it under the law of negligence—

(a) a duty owed to its employees or to other persons working for the organisation or performing services for it;

(b) a duty owed as occupier of premises;

(c) a duty owed in connection with—

(i) the supply by the organisation of goods or services (whether for consideration or not),

(ii) the carrying on by the organisation of any construction or maintenance operations,

(iii) the carrying on by the organisation of any other activity on a commercial basis, or

(iv) the use or keeping by the organisation of any plant, vehicle, or other thing;

(d) a duty owed to a person who, by reason of being a person within subsection (2), is someone for whose safety the organisation is responsible.

(2) A person is within this subsection if—

(a) he is detained at a custodial institution or in a custody area at a court or police station;

(aa) he is detained in service custody premises;

(b) he is detained at a removal centre or short-term holding facility;

(c) he is being transported in a vehicle, or being held in any premises, in pursuance of prison escort arrangements or immigration escort arrangements;

(d) he is living in secure accommodation in which he has been placed;

(e) he is a detained patient;

...

(4) A reference in subsection (1) to a duty owed under the law of negligence includes a reference to a duty that would be owed under the law of negligence but for any statutory provision under which liability is imposed in place of liability under that law.

(5) For the purposes of this Act, whether a particular organisation owes a duty of care to a particular individual is a question of law. The judge must make any findings of fact necessary to decide that question.

(6) For the purposes of this Act there is to be disregarded—

(a) any rule of the common law that has the effect of preventing a duty of care from being owed by one person to another by reason of the fact that they are jointly engaged in unlawful conduct;

(b) any such rule that has the effect of preventing a duty of care from being owed to a person by reason of his acceptance of a risk of harm.

6.5.3 Gross breach

Corporate Manslaughter and Corporate Homicide Act 2007, s8

(1) This section applies where—

(a) it is established that an organisation owed a relevant duty of care to a person, and

(b) it falls to the jury to decide whether there was a gross breach of that duty.

(2) The jury must consider whether the evidence shows that the organisation failed to comply with any health and safety legislation that relates to the alleged breach, and if so—

(a) how serious that failure was;

(b) how much of a risk of death it posed.

(3) The jury may also—

(a) consider the extent to which the evidence shows that there were attitudes, policies, systems, or accepted practices within the organisation that were likely to have encouraged any such failure as is mentioned in subsection (2), or to have produced tolerance of it;

(b) have regard to any health and safety guidance that relates to the alleged breach.

(4) This section does not prevent the jury from having regard to any other matters they consider relevant.

Case law in this area is limited:

***Cotswold Geotechnical Holdings Ltd* [2011]**

***Wells* [2014]**.

6.5.4 Causation

This implies the usual principles of causation.

6.6 Evaluation and reform

6.6.1 Legal certainty and legal clarity

(1) Constructive act manslaughter has an internal logic to it. Firstly, find the base offence; check the requirements of the base offence including any justification are made out. Secondly, check the reasonable person test and finally check the causation test. As we note below in relation to the case of ***Grey*** even this relatively straightforward piece of law has caused difficulties for judges at first instance. However, overall it seems legally certain, clear and logical.

(2) Gross negligence manslaughter is a logical route to attribute liability where there has been a wholesale departure from the standard of behaviour expected. There has in recent years been welcome clarification of what is meant by the

term gross and how exceptionally bad the error must be. It is also helpful that the Law Commission's proposal on the threshold has been endorsed by the Court of Appeal in recent authorities culminating in ***Broughton***. The law appears to be in a healthy position albeit there is a significant reliance on the jury.

(3) In relation to gross negligence manslaughter it is noted by Karl Laird re

***Kuddus* [2019]**:

"Although the issues discussed in this note may arise only in rare cases, it is submitted that there is much more work to do in the future on both of them. One practical consequence of the court's analysis in this case is that the expert evidence will not only take on even greater importance in determining whether there was a serious and obvious risk of death, but it will be extremely complex and may therefore be difficult for juries to comprehend. Trial judges will have to be alive to this issue, to ensure that the evidence is explained to the jury in a comprehensible way."[8]

6.6.2 Equality before the law: protected characteristics and socio-economic barriers

(1) In relation to constructive act manslaughter there does not appear to be any equality barriers to this offence.

(2) In relation to gross negligence manslaughter it is clear that the recent case law has evolved the definition of gross and has also restrained the worst excesses of leaving to the jury the open textured decision in relation to whether it is reasonably foreseeable that the breach gives rise to a serious and obvious risk of death.

(3) The offence of causing or allowing the death or serious physical harm of a vulnerable adult is an important addition to the canon of the prosecutor seeking to prosecute in a domestic context the causation of death of a child. It is submitted it is a welcome improvement on the previous law and its success is in part shown by the volume of prosecutions under this legislation.

(4) Corporate manslaughter is a necessarily complex offence. The statute is carefully thought out. It is not without problems in terms of the reality of enforcement. Some have argued that there is also an anthropomorphic error here namely that a corporation is not an individual. The criminal law locus classicus would deal with the individual rather than the corporation. However it is important to note there may be a deterrent effect by virtue of having the statute in force.

8 Karl Laird, "Gross negligence manslaughter: R. v Kuddus (Mohammed Abdul) Court of Appeal (Criminal Division)" [2019]

It is hoped that the shadow of the legislation leads to a culture of health and safety and avoidance of death in the workplace.

6.6.3 Fair warning; fair labelling and sufficient breadth principles

(1) Fair warning

It seems although the first two of the four offences, although from common law, are relatively clearly defined and do give fair warning to the potential offender.

(2) Fair labelling

Again the law seems to be positive here that there is a fair labelling of constructive act manslaughter. The other three offences all appear to correctly label D. The only query would be for corporate manslaughter whereas mentioned above – is there an anthropomorphic error?

(3) Sufficient breadth

There appears to be sufficient breadth to capture offending. The advantage of the common law offences is they can of course evolve. It is very clear in recent years that there has been an evolution particularly in relation to gross negligence manslaughter (initially an expansion of scope and then a retraction of scope).

The two statutory offences of causing or allowing corporate manslaughter appear to sufficiently broadly capture wrongdoing. In particular in relation to causing or allowing death the new offence appears to capture what was a *lacuna* in the previous law.

(4) Practicality, cost, and expense

(a) Practicality

The law appears to be practical although the case of ***Grey*** (discussed below) seems to be a rare example of significant errors by the judge. It may be anomalous in the sense that it was simply a fundamental and foundational error by the specific judge.

(b) Avoid undue cost and expense

The law here appears to have a ringing endorsement here as there is clarity in relation to most areas. The only area where there may be evolution which may cause costs and expense would be a welcome Supreme Court judgment to confirm the **newer** elements of gross negligence manslaughter.

6.6.4 Human rights: autonomy and welfare principles

The **Art 7 ECHR** legal certainty discussion has been tested and it is notable that the Court of Appeal is clear in relation to the guidelines on each of these events. In terms of equality, **Art 14 ECHR**, there does not appear to be an issue of discrimination save as so often it would be easier to prosecute an individual than a corporate entity.

6.6.5 International comparators and reform: practicality principle and politics

- **Comparators**

None specified at this stage – see the Law Commission report below:

Law Commission, Murder, Manslaughter and Infanticide (Law Com No 304, 2006)

The Law Commission proposes significant reform:

- **Constructive act manslaughter**

The Law Commission proposed re-labelling this as criminal act manslaughter. The requirements of which would be:

> "i. The Commission of a criminal act
>
> ii. with intention by the defendant to cause injury
>
> iii. the defendant being aware that the action involved a serious risk of causing some injury."

This realigns the test to a subjective test rather than a reasonable person test on dangerousness. This does not appear to be a significant change in the law. However statutory intervention may assist in terms of clarity.

- **Gross negligence manslaughter**

The Law Commission proposed:

"i. Where a person has a duty to another person

ii. The defendant breaches the duty by conduct falling far below what is reasonably expected of them in the circumstances

iii. The defendant causes the death of another and

iv. That the risk would be obvious to a reasonable person in the defendant's position and the defendant is capable of appreciating the risk."

Notably the case law of Lord Justice Leveson has endorsed what the reform proposals are and in fact brought them into the common law.

Finally it is noted that both causing and allowing the death and corporate manslaughter emerge from earlier carefully thought-out reform proposals preceded by Law Commission reports.

In the News

The cyclist on the footpath

Please read these two articles.

1. Brian Farmer & PA Media, "Auriol Grey has cyclist manslaughter conviction overturned" BBC News (8 May 2024)

   <https://www.bbc.co.uk/news/uk-england-cambridgeshire-68975335> accessed 06 April 2025

   Please note the video shows the aspect shortly before the victim's death.

2. Jessica Murray and agencies, "Woman who caused cyclist to fall into car's path has manslaughter conviction quashed" *The Guardian* (London, 8 May 2024)

   <https://www.theguardian.com/uk-news/article/2024/may/08/woman-who-caused-cyclist-to-fall-into-cars-path-has-manslaughter-conviction-quashed> accessed 06 April 2025

3. The case of ***Auriol Grey* [2024]** is tragic on number of levels

   Facts

   i. D was on a footpath when a cyclist was cycling along the same footpath in the opposite direction.

   ii. D was a person with numerous physical and learning difficulties who shouted at V to get off the footpath.

   iii. There was no physical contact between D and V. D was alleged to be shouting, swearing and gesticulating.

   iv. During the trial the prosecution case was put on the basis of a constructive act manslaughter based on an underlying assault (this was implicit but not explicit).

   v. There was no mention of a defined base offence assault.

vi. There was no mention of any potential defence of self defence or accident.

vii. The reasonable person test was not fully addressed.

viii. D was convicted of constructive act manslaughter.

Court of Appeal decision and reasoning

Allowing the appeal due to the absence of a base offence and the misdirections at trial.

i. For constructive act manslaughter there is the requirement of a base defence.

ii. In this case no base offence was identified or defined for the jury. The only potential offence would be one of common assault. But it was clear that in relation to this neither a broad battery assault nor a narrow psychic assault was made out.

iii. The Court of Appeal was so critical that it said the case should never have been left to the jury. There was not a proper basis on which the defendant could be convicted.

4. It is submitted the case is a very good example of why accuracy on the law is so important. It is of foundational importance to understand the elements and principles that relate to criminal offences. One would hope by the end of reading this chapter students are confident as to the core principles that are required in order to prove the criminal offences of involuntary homicide.

6.7 Summary

- **Constructive act manslaughter (CAM)**

  We have seen here the relatively straightforward offence of constructing an underlying criminal offence, combined with an objectively physical dangerous action that causes death. The classic example is one-punch manslaughter.

- **Gross negligence manslaughter (GNM)**

  We have seen in relation to gross negligence manslaughter where the omission to act can lead to prosecution where the breach is gross. The law in relation to the duty of care is clear. The law in relation to gross breach has been clarified to make it clear that it's an exceptionally bad threshold. Finally, the decisions in relation to it being reasonably foreseeable that the breach gives rise to a serious and obvious risk of death are welcomed, to clarify the high threshold required. The cases in relation to causation will also show that this offence is now more difficult to prosecute than perhaps it was thought to be.

- **Causing or allowing the death of or serious physical harm to a child or vulnerable adult (CAD)**

  This is a welcome addition to the Canon of manslaughter. It allows for the context of the relationships within the same household to be examined where there is causation of death.

- **Corporate manslaughter (CM)**

  Corporate manslaughter has also been a welcome addition to the count of manslaughter. It is however difficult to prosecute due to the same issues of identification that pre-existed the statute. That said the shadow effect on the deterrent effect of the legislation is potentially significant. There does remain a moot point whether there is an anthropomorphic error labelling a corporation with what would normally be an individual's culpability.

- **Evaluation framework**

  We have reviewed the evaluation framework and it seems in this area there are a number of positives with some small areas for corrections and clarifications.

Further reading

Elaine Freer, "We Need to Talk About Charlie: Putting the Brakes on Unlawful Act Manslaughter" (2018) *Criminal Law Review 612.*

Gavin Leigh, "Deconstructing unlawful act manslaughter" (2017) *Journal of criminal law 112*

Catherine Crosby "Gross Negligence Manslaughter Revisited: Time for a Change of Direction?" (2020) *84 Journal of Criminal Law 228.*

Glenys Williams, "Gross Negligence Manslaughter And Duty Of Care In 'Drugs' Cases: R v Evans" (2009) *Criminal Law Review 631.*

Susanna Menis, "The Fiction of the Criminalisation of Corporate Killing" (2017) 81 *Journal of Criminal Law 46.*

CHAPTER 7

Offences against the person

7.1 Introduction

7.1.1 The problem

The law relating to non-fatal assaults is based upon an archaic mix of statutory and common law provisions. Unfortunately even the statutory provisions are a messy combination of previous common law offences with undue specificity.

The main statute is the **Offences against the Person Act 1861** (**OPA 1861**). It is an assortment of offences. Unfortunately it was not a codification exercise more of a consolidation of the existing variety of offences. In the statute there is no systematic attempt as to legal certainty or clarity. It is widely agreed **OPA 1861** needs reform and codification. The reform proposals at the end of this chapter show reform in this area would be a very "easy win".

The main offences are common law assault and battery; statutory actual bodily harm (**s47 ABH**); statutory grievous bodily harm (**s20 GBH**) and statutory grievous bodily harm with intent (**s18 GBH with intent**). In the last 27 years Parliament has added to the statute book legislation specifically aimed at the activities of those who "harass", "stalk" and exercise "coercive control".

Where D has assaulted V the usual trinity is engaged.

1. Harm: Establish what level of harm has been caused
2. Fault: Establish what level of fault can be proven
3. Justification: Establish whether a legally permissible justification exists. The main issue here frequently links to the **Chapter 13** denial of fault of the intoxicated defendant and the **Chapter 14** justification defence of self defence.

7.1.2 The reality

Thankfully the archaic complexity of **OPA 1861** is ameliorated by the case law. Since the 1990s the archaic terms have often been simplified by the case law to create legal certainty and clarity.

Lets focus on some common terms.

- "Assault": This is a narrow psychic assault, i.e. Where D causes V to apprehend immediate physical violence.
- "Battery": This is a broad battery assault, i.e. Where D caused non-consensual physical harm to V.
- "Actual bodily harm": The causation of some harm.
- "Grievous bodily harm": The causation of serious harm.
- "Wounding": The causation of a breaking of the skin (e.g. a stabbing).
- "Maliciously": This is a composite word incorporating "Intentionally" in the direct and indirect sense (see **Chapter 4**) **or** "Recklessly" (in the subjective "G" sense see **Chapter 4**).
- "Inflicting/occasioning": This is synonymous with causation in fact; causation in law and without a break in the chain of causation (see **Chapter 3**).

Aims of this chapter

By the end of this chapter you can be expected to know and be able to evaluate the law on offences against the person:

- Common assault.
- Actual bodily harm.

- Causing grievous bodily harm.
- Causing grievous bodily harm with intent.
- Consent.
- Other assault related offences.
- Racially aggravated assaults.
- Specific evaluation themes will be discussed.

7.1.3 Summary of the main non-fatal offences against the person

General Principle CPS Offences Against the Person Charging Standard[2]

1. **Start by determining the level of injury** i.e. Is the injury consistent with Battery, ABH or GBH?

Consider with reference to the victims age, health and any other relevant factors

2. **Take a step back** and **considering all of the circumstances**, select the appropriate charge

"Prosecutors should select charges which:

- reflect the seriousness and extent of the offending
- give the court **adequate powers to sentence** and impose appropriate post-conviction orders;
- **enable the case to be presented in a clear and simple** way.

This underlines that the **level of injury is not determinative** and prosecutors **must consider all the circumstances of the offending."**

2 https://www.cps.gov.uk/legal-guidance/offences-against-person-incorporating-charging-standard [Accessed 11/04/2025; CPS Last Updated 31/10/2024]

General Principle CPS Offences Against the Person Charging Standard[2]			
Common Assault (Both Common Law offences but charged under s39 Criminal Justice Act 1988)			Examples • grazes • scratching • abrasions • minor bruising • swelling • reddening of the skin • superficial cuts
(i) Narrow psychic assault	Where D causes V to apprehend immediate physical violence	Intention or Subjective Recklessness as to cause V to apprehend immediate and unlawful violence (whether such apprehension is so caused)	
(ii) Broad battery assault	Where D has non-consensual physical contact with V	Intention or Subjective Recklessness as to using some force against V	
Actual Bodily Harm s47 OPA 1861	Causing Actual bodily harm	Same as Common assault N.B. No requirement to foresee ABH	Examples • damaged teeth or bones • extensive or severe bruising • cuts requiring suturing • loss of consciousness
Causing Grievous Bodily Harm s20 OPA 1861	Causing a Wound or GBH	Same as Common assault + Intention or Subjective Recklessness as to the risk of some harm N.B. No requirement to foresee GBH	Examples • life changing injuries • significant or sustained medical treatment is required (for instance, intensive care or a blood transfusion) even if full or relatively full recovery follows.

General Principle CPS Offences Against the Person Charging Standard[2]			
Causing Grievous Bodily Harm With Intent s18 OPA 1861	Causing a Wound or GBH	Intention to do GBH to any person. [Other forms e.g., intent to resist arrest; intent to prevent the lawful apprehension of any other person rarely charged and not explored here]	Consider • selection and use of a weapon, severity and duration of attack, making prior threats or planning a serious attack • a particularly serious way of committing an assault (e.g. kicking on the floor, headbutting), • a vulnerable victim, • repeated conduct, • the making of threats, multiple incidents, • significant pre-meditation, or • a relevant past history • The severity of a wound …a wound requiring life-saving surgery would usually be charged contrary to section 20/18 • Where a knife is used to wound, section 20/18 is almost always the appropriate charge.

7.1.4 Sentencing summary

Offence	Maximum sentence	Maximum sentence – racially or racially aggravated offence	Sentencing Council Guideline
Common assault / battery – s39 Criminal Justice Act 1988	6 months' imprisonment and/or fine not exceeding level 5	2 years' imprisonment and/or a fine (triable either way)	Common assault / Racially or religiously aggravated common assault[3]
s47 Offences Against the Person Act 1861	5 years' imprisonment	7 years' imprisonment and/or a fine (triable either way	Assault occasioning actual bodily harm / Racially or religiously aggravated ABH[4]
s20 Offences Against the Person Act 1861	5 years' imprisonment	7 years' imprisonment and/or a fine (triable either way	Inflicting grievous bodily harm/Unlawful wounding / Racially or religiously aggravated GBH/Unlawful wounding[5]
s18 Offences Against the Person Act 1861	Life imprisonment	N/a	Causing grievous bodily harm with intent to do grievous bodily harm / Wounding with intent to do GBH[6]

3 Sentencing Council, 'Common assault / Racially or religiously aggravated common assault/ Battery/ Common assault on emergency worker' (1 July 2021) <https://www.sentencingcouncil.org.uk/offences/crown-court/item/common-assault-racially-or-religiously-aggravated-common-assault-common-assault-on-emergency-worker/> accessed 06 April 20254

4 Sentencing Council, 'Assault occasioning actual bodily harm / Racially or religiously aggravated ABH' (1 Jult 2021) https://www.sentencingcouncil.org.uk/offences/crown-court/item/assault-occasioning-actual-bodily-harm-racially-or-religiously-aggravated-abh/ accessed 06 April 2025

5 Sentencing Council, 'Inflicting grievous bodily harm/ Unlawful wounding/ Racially or religiously aggravated GBH/ Unlawful wounding' (1 July 2021) <https://www.sentencingcouncil.org.uk/offences/crown-court/item/inflicting-grievous-bodily-harm-unlawful-wounding-racially-or-religiously-aggravated-gbh-unlawful-wounding/> accessed 06 April 2025

6 Sentencing Council, 'Causing grievous bodily harm with intent to do grievous bodily harm / Wounding with intent to do GBH' (1 July 2021) <https://www.sentencingcouncil.org.uk/offences/crown-court/item/causing-grievous-bodily-harm-with-intent-to-do-grievous-bodily-harm-wounding-with-intent-to-do-gbh-2/> accessed 06 April 2025

7.2 Common assault [Common law]

7.2.1 Distinguishing and charging narrow psychic and broad battery assaults

The first category is narrow psychic assault (NPA): where D causes V to apprehend immediate physical violence. The second category is broad battery assault (BBA): where D has non-consensual physical contact with V. When discussing assault, always be specific as to the sense in which you are using the term assault: Is it NPA or BBA?

a) Statute, mode of trial and penalty

s39 Criminal Justice Act 1988

"Common assault and battery shall be summary offences and a person guilty of either of them shall be liable ... to imprisonment for a term not exceeding six months."

b) How is assault and battery charged?

DPP v Little; DPP v Taylor [1992]

A charge sheet alleging assault and battery could be bad for duplicity (i.e. double). Therefore, the prosecution should be more specific and charge the most accurate version

- Narrow psychic assault (NPA) should be charged as common assault.
- Broad battery assault (BBA) should be charged as assault by beating.

The case of ***Ward* [2020]** states *obiter* a charge of "common assault" "*may*" be valid for a battery provided it was clear what D was accused of. In most cases BBA is an offence and so assault by beating should be charged.

c) CPS charging standard

See above in the Introduction some examples from the CPS Offences Against the Person Charging Standard.

7.2.2 Narrow psychic assault – Where D causes V to apprehend immediate physical violence

a) **Conduct or words or both (*actus reus*)**

Narrow psychic assault may be committed by conduct or words.

Conduct

For example, D terrified V by staring through the window of her ground floor flat. The court upheld the conviction. Despite D being outside the building, there was evidence to suggest that V was terrified by the prospect of some immediate violence. *Obiter* the court stated it was not necessary for the prosecution to establish precisely what V feared would happen. A general apprehension of violence was sufficient (***Smith* (1983)**).

Similarly where D pointed an imitation gun at V intending this as a joke. V thought it was real and apprehended immediate physical violence. Even though D thought it was a joke, an assault was nevertheless committed if V is sufficiently frightened (***Logdon* [1976]**).

Words alone

Where the victim suffered psychiatric injury by virtue of words alone this was sufficient to amount to a narrow psychic assault (***Chan-Fook* [1994]**).

In the important case of ***Burstow; Ireland* [1998]** the facts were in ***Burstow*** where D and V historically had a friendship. V broke off the friendship with D. D harassed V over a lengthy period. D made numerous abusive phone calls. As a result of Ds conduct V suffered a severe depression. D was charged with **s20 OPA 1861**. The facts in *Ireland* were D telephoned the Vs and remained silent on the phone. V suffered psychiatric illnesses caused by Ds conduct. The question in both cases was: Did this type of behaviour amount to "immediate and unlawful violence"?

The House or Lords stated Ds could be charged with "narrow psychic" assault based on medical evidence (namely in ***Burstow*** on the basis of the abusive calls and in *Ireland* the silence the words/conduct were sufficient for V to apprehend immediate physical violence).

Per Lord Steyn:

> *"The proposition that **a gesture may amount to an assault but that words can never suffice is unrealistic and indefensible**. A thing said is also a thing done...*
>
> *"...there is no reason why a telephone caller who says to a woman in a menacing way "I will be at your door in a minute or two" may not be guilty of an assault if he causes his victim to apprehend immediate personal violence. ... the silent caller...intends by his silence to cause fear and he is so understood. The victim is assailed by uncertainty about his intentions.*[7]

7 Burstow; Ireland [1998]

"Neuroses must be distinguished from simple states of fear, or problems in coping with everyday life. Where the line is to be drawn must be a matter of psychiatric judgment. ...the statute must be interpreted in the light of the best current scientific appreciation of the link between the body and psychiatric injury."[8]

b) Immediacy (*actus reus*)

Words which condition the threat can remove the immediacy and thus the assault.

For example, in ***Tuberville v Savage* (1669)**, where D argued with V. D placed his hand on his sword stating: "If it were not assize-time, I would not take such language from you."

The court held he was not guilty of assault as there was no possibility of immediate violence when the words were so conditioned.

In ***Constanza* [1997]** D sent 800 letters to V and harassed V causing psychiatric damage. The court held the immediacy was made out by the continuing nature of the threat. V feared she may be attacked at any time.

c) Intention or subjective recklessness as to cause V to apprehend immediate and unlawful violence (*mens rea*)

***Savage & Parmenter* [1992]** is the leading authority. In *Savage* D was charged with unlawful wounding contrary to **s20 OPA 1861**. D had wanted to throw the contents of a glass of beer over V. D's grip slipped and D threw the glass at V. V suffered cuts consistent with GBH. D denied it was her intention to throw the beer over V. In *Parmenter* D injured a child V through rough dealings. D stated he was not aware he would harm V. The question for the court was: what is the *mens rea* for offences against the person?

The House of Lords held:

"[1] For common assault whether by a narrow psychic assault or a broad battery assault the mens rea was intention or subjective recklessness. For NPA as to intention or recklessly causing V to apprehend immediate physical violence and for BBA Intention or subjective recklessness as to using some force against V

[2] For s.47 Actual Bodily Harm (ABH) the only Mens rea was that necessary for common assault. s.47 has no express additional Mens Rea as to causing ABH. Therefore once the causation of the assault is established the prosecution only need to show it caused ABH and that D has the mens rea for the underlying assault.

---

8 Burstow; Ireland [1998]

[3] For s.20 Causing Grievous Bodily Harm (GBH) the only Mens rea was that necessary was for the underlying narrow psychic assault or a broad battery assault (i.e., intention or subjective recklessness) and ***foresight of some harm*** *albeit not serious harm."*

7.2.3 Broad battery assault – Where D has non-consensual physical contact with V

Broad battery assault is where D has non-consensual physical contact with V. We will now look at the requirements.

a) Non consensual contact: there is no need for an injury (*actus reus*)

The High Court has confirmed for battery all that is required is "*non-consensual physical contact". There is no need for any injury (***Austen* [2017]**). This means that any contact whether it is a tickle with a feather or a punch with a fist will be covered.*

b) Caused directly or indirectly (*actus reus*)

The cause of the battery can be direct or indirect; and via a weapon or object.

Directly

Battery was defined as "touching of another in anger" and is usually committed directly, e.g. by direct physical contact from human to human, for example a punch (***Cole v Turner* (1704)**).

Indirectly

***Martin* (1881)** is a famous example where D switched off the theatre lights in a full theatre. D placed an iron bar across the exit doors. D then shouted fire. V's were injured as they tried to escape. It was unsurprisingly held this this could amount to the causation of indirect battery and D would be guilty of the assaults caused.

In ***K* (1990)** D a schoolchild placed acid in a dryer in the bathroom. V used the dryer and was injured. The court upheld liability on the basis of causation of an indirect assault.

D had a hypodermic needle in his pocket. D falsely assured V (a police officer) he had no "sharps". V was stabbed by the hypodermic needle. The High Court unsurprisingly stated this was causation of an indirect assault and upheld liability (***Santa-Bermudez* [2003]**).

With a weapon

An example of a weapon is the obvious such as a brick, a knife, a knuckle duster.

With an object

An example would be placing a car on a police officer's foot (***Fagan* [1969]** – see **Chapter 3** for a case summary).

c) Intention or subjective recklessness as to using some force against V (*Mens rea*)

See ***Savage & Parmenter* [1992]** (above).

d) The exemption for everyday touching

There is an important exemption for everyday touching. This covers the situation where you bump into somebody by accident, you need to draw somebody's attention by tapping them on the shoulder or you perhaps touch the person on the elbow to move them forward if you are working as a security guard at a football match.

The common law deems consent to the usual everyday contacts which are therefore not unlawful (***Wilson v Pringle* [1986]**). Thus the mere laying on of hands to attract attention is no battery. In ***Coward v Baddeley* (1859)** Pollock, C. B. stated:

> *"Suppose two persons were walking near each other, and one turned round, and in so doing struck the other: surely that would not be a battery...*
>
> *Touching a person so as merely to call his attention, whether the subject of a civil action or not, is not the ground of criminal proceeding[s]."*

This was confirmed by ***Collins v Wilcock* [1984]** which stated everyday touching such as bumping into someone on the tube is not an offence or tort of "battery". A more recent example is ***Pegram* [2019]** which confirmed a police officer drawing attention by holding a protesters arm was everyday touching.

7.3 Actual bodily harm (s47 OPA 1861)

7.3.1 Introduction

a) s47 OPA 1861

> *Whosoever shall be convicted on indictment of any assault occasioning actual bodily harm shall be liable...[to imprisonment of up to 5 years].*

b) CPS charging standard

See above in the **Introduction** examples from the CPS Offences Against the Person Charging Standard.

7.3.2 Elements

a) Underlying assault (*actus reus* – see above)

Either a narrow psychic or a broad battery.

b) Causing actual bodily harm (*actus reus*)

Occasioning is to be read in the modern era as simply causing actual bodily harm. It therefore must be shown that the ABH resulted from the assault or battery. See in **Chapter 3** the case of ***Roberts* (1971)** (the passenger in the car escaping the predatory driver).

Actual bodily harm has been defined as "*any hurt or injury calculated to interfere with the health or comfort of the [victim]. Such hurt or injury need not be permanent, but must, no doubt, be more than merely transient and trifling.*" (***Donovan* [1934]** per Swift J). In the case of ***Miller* [1954]** Lynskey J confirmed ABH included "*any hurt or injury calculated to interfere with the health or comfort of the [victim]*".

More recently ***DPP v Smith* [2006]** was a case where D cut the ponytail from the hair of V (his ex-partner). D was charged with ABH. The High Court held the cutting of the hair was ABH. There was no requirement to prove V felt pain. Bodily in this context meant the whole body "*organs, nervous system, brain and hair*".

Sir Igor Judge stated:

> *"[ABH] was not limited to "harm to the skin, flesh and bones of the victim" [and] physical pain consequent on an assault is not a necessary ingredient of this offence.*
>
> *[In relation to hair]... whether it is alive beneath the surface of the skin or dead tissue above the surface of the skin, the hair is an attribute and part of the human body. It is intrinsic to each individual and to the identity of each individual.*
>
> *I note that an individual's hair is relevant to his or her autonomy. Some regard it as their crowning glory. Admirers may so regard it in the object of their affections. Even if, medically and scientifically speaking, the hair above the surface of the scalp is no more than dead tissue, it remains part of the body and is attached to it. While it is so attached, in my judgment it falls within the meaning of "bodily" in the phrase "actual bodily harm". It is concerned with the body of the individual victim"'*

c) Intention or subjective recklessness – *no* requirement to reasonably foresee ABH (*Mens Rea*)

It is not necessary for D to have foreseen that actual bodily harm would be caused to the victim as a result of his assault. All that is necessary is the intention or subjective recklessness per common assault i.e.

- Narrow psychic assault: Intention or subjective recklessness as to cause V to apprehend immediate and unlawful violence (whether such apprehension is so caused).
- Broad battery assault: Intention or subjective recklessness as to using some force against V.

See *Savage & Parmenter* [1992] (above).

7.4 Causing grievous bodily harm (s20 OPA 1861)

7.4.1 Introduction

There are two formulations of causing GBH:

a) The "grievous bodily harm" formulation

Whosoever shall.... inflict any grievous bodily harm upon any other person, either with or without any weapon or instrument.

b) The "wounding" formulation

Whosoever shall unlawfully wound... either with or without any weapon or instrument.

c) CPS Charging Standard

See above in the **Introduction** examples from the CPS Offences Against the Person Charging Standard.

7.4.2 Elements

a) Underlying assault (*actus reus*)

Either a narrow psychic or a broad battery – see above under common assault.

b) Causing either GBH or wounding (*actus reus*)

Inflicting is synonymous with causing

This was a problem area because the statute states "*inflicting*" (***Martin* (1881)**. However in the modern era all that is required is causation. In ***Burstow & Ireland* [1998]** (for the facts see above) Lord Steyn stated:

> *"The problem is one of construction. The question is whether as a matter of current usage the contextual interpretation of "inflict" can embrace the idea of one person inflicting psychiatric injury on another. One can without straining the language in any way answer that question in the affirmative. I am not saying that the words "cause" and "inflict" are exactly synonymous. They are not. What I am saying is that in the context of the Act of 1861 one can nowadays quite naturally speak of inflicting psychiatric injury. Moreover, there is internal contextual support in the statute for this view. ... this should be a very practical area of the law. The interpretation and approach should so far as possible be adopted which treats the ladder of offences as a coherent body of law."*[9]

Either GBH or wounding (*actus reus*)

Firstly, grievous bodily harm means really serious harm or serious harm

(***Smith* [1961]**; ***Saunders* [1985]**; ***Doyle* [2004]**).

Secondly, wounding means any injury that breaks the skin. In ***Eisenhower* [1984]**, a pistol shot striking near the eye caused it to fill with blood. This was held not to be a wound as the bleeding was internal. In order to constitute a "*wound*" such injury requires a rupture of the dermis and epidermis, i.e. not just a scratch, graze, or bruising.

c) Intention or subjective recklessness as to some harm (*mens rea*)

The provision required intention or subjective recklessness as to some harm. There is no requirement to reasonably foresee GBH or wounding (***Savage & Parmenter* [1992]** – see above under common assault for full case note. In rare cases the issue of "recklessness" arises. ***Brady* [2006]** emphasised the importance of a clear jury direction on subjective recklessness.

In the case of ***Cunningham* [1957]** Byrne, J confirmed "Maliciously":

> *"...Not be taken in old vague sense of wickedness in general but requiring either:*
>
> *(1) an actual intention to do the particular kind of harm that in fact was done;*
>
> *OR*
>
> *(2) recklessness as to whether such harm should occur or not (i.e. [D] has foreseen that the particular kind of harm might be done and yet has gone on to take the risk of it)."*

---

9 Burstow & Ireland [1998]

***Mowatt* [1967]** confirmed D must foresee only some physical harm. Diplock LJ stated:

> *"[I]t is quite unnecessary that [D] should have foreseen that his unlawful act might cause physical harm of the gravity described in the section, i.e., a wound or serious physical injury.*
>
> *It is enough that he should have foreseen that some physical harm to some person, albeit of a minor character, might result.'*

7.5 Causing grievous bodily harm with intent (s18 OPA 1861)

7.5.1 Introduction

a) Full form

In its full form under **s18** there are four different versions, namely:

- *wounding with intent to do grievous bodily harm (GBH);*
- *causing grievous bodily harm with intent to do so;*
- *maliciously wounding with intent to resist or prevent the lawful apprehension etc. of any person; or*
- *maliciously causing grievous bodily harm with intent to resist or prevent lawful apprehension etc. of any person.*

b) Main focus

The two main formulations and our focus are wounding and GBH. Firstly *the "wounding" formulation:*

> *Whosoever shall...wound... with intent...to do some...grievous bodily harm to any person... [shall be guilty of an offence.]'. Secondly, the 'grievous bodily harm' formulation: 'Whosoever shall... cause grievous bodily harm to any person... with intent...to do some...grievous bodily harm... [shall be guilty of an offence.]'. The other forms i.e. intent to resist arrest and intent to prevent the lawful apprehension of any other person are rarely charged and not explored.*

c) Alternatives

From a process perspective it is important to note that the alternative verdicts exist. The jury can acquit D charged with **s18** and substitute a conviction for a lesser offence such as **s20** (**s6(3) Criminal Law Act 1967**).

d) CPS Charging Standard

See above in the **Introduction** examples from the CPS Offences Against the Person Charging Standard.

7.5.2 Elements

a) Underlying assault (*actus reus*)

The underlying assault either a narrow psychic or a broad battery (see under common assault for details) must be proven. The majority of the offences are based on a broad battery.

b) Causing either GBH or wounding (*actus reus*)

This aspect is discussed above under **s20**, i.e. causation of the harm (either GBH or wounding).

c) Intention to do grievous bodily harm to any person (*mens rea*)

This is a high threshold, namely a specific intention to cause grievous bodily harm.

In ***Mowatt*** **[1967]** Diplock LJ confirms "*the word 'maliciously' adds nothing*" and the jury do not need to be directed on it'. In ***Midmore*** **[2017]** Ds had thrown sulphuric acid into their victim's face, the trial judge had been correct to admit a text message sent by one of them containing a photo of the acid with the caption "this is the one face melter" as evidence of their intention to use the acid to cause the victim serious harm.

7.6 Consent

7.6.1 The role of consent in criminal law generally

Consent would normally negate liability, i.e. an otherwise illegal action becomes legal where you consent to it. However in the criminal law the exact position depends on the offence area and the relevant policy considerations. To take some examples:

- **Chapter 2**: Criminal damage. Can consent negate liability? Yes, no offence.
- **Chapter 7**: Assault. Can consent negate liability?

  #Yes consent can negate liability regarding common assault

  #No consent cannot negate liability regarding ABH and above unless the consent falls into an exceptional category

- **Chapter 8**: Sexual offences. Can consent negate liability?

  Firstly, penetration requires consent. Secondly with two adults if Vs consent exists then there is no sexual offence (this excludes situations where the complainant is legally incapable of giving consent for example a child under 16). Finally a *mens rea* aspect is whether D reasonably believes V is consenting which can also negate liability.

- **Chapter 9** and **10** Theft and fraud. Can consent negate liability? Yes, no offence.

7.6.2 Distinctions between offences against the person and sexual offences

It is important to distinguish **Chapter 6** offences against the person consent from **Chapter 7** sexual offences consent. Different policy considerations mean the law currently takes a divergent approach dependent on the context.

7.6.3 Competing principles: autonomy & freedom v public policy considerations

Please see **Chapter 2** for more discussion of the autonomy/freedom v public policy considerations.

In a nutshell the first consideration is autonomy: the state allows a fair degree of autonomy, respect for freedom of choice and respect for privacy. The second consideration is public policy where the state appears to draw the line at activities that could be regarded as anti-social, or contrary to public policy.

It is important to note this area is mostly governed by the common law with only one recent statute noted below. It is submitted the sustained policy discussion has not been fully explored in the law.

7.6.4 Common assault: Consent is a defence

Consent can be given to common assault level touching (***Brown (Anthony Joseph)*** **[1994]** see below).

7.6.5 Consent - behaviour is within a recognised exceptional category

Chronologically the case law has clarified that for ABH and more serious offences against the person consent is only a defence if the behaviour is within a recognised exceptional category.

Donovan **[1934]** is a case about a male "caning" a female and the issue of consent. The Court of Appeal made it clear the general rule was the consent of V to suffer harm inflicted by D can only provide D with a defence if the harm inflicted does not go beyond the scope of common assault. If the offence goes beyond common assault, consent is no defence unless within a recognised exceptional category.

In the ***Attorney General's Reference (No 6 of 1980)*** **[1981]**, the case was a about a fist fight in the street and the supposed consent of the participants to the injuries caused. Unsurprisingly the Court of Appeal held the consent in this situation was no defence because it was not in the public interest for people to cause each other actual bodily harm for no good reason.

The judgment of Lord Lane CJ is very important, he states:

> *"[1] An essential element of an assault is that an act is done contrary to the will and without the consent of the victim.*
>
> *[2] Exceptions exist such as '...properly conducted games and sports, lawful chastisement or correction, reasonable surgical interference, dangerous exhibitions etc..."*

The law has evolved in ***Brown (Anthony Joseph)*** **[1994]** (see below) and statute has recently in **s71 Domestic Abuse Act 2021** begun to have a role (see below).

a) Reasonable surgical interference

Reasonable surgical interference is an exceptional category. However the law distinguishes situations where there is fraud as to attributes where consent is not normally vitiated and those where there is a fraud as to the nature and quality of the act where fraud does normally vitiate consent.

Fraud as to attributes

In relation to fraud as to attributes the leading authority is ***Richardson (Diane)*** **[1999]**. D (a qualified dentist) was suspended from the Dental Practitioners Register. D continued to treat her patients in spite of her suspension. D was charged on six counts of assault and pleaded guilty because the trial judge had ruled that the apparent consent of the patients (Vs) had been vitiated (taken away) by fraud. The question on appeal was: Did V's consent as to identity give a D a complete defence?

The Court of Appeal allowed the appeal. Firstly, this was a fraud as to attributes but did not vitiate the patients consent as there was no deception as to the nature or identity of the person. Secondly, Vs knew who D was and what she was doing. Whilst D was certainly negligent she did not fall within the boundaries of the criminal law. Finally, a mistake as to identity did not extend to a belief as to a person's professional qualifications and attributes. The patients had been fully aware of the Ds true identity. Ds conduct, although clearly reprehensible, did not found a basis of criminal liability in the field of offences against the person. It was noted *obiter* if there had been unnecessary surgery then that would amount to an offence.

One can therefore state a mistake as to the nature of the actions of the dentist would have vitiated consent but a mistake as to the quality of the actor's attributes will not vitiate consent to the act.

The case can usefully be contrasted with ***Melin* [2019]**. In that case botox injections were administered by an unqualified person. The injections caused really serious harm. The botox injectors did not require a qualification but D who was injecting purported to be medically qualified.

The question on appeal was: Did D's deception as to attributes (qualification) vitiate the consent? The court answered where the deception as to attributes were material to Vs consent then the fraud existed and vitiated the consent. In this case one of the Vs would not have consented to the procedure so their consent was vitiated and the offence for that V proven.

Fraud as to the nature and quality of the act

If in contrast the fraud related to the nature and quality of the act then that form of fraud would vitiate consent.

An obvious and distressing example of fraud is ***Tabussum* [2000]** where D, purporting to be a medic, stated he was completing a breast cancer survey. The innocent Vs "consented" to the touching of their breasts. The Vs obviously consented on the basis the survey was for medical purposes. D was charged with what would now be called a sexual assault and convicted at trial. The question for the Court of Appeal was: whether Vs consent was valid as to the nature and quality of the actions?

The Court of Appeal unsurprisingly stated Vs consent was vitiated by the fraud as to the nature and quality of the actions. The appeal was dismissed on the basis the nature of the action was of a different nature to that which was consented to. As Rose LJ stated p337: *"[t]hey were consenting to touching for medical purposes, and not to indecent behaviour, that is, there was consent to the nature of the act, but not its quality."*

b) Ritual circumcision, tattooing, earpiercing

Ritual circumcision, tattooing, ear piercing is a recognised exceptional category. For a somewhat surprising example see ***Wilson* [1997]** where D (the husband) branded

V's (his wife) buttocks. A medic notified the police. D was charged with assault and stated the defence of consent. In the Court of Appeal the case proceeded on the agreed factual basis that V consented to branding and indeed instigated it as V believed it to be a desirable personal adornment. The court held this was consensual and therefore not a matter for criminal investigation. The court stated: "*Brown was not authority for the proposition that consent was no defence to a charge under* ***S.47*** *...in all circumstances where actual bodily harm was deliberately inflicted." The case is to be contrasted with* **Brown** *(see below). It is submitted there is no logical difference between the cases and perhaps the inarticulate major premise was that in* **Brown** *the activity related to a group of homosexual men engaging in a minority activity with perhaps limited public support whereas* ***Wilson*** *concerned a heterosexual couple.*

The case stands perhaps on its facts alone but appears confined by ***BM* [2019]** and probably does not **withstand s71 Domestic Abuse Act 2021**. The recent authority of ***Hobday* [2025]** is helpful. On the facts D was convicted of assault occasioning actual bodily harm. D approached V, a 17-year-old. They engaged in consensual sexual intercourse and D carved his initials onto Vs buttock using a unsterile Stanley knife. The Court of Appeal upheld the conviction and stated that ***Wilson*** should not be followed. It appears to state the ***Wilson*** was a case that was decided on its facts. This disapproval of ***Wilson*** appears to render ***Wilson*** outdated. It is to be welcomed.

In ***BM* [2019]** D was a tattooist and body modifier. D had removed various ears, nipples, and split the tongue of Vs. All of the Vs had consented. D was charged with GBH. Firstly, the court held following ***Brown*** that the consent of V's was not a defence unless it fell within the exceptional categories which this did not as it was beyond the tattooing exception. Secondly, this form of extreme body modification, such as the removal of an ear or nipple, or tongue splitting, performed on a consenting adult by a practitioner with no medical training or qualification, could not form an exception to the general rule that consent was no defence to causing actual bodily harm or above. Lord Burnett CJ distinguished: "*Tattooing, boxing, and piercing are long accepted and deeply embedded in our law and general culture' but 'Body modifications are extreme and dangerous operations which cannot be considered analogous to mere tattooing*".

He went on to say at [41]:

> "*New exceptions should not be recognised on a case by case basis, save perhaps where there is a close analogy with an existing exception to the general rule established in the Brown case. The recognition of an entirely new exception would involve a value judgement which is policy laden, and on which there may be powerful conflicting views in society. The criminal trial process is inapt to enable a wide-ranging inquiry into the underlying policy issues, which are much better explored in the political environment.*"

c) Horseplay

Horseplay is in effect a quasi-contractual agreement between individuals to involve themselves in "rough and tumble". The rationale seems to be "I'll indulge by giving you permission to behave recklessly towards me with my consent for the sake of mutual fun". It has a not dissimilar logic to that of engaging in sport.

In ***Jones (Terence)*** **(1986)** Ds tossed Vs in the air and let them fall. V1 suffered a ruptured spleen and V2 a broken arm. The trial judge did not allow the issue of consent to go to the jury given the serious injuries. The Court of Appeal stated the defence of consent based on the "horseplay" exception should have been left to the jury.

In ***Aitken*** **[1992]**, D was an RAF officer drunkenly playing in the RAF "mess" area. D set V alight with his consent in a fireproof outfit. Unfortunately V suffered serious burns. D was charged with **s20**. The Court of Appeal overturned the conviction based on the "horseplay exception". The court confirmed it was not a "*bully's charter*" and could only exist where there is by D a genuine belief V is consenting.

d) Sports

Sports players of course routinely give consent to contact provided it is part and parcel of the sport.

In ***Billinghurst*** **[1978]** a case about a rugby match where in a "off ball" incident, D punched V breaking his jaw. The judge at first instance confirmed that players are deemed to consent to force "*of a kind which could reasonably be expected to happen during a game*" but that a rugby player has no unlimited licence to use force and that "*there must obviously be cases which cross the line of that to which a player is deemed to consent*". The commentary in the *Criminal Law Review* gives the helpful example of cricket:

> *"If in a cricket match, a fast bowler bowls and hits his opponent on head and causes serious bodily harm, it may well be that the batsman validly consented to run the risk of that kind of harm; but the position is entirely different if, when the ball is "dead", the bowler throws it at the batsman's head."*

In ***Barnes*** **[2004]** the court held that the public interests in terms of health and society of sports means some consent to force within the game is a necessary exception. On the facts the group of amateur footballers were playing when D tackled V in a very late high tackle. D was charged with **s20**.

The Court of Appeal held firstly, consent was a defence to legitimate sports activity if the force was of a kind that was expected. Secondly, considerations including level of the game; nature of the act, degree of force used, risk of injury and the mental aspect of D were relevant. Thirdly, Criminal cases should be reserved for the most serious fouls as otherwise normally the more appropriate course would be internal disciplinary routes. Instinctive errors and misjudgements are inevitable in the heat of a match. For example Lord Woolf stated it would be legitimate to travel going for the ball. It would be illegitimate going for the opponent.

e) Dangerous exhibitions

Lord Lane CJ in ***A-G's Ref (No. 6 of 1980)*** (above) identified an exception covering "*dangerous exhibitions*" which appears to include for example the volunteer at a knife throwing event where an innocent miss throw would appear to be exempt.

f) Sado-masochism

The leading authority in this area is ***Brown (Anthony Joseph)*** **[1994]**. The facts were that the Ds were male sadomasochists engaging in bondage, domination and sadomasochism (BDSM). Ds had with consent committed assaults on each other for pleasure. They were charged with variously **s47 ABH** and **s20 GBH**. Their defence was that of consent in that they enthusiastically engaged in the acts.

The House of Lords by a majority of 3:2 (with notable dissents from Lord Mustill and Lord Slynn) held consent was no defence to a charge of **s47 ABH** or above.

Firstly, consent did provide a defence to common assault. Secondly, consent provided no defence to offences of ABH or above unless it fell within one of the recognised public interest exceptions. Thirdly, the court could not and did not find a new public interest exception in allowing BDSM. Finally, the court stated the risk of HIV infection, withdrawal of consent and to societies morals was too high a risk.

The majority saw the issue as a defence of consent. The minority (Lord Mustill and Slynn) saw the issue as one of privacy and absence of consent being an aspect of the *actus reus* for the prosecution to disprove.

Majority judgment Per Lord Templeman: (at 231, 234 and 236):

> *"In some circumstances violence is not punishable under the criminal law.*
>
> *[1] When no actual bodily harm is caused, the consent of the person affected precludes him from complaining. There can be no conviction for the summary offence of common assault if the victim has consented ...*
>
> *[2] Even when violence is intentionally inflicted and results in ... wounding or serious bodily harm [D] is entitled to be acquitted if the injury was a foreseeable incident of a lawful activity in which the person injured was participating. [He then lists examples of lawful Activity including: Surgery; Ritual [male] circumcision; tattooing; ear piercing and violent sports including boxing are lawful activities.*
>
> *[3] The question whether the defence of consent should be extended to the consequences of sado-masochistic encounters can only be decided by consideration of policy and public interest... .*

[4] It is an offence for a person to abuse his own body and mind by taking drugs. Although the law is often broken, the criminal law restrains a practice which is regarded as dangerous and injurious to individuals and which if allowed and extended is harmful to society generally

*[5]...**Society is entitled and bound to protect itself against a cult of violence**. Pleasure derived from the infliction of pain is an evil thing. Cruelty is uncivilised. ...such violence is injurious to the participants and unpredictably dangerous. **I am not prepared to invent a defence of consent for sado-masochistic encounters which breed and glorify cruelty** and result in offences under sections 47 and 20 of the Act of 1861."*

Majority judgment Per Lord Jauncey of Tullichettle (at 246):

*"My Lords I have no doubt that **it would not be in the public interest that deliberate infliction of actual bodily harm during the course of homosexual sadomasochistic activities should be held to be lawful**...If it is to be decided that such activities as the nailing by A of B's foreskin or scrotum to a board or the insertion of hot wax into C's urethra followed by the burning of his penis with a candle or the incising of D's scrotum with a scalpel to the effusion of blood are injurious neither to B, C and D nor to the public interest then it is for Parliament with its accumulated wisdom and sources of information to declare them to be lawful."*

Majority judgment Per Lord Lowry (at 255):

*"... the reason for the proposed exemption [put forward by Ds is] that both those who will inflict and those who will suffer the injury wish to satisfy a perverted and depraved sexual desire. **Sadomasochistic homosexual activity cannot be regarded as conducive to the enhancement or enjoyment of family life or conducive to the welfare of society."***

Minority judgment Per Lord Mustill (dissenting, at 273):

*"What I do say is that **these are questions...of private morality; that the standards by which they fall to be judged are not those of the criminal law;** and that if those standards are to be upheld the individual must enforce them upon himself according to his own moral standards or have them enforced against him by moral pressures exerted by whatever religious or other community to whose ethical ideals he responds. The point from which I invite your Lordships to depart is simply this, that **the state should interfere with the rights of an individual** to live his or her life as he or she may choose **no more than is necessary to ensure a proper balance between the special interests of the individual and the general interests of the individuals who together comprise the populace at large.**"*

The House of Lords' decision was vindicated by the European Court of Human Rights:

Laskey, Jaggard and Brown v United Kingdom (1997)

The European Court of Human Rights unanimously upheld the judgment ruling that this position was consistent with the **ECHR Art 8(2)** qualification on the right to privacy and family life to the extent the limitation on defence of consent to injury of common assault level could be viewed as necessary in a democratic society for preservation of health or morals. The risk of physical injury undermined "the respect which human beings should confer upon each other".

This case is open to a significant amount of academic critique.

1. The first view in the majority judgment is the defence *onus* view, *i.e. placing a burden on the defendant that* consent is a defence for D to evidence. This view does not see the absence of consent as an aspect of *actus reus* or *mens rea* but merely as a separate defence which D has the onus of showing.

2. The second view which is predominant in the academic community (and is the minority judgment in the case of ***Brown***) is the *actus reus* view, i.e. the burden should be on the prosecution to prove beyond reasonable doubt the absence of consent. Indeed this was the approach taken in ***K* [2002]** and ***Andrews* [2003]**.

The case of ***Brown*** is also open to critique on equality criteria. When contrasted with the case of ***Wilson*** which involves a heterosexual couple branding of the wife's buttocks, as opposed to homosexual men, the case seems open to rigorous charges of double standards. Is there in reality any meaningful difference between the two situations? The result seems to have been achieved by **s71 Domestic Abuse Act 2021**.

In ***Emmett* (1999)** the facts were a husband and wife engaged in sadomasochistic acts within the privacy of their home. In this situation the husband poured fluid onto the wife's breasts and set fire to it. It was held in this case that consent was no defence to the two offences of ABH above. ***Meachen* [2006]** was decided to similar effect.

g) School teachers

A teacher employed in a special school did not impliedly consent to violence (***H v CPS* [2010]**).

h) Sexual intercourse involving somebody living with HIV or another STI

There are complex variables in relation to sexual intercourse where one party has a sexually transmitted infection, such as HIV. In this situation the law has to differentiate the consents involved. Firstly, there is a consent to sexual intercourse: if there is an absence of consent in this situation this would amount to the sexual offence such as rape explained in **Chapter 8**. Secondly, the potential transmission of a sexually transmitted infection is subject to the law on offences against the person.

The old position at law was laid out in ***Clarence*** (1888) which is no longer good law. The new position is explained in ***Dica* [2004]**. In ***Dica***, the facts were D was HIV positive. D engaged in consensual sexual intercourse with two V's. Both V's were not aware of D's HIV diagnosis. Both V's became infected with HIV. D was charged with GBH contrary to **s20 OPA 1861**. The trial judge held that even if they were aware of his status then consent would be no defence to **s20**. The question on appeal was: could V consent to the HIV infection if she were aware of the risk?

The Court of Appeal in a very significant ruling ordered a re-trial regarding an error in the judge's direction. The decision held:

> *"[1] The intercourse was not rape as there was no deception as to the nature and quality of the sexual act itself.*
>
> *[2] V could consent to the risk of transmission. Thus if V were aware D had HIV and V had consented to the risk of transmission there would be no liability.*
>
> *[3] In circumstances where D were aware he had HIV and V was NOT aware D had HIV then V had not consented to the risk of D deliberately/intentionally spreading HIV for s.18 OPA 1861."*

N.B.

Per Judge J (at para 51)

> *'[1] The problems of criminalising the consensual taking of risks like these include the sheer impracticability of enforcement and the haphazard nature of its impact.*
>
> *[2] The process would undermine the general understanding of the community that sexual relationships are pre-eminently private and essentially personal to the individuals involved in them.*
>
> *[3] If adults were to be liable to prosecution for the consequences of taking known risks with their health, it would seem odd that this should be confined to risks taken in the context of sexual intercourse, while they are nevertheless permitted to take the risks inherent in so many other aspects of everyday life, including, again for example, the mother or father of a child suffering a serious contagious illness, who holds the child's hand, and comforts or kisses him or her goodnight...In our judgement, interference of this kind with personal autonomy, and its level and extent, may only be made by Parliament."*

This was confirmed In ***Konzani* [2005]**. D, knowing he was HIV positive, had sex with three V's who did not know his HIV status. Each V contracted HIV. D was charged with **s20**. D's defence was V's consented to unprotected sex and therefore the risk of infection. The V's perspective was they did not know of the HIV status and therefore could not consent. The Court of Appeal dismissed the appeal and upheld the conviction stating

V's consent was materially vitiated by the failure to disclose by D his HIV status. However if D had an honest belief in V's alleged consent, that would afford him a defence.

Judge LJ at [41] stated:

> *"There is a critical distinction between taking a risk of the various, potentially adverse and possibly problematic consequences of sexual intercourse, and giving an informed consent to the risk of infection with a fatal disease."*

***B* [2007]** confirmed D's failure to disclose his HIV status did not vitiate the consent to sex. Latham LJ stated at [17]:

> *"Where one party to sexual activity has a sexually transmissible disease which is not disclosed to the other party any consent that may have been given to that activity by the other party is not thereby vitiated. The act remains a consensual act. However, the party suffering from the sexual transmissible disease will not have any defence to any charge which may result from harm created by that sexual activity, merely by virtue of that consent, because such consent did not include consent to infection by the disease."*

It is important to note, in ***McNally* [2013]** the Court of Appeal suggested that the case of **B** did not rule out the situation where a deliberate lie may be capable of vitiating sexual offences consent – although this point may need to be reconsidered in light of the judgment in ***Lawrance* [2020]** discussed below.

Similar considerations to apply:

- Gonorrhoea: ***Marangwanda (Peace)* [2009]** this was a sentencing appeal about the tragic transmission by an adult who knew their gonorrhoea status to the children of the home. The initial charge had been a sexual offence which was "pled out" to an assault[10].
- Herpes: In ***Golding* [2014]** it was confirmed the same position existed in relation to the transmission of incurable genital herpes.
- Campaigns of knowing transmission occur, such as the much published case of ***Rowe* [2018]; [2019]**.

In ***Lawrance* [2020]** (which will be explored fully at **Chapter 8** regarding sexual offences consent) Lord Burnett CJ confirmed the transmission of an STD through sexual intercourse is a consequence of the intercourse and can lead to liability for an offence against the person e.g. **s20** or **s18 OPA 1861**. Hower, the transmission is not part of the performance of the sexual act and the deception as to the STD did not vitiate consent under the **s74 Sexual Offences Act 2003**. Helpfully there is

10 Cameron Giles, "A Sexual Harm? HIV Transmission, 'Biological' GBH and Ancillary Sentencing Provisions in England and Wales" (2021) 85(3) Journal of Criminal Law 209

detailed and helpful CPS Policy on prosecuting the intentional or reckless transmission of infections[11].

i) Statute: consent in the context of serious harm for sexual gratification

s71 Domestic Abuse Act 2021 restates in statute law the general proposition (established in the case of ***Brown (Anthony Joseph)*** **[1994]**) that *a person may not consent to the infliction of serious harm (GBH, Wounding or ABH) and, by extension, is unable to consent to their own death.* It also reflects the exception in relation to consent in cases involving the transmission of sexually transmitted infections.

s71 Domestic Abuse Act 2021:

(1) *This section applies for the purposes of determining whether a person ('D') who inflicts serious harm on another person ('V') is guilty of a relevant offence.*

(2) *It is not a defence that V consented to the infliction of the serious harm for the purposes of obtaining sexual gratification (but see subsection (4)).*

(3) In this section—

'relevant offence' means an offence under section 18, 20 or 47 of the Offences Against the Person Act 1861 ('the 1861 Act');

'serious harm' means-

(a) *grievous bodily harm, within the meaning of section 18 of the 1861 Act,*

(b) *wounding, within the meaning of that section, or*

(c) *actual bodily harm, within the meaning of section 47 of the 1861 Act.*

(4) *Subsection (2) does not apply in the case of an offence under section 20 or 47 of the 1861 Act where-*

(a) *the serious harm consists of, or is a result of, the infection of V with a sexually transmitted infection in the course of sexual activity, and*

(b) *V consented to the sexual activity in the knowledge or belief that D had the sexually transmitted infection.*

(5) *For the purposes of this section it does not matter whether the harm was inflicted for the purposes of obtaining sexual gratification for D, V, or some other person.*

(6) *Nothing in this section affects any enactment or rule of law relating to other circumstances in which a person's consent to the infliction of serious harm may, or may not, be a defence to a relevant offence.*

---

11 Crown Prosecution Service, 'International or Reckless Transmission of Infection' (29 March 2023) <https://www.cps.gov.uk/legal-guidance/intentional-or-reckless-sexual-transmission-infection> accessed 06 April 2025

7.7 Other assault related offences

7.7.1 Harassment

s1 Protection from Harassment Act 1997:

"S.1(1) A person must not pursue a course of conduct-

(a) which amounts to harassment of another, and

(b) which he knows or ought to know amounts to harassment of the other.

S.1 (2) For the purposes of this section, the person whose course of conduct is in question ought to know that it amounts to harassment of another if a reasonable person in possession of the same information would think the course of conduct amounted to harassment of the other.

S.1(3) Subsection (1) does not apply to a course of conduct if the person who pursued it shows-

(a) that it was pursued for the purpose of preventing or detecting crime,

(b) that it was pursued under any enactment or rule of law or to comply with any condition... or requirement imposed by any person under any enactment, or

(c) that in the particular circumstances the pursuit of the course of conduct was reasonable."

a) *Actus reus*: "A person must not pursue a course of conduct which amounts to harassment of another"

Conduct is defined widely in **s7(4)** to include speech.

There must be at least two incidents to establish a course of conduct.

The two incidents must be linked, i.e. there must be some connection between the incidents.

***Patel* [2005]**

***Lau v DPP* [2000]**

***Curtis* [2010]**

It is not necessary to show that the victim suffered harassment twice: as long as there are at least two items of conduct which caused the victim harassment at least once. ***Kelly* [2003]**.

b) *Actus reus:* The course of conduct must amount to harassment

s7(2) states that references to harassing a person include alarming them or causing them distress. This is an inclusive, not exhaustive, list.

Harassment is a persistent and deliberate course of unreasonable and oppressive conduct, targeted at another person, which is calculated to and does cause that person alarm, fear or distress.

***Hayes v Willoughby* [2013]**

A person can be harassed by words communicated to a third party:

***DPP v Kellett* [2001]**

***King v DPP* [2001]**

***DPP v Hardy* [2008]**

Conduct can amount to harassment even where the victim has chosen to enter the defendant's presence (***James* [2009]**).

The courts are reluctant to allow the Act to be used in a way that inhibits free speech:

***Trimingham v Associated Newspapers* [2012]**

***Pegram v DPP* [2019]**

c) *Mens rea: "...which he knows or ought to know* amounts to harassment."

Either subjective or objective *mens rea*:

"the person...ought to know that it amounts to harassment of another if a reasonable person in possession of the same information would think the course of conduct amounted to harassment of the other (section 1(2)).

"Alternatively, if the defendant acts in a way that he knows is harassing the victim, even if a reasonable person would not realise that the conduct was harassing, he can still be convicted of the offence" (***Colohan* [2001]**).

d) Defences

The act sets out a number of statutory defences in **s1(3)** including the prevention and detection of crime and that the conduct of D was reasonable.

7.7.2 Stalking

s2A Protection from Harassment Act 1997

A person is guilty of an offence if – (a) the person pursues a course of conduct in breach of s1(1), and (b) the course of conduct amounts to stalking.

1) *Amounts to stalking* (**s2A(2)**)

A course of conduct amounts to stalking if:

(a) It amounts to harassment of that person.

(b) The acts and omissions involved are ones associated with stalking, and

(c) The person whose course of conduct it is knowing or ought to know that the course of conduct amounts to harassment of the other person.

2) *Acts or omissions associated with stalking* (**s2A(3)**)

(a) Following a person

(b) Contacting, or attempting to contact, a person by any means.

(c) Publishing any statement or other material –

(i) Relating or purporting to relate to a person, or

(ii) Purporting to originate from a person.

(d) Monitoring the use by a person of the internet, email, or any other form of electronic communication

(e) Loitering in any place (whether public or private)

(f) Interfering with any property in the possession of a person

(g) Watching or spying on a person.

This offence is not restricted to traditional stalking.

Its purpose is also to tackle online stalking.

7.7.3 Aggravated harassment

s4 Protection from Harassment Act 1997

1) Definition:

s4(1): *A person whose* ***course of conduct causes another to fear****, on at least* ***two occasions****, that* ***violence will be used*** *against him is* ***guilty*** *of an offence* ***if he***

knows or ought to know that his course of conduct will cause the other so to fear on each of those occasions.

s4(2): *For the purposes of this section, the person whose course of conduct is in question ought to know that it will cause another to fear that violence will be used against him on any occasion if a* ***reasonable person in possession of the same information would think the course of conduct would cause the other so to fear on that occasion.***

s4(3): *It is a* **defence** *for a person charged with an offence under this section to show that-*

(a) his course of conduct was pursued for the purpose of ***preventing or detecting crime****,*

(b) his course of conduct was **pursued under any enactment or rule of law** *or to comply with any condition or requirement imposed by any person under any enactment, or*

(c) the pursuit of his course of conduct was reasonable for the ***protection of himself or another or for the protection of his or another's property****.'*

It is necessary to show:

(i) *"That the defendant pursued a course of conduct that caused harassment"*

Haque **[2011]**.

(ii) *"That there was a course of conduct which, on at least two occasions, led to the victim having cause to fear that violence would be used against her."*

Henley **[2000]**.

7.7.4 Aggravated stalking

s4A Protection from Harassment Act 1997 creates an aggravated form of the offence which applies when the stalking causes fear of violence or serious alarm or distress.

7.7.5 Controlling or coercive behaviour in an intimate or family relationship

s76 Serious crime act 2015:

(1) [D] commits an offence if –

(a) *A repeatedly or continuously engages in behaviour towards another person [V] that is controlling or coercive,*

(b) *at the time of the behaviour, [D] and [V] are personally connected,*

(c) *the behaviour has a serious effect on [V], and*

(d) *[D] knows or ought to know that the behaviour will have a serious effect on [V].*

7.7.6 Administering poison

s23 Offences Against the Person Act 1861

Whosoever shall unlawfully and maliciously administer to or cause to be administered to or taken by any other person any poison or other destructive or noxious thing, so as thereby to inflict upon such person any grievous bodily harm, shall be guilty.

7.7.7 Strangulation or suffocation

Serious Crime Act 2015, s75A (inserted by s7 Domestic Abuse Act 2021)

75A Strangulation or suffocation[12]

(1) A person ("A") commits an offence if—

(a) A intentionally strangles another person ("B"), or

(b) A does any other act to B that—

(i) affects B's ability to breathe, and

(ii) constitutes battery of B.

(2) It is a defence to an offence under this section for A to show that B consented to the strangulation or other act.

(3) But subsection (2) does not apply if—

(a) B suffers serious harm as a result of the strangulation or other act, and

(b) A either—

(i) intended to cause B serious harm, or

(ii) was reckless as to whether B would suffer serious harm.

(4) A is to be taken to have shown the fact mentioned in subsection (2) if—

(a) sufficient evidence of the fact is adduced to raise an issue with respect to it, and

12 Commentary on this provision can be seen in David Ormerod and Rory Kelly, 'Non-Fatal Strangulation and Belief in Consent' [2025] Criminal Law Review 22-40

(b) the contrary is not proved beyond reasonable doubt.

(5) A person guilty of an offence under this section is liable—

(a) on summary conviction—

(i) to imprisonment for a term not exceeding [the general limit in a magistrates' court]2 (or 6 months, if the offence was committed before the coming into force of paragraph 24(2) of Schedule 22 to the Sentencing Act 2020), or

(ii) to a fine, or both;

(b) on conviction on indictment, to imprisonment for a term not exceeding 5 years or to a fine, or both.

(6) In this section "serious harm" means—

(a) grievous bodily harm, within the meaning of section 18 of the Offences Against the Person Act 1861,

(b) wounding, within the meaning of that section, or

(c) actual bodily harm, within the meaning of section 47 of that Act.

7.7.8 Encouraging or assisting serious self-harm

s184 Online Safety Act 2023 creates the offence of encouraging or assisting serious self-harm.

184 Offence of encouraging or assisting serious self-harm

(1) A person (D) commits an offence if—

(a) D does a relevant act ***capable of encouraging or assisting the serious self-harm of another person****, and*

(b) D's act was ***intended to encourage or assist the serious self-harm of another person.***

(2) D "does a relevant act" if D—

(a) communicates in person,

(b) sends, transmits or publishes a communication by electronic means,

(c) shows a person such a communication,

(d) publishes material by any means other than electronic means,

(e) sends, gives, shows or makes available to a person—

(i) material published as mentioned in paragraph (d), or

(ii) any form of correspondence, or

(f) sends, gives or makes available to a person an item on which data is stored electronically.

(3) "Serious self-harm" means self-harm amounting to—

(a) in England and Wales and Northern Ireland, grievous bodily harm within the meaning of the Offences Against the Person Act 1861, and

...and includes successive acts of self-harm which cumulatively reach that threshold.

...

(5) D may commit an offence under this section whether or not serious self-harm occurs.

7.8 Racially aggravated assaults

s29 Crime and Disorder Act 1998:

D Guilty of an aggravated offence if he commits an

(I) offence contrary to S. ***20 or 47 of the Offences Against the Person Act 1861, or common assault****, AND*

(II) the offence is ***S.28 CDA 1998 'Racially Aggravated' =***

(a) at the time of committing the offence or immediately before or after doing so, the ***offender demonstrates towards the victim of the offence hostility based on the victim's membership*** *(or presumed [by the offender] membership)* ***of a racial group****; OR*

(b) the ***offence is motivated (wholly or partly) by hostility towards members of a racial group*** *based on their membership of that group. It is immaterial that the offender may or may not have also been motivated by the fact or presumption that any person or group of persons belongs to any religious group, or any other factor not mentioned in (a) and (b). For the purposes of s.28* ***'racial group'*** *means* ***'a group of persons defined by reference to race, colour, nationality (including citizenship) or ethnic or national origins.***

The whole point of creating these aggravated offences is to provide the courts with greater sentencing powers to reflect the aggravating factor of racial hatred. Hence a conviction under **s20** where the offence is racially motivated carries a maximum penalty of seven years imprisonment (as opposed to five for the basic offence), and a conviction on indictment for racially motivated assault carries the possibility of two years imprisonment, as opposed to the maximum six months where it is tried summarily.

7.9 Evaluation and reform

7.9.1 Legal certainty and legal clarity

The law on offences against the person is undoubtedly the easiest area to critique. The 1861 statute is clearly outdated. It requires codification where there is a consistency of terminology and a systematic review.

It is submitted that broad offences like those in the **Theft Act 1968** can be created within them when it comes to sentencing differential considerations can be made in terms of the harm culpability and role of the individual.

In terms of legal clarity, at the moment terminology such as battery, grievous, occasioning, and wounding are all clearly outdated.

All of that being said it is also the case that in fact the case law of the 1990s has in many circumstances clarified what the law is that made it easier for a judge to direct the jury accurately on the law. It is also clear enough for a jury to interpret.

The legal boundaries on consent remain certain but arguably perhaps the threshold should be moved up to incorporate that an individual could consent to actual bodily harm. This would be consistent with other jurisdictions.

7.9.2 Equality before the law: protected characteristics and socio-economic barriers

The majority of the law here operates with equality before the law at the core. Two themes that are problematic:

- firstly, in relation to domestic violence it is clear that the law should have a cogent focus on protecting those who are the victims of domestic violence. There is a clear evidential link between domestic violence causing injury and domestic violence leading to fatalities;
- secondly the law in relation to consent as explained in the case of ***Brown*** seems to differentiate depending on whether this is a heterosexual or homosexual relationship. It seems clear now that ***Wilson*** is no longer sustainable, and further statutory intervention is required or a Supreme Court judgment reviewing ***Brown*** and ***Wilson***.

7.9.3 Fair warning; fair labelling and sufficient breadth principles

a) Fair warning

Although not binding, the Crown Prosecution Service's website is exceptionally useful in developing policies to assist in scaling the level of harm and attributing which offence to prosecute. It is also very useful in relation to the concept of consent and harassment or stalking.

In terms of the transmission of HIV and other sexually transmitted diseases it is very useful that the Crown Prosecution Service guidance is well drafted and nuanced. All of this arguably means collectively that there is fair warning to the defendant and the community.

The only question would be whether there is such a need for this, specifically in terms of broad categories of offending where there are isolated versions of the offence, such as assaulting a shop worker. It is arguable it is not necessary to have such specific versions of this and this is merely performative theatre by the politicians. The needs can be met by existing legislation and existing sentencing norms being applied.

b) Fair labelling

The labelling of behaviour as battery, ABH, GBH, wounding in the modern era does not fully explain what the situation is, but perhaps just a simple levelling of assaults would be more useful, i.e. low harm; some harm; serious harm; serious harm with intent. Accurate modern terminology may be more empowering and accurate.

c) Sufficient breadth

There appears to be sufficient breadth to capture offending. The only critique would be whether there should be specific offences in relation to specific instances. It is submitted that actually what is necessary is a broad category of offending and then specific and useful sentences in guidelines that can deal with the circumstances of the offence.

d) Practicality, cost, and expense

1) Practicality – Law must be sufficiently practical and enforceable to achieve its goals

On paper, in terms of the statute law, this remains complex. In reality, the House of Lords Supreme Court and Court of Appeal judgments have in fact clarified many of the terms and the law is relatively practical. The law is particularly assisted by the *Crown Prosecution Service Charging Guidance*.

2) Avoid undue cost and expense

The law now settled through the case law does not seem to cause undue cost and expense and this is also notable by the diminished volume of appeals post the 1990s on assaults.

7.9.4 Human rights: autonomy and welfare principles

The position for the purposes of **ECHR Art 8** regarding privacy may be engaged in relation to the consent issues of the consensual sado-masochism. The position in terms of equality is contained in **ECHR Art 14**.

Consent may also need a 2024 review. It seems that ***Brown*** and ***Wilson*** are unsustainable. There is a strong argument to say perhaps the threshold should be moved up to consent being allowed in relation to ABH.

7.9.5 International comparators and reform: practicality principle and politics

a) Comparators

New Zealand has some particularly interesting ideas in relation to consent which are explored.[13]

b) Law Commission

There are significant advantages to a Law Commission review. It would focus on legal certainty, clarity, equality, labelling, human rights and comparators. It would be free from the constraints of fact-based litigation. It could review the whole law and engage in full consultation.

The Law Commission's proposals are found in its report: *Legislating the Criminal Code: Offences Against the Person and General Principles'* (1993) Law Com No 218.

c) Government paper: *Violence: Reforming the Offences Against the Person Act 1861 from 1998*

The government in 1998 published a consultation document which sought to build upon the work of the Law Commission, which included a draft bill.

13 Jennifer Tolmie, 'Consent to Harmful Assaults: The Case for Moving Away from Category Based Decision Making' [2012] Crim LR 656

Clauses 1 to 3 propose new offences to replace **s18**, **20**, and **47** of the **OAPA 1861**. They provide as follows:

Clause 1. Intentionally causing serious injury

(1) *person is guilty of an offence if he* ***intentionally causes serious injury to another****.*

(2) *A person is guilty of an offence if he* ***omits to do an act which he has a duty to do*** *at common law, the omission* ***results in serious injury to another****, and he* ***intends*** *the omission to have that result.*

(3) *An offence under this section is committed notwithstanding that the injury occurs outside England and Wales if the act causing injury is done in England and Wales or the omission resulting in injury is made there.*

(4) *A person guilty of an offence under this section is liable on conviction on indictment to* ***imprisonment for life.***

Clause 2. Recklessly causing serious injury

(1) *A person is guilty of an offence if he* ***recklessly causes serious injury to another****.*

(2) *An offence under this section is committed notwithstanding that the injury occurs outside England and Wales if the act causing injury is done in England and Wales.*

(3) *A person guilty of an offence under this section is liable—*

   (a) on conviction on indictment, to imprisonment for a term not exceeding ***7 years****;*

   (b) on summary conviction, to imprisonment for a term not exceeding ***6 months*** *or a fine not exceeding the statutory maximum or both.*

Clause 3. Intentionally or recklessly causing injury to another

(1) *A person is guilty of an offence if he* ***intentionally or recklessly causes injury to another****.*

(2) *An offence under this section is committed notwithstanding that the injury occurs outside England and Wales if the act causing injury is done in England and Wales.*

(3) *A person guilty of an offence under this section is liable—*

   (a) on conviction on indictment, to imprisonment for a term not exceeding ***5 years****;*

(b) on summary conviction, to imprisonment for a term not exceeding ***6 months*** *or a fine not exceeding the statutory maximum or both.*

Clause 4. Assault

4. - *(1) A person is guilty of an offence if—*

(a) he ***intentionally or recklessly applies force to or causes an impact on the body*** *of another, or*

(b) he ***intentionally or recklessly causes the other to believe that any such force or impact is imminent.***

(2) ***No such offence*** *is committed if the force or impact, not being intended or likely to cause injury, is in the circumstances such as is* ***generally acceptable in the ordinary conduct of daily life and the defendant does not know or believe that it is in fact unacceptable to the other person****.*

(3) A person guilty of an offence under this section is liable on summary conviction to imprisonment for a term not exceeding ***6 months*** *or a fine not exceeding level 5 on the standard scale or both.*

Clause 14. Fault terms

14. - *(1) A person acts* ***intentionally*** *with respect to a result if—*

(a) it is his ***purpose to cause it****, or*

(b) although it is ***not his purpose*** *to cause it,* ***he knows that it would occur in the ordinary course of events*** *if he were to succeed in his purpose of causing some other result.*

(2) A person acts ***recklessly*** *with respect to a result if he is* ***aware of a risk that it will occur and it is unreasonable to take*** *that risk having regard to the circumstances as he knows or believes them to be.*

(3) A person intends an omission to have a result if—

(a) it is his purpose that the result will occur, or

(b) although it is not his purpose that the result will occur, he knows that it would occur in the ordinary course of events if he were to succeed in his purpose that some other result will occur.

(4) A person is reckless whether an omission will have a result if he is aware of a risk that the result will occur, and it is unreasonable to take that risk having regard to the circumstances as he knows or believes them to be.

(5) Related expressions must be construed accordingly.

(6) This section has effect for the purposes of this Act.

Clause 15. Injury

(1) In this Act "injury" means—

(a) ***physical injury, or***

(b) ***mental injury****.*

(2) ***Physical injury*** *does* ***not include anything caused by disease*** *but (subject to that) it* ***includes pain, unconsciousness, and any other impairment of a person's physical condition****.*

(3) ***Mental injury*** *does* ***not include anything caused by disease*** *but (subject to that) it* ***includes any impairment of a person's mental health****.*

(4) In its application to section 1 this section applies without the exceptions relating to things caused by disease.'

d) *Consent*

In the ***Law Commission Consultation Paper No. 139*** *the Law Commission proposed significant liberalisation of law on consent.*

Namely so that consent could be a defence if the injury was less serious than a serious disabling injury (serious disabling injury includes causing serious distress; loss of bodily member or organ; permanent bodily injury or permanent functional impairment; severe or prolonged pain; or serious impairment to mental health or prolonged unconsciousness).

This would greatly extend the kind of injuries to which the victim's consent would provide a defence.

In the News

Brown and the eunuch makers

Please read these two articles. Please note both contain references to extreme but consensual sex related behaviours.

1. Brown and Wilson

Catherine Baksi, "Landmarks in law: when five men were jailed for consensual sex" *The Guardian* (London, 17 February 2021) <https://www.theguardian.com/law/2021/feb/17/landmarks-in-law-when-five-men-were-jailed-for-consensual-sex> accessed 06 April 2025

2. The Eunuch maker

Emine Sinmaz and Kevin Rawlinson, "Man known as 'eunuch maker' who streamed mutilations is jailed for life" *The Guardian* (London, 9 May 2024) <https://www.theguardian.com/uk-news/article/2024/may/09/man-eunuch-maker-streamed-mutilations-jailed-life-marius-gustavson> accessed 06 April 2025

Firstly, it is obvious that a harm level is very relevant to the decision on whether to prosecute.

Secondly, in terms of threshold the eunuch maker appears to be a threshold that few could live with. It is extremely serious harm done to others.

Finally, the question remains, should the threshold be assault, actual bodily harm or grievous bodily harm? It is submitted that on most readings, consent to actual bodily harm should be permissible.

It is also notable that there is a distinction that appears to be drawn between the heterosexual couple in ***Wilson*** and the homosexual activities in both ***Brown*** and the eunuch maker case.

7.10 Summary

We have reviewed

- **Common assault**

  This being the lowest end of the harm threshold. For example, a punch causing a bruise on someone's arm.

- **Actual bodily harm**

  This being the next step up in terms of injury where there is an actual injury that is more than trifling in nature.

- **Causing grievous bodily harm**

  This covers the causation of serious injury.

- **Causing grievous bodily harm with intent**

  This covers the causation of serious injury where it is the aim or purpose of the defendant to cause serious injury.

- **Consent**

  The vexed issue of consent is explored. There are notable exceptions but controversy still exists as to whether the threshold should be that common assault and actual bodily harm should be eligible for the individual to autonomously choose to consent to in the context of, for example BDSM.

- **Other assault related offences**

  There are no numerous statutory offences that support remedies for a variety of wrongs including stalking and harassment.

- **Racially aggravated**

  The specific racially aggravated offences from 1998 offer further deterrents to those who wish to add gratuitous abuse to the assaults.

- **Specific evaluation themes will be discussed**

  The statutory legislation is archaic and the terminology is outdated. There is a definite need for codification of the law for the modern era. The 1998 report offers a sensible solution. However, in terms of the current law, the courts have thankfully interpreted it in a manner which makes it workable.

Further reading

Dennis Baker, "The Moral Limits of Consent in Criminal Law" (2008) *New Criminal Law Review 12:93*

Catherine Elliott and Claire De Than "The Case for a Rational Reconstruction of Consent in Criminal Law" Catherine (2007) *70 MLR 225*

Matthew Gibson, "Getting Their "Act" Together? Implementing Statutory Reform of Offences against the Person" (2017) *Criminal Law Review 597*

David Ormerod and Michael Gunn. "The Second Law Commission Consultation Paper on Consent: Consent—A Second Bash" (1996) *Criminal Law Review 694*

Samantha Pegg, "Not so clear cut: the lawfulness of body modifications" (2019) *7 Criminal Law Review 579*

CHAPTER 8
Sexual offences

8.1 Introduction

In this chapter, we will be exploring a range of sexual offences, including rape and sexual assault, all of which are set out in the **Sexual Offences Act 2003**, as amended. Sexual offences are often considered some of the most serious crimes within the criminal justice system and many of the cases you might encounter when exploring this topic will involve distressing and sensitive situations.

Support for victims of sexual violence

The following support services are available for victims of sexual offences:

- National Domestic Abuse Helpline (Refuge) – 0808 2000 247
- www.mind.org.uk
- The Survivors Trust - https://www.thesurvivorstrust.org
- Supportline – 01708 765200 and www.supportline.org.uk
- https://www.safeline.org.uk/contact-us/

This chapter begins by discussing rape, an offence under **s1 Sexual Offences Act 2003**. We use this offence to explore some of the core concepts, such as consent, capacity and deception which are relevant across many of the other offences discussed in this chapter, as well as other offences found in the 2003 Act. As we will see, consent is key to all of the offences discussed here and, whilst there are other offences – such as those relating to children – within the 2003 Act which do not require the prosecution to prove an absence of consent; the offences discussed here share many other elements with those offences which you will find it useful to understand.

Throughout this chapter, you will see that despite the significance of the reforms in 2003, there are significant ambiguities in the law on consent and sexual offending. You will see that provisions within **ss75–76 Sexual Offences Act 2003** establishing presumptions around the absence of consent and reasonable belief in consent have been the subject of key case law. The consequences of these cases, beyond the individual impact that they have on the complainants and defendants involved, can be seen in debates over potential reforms to the law. The intention of this chapter will be for you to be able to critically evaluate some of these issues, as well as apply the law in practical scenarios.

Aims of this chapter

By the end of this chapter, you will:

- understand how the law approaches the issue of consent in the context of sexual activity;
- know how to apply the law on offences such as sexual assault to complex problem scenarios; and
- be able to critically evaluate key aspects of the law on sexual offences and discuss potential future reforms.

8.2 Rape and consent to sexual activity

As with many of the offences discussed in this chapter, the law on rape was significantly amended by the **Sexual Offences Act 2003 (SOA 2003)** which sought to update the law to reflect a more modern understanding of sexual offending. Prior to 2003, the law on rape was set out **in s1 Sexual Offences Act 1956** which, in its original form, only covered the rape of a woman by vaginal penetration. **s1 SOA 2003** broadens the offence of rape, applying in situations where there is:

- *Penile Penetration*
- *Of the Vagina, Anus or Mouth of Another*

- *Without Consent*
- *And without a Reasonable Belief in Consent*
- *With the Defendant Intending Penile Penetration.*

The Government white paper which preceded **SOA 2003** explained that "[o]ne of the principles underlying our new offences is that they should not be gender specific. However, the offence of rape is clearly understood to be non-consensual penile penetration perpetrated by a man."[1] **SOA 2003** therefore created a separate offence of Causing a Person to Engage in Sexual Activity without Consent, discussed at **8.5**.

Further reading

Whether the **Sexual Offences Act 2003** achieves the aim of creating a framework of sexual offences which is not gender specific has been explored within academic commentary. Consider reading:

Jeremy Robson, Lucy Newman and Andrew O'Hagan, "Redrawing the Boundaries: The Adequacy of the Sexual Offences Act in Addressing Female Sexual Offending" (2021) 85(4) Journal of Criminal Law 253

Despite **SOA 2003**, there are many potential critiques of the law on as serious sexual offences, including rape, including decreased rates of prosecution and conviction in recent years.[2] Sexual offences can be understood as a unique category of offending. Different theories about the wrongfulness at the core of rape and sexual offending include arguments that it: diminishes the autonomy of victims, represents an invasion of personal integrity, dehumanises and objectifies victims, and reinforces and perpetuates broader misogyny and gender-based violence. Critical analysis of the current law needs to take into account the broader context surrounding sexual offences, including misogyny within society, cultural norms regarding sex and sexuality and the stigma often faced by victims of sexual offences. It is important to consider how this context shapes the criminal justice system's response to the wrongfulness of rape, including current prosecution trends, as well as the development of the offence of rape itself.

1 Home Office, Protecting the Public: Strengthening protection against sex offenders and reforming the law on sexual offences (Cm 5668, 2002) para 42

2 See, Rachel George and Sophie Ferguson, 'Review into the Criminal Justice System response to adult rape and serious sexual offences across England and Wales' (Research Report, HM Government 2021)

8.2.1 Penile penetration

For rape to occur, the defendant must physically penetrate the complainant with his penis. **s79(3) SOA 2003** explains that references to body parts within the Act include body parts which have been surgically constructed, therefore this requirement could be satisfied where a defendant has undergone gender reassignment surgery or penile reconstructive surgery. Penetration is deemed to be continuing act from entry to withdrawal (**s79(1)**) meaning that failure to withdraw in situations where the other elements of the offence are satisfied (such as where the complainant no longer consents and the defendant realises this) will constitute an offence.

8.2.2 Of the vagina, anus or mouth

Penetration must be of the complainant's vagina, anus or mouth which, again under **s79(3)**, may be surgically constructed. Although **s1(1)(a)** uses the terminology vagina, **s79(9)** explains that this includes the vulva. Where the defendant does not penetrate the vagina, anus or mouth, there may be liability for sexual assault or, as in cases such as ***Zaheer* [2018]** where such penetration is attempted but does not take place, for attempted rape.

8.2.3 Without consent

Where offences involve adult complainants, i.e. those above the age of consent to sexual activity, the presence of absence of consent is a central issue when determining liability for rape and other sexual offences. The basic definition of consent is set out in **s74 SOA 2003** which explains that "a person consents if he agrees by choice, and has the freedom and capacity to make that choice". However, there are also a number of rebuttable and irrebuttable presumptions regarding consent which may also apply in particular circumstances.

The basic definition places an emphasis on the complainant's **freedom** and **capacity** to make a choice. In both **C [2009]** and **GA [2014]** the courts have been required to evaluate these concepts in situations where there have been questions regarding the complainant's mental capacity to consent. In both cases, the courts have held that consent is context and time specific, with Baroness Hale stating in **C [2009]**, para 27:

> *"[I]t is difficult to think of an activity which is more person and situation specific than sexual relations. One does not consent to sex in general. One consents to this act of sex with this person at this time and in this place. Autonomy entails the freedom and the capacity to make a choice of whether or not to do so."*

In ***Olugboja* [1982]** the complainant had previously been raped by one of the defendant's friends and, partially out of fear, submitted to the defendant when he attempted to have sex with her. The Court of Appeal emphasised at 332 "that there is a difference between consent and submission; every consent involves a submission, but it by no means follows that a mere submission involves consent". Although this case precedes **SOA 2003**, it has been positively cited since 2003 and remains a good authority for the principle that the jury's assessment of consent needs to take into account the circumstances of the complainant's decision.

Further reading

The distinction between consent and submission to sexual activity is also explored in ***PK* [2008]** where the complainant, in a situation of economic desperation, submitted to sexual activity in exchange for £3.25. Cases such as this raise questions about consent and socio-economic vulnerability, which may also arise in the context of long-term intimate partner violence. For further discussion of consent and "chronic" sexual offending, consider reading:

Tanya Palmer, "Failing to See the Wood for the Trees: Chronic Sexual Violence and Criminal Law" (2020) 84(6) *Journal of Criminal Law 573*

The statutory definition of consent, as well as highlighting the importance of freedom and capacity, relies on the concept of agreement. This agreement may, in certain circumstances, be conditional on express or implied circumstances. What these circumstances are, however, is a complex issue, demonstrated by a series of recent cases. In ***Assange v Swedish Prosecution Authority* [2011]** the complainant's consent was conditional on the use of a condom. Without the complainant's knowledge, a condom was not used during penetration and, as a consequence, the court ruled that the complainant was not consenting.

Assange was considered in the later case of ***McNally* [2013]**. In that case, the defendant and the complainant met online and maintained a relationship for a number of years, during which time the defendant presented as male. The complainant met the defendant in-person and engaged in sexual activity multiple times before discovering that the defendant was female. The Court of Appeal (at para 26) held that deceptions regarding gender could vitiate consent to sexual activity, on the basis that the complainant did not have the "freedom to choose whether or not to have a sexual encounter with a girl".

Further reading

The decision in ***McNally* [2013]** has been subject to significant discussion and critique. Consider reading:

Alex Sharpe, "Criminalising Sexual Intimacy: Transgender Defendants and the Legal Construction of Non-Consent" [2014] *Criminal Law Review 207*

Two further cases are key to understanding the current approach to consent, deceptions and agreement to sexual activity. ***R (on the application of Monica) v Director of Public Prosecutions* [2018]** was a case arising out of what has come to be termed the "spy cops" scandal. Monica was in a long-term sexual relationship with an undercover police officer and, after discovering this, sought to challenge the Director of Public Prosecution's decision not to bring a prosecution against the officer. The High Court held that whilst Monica had been deceived as to the officer's identity, she had not been deceived in relation to the ***fundamental nature*** of the sexual act. This approach formed the basis of the Court's judgment in ***Lawrance* [2020]** where the defendant told the complainant that he had undergone a vasectomy when he had, in fact, not done so. The complainant later became pregnant, and the defendant admitted the deception but denied this behaviour constituted an offence. The judgment in ***Lawrance*** distinguishes this kind of deception from that seen in ***Assange*** and other similar cases, on the basis that Lawrance's deception did not misrepresent that penetration would take place without the physical barrier of a condom; with the Court of Appeal finding that deceptions as to fertility are not closely connected with the nature and purpose of sexual activity but instead concerned the risks and consequences of it.

In the News

"Spy cops"

Several allegations of sexual offences have arisen out of the "Spy Cops" scandal. Many of the cases, such as ***Monica***, involve relationships which ended decades ago where the deception only came to light following media revelations in the early 2010s, as highlighted in articles such as:

Paul Lewis and Rob Evans, "Secrets and lies: untangling the UK 'spy cops' scandal" *The Guardian* (28 October 2020)

Whilst **s74 SOA 2003** provides the general definition of consent, there are also a number of presumptions related to consent which the prosecution may utilise. **s75** sets out a number of rebuttable presumptions. Where one of these applies, it is presumed that the complainant did not consent and that the defendant did not have a reasonable belief that the complainant was consenting, unless the defence bring forward evidence to rebut the presumption.

The circumstances which give rise to a rebuttable presumption, set out in **s75(2)**, are:

> **s75(2)(a)**: "any person was, at the time of the sexual act or immediately before it began, **using violence against the complainant** or causing the complainant to fear that immediate violence would be used against the complainant."

s75(2)(b): "any person was, at the time of the sexual act or immediately before it began, causing the claimant to fear that violence was being used, or that immediate violence would be used, against another person."

s75(2)(c): "the complainant was, and the defendant was not, **unlawfully detained** at the time of the sexual act."

s75(2)(d): "the complainant was **asleep or otherwise unconscious** at the time of the relevant act."

s75(2)(e): "because of the complainant's **physical disability** the complainant would not have been able at the time of the sexual act to communicate to the defendant whether the complainant consented."

s75(2)(f): "any person had **administered** or caused to be taken by the complainant, without the complainant's consent, **a substance** which, having regard to when it was administered or taken, was capable of causing or enabling the complainant to be **stupefied or overpowered** at the time of the sexual act."

In ***Ciccarelli* [2011]** the complainant had been asleep at the defendant's house following a party. The defendant entered the room where the complainant was sleeping and had performed sexual acts on the complainant. The defendant attempted to argue that he had a reasonable belief in consent, on the basis that the complainant had been friendly to him earlier in the evening, however the Court rejected this argument outright, holding (at Para 18) that "some evidence beyond the fanciful or speculative had to be adduced to support the reasonableness" of this belief in order to rebut the presumption.

Terminology alert!

Rebuttable and irrebuttable presumptions

The key difference between the presumptions found in **s75** and **s76** is that where either of the circumstances set out in **s76** are found to apply "it is to be conclusively presumed" that the complainant did not consent and the defendant did not reasonably belief that the complainant was consenting. This means that the presumption is **irrebuttable**, the defendant cannot bring forward evidence to counter the presumption. This contrasts with the rebuttable presumption made when the circumstances found in **s75** apply, where a defendant can challenge the presumption with evidence to the contrary.

Another situation where a rebuttable presumption may apply is where the defendant has administered a substance to the complainant. This is discussed in the leading case of ***Bree* [2007]** which highlights the significance of the distinction between voluntary and involuntary intoxication in the context of sexual consent. In ***Bree***

(Para 24) the Court of Appeal explains that whilst **s75(2)(f)** would apply in instances where drinks are spiked (which would amount to involuntary intoxication) it does not extend to situations where there is casual encouragement to drink. In those situations, whether the complainant was consenting would be dependent upon their capacity to make a choice. Intoxication does not inherently eliminate the capacity to consent, however, where a defendant is so drunk that they do lose their capacity any consent would also be vitiated.

s76 SOA 2003 sets out two irrebuttable presumptions. In situations where one of these presumptions applies, the defendant cannot bring forward evidence in an attempt to argue that the complainant was consenting or that they had a reasonable belief in consent (although they may attempt to argue that the circumstances giving rise to the presumption do not exist).

s76(2)(a) applies where the defendant **intentionally deceived** the complainant as to the **nature** or the **purpose** of the sexual act. Several cases which occurred prior to the 2003 legislation, but which apply comparable principles, offer good examples of when this provision might apply. In ***Flattery* [1877]** the defendant deceived the complainant that he was going to perform a medical procedure on her, when in fact he was penetrating her. Similarly, in ***Williams* [1923]** the defendant told the complainant that penetration was a method of improving the complainant's singing voice. In both cases, the courts held that the defendant had deceived the complainant regarding the nature and purpose of the sexual act.

The conclusive presumption of **s76(2)(a)** is narrowly constructed, and case law has made clear that the deception must go to the nature or purpose of the sexual act in order for the provision to apply. In ***Linekar* [1995]** the defendant agreed to pay the complainant, a sex worker, £25 for sexual intercourse, however, after having sex refused to pay. The defendant's conviction was overturned by the Court of Appeal on the basis that there was no deception *as to the nature or purpose of the act* itself.

In ***Jheeta* [2007]** the defendant and the complainant had been in a previously consensual sexual relationship. The defendant started sending the victim anonymous threatening text messages and, after the complainant had approached him for support with the anonymous messages, further messages were sent from the defendant purporting to come from the police. The complainant repeatedly attempted to end the relationship with the defendant, with the defendant then sending messages purporting to come from the police claiming that the defendant had attempted to harm himself and that the complainant was liable to receive a fine if she did not have sexual intercourse with him. The Court of Appeal held that the deceptions perpetrated by the defendant did not relate to the nature or purpose of the sexual act and therefore did not fall under **s76(2)(a)**, however, they did undermine the complainant's freedom to make a choice regarding sex with the defendant, thereby constituting an offence using the general **s74** definition of consent.

Further reading

The narrow construction of **s76(2)(a)** has been an issue in a number of cases since the legislation was enacted. In ***Devonald* [2008]** the provision was considered applicable where the defendant induced the complainant to perform sexual acts on webcam on the basis that the defendant was a young woman when, in fact, he was the father of the complainant's ex-girlfriend. However, this broader application of the presumption was questioned in both ***McNally* [2013]; [2014]** and ***B* [2013]** which restate the narrower interpretation of ***Jheeta* [2007]**. For further discussion which discusses the benefits of this narrower interpretation, consider reading:

Karl Laird, "Rapist or rogue?: Deception, consent and the Sexual Offences Act 2003" [2014] *Criminal Law Review 492*

The second irrebuttable presumption applies under **s76(2)(b)** where the defendant intentionally induces consent to the sexual act "by impersonating a person known personally to the complainant". Prior to 2003, **s1(2) Sexual Offences Act 1956** had provided that impersonation of a husband would vitiate consent by his deceived wife. In ***Elbekkay* [1995]** the Court of Appeal ruled that impersonation of the complainant's boyfriend was capable of vitiating consent at common law. **s76(2)(b)** of the **Sexual Offences Act 2003** now means that impersonation of someone known to the complainant does vitiate consent, irrespective of the relationship between the complainant and the person being impersonated. This provision is only limited in its application by the requirement that the complainant personally know the person being impersonated. This prevents the provision being used where a defendant impersonated, for example, a film star not personally known by the complainant.

8.2.4 Without a reasonable belief in consent

In addition to being required to prove the absence of consent, the prosecution are also required to establish that the defendant lacked a reasonable belief that the complainant was consenting. This area of law was particularly problematic prior to the enactment of the **Sexual Offences Act 2003** as exemplified in the case of ***DPP v Morgan* [1976]**. In ***Morgan***, Morgan and three other defendants were charged in connection with the rape of Morgan's wife. Morgan had encouraged the other defendants to have sex with the complainant, indicating that she would *act* as if she were resisting when, in fact, she was a willing participant. Then, the House of Lords held that the law at the time, which did not impose a requirement of **reasonableness** on a defendant's belief in consent, meant that an honest – albeit unreasonable – belief in consent would avoid liability, although in ***Morgan*** itself it was held that the defendants' beliefs were not honestly held.

This aspect of the law was changed by **SOA 2003**, which does now impose a requirement of reasonableness in relation to any belief in consent. **s1(2)** specifies the assessment of *whether a belief is reasonable is to be determined having regard to all the circumstances, including any steps [the defendant] has taken to ascertain whether [the complainant] consents*. If one of the rebuttable or irrebuttable presumptions found in **ss 75–76** applies, this also establishes that the defendant did not reasonably believe that the complainant was consenting.

Key concepts

HIV, consent to harm and consent to sexual activity

The discussion of HIV transmission as a non-fatal offence against the person in **Chapter 7** highlighted that non-disclosure of HIV status can preclude a defendant claiming a reasonable belief in the complainant's consent to the risk of HIV transmission. Non-disclosure of HIV status does not, however, vitiate consent to sexual activity nor prevent a defendant from holding a reasonable belief in such consent.

The requirement that the defendant's belief in consent be a reasonable one requires an objective assessment of their belief. Where this is an issue during a trial, a jury will be directed to consider whether a reasonable person in the circumstances of the defendant would have believed that the complainant was consenting. Complexities arise when attempting to determine what surrounding circumstances, including circumstances relating to the defendant, are relevant to this assessment: something seen acutely in the context of defendants who are neurodiverse or who have recognised mental health conditions.

In ***M A B v The Queen* [2013]** the defendant was charged with multiple counts of rape. The defendant was suffering from paranoid schizophrenia and other mental health conditions at the time and the court considered whether the defendant's mental health impacted whether his beliefs should be considered reasonable. It concluded that they did not, stating at Para 40 that "beliefs in consent arising from conditions such as delusional psychotic illness or personality disorders must be judged by objective standards of reasonableness and not by taking into account a mental disorder which induced a belief which could not reasonably arise without it."

However, this is not the same as completely discounting all characteristics of the defendant. ***M A B*** also suggests that where a belief is not irrational, a defendant's characteristics may be relevant to the assessment of whether a belief is objectively reasonable. In ***Jacobs* [2023]** the Court of Appeal reinforces this point, stating that whilst the test is an objective one, there may be circumstances in which the defendant's mental state is a relevant circumstance to be taken into account. The judgment stresses that this will be heavily dependent upon the facts of the case rather than such evidence being automatically relevant to the issue. In ***Jacobs*** itself, where the defendant argued that his autism was relevant to the question of whether a belief in consent was reasonable, it was held that the evidence did not support the defendant's argument.

8.2.5 With the defendant intenting penile penetration

Whilst the reasonableness of the defendant's belief in consent is assessed objectively, the final element of rape – the requirement for intent in respect of penile penetration – is assessed subjectively. In many cases this will be readily established on the facts, applying the general principles of intent discussed in **Chapter 4**.

Where there is more than one instance of penetration and this gives rise to separate charges against the defendant, the prosecution will have the burden of proving intent in relation to the kind of penetration specified. In ***Gabbai* [2019]** the defendant was charged with separate counts relating to vaginal, oral and anal penetration. The defendant denied that the oral and vaginal penetration was non-consensual and disputed that anal penetration had occurred, conceding that it may have taken place unintentionally. The jury acquitted on the counts relating to vaginal and oral penetration but convicted the defendant on the count relating to anal penetration. The defendant successfully appealed the conviction on the basis that the trial judge's directions did not make clear that the prosecution needed to establish that the defendant intended to penetrate anally rather than vaginally.

Reflective question

Maria and her boyfriend, Anthony, go out to dinner one Friday night. Whilst at dinner, Anthony goes to the bar and orders two glasses of lemonade with vodka. On taking then back to the table, he does not mention that the drinks are alcoholic. When they get home, Maria falls asleep on the sofa. Anthony goes over to Maria and starts to penetrate her vagina with his fingers. Maria wakes up and whilst she is still startled Anthony penetrates her vagina with his penis. Consider Anthony's potential liability for rape.

As you progress through this Chapter, you may wish to return to this scenario to attempt to identify other potential criminal offences.

8.3 Assault by penetration

Assault by penetration is set out in **s2 Sexual Offences Act 2003** and is similar, in many respects, to the offence of rape. It applies in situations where there is:

- Penetration of the vagina or anus
- The penetration is sexual

- Without consent
- Without a reasonable belief in consent
- With the defendant intending penetration.

8.3.1 Sexual penetration of the vagina or anus

Assault by penetration shares many of the same principles as rape. As with rape, **s79(3) SOA 2003** explains that references to body parts include body parts which have been surgically constructed and **s79(9)** explains that references to the vagina include the vulva. **s79(1)** continues to establish that penetration is a continuing act, meaning the offence can be satisfied where penetration continues once the other elements of the offence are present.

Unlike rape, assault by penetration does not involve penile penetration. The offence is gender neutral and can involve penetration by any part of the defendant's body (other than a penis) or penetration by an object. Also unlike rape, penetration of the mouth is excluded from the offence; although such actions could constitute an offence under **s3**, discussed below.

To constitute an offence, the penetration must be sexual in nature. **Sexual** is defined in **s78** of the Act, which specifies that touching or another activity can be sexual where:

> *Whatever its circumstances or any person's purpose in relation to it, it is because of its nature sexual, or*
>
> *because of its nature it* ***may be sexual*** *and because of its* ***circumstances or purpose*** *of any person in relation to it (or both) it is sexual.*

Touching will be, *because of its nature* is sexual (**s78(a)**), when it is objectively sexual in nature. This means that touching can be defined as sexual even when it is accepted that the defendant did not intend for the touching to be sexual, provided the reasonable person would consider it to be so (***Abdulahi* [2022]**). In ***Hill* [2006]** a case involving intimate partner violence, the defendant penetrated the vagina of the complainant with his finger. Although it was suggested that the purpose of this was a "form of aggressive humiliation rather than a sexual act" (Para 4), the nature of the conduct was such that it was sexual whatever the defendant's purported purpose.

In contrast, some touching will be sexual, under **s78(b)**, because it is potentially sexual, and it is sexual when the circumstances or the purpose of the defendant or another in relation to it is sexual. The phrasing of this section means that it does not apply where the touching is inherently sexual (which would be dealt with via **s78(a)**). In ***H (Karl Anthony)* [2005]** the defendant grabbed the complainant's tracksuit bottoms after making a sexual advance and was charged with sexual assault (see below). **s79(8)** explains that, for the purpose of sexual offending, touching includes touching through clothing. Given that touching somebody's tracksuit bottoms may not always be sexual, but is capable of being, the issue was one capable of being left to the jury to evaluate taking into consideration the circumstances and/or the defendant's purpose.

Reflective question

In the context of assault by penetration, many cases are likely to appear to be sexual by nature, however, there may be borderline cases where it is appropriate to also consider applying **s78(b)**. Consider liability in the following scenario:

Beatrice is a GP who carries out intimate medical examinations on many of her patients. Olivia attends Beatrice's surgery one Thursday morning as she has been experiencing some abdominal pain. Although it is medically unnecessary, for her sexual gratification, Beatrice asks Olivia to stay on the examination bed and proceeds to penetrate Olivia's vagina with her finger.

8.3.2 Consent and intention

As with the offence of rape under **s1**, the absence of consent is an important part of the *actus reus* of assault by penetration and the absence of a reasonable belief in consent is an important part of the *mens rea*. The same definition of consent and rebuttable and irrebuttable presumptions discussed above, under **ss 74–76 Sexual Offences Act 2003**, apply.

Reflective question

Consider the law on consent discussed earlier in this chapter. In the following scenario consider if any conclusive or rebuttable presumptions regarding consent apply and, if so, what the consequences will be:

Frankie and Lewis are in a long-term relationship and live together in a flat in Leeds. One Saturday evening when out with their friends, Lewis orders soft drinks as he is driving to work the following morning. Whilst he is in the bathroom, Frankie orders a double shot of vodka and pours it into Lewis' drink and proceeds to do this again throughout the evening. When they get home, Lewis goes to lie down in the bedroom. Frankie comes in and proceeds to penetrate Lewis' anus with a plastic bottle.

The prosecution will also need to prove, as with rape, that the defendant intended to penetrate the complainant. As we have seen with examples such as ***Hill* [2006]** it is not necessary to establish that the defendant intended this penetration to be sexual.

8.4 Sexual assault

The offence of sexual assault is set out in **s3 SOA 2003**. Sexual assault does not require penetration, although in limited circumstances some penetrative acts might fall under the offence. It employs many of the same principles as seen above with rape and assault by penetration, applying where there is:

- Touching of another person.
- The touching is sexual.
- Without consent.
- And without a reasonable belief in consent.

As you might have noticed, this offence also shares many similarities with the offence of battery (see **Chapter 7**) with the additional requirement that the touching is sexual. Where it is not possible to establish this requirement, you may wish to consider whether a non-fatal offence against the person charge would be appropriate.

8.4.1 Sexual touching

Sexual assault applies the same **s78** definition of "sexual" as seen with the offence of assault by penetration. Unlike that offence, it is not necessary for the defendant to have penetrated the complainant, although penetration not amounting to assault by penetration or rape (such as oral penetration with something other than the defendant's penis) could be addressed as a sexual assault. In ***B* [2007]** it was acknowledged that "touching includes touching in various forms and in particular includes touching amounting to penetration". However, generally touching which does amount to penetration would arguably be better addressed through a **s1** or **s2** offence. Touching which does not amount to penetration is more likely to produce borderline cases requiring the application of **s78(b)** as seen in ***H* (Karl Anthony) [2005]**.

It is not necessary for the complainant to be aware that the touching has taken place in order for the offence to be established. In ***Bounekhla* [2006]** the defendant pressed up against the complainants whilst in nightclubs and proceeded to take his penis out of his trousers and ejaculate on them. Although they were not immediately aware that this had taken place, the offence was established as the touching, although through clothing, was sexual.

8.4.2 Consent and intention

Sexual assault applies the same **s74** definition and principles surrounding of **consent** discussed in relation to rape and sexual assault, above, including the rebuttable and irrebuttable presumptions surrounding consent found in **sections 75–76.**

The prosecution will also need to establish that the defendant intended to touch the complainant (***Heard* [2007]**), however, it is not necessary to establish the defendant's motivations for doing so. In ***Attorney-General's Reference No 1 of 2020* [2020]** the defendant kissed the complainant without her consent. Although both the prosecution and the defence agreed that a kiss could fall under the definition of sexual, the defendant argued that it was also necessary for the prosecution to prove that he intended the kiss to be sexual; something which he denied. The Court of Appeal rejected this argument. It is necessary for the prosecution to prove that the kiss *was* sexual, but it is not necessary for them to prove that the defendant intended it to be sexual.

8.5 Causing a person to engage in sexual activity without consent

The offence of causing a person to engage in sexual activity without consent in set out in **s4 SOA 2003.** In order to establish the offence, the prosecution will need to prove that the defendant:

- Caused another person to engage in an activity
- The activity was sexual
- Without consent
- Without a reasonable belief in consent
- With an intent to cause the complainant to engage in the activity.

8.5.1 Causing a person to engage in sexual activity

The **s4** offence requires the defendant to have caused the complainant to engage in sexual activity. As the explanatory notes to the **SOA 2003** explain, this covers a range of situations where the complainant engages in sexual activity with another person, performs a sexual act on another person, or performs a sexual act on themselves.[3] Both ***Devonald* [2008]** and ***B* [2013]** provide useful examples of the latter situation, involving defendants who caused complainants to engage in sexual acts on webcam. As with the other offences discussed here, the definition

3 Explanatory Notes to the Sexual Offences Act 2003, para 13.

of sexual for the purposes of this offence is based on the definition set out in **s78 SOA 2003**.

It is necessary for the defendant to have caused the complainant to have engaged in sexual activity. Whilst this requires more than mere encouragement, In many cases this will be satisfied through threats or coercive demands, as was seen in ***B* [2013]** where the defendant threatened to release intimate images of the complainant if she did not comply with the demands being made.

8.5.2 Consent and intention

As with the **s3** offence of sexual assault, it is not necessary for the defendant to intend the activity being performed to be sexual; instead *mens rea* for the offence consists of intent to cause the activity and the absence of a reasonable belief in consent. When assessing whether it was the defendant's intent, it will be important to consider the specific facts of the case alongside applying the principles of intent discussed in **Chapter 4**.

Similarly, whether the complainant was consenting will draw upon the definition found in **s74** and the presumptions related to consent, discussed above. In a similar manner to many of the other offences discussed here **s4(2)** specifies that "[w]hether a belief is reasonable is to be determined having regard to all the circumstances, including any steps A has taken to ascertain whether B consents".

8.6 Evaluation and reform

Throughout this chapter there have been several examples of the modernisation of the law on sexual offences implemented through the **Sexual Offences Act 2003**. There have also been statutory developments since 2003, including through legislation which has amended **SOA 2003**. This includes provisions within the **Online Safety Act 2023** which introduced additional offences addressing technologically facilitated sexual offending – such as "cyberflashing", now an offence under **s66A SOA 2003** – and the **Voyeurism (Offences) Act 2019**, which introduced additional offences relating to voyeurism, now found in **s67A SOA 2003**. Prior to the 2024 General Election, Parliament was considering the **Criminal Justice Bill (2024)** which would have made further amendments to the law in these and other areas covering sexual offending.

Significant developments can also be seen in in the cases, discussed above, which have considered the nature of consent in the context of sexual offences. Cases such as ***Assange* [2011]**, ***B* [2013]** and ***Lawrance* [2020]** have each sought to clarify the interpretation of aspects of **ss 74–76**. As these provisions apply across a range of offences found in **SOA 2003**, including the offences discussed in this chapter, the implications of these decisions can be far reaching.

As Simpson notes, the **SOA 2003** sought to provide additional clarity by defining the concept of consent within statute as is done in many other jurisdictions,[4] and subsequent case law has highlighted that these provisions should guide complex cases. In ***Lawrance,*** where the Court of Appeal was required to consider the limits of **s76** as they relate to deceptions connected to sexual activity, it was stressed that:

> *"Arguments about consent in cases of alleged sexual offending sometimes proceed on the assumption that the meaning of "consent" is a matter for development by the common law. That was the position in the nineteenth century when the seminal cases on impersonation and misconduct during medical examinations were decided. It is no longer the position because consent is defined in section 74 of the 2003 Act, with the evidential presumptions found in section 75 and the conclusive presumptions in section 76. Any novel circumstances must be considered by reference to the statutory definition, namely whether the alleged victim has agreed by choice and has the freedom and capacity to make that choice. There is no sign that Parliament intended a sea change in the meaning of consent when it legislated in 2003."*[5]

However, the different interpretations of what negates a complainant's freedom and capacity to make a choice across cases including ***Lawrance*** has been criticised for a lack of clarity notwithstanding that those cases engage with the statutory definition. Murray and Beattie, for example, argue that that the requirement that deceptions be "closely connected" to the nature or purpose of sexual activity in order to undermine consent misinterpret the **SOA 2003** and the focus on sexual autonomy which underpin the act; instead proposing that future reforms should restate the approach taken in ***McNally.***[6]

Others have suggested broader reform to the law on sexual offences. In a chapter of the Criminal Law Reform Now Network's *Reforming the Relationship between Sexual Consent, Deception and Mistake* report of 2023, Williams argues that "we should replace our existing sexual offence of rape and sexual assault with a series of offences of 'rape by stealth', 'rape by force', 'rape by fraud' and others, on the basis that, as with theft, robbery and burglary offences, it would enable greater clarity as well as more specific labelling of offenders.[7] Proposed reforms such as this raise a number of questions about the nature of sexual offending and the law's

---

4 Bethany Simpson, 'Why has the Concept of Consent Proven So Difficult to Clarify?' (2016) 80(2) Journal of Criminal Law 79, 99

5 R v Lawrance [2020]

6 Kyle L Murray and Tara Beattie, 'Conditional consent and sexual offences: revisiting the Sexual Offences Act 2003 after Lawrance' [2021] Criminal Law Review 556, 572-574

7 Rebecca Williams, 'Economic and Sexual Autonomy' in John Child (ed) *Reforming the Relationship between Sexual Consent, Deception and Mistake* (Criminal Law Reform Now Network Report, 2023) 108

response to it. On the one hand, legislation which establishes specific ways in which sexual offences can be committed is not unprecedented. In the United States of America, for example, the **California Civil Code § 1708.5(a)(4) (1872)** states that the non-consensual removal of a condom (often termed "stealthing") is one way in which a person can commit sexual battery. On the other hand, it has also been suggested that labels associated with rape do not always reflect the specific blameworthy behaviour perpetrated by a sexual offender, even though the law might seek to criminalise such behaviour.[8] The censuring aspect of a criminal conviction is especially important in the context of sexual offences, making these labels which are attached to offenders particularly significant.

Achieving clarification of the law, without risking overcriminalisation in an area of acutely serious offences presents significant challenges. Although some have welcomed the reforms achieved by **SOA 2003** as enabling a "common-sense balance to be struck";[9] others have raised concerns about the approach taken in some areas from a human rights perspective.[10] It has been argued that "there may be legislative solutions to mitigate against certain concerns, protecting against cases of racism, transphobia, or other discrimination" whilst enhancing the law so that it is clearer and more certain.[11] However, until such legislative solutions are forthcoming it will be necessary to look at the incremental development and reform of the law through the cases since 2003 when considering practicable ways of addressing concerns about sexual offending.

Activity

Suppose that you are a civil servant advising the newly appointed Home Secretary. Prepare a one-page summary of developments in the law on sexual offending since 2003 which the Home Secretary will need to be aware of ahead of their appearance at a select committee exploring potential reforms to the law.

8 Isabella Glendinning, 'Should Mistaken Consent Still Be Consent? In Defence of an Incremental Understanding of Consent in the Sexual Offences Act 2003' (2021) 85(3) Journal of Criminal Law 223, 225

9 Catarina Sjölin, 'Ten years on: Consent under the Sexual Offences Act 2003' (2015) 79(1) Journal of Criminal Law 20, 35

10 Alex Sharpe, 'European human rights law and the legality of sex offence prosecutions based on deceptions as to gender history' (2024) 44(4) Legal Studies 631

11 Ticiana Alencar, 'Conditional Consent and Sexual Crime: Time for Reform?' (2021) 85(6) Journal of Criminal Law 455, 464

8.7 Summary

This chapter has explored a number of offences created by the **Sexual Offences Act 2003** and the concepts which underpin them. The key points to take away from this chapter are:

- Consent is defined by **s74 Sexual Offences Act 2003** as where there is agreement, by choice and with the freedom and capacity to make that choice.
- In addition to the general **s74** definition, when determining whether a person is consenting, it is necessary to consider a number of rebuttable (**s75**) and irrebuttable (**s76**) presumptions which can determine the issue.
- Some offences require the defnedant's conduct to have been *sexual* in nature, conduct may be sexual because it is objectively sexual, whatever the context, or it may be sexual because the circumstances or somebody's purpose in respect of it make it so.
- Rape is an offence under **s1 Sexual Offences Act 2003** where a defendant intentionally penetrates the vagina, anus or mouth of another person, without their consent and without a reasonable belief in consent.
- **s2 Sexual Offences Act 2003** creates the offence of assault by penetration where a defendant intentionally penetrates the vagina or anus of another person (with something other than the defendant's penis) without the complainant's consent and without a reasonable belief in consent.
- Sexual assault is an offence under **s3 Sexual Offences Act 2003** where the defendant touches another person in a sexual manner, without the complainant's consent and without a reasonable belief in consent.
- **s4 Sexual Offences Act 2003** sets out the offence of causing another person to engage in sexual activity without consent. To be liable, the defendant must intentionally have caused another person to engage in an activity without consent and without the defendant reasonably believing that they were consenting.
- The **Sexual Offences Act 2003** represents a significant development in the law's response to sexual offending, however, it has also been critiqued for a lack of clarity and effectiveness.

Further reading

Bethany Simpson, "Why has the Concept of consent Proved so difficult to clarify?" (2016) *81 Journal of Criminal Law 417*

Kyle L Murray and Tara Beattie, "Conditional consent and sexual offences: revisiting the Sexual Offences Act 2003 after Lawrance" (2021) *Criminal Law Review 556*

Ticiana Alencar, "Conditional Consent and Sexual Crime: Time for Reform?" (2021) *85 Journal of Criminal Law 455*

Karl Laird, "Rapist or Rogue? Deception, Consent and the Sexual Offences Act 2003" (2014) *Criminal Law Review 492*

Cameron Giles and Hannah Bows, "Consent, Sexual Violence and the Law" in Chris Ashford and Alexander Maine (eds) *Gender, Sexuality and Law: A Textbook* (Edward Elgar 2024.

CHAPTER 9

Theft and related offences

9.1 Introduction

9.1.1 Theft and fraud

Chapter 8A and **8B** are very much overlapping in terms of themes. They both relate to property offences.

- **Chapter 9** focuses on theft and related offences. These usually involve D taking, attempting or preparing to take something from V.
- **Chapter 10** focuses on fraud. This usually involves D "conning" or deceiving V out of something or trying to "con" or deceive V out of something.

9.1.2 Criminal v civil law

The criminal law offences relating to theft and fraud do not operate in a legal vacuum. The Civil law concepts of ownership, possession, contract etc co-exist. In civil and criminal law these concepts are complex and evolving. In the civil law they mostly exist at "common law", i.e. through the incremental body of developing case law.

Commentators ideally want the civil and criminal concepts to operate in tandem. i.e. where the civil concept exists it is matched by the criminal concept. Unfortunately sometimes for good reasons the development of the property law aspects in criminal and civil cases is not always harmonious.

Many commentators criticise the criminal law for its policy drive to find wrongdoing sometimes to the cost of sound existing civil law legal principles. However when we see some of the examples one can see why the courts are reluctant to allow D who appears to have "taken" or "conned" V out of property to escape on what would seem to be a technicality. The technicality is often caused by charging the wrong offence. It is submitted the issue is less likely to emerge provided "taking" is charged under the **Theft Act 1968** and "conning" under the **Fraud Act 2006**.

9.1.3 Evolution

Until 1916, theft and fraud/deception were governed largely by common law offences.

From 1916–1968 what we now call theft was governed by enactments including the **Larceny Act 1916** and some retained common law. Terms such as "breaking and entering" were used and remain in common parlance even though that offence has been replaced by the less evocatively named offence of burglary.

Thankfully the Criminal Law Revision Committee (CLRC) reviewed and codified theft as an area of law. The august body mentioned in **Chapter 2** consisted of, amongst others, Professor Glanville Williams, Professor Rupert Cross and Professor Edward Griew. They produced their *Eighth Report: Theft and Related Offences* (Cmnd 2977, 1966).

It was a carefully thought-out precise piece of work which led to some arguably certain, clear and cogent legislation in the form of the **Theft Act 1968**. It simplified the law; structuring theft and fraud/deception-related offences and aligning the harm and culpability principles to avoid undue complexity; undue specificity and technicalities. It is submitted the CLRC paper and the statute are a model for how legislation can be drafted. The fact it remains force over 56 years later is a good indication of how successful it was at capturing successfully the wrongdoing.

9.1.4 Statute v case law

The statute is a carefully thought-out scheme. The statute is largely legally certain, legally clear, has sufficient breadth, labels accurately and fairly (e.g. thief, robber, burglar, handler) and does not trigger equality-based issues (save possibly regarding socio economic differentiation where corporations are less likely to be prosecuted than individual offenders). The amendments made to the **Theft Act 1968** and offences added by the **Theft Act 1978** covered small gaps in the statute exposed by precedents 1968–1977.

Unfortunately, the construction/interpretation of the case law on theft and deception has not always accorded with the aims of CLRC (particularly regarding appropriation). There is a considerable body of case law which has developed indicating the way in which the courts interpret the provisions of the act. There are often policy concerns which impact on the interpretation of the statute.

9.1.5 The approach to this chapter

Normally, as there is limited critique of the law in this area, students are assessed by way of a theft/fraud problem question. The two topics overlap so it is usually worth revising both fully. **Chapters 9** and **10** cover all major forms of offences. The main focus for assessments at most institutions is normally **s1–6 Theft Act 1968** and **s1–5 Fraud Act 2006**.

The chapter takes the approach of:

- maximum exposure to the Acts for awareness of the context and coverage;
- use of case law where it advances the principles on theft or fraud.

Aims of this chapter

By the end of this chapter you can expect to know and be able to evaluate the law on theft-related offending in criminal offences:

- The offence of theft (**s1 Theft Act 1968**)
- Property (P) (*actus reus*) (**s4 Theft Act 1968**)
- Belonging to another (BTA) (*actus reus*) (**s5 Theft Act 1968**)
- Appropriation (A) (*actus reus*) (**s3 Theft Act 1968**)
- Dishonesty (D) (*mens rea*) (**s2 Theft Act 1968**)

- Intention to permanently deprive (IPD) (*mens rea*) (**s6 Theft Act 1968**)
- Robbery (**s8 Theft Act 1968**)
- Burglary (**s9 Theft Act 1968**)
- Other theft-related offences
- Evaluation and reform

9.2 The offence of theft (s1 Theft Act 1968)

s1 Theft Act 1968 Basic definition of theft

(1) *A person is guilty of theft if he dishonestly appropriates property belonging to another with the intention of permanently depriving the other of it; and "thief" and "steal" shall be construed accordingly.*

(2) *It is immaterial whether the appropriation is made with a view to gain or is made for the thief's own benefit.*

(3) *The five following sections of this Act shall have effect as regards the interpretation and operation of this section (and, except as otherwise provided by this Act, shall apply only for purposes of this section).*

Commentary: Elements of theft

Actus reus

s4 *Property*	P	8.02
s5 *Belonging to another*	BTA	8.03
s3 *Appropriates*	A	8.04

Mens rea

s2 *Dishonestly*	D	8.05
s6 *With the intention of permanently depriving the other of it*	IPD	8.06

9.3 Property (P) (*Actus reus*) (s4 Theft Act 1968)

9.3.1 Statute

s4 Theft Act 1968 "Property"

(1) "Property" includes money and all other property, real or personal, including things in action and other intangible property.

(2) A person ***cannot steal land,*** *or things forming part of land and severed from it by him or by his directions,* ***except*** *in the following cases, that is to say—*

(a) when he is a ***trustee or personal representative****, or is authorised by power of attorney, or as liquidator of a company, or otherwise, to sell or dispose of land belonging to another, and he appropriates the land or anything forming part of it by dealing with it in breach of the confidence reposed in him; or*

(b) when he is ***not in possession of the land*** *and appropriates anything forming part of the land by severing it or causing it to be severed, or after it has been severed; or*

(c) when, ***being in possession of the land under a tenancy****, he appropriates the whole or part of any fixture or structure let to be used with the land.*

For purposes of this subsection "land" does not include incorporeal hereditaments; "tenancy" means a tenancy for years or any less period and includes an agreement for such a tenancy, but a person who after the end of a tenancy remains in possession as statutory tenant or otherwise is to be treated as having possession under the tenancy, and "let" shall be construed accordingly.

(3) A person who ***picks mushrooms growing wild on any land, or who picks flowers, fruit or foliage from a plant growing wild on any land, does not*** *(although not in possession of the land)* ***steal what he picks, unless he does it for reward or for sale or other commercial purpose****. For purposes of this subsection "mushroom" includes any fungus, and "plant" includes any shrub or tree.*

(4) ***Wild creatures, tamed or untamed, shall be regarded as property;*** *but a person* ***cannot steal a wild creature not tamed nor ordinarily kept in captivity, or the carcase of any such creature, unless either it has been reduced into possession*** *by or on behalf of another person and possession of it has not since been lost or abandoned, or another person is in course of reducing it into possession.*

9.3.2 What property can be stolen?

a) s4(1) Theft Act 1968, Property = Money and all other property

s4(1) '"Property" includes *money and all other property, real or personal, including things in action and other intangible property.*

Commentary

Most commonly this involved:

- Cash (***Velumyl* [1989]**)
- Drugs (***Smith* [2011]**) where the Court of Appeal held illegal drugs (heroin) are property so illegal drugs can be stolen.
- Moveable objects (e.g. phones, wallets, watches)
- Tickets (***Marshall* [1998]**) where D's collected London Underground Tickets from passengers exiting stations. D's received the tickets for free from passengers who "donated" them. D's then sold the tickets onto other members of the public seeking to travel on the tube at a reduced rate. This caused financial loss to the tube provider, what is now Transport for London.

Elemental analysis

Property	*P*	*YES*	*Physical ticket and chose in action*
Belonging to another	*BTA*	*YES*	*London Underground*
Appropriation	*A*	*YES*	*Assumed the rights of the owner*
Dishonesty	*D*	*YES*	*Knowing it was wrong*
Intention to permanently deprive	*IPD*	*YES*	*Of the chose in action*

The Court of Appeal unsurprisingly upheld the convictions. The re-sales of the ticket amounted to a disposal regardless of the owners' rights. When the traveller purchases the ticket, he contracts and there are rights on both sides. The right not to have the ticket resold was implied into the contract. The right to insist on the way the ticket is used. D's acted regardless of these rights.

The *obiter* was issuing an underground train ticket created a contract between customer and train operator.

"Therefore it is arguable, we suppose, that by the transaction ***each party has acquired a chose in action****.*

"On the side of the purchaser it is represented by a right to use the ticket to the extent which it allows travel on the underground system.

"On the side of [the operator] it encompasses the right to insist that the ticket is used by no one other than the purchaser.

"It is that right which is disregarded when the ticket is acquired by [D] and sold on."

b) s4(2) Theft Act 1968 Land

s4(2): *A person* ***cannot steal land,*** *or things forming part of land and severed from it by him or by his directions,* ***except*** *in the following cases, that is to say—*

(a) when he is a ***trustee or personal representative****, or is authorised by power of attorney, or as liquidator of a company, or otherwise, to sell or dispose of land belonging to another, and he* ***appropriates the land or anything forming part of it by dealing with it in breach of the confidence reposed in him****; or*

(b) when he is ***not in possession of the land*** *and appropriates* ***anything forming part of the land by severing it or causing it to be severed****, or after it has been severed; or*

(c) when, ***being in possession of the land under a tenancy****, he appropriates the whole or part of* ***any fixture or structure let to be used with the land****.*

For purposes of this subsection

"land" does not include incorporeal hereditaments;

"tenancy" means a tenancy for years or any less period and includes an agreement for such a tenancy, but a person who after the end of a tenancy remains in possession as statutory tenant or otherwise is to be treated as having possession under the tenancy, and

"let" shall be construed accordingly.

Commentary

(a) Trustee liability for acquiring/dealing with land in breach of confidence.

(b) Severing fixtures e.g. digging up trees or plants to remove. Picking fruit would not amount to theft.

(c) Tenant severing fixtures or moveable objects from the land, e.g. bathroom sink or bookshelves.

(c) s4(3) Theft Act 1968: mushrooms, flowers, fruit or foliage if done for commercial purpose.

s4(3): *A person who **picks mushrooms growing wild on any land, or who picks flowers, fruit or foliage from a plant growing wild on any land, does not** (although not in possession of the land) **steal what he picks, unless he does it for reward or for sale or other commercial purpose**. For purposes of this subsection "mushroom" includes any fungus, and "plant" includes any shrub or tree.*

Commentary

e.g. Jam makers who pick from hedgerows black berries (also known as bramble).

- Would it be ok if made into jam for home consumption? Yes
- Would it be ok if made into jam for a charity sale? Yes
- Would it be ok if made into jam for commercial sale? No it would not be OK unless given express permission.

d) s4(4) Theft Act 1968: Animals reduced into possession

s4(4): ***Wild creatures, tamed or untamed, shall be regarded as property;** but a person **cannot steal a wild creature not tamed nor ordinarily kept in captivity, or the carcase of any such creature, unless either it has been reduced into possession** by or on behalf of another person and possession of it has not since been lost or abandoned, or another person is in course of reducing it into possession.*

Commentary

There can be no theft of wild creatures.

There can be theft of a wild creature "reduced into possession".

9.3.3 What cannot be stolen?

a) Information

Information cannot be stolen. The leading case is ***Oxford v Moss* (1978)**, where D borrowed an exam paper and copied out the questions. D returned the physical exam paper. The Court of Appeal held this was **not** theft because information is not property. The reasoning appears to be that the other legislation regarding copyright covered this type of behaviour.

b) Services – see s11 Fraud Act 2006 for the offence

Previously obtaining services by deception. Now obtaining services dishonestly.

c) The human body and its products – unless skills and effort added.

The case of ***Sharp* (1857)** established the common law rule that there is *"No property in a corpse"*. This could be contrasted with the persuasive Austrialia precedent of ***Doodeward v Spence* (1907)**; in that case a body underwent a process of mummification. The court held where some *"skill & effort has been exercised"* to preserve a body the product can be property.

Griffiths J stated:

> *"…when a person has by the lawful exercise of work or skill dealt with a human body or part of a human body in his lawful possession that it has acquired some attributes differentiating it from a mere corpse awaiting burial, he acquires the right to retain possession."*

In the rather unusual case of ***Welsh* [1974]** D, a person detained for drink-driving, provided a urine sample to police. D was left alone and poured the sample down the sink. The Court of Appeal held D was properly convicted of perverting the course of justice and theft of the urine sample. The urine sample had as property somewhat ironically been "passed" to the police.

In ***Rothery* (1976)** another person detained for a road traffic offence this time stole their sample. This time it was a blood sample. It was held the blood had been reduced into possession.

In ***Kelly* [1999]** D took approximately 35 body parts from the Royal College of Surgeons. The Court of Appeal confirmed ***Doodeward*** [above] and upheld a conviction for theft. The court held normally there is no property in a corpse. However, where a corpse had undergone a process of the application of human skill designed to preserve it for medical or scientific examination it acquired value and became property.

> *"It may be that if … the question arises, the courts will hold that human body parts are capable of being property for the purposes of the [**s.4 Theft Act 1968**], even without the acquisition of different attributes, if they have a use or significance beyond their mere existence. This may be so if, for example, they are intended for use in an organ transplant operation, for the extraction of DNA or, for that matter, as an exhibit in a trial."*

In ***Yearworth v North Bristol NHS Trust* [2009]** the court *obiter* held a sperm donor could have property interests in their own stored sperm. Now **s5 Human Tissue Act 2004**, has specific offences regarding the improper and unauthorised use, storage or removal of human bodies, organs, and other tissue.

d) Electricity

In ***Low v Blease* (1975)** there was held to be no offence of theft of electricity because electricity is travelling on a circuit and returns to the same point. The court thus held electricity is not property as no intention to permanently deprive could be proved. Thus **s13 Theft Act 1968** is a separate offence of abstracting electricity.

9.4 Belonging to another (BTA) (*Actus reus*) (s5 Theft Act 1968)

9.4.1 Statute

s5 Theft Act 1968, *Belonging to another*

(1) *Property shall be regarded as* ***belonging to any person having possession or control of it or having in it any proprietary right or interest*** *(not being an equitable interest arising only from an agreement to transfer or grant an interest).*

(2) *Where property is* ***subject to a trust****, the persons to whom it belongs shall be regarded as* ***including any person having a right to enforce the trust****, and an intention to defeat the trust shall be regarded accordingly as an intention to deprive of the property any person having that right.*

(3) *Where a person* ***receives property from or on account of another*** *and is* ***under an obligation to the other to retain and deal with that property*** *or its proceeds in a particular way, the property or proceeds shall be regarded (as against him)* ***as belonging to the other****.*

(4) *Where a person* ***gets property by another's mistake*** *and is* ***under an obligation to make restoration (in whole or in part) of the property or its proceeds*** *or of the value thereof, then to the extent of that obligation the property or proceeds shall be regarded (as against him)* ***as belonging to the person entitled to restoration,*** *and an intention not to make restoration shall be regarded accordingly as an intention to deprive that person of the property or proceeds.*

(5) ***Property of a corporation sole shall be regarded as belonging to the corporation*** *notwithstanding a vacancy in the corporation.*

Commentary

Normally not a major issue.

e.g. Theft of an item from a shop. The items clearly belongs to another, namely the shop.

9.4.2 Property belonging to any person having possession, control or propriety right

s5(1): *Property shall be regarded as* ***belonging to any person having possession or control of it or having in it any proprietary right or interest*** *(not being an equitable interest arising only from an agreement to transfer or grant an interest).*

a) The owner need not be known but the indictment must be accurate

In ***Dyke and Munroe*** **[2001]** Ds collected and kept money for a charity. D's then stole the money. The charge was "... stole money belonging to person or persons unknown".

The Court of Appeal noted it is necessary to identify the person who owns the property. It quashed the conviction on the basis of the charge error, namely the money did belong to another, it belonged to the charity in question.

Lord Justice Henry, Para 8:

> *"So the collector of money from the public receives that money subject to the charitable trust and shall treat the money collected as belonging to the beneficiaries of that charity. Accordingly, in our judgment property in the money passes from the donor member of the public to the charity when that money is put in the collecting tin. It is then stolen by whoever acts in a way inconsistent with the charity's ownership of that money. But it is not stolen from the donor public - it was the charity's the moment it was placed in the collecting box."*

b) Possession may be sufficient

In ***Turner (No 2)*** **[1971]** D lodged his car with a garage for repairs. The garage completed repairs but D did not pay the bill. The garage had held on to the car for security. D drove the car away from the garage.

The Court of Appeal upheld the conviction on the basis D was rightly convicted of theft because the garage was the lawful possessor of the property.

Per Lord Parker CJ:

> *"There is no ground whatever for qualifying the words 'possession or control' in any way.*

It is sufficient if it is found that the person from whom the property is taken... was at the time in fact in possession or control."

N.B. Could now be charged with **s3 Theft Act 1978**, making off without payment.

c.f. ***Meredith* [1973]** where a custodian of goods has no right to retain them as against the owner there was no property BTA (custodian was police; owner retrieved car from police yard).

c) Lost property is owned and remains belonging to another

Hibbert v McKiernan [1948]

F: D found lost golf balls on a golf course and sold them

CAH: D was guilty of theft as the golf ball BTA namely the club.

Rostron [2003]

F D with others went onto a golf course at night and with diving apparatus dredged a lake for golf balls

Ch Theft

CAH: Conviction upheld

Golf balls BTA namely the golf club

Golf balls lying at the bottom of a lake may still belong to the club even if they don't intend to dredge the lake.

d) Abandoned Property is no longer belonging to another if clearly abandoned

Williams v Phillips (1957)

H Property left outside for the dustman is not abandoned

N.B. 1. May be abandoned if it has "please feel free to take me"

N.B. 2. Clear potential defence of lack of dishonesty.

R (Ricketts) v Basildon Magistrates' Court [2011]

F Donated items left by donees outside a charity shop

Q Were the items abandoned?

CAH No. Leaving outside a charity shop is not abandoning

The donee's ownership passes to the charity who now own from the point of donation.

e) Retaining a propriety interest

***Marshall*; *Coombes*; *Eren* [1998] – see above.**

F: D's collected London Underground Tickets from passengers exiting stations.

D's then sold the tickets onto other members of the public seeking to travel on the Tube.

CAH London Underground retained a propriety interest.

9.4.3 Trust obligation

s5(2) *Where property is **subject to a trust**, the persons to whom it belongs shall be regarded as **including any person having a right to enforce the trust**, and an intention to defeat the trust shall be regarded accordingly as an intention to deprive of the property any person having that right.*

AG's Ref (No. 1 of 1985) [1986]

F D pub landlord sold his own beer keeping a profit for himself.

V was the brewery who allowed him a tenancy.

CA *obiter*: In some circumstances D could have inadvertently created a constructive trust in relation to profits.

Shadrokh-Cigari (1988)

F: D was guardian of child who was paid $286k by the bank instead of $286.

D persuaded the child to sign authorities instructing the bank to issue bankers drafts in favour of D.

TJH: Conviction of theft because obtained drafts belonging to another (the bank)

CAH: Conviction upheld on two grounds:

1. **s5(2)** bank had created a constructive trust in favour of the bank; and

2. **s5(4)** a fundamental mistake of fact. D had obtained drafts as a result of the bank's mistake and was under an obligation to restore the property or its proceeds.

Re Holmes [2004]

CAH Where property was fraudulently obtained from V.
Proceeds of the fraud may become a constructive trust in V's favour and thus BT V.

9.4.4 Property received on account of another

s5(3): *Where a person* ***receives property from or on account of another*** *and is* ***under an obligation to the other to retain and deal with that property*** *or its proceeds in a particular way, the property or proceeds shall be regarded (as against him)* ***as belonging to the other****.*

Wilson **[1991]**:

CAH: 1. Where the person received the property on account which is legally binding AND

2. D knew there was a legal obligation to deal with the property in a particular way.

Per Farquharson LJ:

> *"Whether a person is under an obligation to deal with property in a particular way* ***can only be established by providing that he had knowledge of that obligation****.*
>
> ***Proof*** *that the* ***property was not dealt with in conformity with the obligation is not sufficient in itself****."*

In ***Arnold*** **[1997]** Potter LJ explained:

> *"****Section 5(3)*** *is in terms which cover property received from another under an obligation falling short of actual trusteeship. If it were not intended to go wider than what has gone before [i.e. s5(2)] it provisions would be* ***otiose****...."*

Breaks **[1998]** stated whether an "*obligation*" arises for the purposes of **s5(3)** or **s5(4)** is to be determined by the civil law, and the trial judge should direct the jury accordingly.

Examples

***Cullen* (1974)**. In this case D was V's lover. V gave D £20 to buy food for V. The court held D was correctly convicted of theft of V's £20 as D had dishonestly spent the money for her own purposes and was guilty.

In ***Hall* [1975]** D, a travel agent, was given a deposit and money for flights from V and others. D's business became insolvent, and no money was refunded. There was no contractual guarantee. D would spend the money on the flights/deposits.

The Court of Appeal held there was a breach of contract but no it was not theft because D was not obliged to spend the specific money on the tickets.

Per Edmund Davies LJ:

> *"Nevertheless, when a client goes to a firm carrying on the business of travel agents and pays them money, he expects that in return he will, in due course, receive the tickets and other documents necessary for him to accomplish the trip for which he is paying, and the firm are under an obligation to perform their part to fulfil his expectation and are liable to pay him damages if they do not.*
>
> *"But, in our judgement,* ***what was not here established*** *was that these* ***clients expected them to "retain and deal" with that property or its proceeds in a particular way****, and that an "obligation" to do so was undertaken by the appellant."*

In ***Davidge v Bunnett* [1984]** D's flatmates gave money for a communal gas bill. D spent the money. The Court of Appeal held D was guilty of theft. Money did not belong to D but BTA.

In ***Wain* [1995]** D was a charity accountant. D was permitted to transfer to his own account and the cheque bounced.

It was held under **s5(3)** D was under an obligation to retain at least the proceeds of the sums collected, if not the actual notes and coins.

The *obiter* stated the exact coins and notes given to D could be spent by him so long as he kept a separate fund for that amount as evidence that he was going to pay it.

Per McGowan LJ:

> *"... it seems to us that by virtue of* ***s5(3)****, [D] was plainly* ***under an obligation to retain, if not the actual notes and coins, at least their proceeds,*** *that is to say the money credited in the bank account which he opened for the trust with the actual property. When he took the money credited to that account and moved it over to his own bank account, it was still the proceeds of the notes and coins donated which he proceeded to use for his own purposes, thereby appropriating them.......****Whether a person*** *in the position of the appellant* ***is a***

__trustee__ is to be __judged on an objective basis__. It is an obligation imposed on him by law. It is not essential that he should have realised that he was a trustee, but of course the question remains as to whether he was acting honestly."[1]

9.4.5 Obligation to restore property obtained by mistake

s5(4):

Where a person __gets property by another's mistake__ and is __under an obligation to make restoration (in whole or in part) of the property or its proceeds__ or of the value thereof, then to the extent of that obligation the property or proceeds shall be regarded (as against him) __as belonging to the person entitled to restoration,__ and an intention not to make restoration shall be regarded accordingly as an intention to deprive that person of the property or proceeds.

Commentary

1. The obligation must be a legally enforceable one

In ***Gilks* [1972]** D backed bet on a horse called "Flying Scot".

V paid out £106.63 by mistake when "Flying Taff" won. D knew the mistake had been made.

Civil: V could not have sued under gaming law as it was not an enforceable debt.

Therefore D was only under a moral obligation.

CAH: Quashed the conviction. Obligation must be a *legally enforceable one.*

A purely moral obligation is not legally enforceable. This obligation is not that any property received should be retained in its original form, but that a separate fund, equal to the value of the property originally received, should be maintained.

Per Cairns J:

"In a criminal statute, where a person's criminal liability is made dependent on his having an obligation, it would be quite __wrong to construe that word so as to cover a moral or social obligation as distinct from a legal one.__"

2. Restitution is at the core of the obligation

***Attorney-General's Reference (No 1 of 1983)* [1985]**

1 Wain [1995]

F: Police Officer was overpaid. D was aware she had been overpaid.

D did nothing to notify V (the Metropolitan Police)

Ch: Theft

CAH: Theft if you do not return the money. D. had "got" a chose in action by mistake.

D was under an obligation to restore "the value" of the overpayment to her employer.

Per Lord Lane CJ: Restoration has the same meaning as restitution.

> *"...under the general principles of* ***restitution****, [D] was obliged to restore or pay for the benefit which she received. Generally speaking [D] in these circumstances [D] is obliged to pay for a benefit received when the benefit has been given under a mistake on the part of the giver as to a material fact. The mistake must be as to a fundamental or essential fact and the payment must have been due to that fundamental or essential fact...* ***there was a legal obligation upon [D] to restore that value to the Receiver when she found that the mistake had been made****."*[2]

3. Example, a pension is paid

***Gresham* [2003]**

F: Mother of D died. D continued to receive a pension from V (pension company) for 10 years.

Ch: Theft

CAH: Conviction upheld. D was under a **s5(4)** duty to return to V.

9.4.6 Corporation

s5(5): *Property of a corporation sole shall be regarded as belonging to the corporation* notwithstanding a vacancy in the corporation.

Commentary

A director can be guilty of theft from their own corporation.

2 Attorney-General's Reference (No 1 of 1983) [1985]

9.5 Appropriation (A) (*Actus reus*) (s3 Theft Act 1968)

9.5.1 Statute

s3 Theft Act 1968:

3.— "Appropriates"

'(1) ***Any assumption by a person of the rights of an owner*** *amounts to an appropriation, and this includes,* ***where he has come by the property (innocently or not) without stealing it****,* ***any later assumption of a right to it by keeping or dealing with it as owner****.*

(2) Where property or a right or interest in property is or purports to be **transferred for value to a person acting in good faith***, no later assumption by him of rights which he believed himself to be acquiring shall, by reason of any defect in the transferor's title, amount to theft of the property.*

9.5.2 Any assumption of the rights of an owner

s3(1):

Any assumption by a person of the rights of an owner *amounts to an appropriation, and this includes, where he has come by the property (innocently or not) without stealing it, any later assumption of a right to it by keeping or dealing with it as owner.*

e.g. Swapping price labels

***Morris* [1984]**

F: D1 swapping price labels in a supermarket to secure purchases at the lower price

D2 similar but detected before payment.

Ch: Theft

HLH: Swapping the price labels on goods was an appropriation.

Ds were assuming the rights of the owner to set the price of the goods.

Per Lord Roskill, who confirmed the statutory wording:

"... any assumption of any right of the owner..."

9.5.3 Examples of the rights

- **Destroying:** Smashing a plate

***Graham* [1997]**

Lord Bingham CJ:

> *"... the principle that theft of a chose in action may be committed when a chose in action belonging to another is destroyed by the defendant's act of appropriation."*

- **Eating:** Food
- **Offering for sale:**

Pitham and Hehl (1977)

F: D's bought stolen furniture from TP (the thief) & were collecting them from V's.

CAH: TP had stolen the furniture by offering it for sale even though not removed.

D could appropriate another's goods where he purported to sell them even though he was not in possession of the goods at that time.

P & H: Convicted of handling stolen goods.

- **Retaining**: Borrowing a library book and not returning.
- **Selling**: Selling someone else's property.
- **Taking**: Removing from a shop.

9.5.4 Purpose

The purpose of the offence is to protect V against D interfering with the enjoyment of his property.

9.5.5 Confirmation vitiated consent is not a full consent

Dobson v General Accident Fire and Life Assurance Corporation plc [1990]s

F: C brought a civil action for breach of contract against D (Insurance Co)

D refused to compensate C, a watch owner, under his household contents insurance for theft.

X had posed as bona fide purchaser.

X gave D a cheque which had been stolen.

C handed over the watch and went to bank D's cheque.

Ds refused to pay on the basis that it was not theft because there could have been no appropriation of the property since the owner had consented to the purchaser taking the items.

TJH: C was a V of theft.

CAH: Upheld TJ finding that X had stolen from C. It was a vitiated consent.

1. Ds were liable for breach of contract because C had only intended to pass property in the goods in return for a valid cheque.

2. Hence when C handed the goods that were handed to X, they were still property belonging to another as against him.

3. There could be an appropriation of C's property even if he appeared to consent to its being taken by another.

4. There was no need, in proving theft, to establish that the taking had been without the consent of the owner (confirming ***Lawrence***).

5. It was no defence for D to say property has passed under voidable contract.

9.5.6 D can appropriate even where he has V's consent

Lawrance v MPC [1972]

In this case V was an Italian student at Victoria Station requesting a taxi to Ladbroke Grove. The normal cost was 52p (approximately in post decimal equivalent). V gave D a £1 note. D said it was not enough. V then offered contents of his wallet to the taxi driver. D, the taxi driver, took another £6. D was charged with theft of £6.48. V had not intended to overpay. D stated V's consent authorised the appropriation.

D claimed, I am dishonest but the offence should be obtaining by deception because V allowed D to take the money.

HLH: *D can appropriate even though V (the owner) consents.* Upheld conviction notwithstanding V consented to D appropriating the excess £6.48.

Per Viscount Dilhorne:

> *"I see no ground for concluding that the* ***omission of the words "without the consent of the owner" was*** *inadvertent and not* ***deliberate****, and to read the subsection as if they were included is, in my opinion, wholly unwarranted.* ***Parliament by the omission of these words has relieved the prosecution of the burden of establishing that the taking was without the owner's consent. That is no longer an ingredient of the offence."***[3]

***Gomez* [1993]**

F: D was assistant manager of a shop.

D persuaded V, the manager of the shop, to accept X (a third party) two stolen cheques.

V was told the cheques were "as good as cash". V accepted the cheques.

D and X obtained £17,000 worth of electrical goods.

Therefore goods were freely given to D.

Ch: Theft

N.B. Now the better charge would be what is now **Fraud Act 2006, s2 Fraud by False Representation** (see **Chapter 10**). X & D made a false representation, knowing it was false and with intention to cause gain to themselves and loss to another.

The transfer of goods was with a vitiated consent.

HL: Question:

"When theft is alleged and that which is alleged to be stolen passes to D with the consent of the V, ***but that [consent] has been obtained by a false representation****,*

Has.

(a) an appropriation *... taken place?* **OR**

(b) must such a passing of property necessarily involve an element of adverse interference *with or usurpation of some right of the owner?"*

HLH: 4:1 Conviction upheld

1. YES, you can appropriate with the owner's consent.

3 Lawrence v Metropolitan Police Commissioner [1972]

2. **D *appropriates* property as soon as he does any act which amounts to the assumption of the rights of an owner, whether or not V has permitted D to take the goods**.

3. Per Lord Keith: ***Lawrence**, good law you can steal with consent.

"There is no material distinction between the facts in ***Dobson** *and those in the present case. In each case the* ***owner of the goods was induced by fraud to part with them to the rogue****. Lawrence makes it clear that consent to or authorisation by the owner of the taking by the rogue is irrelevant...*

Lawrence also makes it clear that it is no less irrelevant that what happened may also have constituted the offence [now replaced by Fraud Act 2006, s.2 Fraud by False Representation]."

4. Per Lord Keith, CLRC Report dismissed:

"In my opinion it serves ***no useful purpose*** *at the present time to seek to construe the relevant provisions of the Theft Act* ***by reference to the report which preceded*** *it, namely the Eighth Report of the Criminal Law Revision Committee on Theft and Related Offences (1966) (Cmnd 2977)."*

5. Contrast Lord Lowry (dissenting): Important to distinguish theft and deception:

"In my opinion, any attempt to reconcile the statement of principle in Lawrence and Morris is a complete waste of time...

[I]t is clear that, whether they succeeded or not, ***both the Criminal Law Revision Committee and the draftsman must have intended to give the word one meaning****, which would be the same in the Act as in the committee's report***.**

To simplify the law, *where possible,* ***is a worthy objective but****, my Lords, I maintain that* ***the law, as envisaged in the report, is simple enough****:* ***there is no problem*** *(and there would have been none in* ***Lawrence, Morris,*** *and the present case)* ***if one prosecutes under*** *[now replaced by Fraud Act 2006, s.2 Fraud by False Representation] all offenders involving obtaining by deception and prosecutes theft in general."*

Commentary: Academics roundly criticise this authority on numerous grounds

1. **CLRC*:*** The decision does not accord the majority view of the CLRC.
2. **Decision is too broad brush and lacks "*animus appropriendi*":** Every acquisition in a supermarket trolley is "appropriation" for criminal law. This is too broad and lacks obvious mental element.
3. **Civil:** This means there is a different test in the civil jurisdiction to that in the criminal jurisdiction.

4. Theft v Fraud: There is now no real distinction between theft and fraud.

If the gravamen of theft is taking property and the gravamen of fraud "conning" or "deceiving", why bother having two separate bodies of law?

9.5.7 Receipt of an indefeasible gift is capable of amounting to appropriation

***Hinks* [2001]**:

F: D befriended V a man with a limited intelligence.

D persuaded V to transfer £60,000 to D's account.

Ch: Theft.

D: He gave me them as gifts

HLQ: Could the acquisition of an indefeasible title to property be capable of amounting to an appropriation of property belonging to another?

HLH: (3:2) YES, the conviction was upheld and theft made out.

1.D can appropriate even though there is a complete and valid transfer of property at civil law and the owner consented.

2.Lord Steyn: "***appropriation****' was a* ***neutral word*** *comprehending 'any assumption by a person of the rights of an owner' was wide enough to encompass gift situations & could be looked at in isolation."*

Note

1. Civil law: Hinks owns the money.

2. Criminal law: Hinks is a thief.

Commentary

1. CLRC argument

Professor John C Smith in **[1998]** at 905 quoted from a memorandum written by the draftsman of the **1968 Act** to the Larceny Sub-Committee of the Criminal Law Revision Committee. The memorandum stated

"I trust the Sub-Committee will not agree with ***Dr [Glanville] Williams when he says....... that a person appropriates for himself property of which another person is the owner every time he gratefully accepts a gift or buys an apple***. If this is what the words mean, then the whole language of the clause ought to be changed, because ***one really cannot have a definition of stealing which relies on the word "dishonestly" to prevent it covering every acquisition of property.***"

Lord Steyn dismissed this as:

"... an interesting bit of legal history.... not relevant to the question before the House."[4]

Instead he relied upon Lord Reid's observations in ***Black-Clawson International Ltd v Papierwerke WAA.G.*** **[1975]** (at p613), where Lord Reid observed that:

"We often say that we are looking for the intention of Parliament, but that is not quite accurate. ***We are seeking the meaning of the words which Parliament used****. We are seeking not what Parliament meant but the true meaning of what they said.*

"...to delve into the intentions of individual members of the Committee, and their communications, would be to ***rely on material which cannot conceivably be relevant****. If statutory interpretation is to be a rational and coherent process a line has to be drawn somewhere. And what Mr. Fiennes [the draftsman of the Theft Act] wrote to the Larceny Sub-Committee was demonstrably on the wrong side of the line."*[5]

2. Conflict between the civil law and the criminal law

Lord Steyn (at 252-253) conceded that there was undoubtedly a conflict between the civil and criminal law although he added that the question did not arise for a decision on the facts. He noted:

*"...****The purposes of the civil law and the criminal law are somewhat different.*** *In theory the two systems should be in perfect harmony. In a practical world there will sometimes be some disharmony between the two systems. In any event, it would be wrong to assume on a priori grounds that the criminal law rather than the civil law is defective. Given the jury's conclusions, one is entitled to observe that [D's]* ***conduct should constitute theft, the only available charge****. The tension between the civil and the criminal law is therefore not in my view a factor which justifies a departure from the law as stated in*

4 Hinks [2001]
5 Hinks [2001]

Lawrence and Gomez. Moreover, these decisions of the House have a marked beneficial consequence. While in some contexts of the law of theft a judge cannot avoid explaining civil law concepts to a jury ...the decisions of the House of Lords eliminate the need for such explanations in respect of appropriation. That is a great advantage in an overly complex corner of the law."

Lord Hobhouse (dissenting) stated too much weight was then placed on dishonesty.

He was "*concerned at the prospect of a criminal conviction based upon conduct*":

> *"....* ***which involves no inherent illegality and may only be capable of being criticised on grounds of lack of morality*** *[i.e. it is dishonest] .... [t]his approach itself raises fundamental questions. An essential function of the criminal law is* ***to define the boundary between what conduct is criminal and what merely immoral****. Both are the subject of the disapprobation of ordinary right-thinking citizens and the distinction is liable to be arbitrary or at least strongly influenced by considerations subjective to the individual members of the tribunal. To treat otherwise lawful conduct as criminal merely because it is open to such disapprobation would be contrary to principle and open to the objection that it fails to achieve the objective and transparent certainty required of the criminal law by the principles basic to human rights.*[6]
>
> *"The truth is that* ***theft is a crime which relates to civil property and, inevitably, property concepts from the civil law have to be used*** *and questions answered by reference to that law....... the [1968] Act at times expressly requires civil law concepts to be applied. Section 1(1) uses the expression "belonging to another". Thus, in some criminal cases, it may be necessary to determine whether the relevant property belonged to the alleged victim or to the defendant."*[7]

3. **Dishonestly appropriates** should be construed as a composite phrase.

Per Lord Hobhouse at 266-267:

> *"Once the donor has done his part in transferring the property to the defendant, the property, [subject to s.5 of the Theft Act 1968]* ***ceases to be "property belonging to another"****. However wide a* ***meaning one were to give to "appropriates", there cannot be a theft.... The donee is not "assuming the rights of an owner": she has them already****."*

---

6 Hinks [2001]
7 Hinks [2001]

9.5.8 Later assumption of right of an owner

This covers the common situation of appropriation followed a later assumption of a right of an owner by keeping or dealing with it.

e.g. Finding a wallet:

- At the time: Intention to hand it in
- Later: Aware it is wrong to retain but do retain it and at this later point intend to permanently deprive.

***Atakpu* [1994]**

F: Ds had hired cars in Germany using false documents.

D's were detained at Customs in UK.

D's were charged with conspiring to steal the cars.

Q: 1. Could property that had been appropriated by D be "*appropriated again*" each time he assumed the right of the owner? AND

2. Was appropriation a "*continuous act*"?

CAH: Appealed successfully, based on the theft being outside the jurisdiction.

1. Applying **Gomez** – the appropriation of the cars took place in Germany even though the hire company was deceived into parting with the possession of them, and they had been stolen outside the jurisdiction.

2. Theft was complete in Europe before they returned. Therefore they were "*no longer in the course of stealing*".

3. "*Continuous Act*": It should be left to the jury to test whether or not D's was still "*on the job*" but on these facts theft was a finite act and ended outside the jurisdiction.

Per Ward J:

"*...it would seem.*

(1) theft can occur in an ***instant by a single appropriation,*** *but it* ***can also involve a course of dealing*** *with property lasting longer and involving several appropriations before the transaction is complete;*

(2) **theft is a finite act-it** has a **beginning, and it has an end**;

(3) at what ***point the transaction is complete*** *is a* ***matter for the jury*** *to decide upon the facts of each case;*

(4) though there may be several appropriations in the course of a single theft or several appropriations of different goods each constituting a separate theft... ***no case suggests that there can be successive thefts of the same property*** *(assuming of course that possession is constant and not lost or abandoned, later to be assumed again)."*

9.6 Dishonesty (D) (*Mens rea*) (s2 Theft Act 1968)

9.6.1 The statute

2. "Dishonestly"

(1) A person's appropriation of property belonging to another is ***not*** *to be regarded as dishonest—*

(a) if he appropriates the property ***in the belief that he has in law the right to deprive the other of it****, on behalf of himself or of a third person; or*

(b) if he appropriates the property ***in the belief that he would have the other's consent*** *if the other knew of the appropriation and the circumstances of it; or*

(c) (except where the property came to him as trustee or personal representative) if he appropriates the property in the belief that ***the person to whom the property belongs cannot be discovered by taking reasonable steps.***

(2) A person's appropriation of property belonging to another may be dishonest ***notwithstanding that he is willing to pay for the property.***

Commentary

1. Positive: It is strange there is no statutory positive definition of what is dishonesty.

The Dictionary definition is: [8]

"dishonest

3. Of conduct, a statement, ...not straightforward or honourable; ...fraudulent, of the nature or involving theft, lying, or cheating"

8 Angus Stevenson (ed), *Shorter Oxford English Dictionary* (6th edn, OUP 2007)

"dishonesty

4. Lack of integrity or straightforwardness; spec. willingness to steal, cheat, lie or act fraudulently"

2. **Negative:** The statute only offers a negative definition of what is **not** dishonesty - see **s2(1)(a),(b),(c).**

3. **For (1)(a),(b),(c) there is no requirement that the belief is reasonable**.

As long as the belief is honestly held that will be sufficient (***Holden*** **[1991]**).

However the more unreasonable the belief the less likely a jury are to believe it.

4. **The test is subjective:** D's belief must be honestly held but need not be reasonably held (***A-G's Reference (No 2 of 1982)*** **[1984]**).

5. The prosecution must prove beyond reasonable doubt D did not so believe:

a) ***"if he appropriates the property in the belief that he has in law the right to deprive the other of it, on behalf of himself or of a third person; or***

 1. Claim of right defence: *"I thought I had the legal right to..."*
 2. Examples

  i. Where you take a coat mistakenly thinking it is your own.
  ii. Thinking you have the right to take things out of a skip; golf balls from the golf club rough/lake.
  iii. Civil debt rights

Robinson [1977]

"F D thought he had a right in law to reclaim a sum owed.

H The belief must be a legal not a mere moral belief."

3. The test is subjective: What D honestly believes, i.e. if D honestly believes he has a right to keep it – he is not dishonest.

b) ***if he appropriates the property in the belief that he would have the other's consent if the other knew of the appropriation and the circumstances of it; or***

 1. **Claim of consent defence:** *"I thought the owner would have consent in the circumstances."*

2. Examples

i. Borrowing a family members clothes.

ii. Taking a cigarette without asking – implied by previous occasions.

iii. Emergency, such as a fire, and you take neighbour's extinguisher to put out the fire.

iv. Borrowing your employer's van for the weekend.

3. The test is subjective: *Holden* [1991]

F: D thought he had V's consent to take scrap tyres.

CAH: Not guilty. Belief need only be honest and need not be reasonable.

c) *"... if he appropriates the property in the belief that the person to whom the property belongs cannot be discovered by taking reasonable steps."*

1. **Claim of inability to discover the owner:** *"I thought I would not be able to discover the owner..."*

2. **Examples**

i. Finding £10 in the street P: YES; BTA: YES – assuming lost not abandoned; A: YES; IPD: YES; D?

Belief "finders keepers".

ii. Finding a pen – as above.

iii. C.f. Finding a wallet with details which identify V.

3. **Reasonable** depends upon the nature of the property and circumstances.

4. **Identifiability**: the more unique the less able D is to use this defence.

d) *"A person's appropriation of property belonging to another may be dishonest notwithstanding that he is willing to pay for the property."*

- Willingness to pay is **irrelevant**: E.g. Take your neighbour's milk bottles and leave £1 or £10 in replacement through their letter box!

P:	Yes
BTA:	Yes

A: Yes

D:

a) Law? NO; b) Consent? No; C) Discover? No

IPD: Using up

9.6.2 Common law

In most cases, where the actions are obviously dishonest by ordinary standards, there will be no doubt about it. It will be obvious that the defendant himself knew that he was acting dishonestly. In practice, it is very rarely necessary to use this test and judges were very reluctant to use it due to its complexity and perhaps over generous indulgence for a dishonest defendant who states: "I did not know what I was doing was wrong by other people's standards."

***Ivey v Genting Casinos (UK) Ltd* [2018]**

F: C (A professional gambler) claimed against D (a casino).

C claimed he was entitled to winnings of £7.7 m.

D responded that C had cheated and was not eligible.

The card game of chance was called Punto Banco.

C (the gambler) used the technique of "edge-sorting", which relied on noting tiny physical differences in the edges of the cards.

C had claimed to be to be superstitious and persuaded the croupier to use the same pack of cards and to turn "lucky" cards around, enabling him to use the technique.

This technique increased his odds of winning.

C stated he believed edge-sorting was an honest technique.

C sued for his winnings.

TJH: 1. (Subjective) Accepted C was genuinely convinced that what he had done was not cheating.

2. (Objective) But on a reasonable person's terms C was cheating.

3. C had thus breached the implied term against cheating in his contract with the casino and was not eligible to receive the prize.

C: C argued that the test of what was cheating was the same for the implied term as for the criminal offence of cheating at gambling in **s42 Gambling**

Act 2005, and that cheating necessarily involved dishonesty, which had not been demonstrated in his case.

CAH: Refused the appeal

SCH: C's conduct was objectively dishonest.

The test of dishonesty is as set out by by Lord Hoffmann in ***Barlow Clowes International Ltd v Eurotrust International Ltd* [2006]**:

"The standard by which the law determines ... [dishonesty] is objective. If by ordinary standards Ds mental state would be characterised as dishonest, it is irrelevant that D judges by different standards."

When dishonesty is in question the fact-finding tribunal must [Apply the two stage test].

[1] Subjective Test – D's state of mind (as a matter of evidence)

Ascertain (subjectively) the actual state of [D's] knowledge or belief as to the facts.

The reasonableness or otherwise of his belief is a matter of evidence (often in practice determinative) going to whether he held the belief, but it is **not** an additional requirement that his belief must be reasonable; **the question is whether it is genuinely held**.

[2] Objective Test – Objective standards of ordinary decent people

"... the question whether his conduct was honest or dishonest is to be determined by the factfinder by **applying the (objective) standards of ordinary decent people.**"

There is no requirement that [D] must appreciate that what he has done is, by those standards, dishonest.

[76] **Lord Hughes in *Ivey* identified the advantages of the *Ivey* test:**

"**1. Legal Certainty:** Pre-Theft Act 1968 position was confirmed by **Ivey**

2. Legal Clarity: It is clearer for the Jury

3. *Breadth and Objectivity:* *Gives legitimacy to the verdict rather than D being able to say their own bizarre view was it was not dishonest i.e.*

[58] '[Under the old law] the less [D's] standards conform to what society in general expects, the less likely he is to be held criminally responsible for his behaviour'

[59] 'There is no reason why the law should excuse those who make a mistake about what contemporary standards of honesty are, whether in the context of insurance claims, high finance, market manipulation or tax

evasion. The law does not, in principle, excuse those whose standards are criminal by the benchmarks set by society, nor ought it to do so."

4. **Civil and Criminal test now aligned**.

***Barton* [2021]**

CAH: Confirmed ***Ivey*** is applicable and thus there is a two-stage test

1. Subjective: What D believed the facts to be?
2. Objective: Whether the conduct of D on the facts they believed to be is dishonest by the standards of ordinary decent people?

Lord Burnett CJ [104]:

> *"Where the Supreme Court itself directs that an otherwise binding decision of the Court of Appeal should no longer be followed and proposes an alternative test that it says must be adopted, the Court of Appeal is bound to follow what amounts to a direction from the Supreme Court even though it is strictly obiter. To that limited extent the ordinary rules of precedent (or stare decisis) have been modified. We emphasise that this limited modification is confined to cases in which all the judges in the appeal in question in the Supreme Court agree that to be the effect of the decision."*

9.7 Intention to permanently deprive

9.7.1 Statute

s6 Theft Act 1968 includes in the *mens rea* intention to permanently deprive (IPD): *With the intention of permanently depriving the other of it*

(1) A person appropriating property belonging to another without meaning the other permanently to lose the thing itself is nevertheless to be regarded as having the intention of permanently depriving the other of it ***if his intention is to treat the thing as his own to dispose of regardless of the other's rights****; and* ***a borrowing or lending of it may amount to so treating it if, but only if, the borrowing or lending is for a period and in circumstances making it equivalent to an outright taking or disposal.***

(2) Without prejudice to the generality of subsection (1) above, ***where a person, having possession or control*** *(lawfully or not)* ***of property belonging***

to another, parts with the property under a condition as to its return which he may not be able to perform**, this (if done for purposes of his own and without the other's authority) **amounts to treating the property as his own to dispose of regardless of the other's rights.

9.7.2 Treat the thing as his own

s6(1): *if his intention is to treat the thing as his own to dispose of regardless of the other's rights.*

***Vinall* [2011]**
Pitchford LJ [16]:

> *"What section 6(1) requires is a state of mind in the defendant which Parliament regards as the equivalent of an intention permanently to deprive ... [It] does not require that the thing has been disposed of, nor does it require that the defendant intends to dispose of the thing in any particular way. No doubt evidence of a particular disposal or a particular intention to dispose of the thing will constitute evidence of the defendant's state of mind but it is, in our view, for the jury to decide upon the circumstances proved whether the defendant harboured the statutory intention."*

1. Cash

Velumyl [1989]

F: D took money intending to return equivalent (not the same money) the next day.

CAH: IPD because had no intention of returning the same notes or coins.

Bagshaw [1988]

CAH: Borrowing gas cylinders = theft because the virtue of cylinders would be gone.

Cahill [1993]

F: D as a joke moved V's newspaper to another house.

CAH: Required something more final such as selling. "To dispose of" implied getting rid of the property by destroying or selling it.

c.f. DPP v Lavender [1994]

F: D had taken two doors from council property undergoing repair.

D used them to replace damaged doors at his girlfriend's flat.

D's girlfriends flat was a council property under a tenancy.

D: No IPD.

Q: Did D have IPD?

HCH: Yes, IPD as D had acted regardless of the council's rights

Professor Sir John Smith QC: Critical of the decision on the basis there was no disposal.

Mitchell [2008]

F: D took V's car.

V's car was not damaged but was abandoned.

CAH: Allowed the appeal. Abandoning the car with the hazard lights on made it likely the car would be reverted to V. Thus no IPD

2. Indictments should be drafted carefully to have sufficient breadth to avoid technicalities

AG's Refs (Nos. 1 & 2 of 1979) [1980]

Roskill LJ at 194:

> *"We see no reason in principle why ... a more imprecise method of criminal pleading should not be adopted ... as for example attempting to steal some or all of the contents of a car or some or all of the contents of a handbag."*

e.g. Easom [1971]

F: D reviewed a handbag.

D realised it contained nothing of value and placed it down.

Ch: Theft of handbag and specified contents.

CAH: Conviction quashed no evidence IPD

AGB: Better charge attempted theft?

3. Professionals

Fernandes [1996]

F: Solicitor transferred clients' money into an unauthorised investment.

CAH: Upheld conviction because someone who "deals" with property, knowing that he is doing so in such a way that he is risking losing it has IPD.

Auld LJ at 176:

> *"...**[the]** critical notion...is whether a D intended "to treat the thing as his own to dispose of regardless of the other's rights"."*

9.7.3 Borrowing

s6(1): *.... a borrowing or lending of it may amount to so treating it if, but only if, the borrowing or lending is for a period and in circumstances making it equivalent to an outright taking or disposal.*

Covers used tickets

***Marshall; Coombes; Eren* [1998] – see above**

F: D's collected London Underground Tickets from passengers exiting stations.

CA: Clear IPD

***DPP v SJ, PI, RC* [2002]**: Borrowed and snapped headphones is IPD.

Covers "kidnapping" property e.g. "I have your watch but will not return it unless you give me £100". Lord Lane confirmed this was IPD:

> *"[the] first part of section 6(1) seems to us to be aimed at the sort of case where a defendant takes things and then offers them back to the owner for the owner to buy if he wishes. If the taker intends to return them to the owner only on such payment, then, on the wording of section 6(1), that is deemed to amount to the necessary intention permanently to deprive."*

(Appears confirmed in ***Raphael and another* [2008]**)

Does not cover borrowing; use and return of film stock without diminution of value

***Lloyd, Bhuee and Ali* [1985]**

F: D projectionist took films home.

D and others copied the film and made "pirate copies".

D returned the film a few hours later with no loss of revenue or usability.

CAH: Conviction quashed. No IPD. This was not outright taking and there had been no decrease in value of the goods of the owner.

Per Lord Lane CJ:

> *"section 6 should be referred to in exceptional cases only. In the vast majority of cases it need not be referred to or considered at all.*
>
> *"It must mean, if nothing else, that there are circumstances in which a defendant may be deemed to have the intention permanently to deprive, even though he may intend the owner eventually to get back the object which has been taken.*
>
> *"Borrowing is ex hypothesi not something which is done with an intention permanently to deprive. This half of the subsection, we believe, is intended to make it clear that* ***a mere borrowing is never enough to constitute the necessary guilty mind.***
>
> ***"UNLESS the intention is to return the "thing" in such a changed state that it can truly be said that all its goodness or virtue has gone...***
>
> *"[T]hat being the case, we turn to inquire whether the feature films in this case can fall within that category. Our view is that they cannot.*
>
> *"The goodness, the virtue, the practical value of the films to the owners has not gone out of the article. The film could still be projected to paying audiences, and, had everything gone according to the conspirators' plans, would have been projected in the ordinary way to audiences at the Odeon Cinema, Barking, who would have paid for their seats. Our view is that those particular films which were the subject of this alleged conspiracy had not themselves diminished in value at all....*
>
> *"[T]hat borrowing, it seems to us, was not for a period, or in such circumstances, as made it equivalent to an outright taking or disposal. There was still virtue in the film."*

e.g. **The *"using up"* value principle**

9.7.4 Gambling or pawning

s6(2): *...where a person, having possession or control (lawfully or not) of property belonging to another, parts with the property under a condition as to its return which he may not be able to perform, this (if done for purposes of his own and without the other's authority) amounts to treating the property as his own to dispose of regardless of the other's rights.*

Commentary

Thus a husband pawning his wife's wedding ring hoping to redeem but not knowing if it would be possible would have IPD.

9.8 Robbery

9.8.1 Statute

s8 Theft Act 1968

(1) *A person is guilty of robbery if he steals, and immediately before or at the time of doing so, and in order to do so, he uses force on any person or puts or seeks to put any person in fear of being then and there subjected to force.*

(2) *A person guilty of robbery, or of an assault with intent to rob, shall on conviction on indictment be liable to imprisonment for life.*

- **Robbery** is essentially an **aggravated form of theft**.
- The aggravating factor being the use of force on the victim, or *threats of force* (violence) made prior to or during the theft.

9.8.2 The elements of theft must be made out

***Robinson* [1977]**

F: D threatened V with a knife to get money he was owed.

He honestly thought he had a legal right to the money.

H: Honest belief, T4 not dishonest and it was not theft and hence NOT robbery (it was assault).

Within **s2(1)(a) TA 1968.**

***Corcoran v Anderton* (1980)**

QBH: Appeal dismissed on grounds that even though V was only momentarily dispossessed of the property, where D tugged her bag causing her to fall to the ground "*there was appropriation accompanied by force*".

Per Watkins J:

> *"..... I think that an "**appropriation" takes place when [D] snatches a woman's handbag completely from her grasp**, so that she no longer has physical control over it because it has...fallen to the ground...the forcible tugging of the handbag itself could in the circumstances be a sufficient exercise of control by [D] so as to amount to an assumption by him of the rights of the owner, [& T4] an appropriation of the property."*

9.8.3 "... uses force on any person."

***Dawson* [1976]**

F: D was pickpocket who merely jostled V's in order to pick their pockets.

H: G "*Any amount of force*" will do, including just threats (e.g. raising your fist and asking for money). The question of whether or not force has been used should be left to the jury.

Lawton LJ: "*...Whether there is any difference between 'violence' or 'force' is not relevant for the purposes of this case; but the word is 'force'. It is a word in ordinary use. It is a word which juries understand.*"

▶ *"any person"* Sufficient to use force on V's possessions e.g.

***Clouden* [1987]**

Handbag

OD: Snatching without resistance should not amount to robbery – Q should be left to the jury.

***P v DPP* [2012]**

HCH: D snatching a cigarette was not sufficient force for a robbery

9.8.4 "...or puts or seeks to put any person in fear of being then and there subjected to force..."

No need for physical contact.

***B v DPP* [2008]**

It does not matter if D was actually in fear.

9.8.5 "...before or at the time of ...stealing"

Theft is a continuous act and the jury decides when it finishes.

***Hale* (1978)**

F: D1 & D2 broke into V house.

Ch: Robbery

CAH: Appropriation could be a continuing act.

The point at which it ceased was to be determined by the jury on the facts of each case.

Per Eveleigh LJ:

> *".... the act of appropriation does not suddenly cease. It is a continuous act, and it is a matter for the jury to decide whether or not the act of appropriation has finished."*

***Atakpu* [1994] QB 69 – See above**

***Lockley* [1995]**

H: Included violence used after the threat in order to restrain the V and aid get-away. This is where the "*violence is used as part of the process of the theft*".

9.8.6 *"...in order to do so [i.e. steal] ...."*

***Shendley* [1970]**

H: No such thing as a robbery without violence.

9.9 Burglary

9.9.1 Statute

s9 Theft Act 1968

(1) A person is guilty of burglary if—

(a) he enters any building or part of a building as a trespasser and ***with intent*** *to commit any such offence as is mentioned in subsection (2) below; or*

(b) ***having entered*** *any building or part of a building as a trespasser* ***he steals*** *or attempts to steal anything in the building or that part of it* ***or*** *inflicts or attempts to inflict on any person therein any grievous bodily harm.*

(2) *The offences referred to in subsection (1) (a) above are offences of stealing anything in the building or part of a building in question, of inflicting on any person therein any grievous bodily harm [...]1 therein, and of doing unlawful damage to the building or anything therein.*

(3) *A person guilty of burglary shall on conviction on indictment be liable to imprisonment for a term not exceeding—*

(a) *where the offence was committed in respect of a building or part of a building which is a dwelling, fourteen years;*

(b) *in any other case, ten years.*

(4) *References in subsections (1) and (2) above to a building, and the reference in subsection (3) above to a building which is a dwelling, shall apply also to an inhabited vehicle or vessel, and shall apply to any such vehicle or vessel at times when the person having a habitation in it is not there as well as at times when he is.*

9.9.2 Context

Burglary replaces the old offence of "breaking and entering". NOW: two forms of burglary:

(1) Where D enters as a trespasser with intent to commit one of three specified offences.

(2) Where D has entered as a trespasser and gone on to commit theft or GBH.

9.9.3 What is a building for these purposes?

E.g. Not tent, size, permanence, structure etc.

***Stevens v Gourley* (1859)**

Byles J: *"a structure of considerable size and intended to be permanent or at least endure for a considerable length of time."*

***Norfolk Constabulary v Seekings and Gould* [1986]**

F: Lorry trailer was used for storage & supplied electricity.

H: Not to constitute a building

9.9.4 "Part of a building..."

Move from one part of a building to another.

***Walkington* [1979]**

F: D walked behind the cash desk in a department store and opened the cash till.

CAH: The area inside the partition represented a "part of a building" from which the public had been impliedly excluded. Convicted of **s9(1)(a) *C.f. *Laing* [1995]**

Department store-stock area-Q: Was D a trespasser? CAH: No evidence of intent on entry acquitted.

9.9.5 *"As a trespasser..."*

Trespasser is someone who has no permission or right to be in the building.

a) Who gives permission?

***Collins* [1973]**

F: Women invited naked man through her bedroom window to have sex.

V thought it was her boyfriend.

Ch: Burglary with intent to commit rape.

CAH: Permission to enter, therefore no trespass – therefore no burglary. Entry must be substantial and effective and requires proof of MR.

Per Edmund Davies LJ at 107:

> *"The point was raised that [V] not being the tenant or occupier of the dwellinghouse and her mother being apparently in occupation, [V] could not in any event have extended an effective invitation to enter, so that, even if she had expressly and with full knowledge of all material facts invited the appellant in, he would nevertheless be a trespasser. Whatever be the position in the law of tort, to regard such a proposition as acceptable in the criminal law would be unthinkable.*
>
> *"...there cannot be a conviction for entering premises "as a **trespasser**" within the meaning of **S.9 TA** unless the **person entering does so knowing that he is a trespasser and nevertheless deliberately enters**, **or**, at the very least, **is reckless** as to whether or not he is entering the premises of another without the other party's consent.'* ***Cunningham recklessness –** Subjective.*

Rejected the proposition that D could enter a building with permission, but then become a trespasser within **s9** simply by exceeding the permission. e.g. Deciding after entry to rape or steal.

*"...We are entirely in agreement with the view...that the common law doctrine of trespass ab initio has no application to burglary under the **Theft Act 1968**'.*

b) The scope of the permission

***The Carlgarth* [1927]**

Per Scrutton LJ:

> *"When you invite a person into your house to use the staircase you do not invite him to slide down the banisters."*

c) Where D has permission to enter for one purpose but enters intending to do something different

***Jones and Smith* [1976]** – If D has a secret dishonest intent at the time of entry to V's house, D will be trespassing, as he will be entering for a purpose in excess of his permission to so.

F: D's who visited house of S's father and stolen his TV set – convicted under **s9(1)(b)** and appealed on the basis of permission to go into the house and thus could not have been trespassing.

CAH: D's rightly convicted under **s9(1)(b)** on the basis a person enters a building as a trespasser where he realises, he has exceeded his permission, or is reckless as to whether he has done so.

Per James LJ at 59:

> *"......it is our view that **a person is a trespasser for the purpose of section 9(1)(b)** of the Theft Act 1968, **if he enters premises of another knowing that he is entering in excess of the permission that has been given to him, or being reckless as to whether he is entering in excess of the permission** that has been given to him to enter, providing the facts are known to the accused which enable him to realise that he is acting in excess of the permission given or that he is acting recklessly as to whether he exceeds that permission, then that is sufficient for the jury to decide that he is in fact a trespasser."*

9.9.6 What constitutes an "entry" for these purposes?

***Collins* [1973]** Per Edmund Davies LJ at 106-107

> *"Unless the jury were entirely satisfied that the appellant made an **effective and substantial entry into the bedroom** without the complainant doing or saying anything to cause him to believe that she was consenting to his entering*

it, he ought not to be convicted of the offence charged. The point is a narrow one, as narrow maybe as the windowsill which is crucial to this case."

***Brown* (1985)**

Leaning into broken shop window to extract goods was enough to constitute entry.

***Ryan* [1996]**

D was found with his head and right arm trapped in window of a house.

H: Irrelevant that D had become trapped and unable to proceed to stealing anything from within.

E.g. Fishing rod is sufficient.

9.9.7 *Mens rea*

a) *Mens rea* under s9(1)(a)

It must be proved:
1. *Intention or subjective recklessness* as to trespassing AND
2. D had *intention* to steal etc

***Collins* [1973]** Per Edmund Davies LJ

"(1) :.... there cannot be a conviction for entering premises "as a trespasser" within the meaning of section 9 of the Theft Act unless the person entering does so ***knowing*** *that he is a trespasser and nevertheless deliberately enters,* ***or****, at the* ***very least, is reckless*** *as to whether or not he is entering the premises of another without the other party's consent."*

- **s9(1)(a)** The ulterior intent: D enters with *intent to steal*, inflict on any person therein any *grievous bodily harm*, or do *unlawful damage* to the building...

***AG's Refs (Nos. 1 & 2 of 1979)* [1980]**

CAH: D can incur liability under **s9(1)(a)** for entering as a trespasser with intent to steal regardless of whether there is any property to steal in the building.

The essence of the offence is D's state of mind at the time of entry.

The intent to steal can exist quite independently of any property that he can, or wants to, steal.

Intention was sufficient if the indictment did not allege D intended to steal specific items.

b) *Mens rea* under s9((1)(b)

...having entered any building or part of a building as a trespasser [D] ***...steals or attempts to steal anything in the building*** *OR that part of it or* ***inflicts or attempts to inflict*** *on any person therein any* ***GBH****.*

It must be proved that:

1. Intention or subjective recklessness as to trespassing; and
2. The MR for the ulterior crime – theft, GBH etc.
3. ***Jenkins; Wilson*** **[1984]**

CAH: D could be guilty under **s9(1)(b)** where he entered a house as a trespasser and was observed by an occupant of whose presence, he was unaware.

9.10 Other theft related offences

9.10.1 Aggravated burglary

s10 Theft Act 1968

(1) A person is guilty of aggravated burglary if he commits any burglary and at the time has with him any firearm or imitation firearm, any weapon of offence, or any explosive; and for this purpose—

(a) "firearm" includes an airgun or air pistol, and "imitation firearm" means anything which has the appearance of being a firearm, whether capable of being discharged or not; and

(b) "weapon of offence" means any article made or adapted for use for causing injury to or incapacitating a person, or intended by the person having it with him for such use; and

(c) "explosive" means any article manufactured for the purpose of producing a practical effect by explosion or intended by the person having it with him for that purpose.

(2) A person guilty of aggravated burglary shall on conviction on indictment be liable to imprisonment for life.

9.10.2 Removal of articles from places open to the public

s11 Theft Act 1968

(1) Subject to subsections (2) and (3) below, where the public have access to a building in order to view the building or part of it, or a collection or part of a collection housed in it, any person who without lawful authority removes from the building or its grounds the whole or part of any article displayed or kept for display to the public in the building or that part of it or in its grounds shall be guilty of an offence. For this purpose "collection" includes a collection got together for a temporary purpose, but references in this section to a collection do not apply to a collection made or exhibited for the purpose of effecting sales or other commercial dealings.

(2) It is immaterial for purposes of subsection (1) above, that the public's access to a building is limited to a particular period or particular occasion; but where anything removed from a building or its grounds is there otherwise than as forming part of, or being on loan for exhibition with, a collection intended for permanent exhibition to the public, the person removing it does not thereby commit an offence under this section unless he removes it on a day when the public have access to the building as mentioned in subsection (1) above.

(3) A person does not commit an offence under this section if he believes that he has lawful authority for the removal of the thing in question or that he would have it if the person entitled to give it knew of the removal and the circumstances of it.

9.10.3 Taking motor vehicle without authority

s12 Theft Act 1968

(1) Subject to subsections (5) and (6) below, a person shall be guilty of an offence if, without having the consent of the owner or other lawful authority, he takes any conveyance for his own or another's use or, knowing that any conveyance has been taken without such authority, drives it or allows himself to be carried in or on it.

9.10.4 Aggravated vehicle taking

s12A Theft Act 1968

(1) Subject to subsection (3) below, a person is guilty of aggravated taking of a vehicle if—

(a) he commits an offence under section 12(1) above (in this section referred to as a "basic offence") in relation to a mechanically propelled vehicle; and

(b) it is proved that, at any time after the vehicle was unlawfully taken (whether by him or another) and before it was recovered, the vehicle was driven, or injury or damage was caused, in one or more of the circumstances set out in paragraphs (a) to (d) of subsection (2) below.

(2) The circumstances referred to in subsection (1)(b) above are—

(a) that the vehicle was driven dangerously on a road or other public place;

(b) that, owing to the driving of the vehicle, an accident occurred by which injury was caused to any person;

(c) that, owing to the driving of the vehicle, an accident occurred by which damage was caused to any property, other than the vehicle;

(d) that damage was caused to the vehicle.

(3) A person is not guilty of an offence under this section if he proves that, as regards any such proven driving, injury or damage as is referred to in subsection (1)(b) above, either—

(a) the driving, accident or damage referred to in subsection (2) above occurred before he committed the basic offence; or

(b) he was neither in nor on nor in the immediate vicinity of the vehicle when that driving, accident or damage occurred.

9.10.5 Abstracting of electricity

s13 Theft Act 1968

13. Abstracting of electricity.

A person who dishonestly uses without due authority, or dishonestly causes to be wasted or diverted, any electricity shall on conviction on indictment be liable to imprisonment for a term not exceeding five years.

9.10.6 False accounting

s17 Theft Act 1968

17.— False accounting.

(1) Where a person dishonestly, with a view to gain for himself or another or with intent to cause loss to another,—

> (a) *destroys, defaces, conceals, or falsifies any account or any record or document made or required for any accounting purpose; or*
>
> (b) *in furnishing information for any purpose produces or makes use of any account, or any such record or document as aforesaid, which to his knowledge is or may be misleading, false, or deceptive in a material particular; he shall, on conviction on indictment, be liable to imprisonment for a term not exceeding seven years.*

(2) *For purposes of this section a person who makes or concurs in making in an account or other document an entry which is or may be misleading, false or deceptive in a material particular, or who omits or concurs in omitting a material particular from an account or other document, is to be treated as falsifying the account or document.*

9.10.7 Blackmail

a) Statute

s21 Theft Act 1968

(1) *A person is guilty of blackmail if, with a view to gain for himself or another or with intent to cause loss to another, he makes any unwarranted demand with menaces; and for this purpose a demand with menaces is unwarranted unless the person making it does so in the belief—*

> (a) *that he has reasonable grounds for making the demand; and*
>
> (b) *that the use of the menaces is a proper means of reinforcing the demand.*

(2) *The nature of the act or omission demanded is immaterial, and it is also immaterial whether the menaces relate to action to be taken by the person making the demand.*

(3) *A person guilty of blackmail shall on conviction on indictment be liable to imprisonment for a term not exceeding fourteen years.*

b) The nature of the demand

Reasonable person objective test

The demand can be in the form of words, actions or omissions and can be express or implied.

***Collister and Warhurst* (1955)**

F: 2 PO discussed within earshot of V that payment of some money might lead them to drop what were bogus indecency charges.

H: It was "*obvious*" to V and would have been "*obvious*" to the reasonable man, that a demand was being made even though it was never directly addressed to V.

***Treacy* [1971]**: Posted T to V outside jurisdiction

H: OK, offence if issued in UK.

c) With menaces

Reasonable person objective test

***Lawrence (1971) "menaces"**

H: Ordinary English word no elaboration (x) where what would not normally be menacing to an ordinary person was menacing to V.

***Thorne v Motor Trade Association* [1937]** Per Lord Wright at 817:

> *"I think the word "menace" is to be liberally construed and* ***not as limited to threats of violence but as including threats of any action detrimental to or unpleasant*** *to the person addressed."*

Therefore wide enough to include threats to reveal a person's criminal record, adultery, medical details, or to adversely affect an individual's business or property.

***Harry* [1974]**

F: A student had suggested to a shopkeeper that if he were to make a £50 contribution to the college's Rag Week fund, the shop would be "immune" from Rag Week activities.

TJH: Not satisfied that there were any menaces within the meaning of the act.

***Clear* [1968]**

H: Actions of D should be considered in light of the effect they would have on the ordinary person of reasonable fortitude, per Sellers LJ at 679

> *"Words or conduct which would not intimidate or influence anyone to respond to the demand would not be menaces...but* ***threats and conduct of such a nature and extent that the mind of an ordinary person of normal stability and courage might be influenced*** *or made apprehensive so as accede unwillingly to the demand would be sufficient of a jury's consideration..."*

In ***Garwood* [1987]** V not influenced evidence – normal person would have been made out. Per Lord Lane CJ at 322:

> *"... where the threats in fact affected the mind of [V], although they would not have affected the mind of a person of normal stability...* ***the existence of menaces is proved providing that [D] was aware of the likely effect*** *of his actions upon the victim."*

Menaces will be found where D has special personal knowledge of V's vulnerability such as their age e.g. Grandmother: ***Lambert* [2009]**.

d) *"...with a view to gain for himself or another or with intent to cause loss to another..."*

S.34(2) 'For the purposes of this Act-

> *(a) "gain" and "loss" are to be construed as extending only to gain or loss in money or other property, but as extending to any such gain or loss whether temporary or permanent; and –*
>
> > *(i) "gain" Includes a gain by keeping what one has, as well as a gain by getting what one has not; and*
> >
> > *(ii) "loss" includes a loss by not getting what one might get, as well as a loss by parting with what one has...'*

E.g.

1. D threatens to reveal V's adultery to V's W unless V repays D the £100 which he owes him.

A: This demand is made by D with a view to "gain" even though D is trying to recover that to which he had a right in any event.

2. D makes such a threat to V unless V relinquishes his right to sue D for the money owed by D to V, here V's "loss" is not seeing what he might get.

A: Offence ***Parkes* [1973]**.

e) **Unwarranted**

Subjective. Replaces dishonesty = Unjustified

***Harvey* (1981)**

F: Drug deal, not proper drugs. D had threatened to kill members of V's family if he did not return £20K that he had obtained from D by deception.

TJ: Directed jury that, as a matter of law, such threats could not be a "proper" means of enforcing his demand for the return of the money.

CAH: Upheld conviction, emphasising that a D could not claim that the means adopted were "proper" whilst he also knew that they would involve the commission of serious criminal offences.

Per Bingham J at 142:

"1) 'In order to exonerate a defendant from liability <u>his belief</u> must be [NOT RP] that'

2) 'The use of the menaces is a "proper" means of reinforcing the demand."

Bingham J goes on to state that:

""Proper" is an unusual expression to find in a criminal statute.......... no act which was not believed to be lawful could be believed to be proper within the meaning of the subsection. Thus no assistance is given to any defendant, even a fanatic or a deranged idealist, who knows or suspects that his threat, or the act threatened, is criminal, but believes it to be justified by his end or his peculiar circumstances.

"The test is not what he regards as justified, but what he believes to be proper*. And where, as here, the threats were to do acts which any sane man knows to be against the laws of every civilised country no jury would hesitate long before dismissing the contention that the defendant genuinely believed the threats to be a proper means of reinforcing even a legitimate demand."*[9]

N.B. Not by reference to D's own moral beliefs

f) **N.B. The relationship between blackmail and robbery**

Overlaps, e.g. a Highwayman who points a gun at V and declares "your money or your life" and thus induces handing over of valuables.

Separates **s8** which requires a person to be put in fear of being *then and there subjected to force.*

***Bevans* (1988)**

F: D threatened to shoot Dr if he did not provide D with the pain-killing drug morphine injection. The substance demanded was property.

H: Convicted on the basis that his demand had been made with a view to gain. Per Jones J:

9 Harvey (1981)

"It seems ***difficult, if not impossible****, to argue that* ***the liquid which constituted the substance which was to be injected into the appellant s body was not property****. It clearly was. There has been no dispute but that if an ampoule containing the liquid had been handed over to the appellant instead of being transferred to a syringe and injected into his body, he would have got property in that sense.* ***This Court can see no difference between the liquid being contained in the syringe before it is passed into his body and the liquid being contained in an ampoule.*** *There can be no question but that that morphine was property........****[I]t is nothing to the point that his ultimate motive was the relief of pain through the effect which that morphine would have upon his bodily processes."***

C.f. Services unless for monetary value.

9.10.8 Handling stolen goods

s22 Theft Act 1968

(1) *A person handles stolen goods if (otherwise than in the course of the stealing) knowing or believing them to be stolen goods he dishonestly receives the goods, or dishonestly undertakes or assists in their retention, removal, disposal, or realisation by or for the benefit of another person, or if he arranges to do so.*

(2) *A person guilty of handling stolen goods shall on conviction on indictment be liable to imprisonment for a term not exceeding fourteen years.*

9.10.9 Going equipped for stealing

s25 Theft Act 1968

(1) *A person shall be guilty of an offence if, when not at his place of abode, he has with him any article for use in the course of or in connection with any [burglary or theft]1 .*

(2) *A person guilty of an offence under this section shall on conviction on indictment be liable to imprisonment for a term not exceeding three years.*

(3) *Where a person is charged with an offence under this section, proof that he had with him any article made or adapted for use in committing a [burglary or theft]1 shall be evidence that he had it with him for such use.*

[...]2

(5) *For purposes of this section an offence under section 12(1) of this Act of taking a conveyance shall be treated as theft [...]3.*

9.11 Evaluation and reform

9.11.1 Legal certainty and legal clarity

Legal certainty provides the law must be sufficiently available, certain and enable the individual to know the legal boundaries of their actions and potential consequences of breach[10]. Legal clarity provides that the law must be accessible, clear, intelligible, and predictable[11]. In an accessorial liability case the jury is the tribunal of fact governed by the directions on the law given by the judge. The research shows juries need clear and cogent guidance[12]. It is axiomatic: clear law is needed to give clear guidance.

The significant advantage of the current law is the CLRC systematically codified and defined terms.

Property: belonging to another.

Appropriation: dishonesty and intention to permanently deprive both have relatively certain and clear meanings.

Appropriation includes even gifts. Case law is now of limited importance by virtue of the **Fraud Act 2006** offences (see **Chapter 9**).

Dishonesty is of relatively low importance given it is usually obviously dishonest or obviously not dishonest and the case of ***Ivey*** has cleared up the lacune which existed.

9.11.2 Equality before the law: protected characteristics and socio-economic barriers

Equality provides that equality before the law (including disability, gender, gender identity, race, sexual orientation, and socio economic) is relevant and impacts on the unequal power relationships in society and has a significant impact on the system.

---

10 Richard Buxton, "The Human Rights Act and the substantive criminal law" (2000) Criminal Law Review 331, 332

11 Rimmington; Goldstein [2005]; [2006]

12 Alan Travis, "The verdict on juries: fair, effective and efficient" *The Guardian* (London, 17 February 2010) <https://www.theguardian.com/uk/2010/feb/17/juries-fairness-research> accessed 06 April 2025, Cheryl Thomas, 'Are juries fair?' (Ministry of Justice Research Series 1/10, February 2010) <https://www.ucl.ac.uk/judicial-institute/sites/judicial-institute/files/are_juries_fair.pdf> accessed 06 April 2025, Cheryl Thomas, "Ethnicity and the fairness of jury trials in England and Wales 2006-2014" [2017] Crim Law Review 860

The protected characteristics are not challenged by the current law.

The only issue is socio-economic and that largely relates not to the law but to the enforcement of the law. It is trite but obvious that ease of prosecution for a shop-lifter who steals razor blades is significantly easier to investigate and prosecute than a City of London Fraud.

9.11.3 Fair warning; fair labelling and sufficient breadth principles

a) Fair warning

The law should give fair warning to the community of the consequences. There is a strong argument many of the young people caught up in so called "gang crime" or "organised crime groups" have little insight in relation to the likely consequences. The Crown Prosecution Service has responded with guidance on charging.[13]

The well established statutory principles do not appear to have given rise to difficulties.

b) Fair labelling

Fair labelling involves labelling criminal offences at a macro scale to indicate categorisation, indicative punishment scales and specialist ancillary orders[14]. Fair labelling involved labelling at a micro scale – it helps with categorising the wrongdoing with a public label which has a communicative value to wider society[15].

Returning to the CLRC work, the labels in terms of Theft equals Thief; Robbery equals Robber; Burglary equals Burglar. All appear to accord with good clear labelling.

c) Sufficient breadth

There appears to be sufficient breadth to capture wrongdoing.

Supplemented by the **Fraud Act 2006**, the current law appears to be sufficiently broad to capture wrongdoing without being too narrow as to exclude good sensible labelling.

---

13 Crown Prosecution Service, "Theft Act Offences" (CPS, 12 September 2024) <https://www.cps.gov.uk/legal-guidance/theft-act-offences> accessed 06 April 2025

14 James Chalmers and Fiona Leverick, "Fair Labelling in Criminal Law" (2008) 71 Modern Law Review 217, 221-222

15 James Chalmers and Fiona Leverick, "Fair Labelling in Criminal Law" (2008) 71 Modern Law Review 217, 221-222

d) Practicality, cost, and expense

1) Practicality: the law must be sufficiently practical and enforceable to achieve its goals.

   The law remains complex on appropriation but the actual "gift" issue is rare.

   The law on dishonesty has been significantly improved by ***Ivey*** but it is still surprising there is no positive definition of this important term. It may be this leaves too much to the jury?

2) Avoid undue cost and expense

   The law now settled in statute and case law terms appears to not cause undue cost or expense.

9.11.4 Human rights: autonomy and welfare principles

The position for purposes of **ECHR Art 7** legal certainty seems to be clear and no other significant issues arise. **Protocol 1**, **Art 1** the protection of possessions is also respected.

9.11.5 International comparators and reform: practicality principle and politics

a) Comparators

None are utilised here.

b) Law Commission

No current proposals.

In the News

The duke

1. Please read this article:

Alan Travis, "Revealed: 1961 Goya "theft" from National Gallery was a family affair" The Guardian (30 November 2012)

<https://www.theguardian.com/artanddesign/2012/nov/30/1961-goya-crime-national-gallery>

2. Please read this film Review of *The Duke*

Mark Kermode, "The Duke review – Jim Broadbent excels in true tale of art-stealing pensioner" *The Guardian* (27 February 2022)

<https://www.theguardian.com/film/2022/feb/27/the-duke-review-roger-michell-jim-broadbent-helen-mirren-kempton-bunton-theft> accessed 06 April 2025

3. Applying your knowledge of the law of theft utilising the elements. Why was Kempton Bunton acquitted of the theft of the painting itself?

9.12 Summary

You should now be familiar with the following offences and be able to critically evaluate aspects of the law

- The offence of **Theft (s1 Theft Act 1968)**

  We have in this chapter focused on the offence of theft and the sister offences within the same statute.

- **Property** (P) (*actus reus*) (**s4 Theft Act 1968**)

  We have looked at the very well defined definition of what is property and what is not property for the purposes of the act.

- **Belonging to another** (BTA) (*actus reus*) (**s5 Theft Act 1968**)

  We have reviewed when property belongs to another which mostly accords with good sense.

- **Appropriation** (A) (*actus reus*) (**s3 Theft Act 1968**)

  We have looked at the issue of appropriation which is often straightforward in terms of taking. However in terms of the issue of a gift we have looked at the case law and why the higher courts have tended to favour the prosecution argument that even a gift can amount to an appropriation.

- **Dishonesty** (D) (*mens rea*) (**s2 Theft Act 1968**)

  We have reviewed the recent change in the law to move towards an objective test of dishonesty.

- **Intention to permanently deprive** (IPD) (*mens rea*) (**s6 Theft Act 1968**)

  We have looked at the relatively straightforward law in relation to intention to probably deprive.

- **Robbery** (**s8 Theft Act 1968**)

  We have reviewed the aggravated form of theft where there is threat of force for use of force.

- **Burglary** (**s9 Theft Act 1968**)

  We have looked at the addition of trespass to the theft to render it a burglary.

- **Other theft-related offences**

  We have reviewed some of the other very specific offences.

- **Evaluation and reform**

  We have noted with some satisfaction that the criminal law revision committee which led to the **Theft Act 1968** has written some very good legislation which has stood the test of time.

Further reading

Kenneth Campbell, "The Test of Dishonesty in R v Ghosh" (1984) 43 *Cambridge Law Journal 349*

Matthew Dyson Matthew and Paul Jarvis, "Poison Ivey or Herbal Tea Leaf?" (2018) *134 Law Quarterly Review 198*

Simon Gardner "Property and Theft" (1998) *Criminal Law Review 35*

Andrew Halpin "The Test for Dishonesty" (1996) *Criminal Law Review 283*

Stephen Shute "Appropriation and The Law Of Theft" (2002) *Criminal Law Review 445*

CHAPTER 10

Fraud Act 2006 and related offences

10.1 Introduction

10.1.1 Introduction

The **Fraud Act 2006** is a relatively recent piece of legislation. It covers:

Fraud Act 2006

Fraud

s. 1 Fraud

s. 2 Fraud by false representation

s. 3 Fraud by failing to disclose information.

s. 4 Fraud by abuse of position

s. 5 "Gain" and "loss"

s. 6 Possession etc. of articles for use in frauds

s. 7 Making or supplying articles for use in frauds.

s. 8 "Article"

s. 9 Participating in fraudulent business carried on by sole trader etc.

s. 10 Participating in fraudulent business carried on by company etc.: penalty.

Obtaining services dishonestly

s. 11 Obtaining services dishonestly.

10.1.2 Pre-fraud act 2006 offences

Prior to the **Fraud Act** existing, there were a number of statutory offences:

- *Obtaining property by deception* **s15(1) Theft Act 1968**
- *Obtaining a pecuniary advantage by deception* **s16 Theft Act 1968**
- *Obtaining services by deception* **s1(1) Theft Act 1978**
- *Evasion of a liability by deception* **s2(1)(a)-(c) Theft Act 1978**

These have all been replaced by the **Fraud Act 2006**.

10.1.3 Why was change needed?

The problem under the old law was regarding the proof and an operative deception, i.e. the prosecution had to usually prove the deception caused the obtaining (see cases ***Davies v Flackett* [1973]**; ***Charles* [1976]**).

The harm aspects are limited under the new law and relatively easy to prove.

The new offences are at their core focused on the fault element of dishonesty.

Aims of this chapter

By the end of this chapter you can be expected to know and be able to evaluate the law on fraud:

- **The Fraud Act 2006:** Offence(s) and common terms
- Fraud by false representation (**s2 Fraud Act 2006**)

- Fraud by failing to disclose information (**s3 Fraud Act 2006**)
- Fraud by abuse of position (**s4 Fraud Act 2006**)
- Possession of articles for use in frauds (**s6 Fraud Act 2006**)
- Making or supplying articles for use in frauds (**s7 Fraud Act 2006**)
- Obtaining services dishonestly (**s11 Fraud Act 2006**)
- Evaluation Framework.

10.2 The Fraud Act 2006 offence(s) and common terms

10.2.1 The new offences and concepts (s2 Fraud Act 2006)

s1 Fraud Act 2006, Fraud

(1) A person is guilty of fraud if he is in breach of any of the sections listed in subsection (2) (which provide for different ways of committing the offence).

(2) The sections are–

(a) section 2 (fraud by false representation),

(b) section 3 (fraud by failing to disclose information), and

(c) section 4 (fraud by abuse of position).

(3) A person who is guilty of fraud is liable–

(a) on summary conviction, to imprisonment for a term not exceeding 12 months or to a fine not exceeding the statutory maximum (or to both);

(b) on conviction on indictment, to imprisonment for a term not exceeding 10 years or to a fine (or to both).

(4) Subsection (3)(a) applies in relation to Northern Ireland as if the reference to 12 months were a reference to 6 months.

10.2.2 Common terms

a) Gain and loss

s5 Fraud Act 2006

(1) The references to gain and loss in sections 2 to 4 are to be read in accordance with this section.

(2) "Gain" and "loss" –

(a) extend only to gain or loss in money or other property;

(b) include any such gain or loss whether temporary or permanent;

and "property" means any property whether real or personal (including things in action and other intangible property).

(3) "Gain" includes a gain by keeping what one has, as well as a gain by getting what one does not have.

(4) "Loss" includes a loss by not getting what one might get, as well as a loss by parting with what one has.

Commentary

D's intention must be to cause gain or loss and the jury require direction e.g. ***Gilbert* [2012]**

b) Dishonesty

s2 Theft Act 1968, not applicable but common law ***Ivey v Genting Casinos* (UK) Ltd [2018]** is applicable (see **Chapter 9**).

10.3 Fraud by false representation (s2 Fraud Act 2006)

(1) A person is in breach of this section if he–

(a) dishonestly makes a false representation, and

(b) intends, by making the representation–

(i) to make a gain for himself or another, or

(ii) to cause loss to another or to expose another to a risk of loss.

(2) A representation is false if–

(a) it is untrue or misleading, and

(b) the person making it knows that it is, or might be, untrue or misleading.

(3) *"Representation" means any representation as to fact or law, including a representation as to the state of mind of–*

  (a) *the person making the representation, or*

  (b) *any other person.*

(4) *A representation may be express or implied.*

(5) *For the purposes of this section a representation may be regarded as made if it (or anything implying it) is submitted in any form to any system or device designed to receive, convey, or respond to communications (with or without human intervention).*

Commentary

See, for example, ***Holt and Lee* [1981]**; ***Jackson* [1983].**

10.3.1 D makes a false representation (*actus reus*)

s2(3): *"Representation" means any representation as to fact or law, including a representation as to the state of mind of-*

(a) *the person making the representation, or*

(b) *any other person.'*

s2(2): *'A representation is false if-*

(a) *it is untrue or misleading, and*

(b) *the person making it knows that it is, or might be, untrue or misleading*

s2(4) *A representation may be express or implied.*

***Varley* [2019]** Gross LJ:

[108] *"The actus reus, the conduct element of the offence, is the making of an objectively untrue or misleading representation. The mens rea, or mental element is made up of the requisite knowledge, dishonesty and intention. The actus reus is therefore contained in s.2(2)(a), with the mens rea found in s. 2(2)(b), s. 2(1)(a) and s. 2(1)(b)."*

10.3.2 Knowledge that the representation was false or that it might be (*actus reus*)

***Augunas* [2013]** CAH This is a subjective question.

Not ought/RP but D must have known.

10.3.3 Intention to make gain or cause loss – (*mens rea*)

See above under common terms.

10.3.4 Dishonesty (*Mens rea* – see above)

The law is thankfully:

1) legally certain;
2) legally clear;
3) fairly labels.

This means very limited need for appeal litigation. Thus very limited case law but:

Examples include:

***Oxford Cap & Gown: Barnard* (1837)**

F D dressed up as though he were member of the University of Oxford in cap and gown.

D's purpose was to secure a reduction in the price.

D secured a credit arrangement, i.e. use now and pay later.

H D's Conduct was a representation.

Eating the food: *Ray* [1974]

F D who was seated in a Chinese restaurant.

Finished eating and left without payment.

H D sitting in the restaurant consuming the food amounted to a representation.

Namely that he was an honest customer.

Creditworthiness: *MPC v Charles* [1977]

F D obtained a financial advantage using a cheque with a cheque card.

D was in fact overdrawn.

HLH Implied representation as to creditworthiness.

Mileage on the odometer: *King* [1979]

F Car salesman says the odometer "may not be correct".

Lie He knew it was incorrect.

H Statement was therefore a misrepresentation.

Credit limitation: *Lambie* [1982]

F D obtained a financial advantage.

D used a credit card she knew was over the limit.

D Shop is guaranteed payment thus no representation was operative.

HLH Dismissed the appeal. Followed ***Charles***. Deception was operative.

Falsifying identity for driving test: *Idress v DPP* [2011]

F Turning up to the driving test for someone else.

H Representation by conduct to make a gain namely to pass the test.

Lying as to enforceability: *Whatcott* [2019]

F D demanded money under a contract he knew was not enforceable.

H Operative representation.

10.4 Fraud by failing to disclose information (s3 Fraud Act 2006)

A person is in breach of this section if he–

(a) dishonestly fails to disclose to another person information which he is under a legal duty to disclose, and

(b) intends, by failing to disclose the information–

(i) to make a gain for himself or another, or

(ii) to cause loss to another or to expose another to a risk of loss.

(1) D under a legal duty to disclose information to another person (*actus reus*)

1. Silent deceptions where there is a legal duty ***Razoq* [2012]**; ***D* [2019]**.
2. Legal duty is for the judge to determine.

3. The statute does not discuss but the Law Commission does (Cm. 5560, 2002)

"7.28 ***... Such a duty may derive from statute*** (such as the provisions governing company prospectuses), ***from the fact that the transaction in question is one of the utmost good faith*** (such as a contract of insurance***), from the express or implied terms of a contract***, from the ***custom of a particular trade or market, or from the existence of a fiduciary relationship between the parties*** (such as that of agent and principal).

"7.29 For this purpose ***there is a legal duty to disclose information not only if the defendant's failure to disclose it gives the victim a cause of action for damages,*** but also if ***the law gives the victim a right to set aside any change in his or her legal position to which he or she may consent as a result of the non-disclosure***.

"For example, a person in a fiduciary position has a duty to disclose material information when entering into a contract with his or her beneficiary, in the sense that a failure to make such disclosure will entitle the beneficiary to rescind the contract and to reclaim any property transferred under it."[1]

e.g.1 ***El Mashta* [2010]**

Continuing to receive asylum support when employed.

e.g.2 Trust Trustee & beneficiary

e.g.3 Solicitor Solicitor & client

(2) D fails to disclose that information This forms part of the *actus reus*.

(3) Intention to make gain or cause loss This forms part of the *mens rea* - see above.

(4) Dishonesty This forms part of the *mens rea* - see above.

10.5 Fraud by abuse of position (s4 Fraud Act 2006)

(1) A person is in breach of this section if he–

(a) occupies a position in which he is expected to safeguard, or not to act against, the financial interests of another person,

(b) dishonestly abuses that position, and

1 Law Commission, *Fraud* (Law Com No 276, 2002) paras 7.28-7.29

(c) intends, by means of the abuse of that position–

(i) to make a gain for himself or another, or

(ii) to cause loss to another or to expose another to a risk of loss.

(2) A person may be regarded as having abused his position even though his conduct consisted of an omission rather than an act.

Commentary

(1) D occupies a position of trust (*actus reus*)

1. Aimed at fiduciary relationships, e.g. trustees (trustee and beneficiary), employers (employer and employee), solicitors (solicitor and client), and professionals (professional and client/patient).

***Valujevs* [2014]**

F Gang masters who controlled agricultural workers.

D's made deductions from V's wages and made V's paid inflated rents.

CAH This conduct is within **s4**.

1. Decision for jury whether a reasonable person would see that expectation of trust.

Indicative of legal and moral duty.

2. Collecting V's pay was sufficient.

2. Employees

***Marshall* [2009]**

F D manager of a care home

D had control of resident's (V's) finances.

D took over £7,000 for herself.

Ch Fraud abuse of position of trust

CAH Upheld sentence

(2) D abuses that position of trust (*actus reus*)

NB s4(2) *A person may be regarded as having abused his position even though his conduct consisted of an omission rather than an act.*

***Pennock* [2014]**

F D's (H & W) open a joint account with V's Uncle aged 90

£100K of uncle's money siphoned off to buy H & W daughter's property.

CAH Appeal allowed due to misdirection regarding joint accounts.

1. Abuse of position = '"uses incorrectly" or "puts to improper use" contrary to the expectations of the role

(3) Intention to make gain or cause loss – This forms part of the *mens rea* – see above.

(4) Dishonesty This forms part of the *mens rea* – see above.

10.6 Possession of articles for use in frauds (s6 Fraud Act 2006)

(1) A person is guilty of an offence if he has in his possession or under his control any article for use in the course of or in connection with any fraud.

(2) A person guilty of an offence under this section is liable–

(a) on summary conviction, to imprisonment for a term not exceeding 12 months or to a fine not exceeding the statutory maximum (or to both);

(b) on conviction on indictment, to imprisonment for a term not exceeding 5 years or to a fine (or to both).

(3) Subsection (2)(a) applies in relation to Northern Ireland as if the reference to 12 months were a reference to 6 months.

Actus reus

(1) **D has in his possession or under his control**

E.g. Scamming items may include fake notes, decoding machines or phones or other items.

***Nimley* [2010]**

D recording cinema films on his phone.

(2) **Any article for use in the course of or in connection with any fraud**

"Article" includes any program or data held in electronic form: **s8(1)**.

(3) ***Mens rea***

No *mens rea* specified although Attorney-General and Solicitor-General confirmed not an offence of strict liability. The courts could interpret the *mens rea* to be either:

A) intent to use the article for fraud

or

B) intent to use the article for fraud in the future.

10.7 Making or supplying articles for use in frauds (s7 Fraud Act 2006)

(1) A person is guilty of an offence if he makes, adapts, supplies, or offers to supply any article–

(a) knowing that it is designed or adapted for use in the course of or in connection with fraud, or

(b) intending it to be used to commit, or assist in the commission of, fraud.

(2) A person guilty of an offence under this section is liable–

(a) on summary conviction, to imprisonment for a term not exceeding 12 months or to a fine not exceeding the statutory maximum (or to both);

(b) on conviction on indictment, to imprisonment for a term not exceeding 10 years or to a fine (or to both).

(3) Subsection (2)(a) applies in relation to Northern Ireland as if the reference to 12 months were a reference to 6 months.

(1) ***Actus reus***

This is where D makes, adapts, supplies, or offers to supply any article. This includes any program or data held in electronic form: **s8(1)**.

(2) ***Mens rea***

The elements of *mens rea* are:

- knowing that it is designed or adapted for use in the course of or in connection with fraud; and
- intending it to be used to commit or assist in the commmission of fraud.

10.8 Obtaining services dishonestly (s11 Fraud Act 2006)

(1) A person is guilty of an offence under this section if he obtains services for himself or another–

(a) by a dishonest act, and

(b) in breach of subsection (2).

(2) A person obtains services in breach of this subsection if–

(a) they are made available on the basis that payment has been, is being or will be made for or in respect of them,

(b) he obtains them without any payment having been made for or in respect of them or without payment having been made in full, and

(c) when he obtains them, he knows–

(i) that they are being made available on the basis described in paragraph (a), or

(ii) that they might be, but intends that payment will not be made or will not be made in full.

(1) ***Actus reus***

The elements are:

- D committed an act causing the obtaining of a service;
- the service was provided on the basis that payment had been or would be made for it; and
- D failed to pay for the service or failed to pay in full for it.

(2) ***Mens rea***

The elements are:

- D knew that the service was provided on the basis that it had been or would be paid for;
- D intended to make a gain or cause loss; and
- D was dishonest.

10.9 Evaluation framework

10.9.1 Legal certainty and legal clarity

The preceding commentary makes it very clear that the law under the **Fraud Act 2006** is legally certain and clear. There have in fact been very few appeals.

10.9.2 Equality before the law: protected characteristics and socio-economic barriers

See **Chapter 9** commentary. There is a clear discussion to be had regarding the differential enforcement of laws. However in relation to the law itself there does not seem to be any equality-based issue.

10.9.3 Fair warning; fair labelling and sufficient breadth principles

a) Fair warning

The law should give fair warning to the community of the consequences. The law is broad but is predictable in the sense of a "con" attracting liability.

b) Fair labelling

If fraud means wrongful deception for financial gain then the new law seems to capture and label accurately the various forms of fraud.

c) Sufficient breadth

There appears to be sufficient breadth to capture offending.

The law is broader in remit than its predecessor but it is submitted this is welcome to readily capture wrongdoing.

d) Practicality, cost, and expense

1) Practicality – the law is less complex than its predecessor.
2) Avoid undue cost and expense – there have been very few appeals which may indicate at first instance the law is working well.

10.9.4 Human rights: Autonomy and welfare Principles

The position for purposes of **ECHR Art 7** legal certainty seems to have improved as the law is clear and with no apparent lacunae.

The **Protocol 1 Art 1** Right to possession of property is protected.

10.9.5 International comparators and reform: practicality principle and politics

a) Comparators

None relevant save see those within the Law Commission Report.

b) Law Commission

The Act was constructed post the Law Commission, *Fraud* (Law Com No 276, 2002) report and there are no current calls for reform.

In the News

Online fraud making money from fake adverts with "Martin Lewis"

Please see these two links:

1. James Tapper, "Martin Lewis: "There's an epidemic of scams, but fraudsters are getting off scot-free" *The Guardian* (2 May 2021)

   <https://www.theguardian.com/money/2021/may/02/martin-lewis-theres-an-epidemic-of-scams-but-fraudsters-are-getting-off-scot-free> accessed 06 April 2025

2. Kit Sproson, "Martin Lewis scam adverts" (Money Saving Expert, 7 January 2025)

   <https://www.moneysavingexpert.com/shopping/fake-martin-lewis-ads/> accessed 06 April 2025

You are approached by an elderly lady called Margaret Smit.

She is a fan of Martin Lewis, the real money saving expert.

She has been approached by text message to buy protection insurance.

She has paid £500 to protect her new laptop.

Unfortunately this was a scam. She wants to report it to the police. How would you prosecute this crime? What offences? What elements?

10.10 Summary

You should now be confident with the following offences:

- The **Fraud Act 2006** offence(s) and common terms

  We have looked at what is meant by the common terms of gain and loss.
- Fraud by false representation (**s2 Fraud Act 2006**)

  We have reviewed where someone knowingly makes a false representation.
- Fraud by failing to disclose information (**s3 Fraud Act 2006**)

  We have reviewed the duty to disclose in specified circumstances.
- Fraud by abuse of position (**s4 Fraud Act 2006**)

  We have reviewed the abuse of position of trust.
- Possession of articles for use in frauds (**s6 Fraud Act 2006**)

  We have briefly reviewed what articles could be used.
- Making or supplying articles for use in frauds (**s7 Fraud Act 2006**)

  We have briefly reviewed the supplying of articles for fraud.
- Obtaining services dishonestly (**s11 Fraud Act 2006**)

We have briefly reviewed obtaining services.

- Evaluation framework

  In fact there is limited critique as the law fulfils positively most of the criteria of value. The only critique may be that too much rests on dishonesty.

Further reading

Jennifer Collins, "Fraud by Abuse of Position: Theorising Section 4 of the Fraud Act 2006" (2011) *Criminal Law Review 513*

Jennifer Collins, "Exploitation of Persons and the Limits of the Criminal Law" (2017) *Criminal Law Review 167*

Michael Levi, and John Burrows, "Measuring the Impact of Fraud in the UK" (2008) *48(3) British Journal of Criminology 293*

Neil MacEwan, "A Tricky Situation: Deception in Cyberspace" (2013) *Journal of Criminal Law 417*

David Ormerod, "The Fraud Act 2006—Criminalising Lying?" (2007) *Criminal Law Review 193*

CHAPTER 11

Drugs offences

11.1 Introduction

This chapter explores a range of offences established by the **Misuse of Drugs Act 1971** (**MDA 1971**) including possession and possession with intent to supply. Offences related to the creation, possession and supply of controlled substances are often the subject of debate and commentary in the press, public and Parliament. Some of these debates have expressed concern over the ability of the law to respond to the evolving landscape of drug use in modern society. This has shaped the development of the law, including through the **Psychoactive Substances Act 2016** (**PSA 2016**) which is discussed later in this chapter.

This chapter begins by discussing how **MDA 1971** establishes three classes of controlled drug, the possession or supply of which is limited by the Act. Whilst this classification does not change whether a defendant is guilty of an offence, classification has significant implications in relation to sentencing, and some proposals for reform of the law focus on specific substances or categories of substance. The chapter then looks at the elements of possession, before going on to consider offences relating to drug "dealing": supply and possession with intent to supply.

Throughout the chapter, you will see that **MDA 1971** is, at times, ambiguous and there has been a significant amount of development through case law in order to provide some clarity to the law. You will see that some of these developments raise questions about how policing is carried out in relation to drugs offences and changing patterns of prosecution and conviction. Towards the end of the chapter, we will consider some potential critiques of the current law and proposals for the reform, or abolition, of certain drug offences.

Aims of this chapter

By the end of this chapter, you will:

- Understand how the law categorises different controlled substances and the implications of these categories.
- Know how to apply offences of possession and possession with intent to supply, as well as other offences, in practical scenarios.
- Be able to critically evaluate key aspects of contemporary drugs-related offences and discuss potential future reforms.

11.2 Classification

The **Misuse of Drugs Act 1971** is only applicable to substances identified within the legislation. This means that a variety of substances which we might consider "drugs" are not covered by the offences listed here, but instead by parts of other legislation. For example, **reg 214** of the **Human Medicines Regulations 2012** establishes limits on the sale of prescription drugs, including many which are not substances controlled by **MDA 1971**.

s2 MDA 1971 specifies that the term "controlled drug" applies to a substance listed in **Sch 2** or which is temporarily specified as such by the government under the procedure set out in **s2A**. Controlled drugs are separated into **Class A**, listed in **Sch 2, Pt I**; **Class B,** listed in **Sch 2, Part II**, and **Class C**, listed in **Sch 2, Part III**. Substances are often added to or moved between these classes by secondary legislation. For example, Ketamine was moved from Class C to Class B by the **Misuse of Drugs Act 1971 (Ketamine etc.) (Amendment) Order 2014.**[1]

1 Recently, the Government have considered further upgrading Ketamine to a Class A substance. See, Rajeev Syal, "Home Office may reclassify ketamine in response to record levels of use" (*The Guardian*, 7 January 2025) <https://www.theguardian.com/society/2025/jan/07/home-office-may-reclassify-ketamine-in-response-to-record-levels-of-use>

Activity

Let's take an example

Hundreds of substances are categorised within **Sch 2 MDA 1971**. Commonly known substances in each class include:

Class A: Cocaine,[2] Morphine,[3] LSD and Ecstasy.[4]

Class B: Ketamine, Cannabis, GBL and GBH.

Class C: Diazepam, Khat and Nitrous Oxide.

An extended list of substances can be found at the link below. Look at this list and try to identify other substances you have heard of:

https://www.gov.uk/government/publications/controlled-drugs-list--2/list-of-most-commonly-encountered-drugs-currently-controlled-under-the-misuse-of-drugs-legislation

As you might find, the scientific language used within the legislation differs from the commonly used names for many substances. Consider looking at this list produced by FRANK which gives both scientific and commonly used names for substances:

https://www.talktofrank.com/drugs-a-z#N

Whether a substance is in Class A, B or C is particularly important at the sentencing stage of a prosecution. **Sch 4 MDA 1971** establishes different statutory maximum sentences for the offences discussed in this chapter based on the class of substance involved. For example, a defendant convicted of possession of a Class C substance by a Crown Court would be subject to a maximum sentence of two years in custody, however, if the substance was Class A the potential maximum would increase to seven years in custody.

Where a substance is not listed within **Sch 2**, possession or distribution of it is not criminalised by the **MDA 1971**. This does not prevent liability where a defendant supplies, or is in possession of, a substance where the chemical structure is

---

2 Including commonly known substances such as crack cocaine and powder cocaine.

3 Commonly known as Heroin.

4 Commonly known as MDMA and Molly.

the same but in a different orientation to a controlled substance (referred to as a "stereo-isometric" form of the substance) as in ***Watts* [1984]**. However, until 2016, substances with a different chemical structure, even where they produced a similar effect, were not criminalised. Concern over these so-called "legal highs" resulted in the **PSA 2016** which criminalises supply and possession with intent to supply of substances which it describes as being "capable of producing a psychoactive effect" (**s2**) when consumed.

In the News

"Legal highs"

The **Psychoactive Substances Act 2016** prohibited the production and supply of what have now been termed "new psychoactive substances". However, some have expressed concern that this has not lowered demand and that criminalisation prevents regulation to reduce the risks associated with drug use:

Paul Pigott, "Psychoactive drugs bought at 'click of a button' online" *BBC News* (26 May 2021)

11.3 Possession

Possession is the most commonly recorded drugs offence in England and Wales according to the UK Government's 2022 white paper *Swift, Certain, Tough: New Consequences for Drug Possession*, which advocated for a new police and sentencing response to possession to bring rates of offending down.[5] **s5(1)–(2) Misuse of Drugs Act 1971** establishes the offence of possession where:

- the defendant has possession of a controlled substance (*the actus reus*);
- with knowledge that it is in their possession (the *mens rea*).

11.3.1 Possession

The distinction between the *mens rea* and the *actus reus* of possession was emphasised in ***Lambert (Steven)* [2002]**, which explained (at **Para 61**):

> *"The physical element [of possession] involves proof that the thing is in the custody of the defendant or subject to his control."*

---

5 Home Department, *Swift, Certain, Tough: New consequences for Drug Possession* (CP 723 2022)

This approach reflects the wording of **s37(3) MDA 1971** and the inclusion of both custody and control of the substance means that multiple defendants may be physically in possession of a substance at the same time.

In ***Peaston* [1978]**, the defendant appealed his conviction for possession of a Class B drug which he had ordered, and which had been posted through the letterbox of the property he was renting. The Court of Appeal held that although he had not opened the envelope containing the drug, until prompted to do so by the police, he was in possession of the drugs from the point at which they had been posted through the letterbox.

However, mere presence on the defendant's property will not, in isolation, be sufficient to demonstrate control over the substance. In ***Adams v DPP* [2002]**, heroin was found on a sofa in the property shared by the defendant and her partner. The heroin appeared to have been brought into the flat by one of two visitors, who were also present at the time that the heroin was discovered by police. Although the defendant was aware and permitted the heroin to be brought into the flat, the High Court determined that this did not amount to control over the drug itself.

11.3.2 Knowledge of possession

The mental element of the offence requires the defendant to have knowledge that the substance is in his or her possession. Factually, a defendant may lack this knowledge where they are not aware of the item's existence. In a notable example given in ***Warner v Metropolitan Police Commissioner* [1969]** at 299, the House of Lords emphasised that where *"someone surreptitiously puts something into my pocket, I am not in possession of it until I know it is there"*. However, this does not prevent liability where the defendant had knowledge that the substance was in their possession but has subsequently forgotten, as was the case in ***Martindale* [1986]**.

***Lambert (Steven)* [2002]** makes it clear that knowledge of possession does not require the defendant to know what the substance is or that the substance is a controlled drug (para 122). In ***Searle v Randolph* [1972]** the defendant was found to be in possession of cigarettes containing cannabis. The court held that the defendant need only have knowledge that he possessed the cigarettes, not that they contained cannabis, to be liable for possession.

Searle was distinguished from ***Marriott* (1971)** where the defendant was charged with possession of cannabis resin when trace amounts were detected on the blade of a pen knife in his possession. Whilst in ***Searle*** the defendant was aware that a substance was in his possession, but was mistaken as to its nature, the defendant in ***Marriott*** argued he was unaware of the presence of a substance at all. The court held that knowledge that he possessed the pen knife was insufficient: the defendant was also required to be aware that something was on the blade.

Reflective question

***Lambert (Steven)* [2002]** is the key authority when applying the mental element of possession. At para 39, the House of Lords explains that a defendant in possession of a container is presumed to have knowledge of the contents of the container, unless there is evidence to the contrary. Apply this principle to discuss liability in the following scenario:

Peter is arrested at Waterloo station with a suitcase in his possession. When searched by the police, 3g of cocaine is discovered in Peter's coat pocket and 20g of cannabis is discovered in the lining of the suitcase. Peter maintains that the suitcase was left unattended when he was on the train and that the cannabis was placed there by an unknown person.

A defence exists under **s28(3)(b)(i) MDA 1971** where the defendant does not believe or suspect, or have reason to suspect, that the substance in their possession is a controlled substance. This does not apply where a defendant believes or suspects the substance to be a different controlled substance. Similarly, where a defendant is entitled to possess a controlled substance(s) but is charged with possession of a different controlled substance, a defence can be claimed under **s28(3)(b)(ii)** where the defendant establishes that they believed the substance to be the one they were entitled to possess.

11.3.3 Joint possession

Where the prosecution alleges joint possession of a substance, it is necessary for each defendant to have had custody of some of the substance or sufficient control over it. Knowledge of the existence of the substance is not, by itself, sufficient evidence of control (***Bland* [1988]**). Instead, an emphasis has been placed on the need for each defendant to have a degree of control over the substance (***Lemma* [2012]**).

11.3.4 Quantities

There is no minimum quantity of a controlled substance which is necessary for a defendant to be liable, although as demonstrated by ***Marriott* (1971)** a very low quantity might suggest a lack of knowledge of the substance. Where the defendant has only a low quantity of a Class B or C substance in their possession, this may also influence the Crown Prosecutor when making a decision about the public interest in bringing a prosecution. Conversely, a large quantity in the defendant's possession might be evidence of an intention to supply, where the quantities involved go beyond what would be considered reasonable for personal use.

11.3.5 Defences

A statutory defence is established by **s5(4)(a) MDA 1971** in situations where a defendant takes possession of a substance for the purpose of preventing another from committing an offence in relation to it. This could apply, for example, where a teacher takes cannabis into their possession after discovering it on a student for the purpose of preventing the student from possessing it.

In order to be able to claim the defence, the defendant must make all reasonable attempts to destroy the substance or hand it to appropriate authorities *as soon as possible*. In ***Murphy* [2002]** the defendant discovered cannabis in his father's car. The defendant buried the drugs, claiming that this amounted to a reasonable attempt to destroy the cannabis. The Court of Appeal held that burial did not amount to destruction given that it was not sufficiently permanent in nature.

A similar defence arises under **s5(4)(b)** where the defendant takes possession of the substance for the purpose of handing the substance to appropriate authorities entitled to take possession of the substance. As with the defence under **s5(4)(a)**, the use of this defence is extremely narrow and fact specific.

Whilst a defendant might attempt to rely upon a general defence of necessity (see **Chapter 14**), on the basis that substances – particularly cannabis – are necessary for pain relief, the law here is complex. ***Quayle* [2005]** and ***Altham* [2006]** both indicate that pain relief does not give rise to a necessity defence. However, this principle was decided prior to some cannabis products becoming available on prescription under the **Misuse of Drugs (Amendments) (Cannabis and Licence Fees) Regulations 2018**. Whilst this does not decriminalise the possession of cannabis, which has not been properly prescribed, arguably this has the potential to shape future necessity-based arguments.

11.4 Supply and possession with intent to supply

11.4.1 Supply and offering to supply

Several offences relating to the supply of controlled substances are set out in **s4(3) Misuse of Drugs Act 1971** which makes it an offence for the defendant:

> *(a) to supply or offer to supply a controlled drug to another [...]; or*
>
> *(b) to be concerned in the supplying of such a drug to another [...]; or*
>
> *(c) to be concerned in the making to another [..] an offer to supply such a drug.*

In ***Martin and Brimecome* [2014]** the court explained supply "*refers to the entire process of supply*" (para 16). This aligns with **s37(1) MDA 1971** which defines supplying as including acts of distribution.

The distinction between the three offences is best explained in ***Coker* [2019]** at para 25, which states:

> *"Section 4(3) of the Act gives rise to three separate and distinct offences. Section 4(3)(a) deals with "supply" or an "offer to supply". Subsections 4(3)(b) and (c) broaden the ambit of the section by applying to those who are "concerned in" either the supply or an offer to supply controlled drugs."*

In ***Osman* [2023]** the Court of Appeal emphasised that the consequence of the distinction between the three offences explained in ***Coker*** was that being concerned with supply could not be used interchangeably with being concerned with offering to supply.

For example, a defendant may be concerned with supply without being concerned with the offer to supply itself, where they are involved in transporting substances or acting as a "middleman" in the supply chain. Similarly, a defendant may be concerned with making offers to supply, for example introducing a would-be customer to a dealer (as in ***Blake* (1979)**) without substances actually being supplied.

Reflective question

Many cases will involve multiple defendants who have all been involved in some way with the supply or offer to supply drugs. Co-defendants cannot be charged with the supply of drugs to one another but will be liable for offences where they provide drugs which are supplied to non-defendants (***Abi-Khalil* [2017]**). With this in mind, consider liability in the following scenario:

Hugh is a university student. To celebrate the end of exam season, he decides to order some drugs ahead of a night out. He texts Em, his dealer, who says he would be able to get Hugh some ecstasy and MDMA tablets. Em rings Eddie, who provides Em with the tablets. Em delivers these to Hugh, who then shares them with his course mates on their night out.

The offences in **s4(3)**, as with other offences discussed in this chapter, are subject to an exception, set out in **s7 MDA 1971**, which enables the government to licence professionals such as doctors, dentists and pharmacists to manufacture, prescribe and supply some controlled substances in their professional capacity.

11.4.2 Possession with intent to supply

It is not necessary for the defendant to have the substance in their possession to commit one or more of the **s4(3)** offences (***Mitchell* [1992]**). Where a defendant does have the substance in their possession, they may be liable for an offence under **s5(3) MDA 1971** which arises where:

- the defendant possesses the substance; and
- the defendant intends to supply it to another.

Possession is established using the same principles as the **s5(1)-(2)** offence, discussed above. However, for the purpose of the **s5(3)** offence, it does not matter if the defendant is normally entitled to possess the substance. Intent to supply to another can be demonstrated through specific evidence that the defendant intended to supply a specific person, or through evidence that the defendant was engaged in trade of drugs, both of which can be seen in various leading cases.

In ***Maginnis* [1987]** the defendant had a quantity of cannabis resin in his car, which he stated had been left there by an unnamed friend who was due to collect it. The House of Lords held that the intent to return the cannabis constituted an intent to supply, notwithstanding that the cannabis did not belong to the defendant. This case also serves to demonstrate that supply need not be for financial (or any other) gain.

In ***Gordon* [1995]** the Court of Appeal held that evidence of drug paraphernalia or other evidence which might support the inference that the defendant intended to buy and sell drugs is admissible during trial but requires careful directions to be given to the jury. In particular, whilst quantities of money might support an inference that the defendant is currently engaged in drug dealing, it is also necessary to consider any innocent explanation for it put forward by the defendant.

It is not necessary for the sums of money involved to be large in order for them to have evidential value, this will depend on the context of the case and, in particular, the defendant's honest sources of income (***Moutousamy* [2003]**). Similarly, whilst the quantity of drugs involved can be evidence either that the drugs were for personal use (where a **s5(1-2)** charge might be appropriate) or for supply, this is not necessarily conclusive – although an exceptionally large quantity might undermine a defendant's claim that it was all for their own personal use! It is not necessary for the supply to be a commercial transaction or, more generally, to the defendant's benefit.

Activity

Suppose that you are a Crown Prosecutor, what evidence might you consider relevant when deciding whether to charge a defendant with mere possession or with possession with intent to supply?

After making a list of these factors, compare your list to the one listed on the CPS website here:

https://www.cps.gov.uk/legal-guidance/drug-offences

11.5 Other drugs offences

11.5.1 Permitting a premises to be used for certain drugs offences

As we have seen, a defendant who is aware that a controlled substance is in their home is not automatically deemed to have sufficient control to be in possession of it (***Adams v DPP* [2002]**). However, a separate offence under **s8 MDA 1971** does apply in situations where:

- *The defendant is either the occupier or concerned in the management of a premises; and*
- *He knowingly permits one or more of the following to take place on those premises:*
    - *Production or attempted production of a controlled substance; or*
    - *Supply or attempted supply of a controlled substance to another; or*
    - *The preparation of opium for smoking; or*
    - *The smoking of cannabis, cannabis resin or prepared opium.*

MDA 1971 does not define who is an occupier and case law makes clear that the term should be given something close to its everyday meaning. It is not necessary for the defendant to be the legal owner of the property: someone who lives in the property and has the ability to exclude others from the property would be an occupier for the purpose of the offence (***Tao* [1977]**).

Similarly, a defendant may be concerned with the management of a property without having any legal right to be there. In ***Josephs and Christie* (1977)** the defendants were squatters in a house owned by the local authority. The defendants used the property to host a "card school", with control over who attended. The Court of Appeal held that the defendants had sufficient control over what went on at the property that they were concerned in the management of it.

In the News

"Cuckooing"

In recent years, there has been increasing acknowledgment that drug offences may take place in the homes of vulnerable individuals who are pressured or threatened into permitting offences to take place. Politicians from multiple political parties have called for this practice of "cuckooing" to become an offence in its own right:

Robert Booth, "Jess Phillips and Iain Duncan Smith lead calls to criminalise 'cuckooing'" *The Guardian* (26 February 2023)

In order to commit a **s8** offence, the defendant must knowingly permit the offence to happen. Of course, this excludes liability where a defendant genuinely has no knowledge of the offence; however, a defendant who is wilfully ignorant of obvious offences being committed, and does little to prevent them, may be liable (***Thomas and Thomson* (1976)**). Where a defendant argues that they did not permit the offence and that this is demonstrated by their efforts to discourage the offence, it is a question for the jury as to whether these steps were sufficient to prevent liability (***Brock and Wyner* [2001]**).

11.5.2 Production

The offence of producing or being concerned in the production of a controlled substance is set out in **s4(1)–(2) MDA 1971**. As with many of the other offences discussed in this chapter, **s7 MDA 1971** provides an exception where the producer is licenced to produce the substance as a regulated pharmaceutical manufacturer.

Production includes both manufacturing and cultivation of substances (**s37(1)**). It also includes converting one substance to another, as was the case in ***Russell* (1992)** which involved the production of "crack" cocaine. The defendant may only be involved in one stage of the production process, such as the preparation of cannabis from harvested cannabis plants (***Harris and Cox* [1996]**). Similarly, a defendant may play a more limited role, such as cleaning the site of the manufacturing, and still be liable but only if they are sufficiently aware of what is going on to make them a part of the production (***Dunn* [2008]**).

11.6 Evaluation and reform

The current legal framework around supply and possession of controlled drugs has seen little reform since 1971, save for the **Misuse of Drugs Regulations 2001** and the **Psychoactive Substances Act 2016. MDR 2001** has seen significant criticisms for a lack of clarity, particularly around the exemptions afforded to healthcare professionals.[6] Meanwhile, whilst **PSA 2016** was introduced to address the limitations of **MDA 1971** in responding to new substances, some have suggested that its scope lacks certainty and clarity, which may unevenly impact minority groups such as LGBTQ+ men[7] and minority religious communities.[8]

---

6 Cathal T Gallagher, "The Misuse of Drugs Regulations 2001: A case study in poor legislative drafting" (2022) 8 Drug Science 1

7 Chris Ashford, "Queer Intimacies and Criminal Law: Queer Legal Praxis and the UK Poppers Ban" in Joseph J Fischel and Brenda Cossman (eds) *Enticements* (New York University Press 2024)

8 Charlotte Walsh, "Caught in the crossfire: Plant medicines and the Psychoactive Substances Act 2016" (2017) 1(2) Journal of Psychedelic Studies 41

It has often been suggested that the law currently places too much emphasis on criminalisation and makes insufficient efforts to address drug use as a public health problem.[9] In 2023, the House of Commons Home Affairs Select Committee's *Drugs* report acknowledged arguments that **MDA 1971** "has failed to prevent drug use and failed to reduce drug-related deaths and drug-related offending" at the same time.[10] The report recommends that future reform "balances its criminal justice response to drugs with an increased public health response that seeks to prevent and treat drug use and tackle the root causes of drug use".[11]

At present, the criminal justice system does pursue some public health aims, including efforts to deter people away from drug use by police without resorting to prosecution.[12] However, there are strong indications that this operates as part of a drugs policy which has an unequal impact dependent upon race. For example, Shiner et al discuss developments in stop and search, arrest and prosecution policies and suggest that "[d]rug policing is a key driver of ethnic disparities throughout the criminal justice system".[13] Similarly, Brown and Wincup's work on vulnerability and drug use suggests that the current policy approach is too narrowly focused on the "problem" of drug use, without engaging with the much more broad socio-economic and structural factors surrounding drug usage.[14]

Proposed reforms to the law on drug offences are often wide reaching, particularly in the context of possession offences. Stevens et al propose the repeal of **s5(1)–(2) MDA 1971** in what they describe as a '"modest proposal"' that they suggest would reduce racial inequalities within the criminal justice system and reduce stigma around drug use, encouraging drug users to explore desistance support.[15] Similar reform proposals are often seen globally, although few jurisdictions fully implement them. An exception to this can be seen in Portugal, where possession was fully decriminalised in 2001, a reform which has been linked to positive health outcomes and reduced crime rates.[16]

---

9 Ellicia Schacht, "Ending the 'War on Drug Users': Abandoning the Criminal Justice Approach to Drug Use in the UK in Favour of a Public Health Model" (2021) 10 Manchester Review of Law, Crime and Ethics 48

10 Home Affairs Committee, *Drugs* (2022-2023, HC 198) 10

11 Home Affairs Committee, *Drugs* (2022-2023, HC 198) 72

12 Matthew Bacon, "Desistance from criminalisation: police culture and new directions in drug policing" (2022) 32 Policing and Society 522

13 Michael Shiner, Zoe Carre et al, "The Colour of Injustice: 'Race', drugs and law enforcement in England and Wales" (StopWatch & Release, 2018) 61

14 Kate Brown and Emma Wincup, "Producing the vulnerable subject in English drug policy" (2020) 80 International Journal of Drug Policy 102525

15 Alex Stevens, Niamh Eastwood and Kirstie Douse, "In defence of the decriminalisation of drug possession in the UK" (2024) 10 Drug Science, Police and Law

16 Susana Ferrera, "Portugal's radical drugs policy is working. Why hasn't the world copied it?" *The Guardian* (5 December 2017)

However, less attention is often given to the complexities of supply-based offences. Cases such as ***Maginnis* [1987]** and ***Dunn* [2008]** have explored situations where the label of "producer" or "supplier" is given to someone who may not be a career drug-dealer. In their research, Hoyle et al discuss patterns of "social supply", particularly among young people, where offenders supply only within their own social circle, which they argue should be seen as distinct from supply as currently framed within **MDA 1971**.[17] Similarly, the wide scope of **s8 MDA 1971** has resulted in situations such as ***Brock and Wyner* [2001]** where a defendant becomes liable following only minimal involvement, potentially with little foresight of the likely consequences of another's actions.

Significant reform to the law on drugs offences does not appear immediately forthcoming. This is despite notable calls to do so from organisations and individuals within Parliament, the healthcare professions and the criminal justice system as part of a "50 Years of Failure" campaign which marked the 50th anniversary of **MDA 1971** in 2021.[18] However, some have advocated for more gradual change, through steps such as declassifying or downgrading particular substances, which may also begin to address some of the concerns regarding the current law outlined here.[19]

Reflective question

Compare and contrast the different offences discussed in this chapter. Do you think that each offence serves a distinct purpose and are there suitable alternative approaches which address behaviour which is concerning?

---

17 Leah Hoyle, Ross Coomber and Jason Lowther, "Crushing a Walnut With a Sledge Hammer? Analysing the Penal Response to the Social Supply of Illicit Drugs" (2013) 22 Social & Legal Studies 553

18 Adam Clarkson, "Misuse of Drugs Act turns 50 with reform calls" *BBC News* (27 May 2021) < https://www.bbc.co.uk/news/uk-england-tyne-57259815>; BMJ,"50 years of failure in UK in UK drug policy must end" (BMJ 29 September 2021) < https://www.bmj.com/company/newsroom/50-years-of-failure-in-uk-drug-policy-must-end/>

19 Toby Seddon, "From law to regulation: re-appraising the misuse of Drugs Act 1971" (2021) 21 Drugs and Alcohol Today 289

11.7 Summary

This chapter explored a range of offences established by the **Misuse of Drugs Act 1971**. The key points to take away from this chapter are:

- **MDA 1971** establishes the category of "controlled drug" in **s2** and three categories – Class A, Class B and Class C – into which drugs are categorised in **Sch 2**.
- Drugs which are not listed in **Sch 2** are not subject to **MDA 1971**. However, concern over new so-called "legal highs" led to the **Psychoactive Substances Act 2016** which criminalised supply and possession with intent to supply of these substances.
- **Possession** of a controlled substance is an offence under **s5(1)-(2) MDA 1971** and requires the defendant to have custody or control of the substance and knowledge it is in their possession.
- **Possession with intent to supply** is an offence under **s5(3) MDA 1971**. The defendant needs to satisfy the requirements of the possession offence and intend to supply it to another. The supply need not be a commercial transaction.
- **Supply** of a controlled substance is an offence under **s4(3) MDA 1971**. The defendant must either supply or offer to supply, or alternatively be concerned in supplying or making an offer to supply, another person with a controlled substance.
- These offences, as well as others such as permitting a premises to be used for drug offences under **s8 MDA 1971**, have been critiqued for being overly inclusive and potentially over criminalising, possibly contributing to unequal experiences within the criminal justice system.

Support for those experiencing drug addiction

The following support services are available for those experiencing issues with drug use and addiction:

- NHS: https://www.nhs.uk/live-well/addiction-support/drug-addiction-getting-help/
- FRANK: https://www.talktofrank.com/
- Withyou: https://www.wearewithyou.org.uk/
- Mind: https://www.mind.org.uk/information-support/types-of-mental-health-problems/recreational-drugs-alcohol-and-addiction/drug-and-alcohol-addiction-useful-contacts/
- Turning point: https://www.turning-point.co.uk/support-we-offer/drugs-and-alcohol

Further reading

Alex Stevens, Niamh Eastwood and Kirstie Douse, "In defence of the decriminalisation of drug possession in the UK" (2024) *10 Drug Science, Police and Law*

Ellicia Schacht, "Ending the 'War on Drug Users': Abandoning the Criminal Justice Approach to Drug Use in the UK in Favour of a Public Health Model" (2021) *10 Manchester Review of Law, Crime and Ethics 48*

Michael Shiner, Zoe Carre et al, "The Colour of Injustice: 'Race', drugs and law enforcement in England and Wales" (*StopWatch & Release*, 2018)

Nigel Stone, "Child Criminal Exploitation: 'County Lines', Trafficking and Cuckooing" (2018) *18 Youth Justice 285*

Mark Monaghan, "Drug Policy Governance in the UK: Lessons from changes to and debates concerning the classification of cannabis under the 1971 Misuse of Drugs Act" (2014) *25 International Journal of Drug Policy 1025*.

CHAPTER 12
Environmental offences

12.1 Introduction

In recent years, Parliament has passed the **Environment Act 2021** (**EA 2021**) and other legislation,[1] which it has done so with the stated aim of addressing the changing climate and regulating new environment-focused technologies such as heat pumps and hydrogen fuel which aim to lower the UK's carbon emissions.[2] "Priority" areas identified by in **s1(3) EA 2021** include:

(a) *Air quality;*

(b) *Water;*

(c) *Biodiversity;*

(d) *Resource efficiency and waste reduction.*

---

1 Such as the Energy Act 2023.
2 See, Department for Energy Security and Net Zero, "New laws passed to bolster energy security and deliver net zero" (*Gov.UK* 26 October 2023) <https://www.gov.uk/government/news/new-laws-passed-to-bolster-energy-security-and-deliver-net-zero>

Although much of this legislation goes beyond the scope of the criminal law, it often turns to criminal law as an enforcement mechanism for specific issues, particularly relating to waste reduction and management. However, as this chapter discusses, the ways in which it takes place often result in debate over whether environmental offences are "truly criminal" or not.[3]

This chapter starts by setting out the regulatory framework which is established by the **Environmental Permitting (England and Wales) Regulations** (**SI 2016/1154**). These regulations, enforced in England by the Environment Agency, require those undertaking specified activities which pose a risk to the environment to obtain authorisation from the Environment Agency before doing so and establish offences where a defendant does not have a permit, or exceeds it. As we will see, this regulatory regime exists alongside a range of statutory offences under the **Environmental Protection Act 1990** which apply whether or not a defendant is undertaking a regulated activity.

Throughout this chapter, you will find that the scope of the law in this area is broad and it is possible for multiple defendants, both individuals and corporate offenders, to commit an offence in relation to a specific incident of offending. You will see how the law has evolved, particularly in the context of nuisances, where the common law offence of public nuisance was first curtailed by the introduction of statutory nuisance and later abolished by the introduction of a statutory offence in the **Police, Crime, Sentencing and Courts Act 2022**. Later on in this chapter, we will consider how the use of criminal law, and alternatives to prosecution, can be critically evaluated.

Aims of this chapter

By the end of this chapter, you will:

- Understand the overarching regulatory framework related to the processing of controlled waste in England and Wales.
- Know how to apply the law on offences such as the unauthorised deposit of waste to complex problem scenarios.
- Be able to critically evaluate key aspects of the use of criminal law as an enforcement mechanism for environmental issues.

3 Julie Adshead, "Doing Justice to the Environment" (2013) 77(3) Journal of Criminal Law 173, 173

12.2 Environmental permitting offences

Waste management and other aspects of waste processing are subject to complex regulatory frameworks under the 2016 Regulations, which give the Environment Agency, in England,[4] the authority to permit certain – otherwise prohibited – activities, as well as to make plans to manage emissions (**reg 67**) require the disclosure of information (**reg 61**) and maintain a public register of regulated operators (**Sch 27**) among other powers. The Environment Agency can also place conditions on an operator who is granted permission and require third parties to agree to works required as part of these conditions (**reg 15**).

In the News

"Fracking"

Hydraulic fracking, which used high-pressure water to extract fossil fuel, has been a source of controversy in recent years. Following the UK's decision to leave the European Union, the possibility of a divergence from the cautious approach taken in EU regulatory approaches to fracking has been a point of particular debate and discussion. Consider reading:

Shashi Kant Yadav and Rosalind Malcolm, "Fracking review suggests UK has softened precautionary principle since leaving EU – here's why it matters" *The Conversation* (5 May 2022)

Under the **Environmental Permitting (England and Wales) Regulations (SI 2016/1154)**, **reg 38** a person commits and offence where they themselves contravene, cause or knowingly permit the contravention of **reg 12**, which specifies that:

> *(1) A person must not, except under and to the extent authorised by an environmental permit—*
>
> *(a) Operate a regulated facility,*
>
> or
>
> *(b) Cause or knowingly permit a water discharge activity or groundwater activity.*

A number of offences therefore arise from this provision, covering situations where a defendant carries out an activity entirely without a permit and situations where

4 In Wales, this function is carried out by Natural Resource Wales.

a defendant holds a permit but exceeds what they are permitted to do.[5] Where it is alleged that the defendant themselves contravened the relevant regulation, the offence is one of *strict liability*.

12.2.1 Regulated facilities and activities

The offence stemming from **reg 12(1)(a)** covers situations where a defendant operates a regulated facility. These facilities encompass any of the following regulated categories, set out in **reg 8**:

- *Installations and mobile plants where combustion, oil and gas, metal production and processing, mineral production and processing (including the processing of asbestos), chemical industry, waste management, carbon capture and other processes are carried out (see* **Sch 1(1)***).*
- *Facilities used for the processing, recovery and disposal of waste* (**reg 2**)*, including waste from mining extraction processes* (**Sch 20(2)**).
- *Facilities used for the accumulation, keeping or disposal of materials which the person concerned knows or has reasonable grounds to believe to be radioactive* (**Sch 23 Part 2(11)**).
- *Facilities which discharge polluted or waste matter, including liquid waste and sewage, to inland or coastal waters* (**Sch 21(3)**) *or any pollutant to groundwater, whether directly or indirectly* (**Sch 22(3)**).
- *Facilities which incinerate non-hazardous waste of quantities no greater than 10 tonnes per day/3 tonnes per hour* (**reg 2**).
- *Facilities which undertake manufacturing or commercial processes involving solvents, such as the manufacturing of synthetic rubber.*[6]
- *Facilities used in a manner affecting main rivers,*[7] *drainage works, flood plains, sea defences, such as dredging and desilting or quarrying and construction near to such rivers* (**reg 25(3)**).

---

5 Department for Environment, Food and Rural Affairs, "Environmental permitting: Core guidance: For the Environmental Permitting (England and Wales) Regulations 2016 (SI 2016 No 1154)" (March 2020) <https://assets.publishing.service.gov.uk/media/5fb3a39dd3bf7f37d7e7270e/environmental-permitting-core-guidance.pdf

6 European Council and Parliament Directive 2010/75/EU of 24 November 2010 on Industrial Emissions OJ L334, Ch 5 and Annex VII (to the extent retained by the European Union (Withdrawal) Act 2018).

7 Main rivers are specific rivers identified on the main river map for England/Wales: see Water Resources Act 1991, s113

- *Facilities where combustion is used for electricity generation, where the thermal input of the plant or generation is above 1 but below 50 megawatts.*[8]

The offence created by **reg 12(1)(b)** covers situations where there is the discharge of polluted or waste matter to inland or coastal waters (**Sch 21(3)**) or direct or indirect pollution to groundwater (**Sch 22(3)**), where the defendant has caused or knowingly permitted this discharge or pollution, whether or not the defendant has operated the facility which does so.

Sch 3 of the **2016 Regulations** provide limited exceptions, where the activities listed above can be carried out without the need for a permit. For example, in limited circumstances, vehicle tyres which have reached the end of their useful life can be used in construction without the need for a permit.[9] The scope of these exemptions are often narrow in application. In ***R (on the application of Cleansing Services Group Limited) v Environment Agency*** **[2019]**, the Court of Appeal rejected arguments by a septic tank drainage company that the screening of debris from sludge that they had collected and were storing was exempt from regulation. Exemptions covering the storage of sludge did not extend to filtering the sludge when it was put into temporary storage, which amounted to a form of treatment (see **para** [**51**]).

12.2.2 Operating without a permit or exceeding permission

Whether a permit has been granted will be a question of fact in each individual case. This makes allegations that the defendant has operated entirely without a permit comparatively straightforward. This issue will be more complex, however, where there is disagreement over whether the defendant has exceeded the authorisation given to them in a permit.

Permits will, subject to limited exceptions, include a map or suitable description of the regulated facility (**reg 14**). The permit may also attach a number of conditions

8 Environmental Permitting (England and Wales) Regulations 2016/1154, Sch 25A(2) and 25B(2). For existing combustion plants between 1-5 megawatts, this provision does not apply until 1 January 2029. For certain categories of generator, with low emission rates of nitrogen oxides, this provision does not apply until 1 January 2030.

9 Environmental Permitting (England and Wales) Regulations 2016/1154, Sch 22, Pt 1(2)(3)

which the operator of the facility must meet (**reg 15**) which may take the form of standard rules developed by the regulator and ministers.[10]

In ***R (on the application of Squire) v Shropshire Council and Matthew Bower* [2019]** the Court of Appeal explained that assessing the conditions should be read *"objectively and in their full context, without straining their natural and ordinary meaning beyond what the context requires, but with appropriate caution where, as here, a breach of condition may lead in the end to criminal proceedings"*. Where specific conditions are imposed on a mandatory basis, the defendant cannot evade liability by demonstrating that comparable or better measures were taken instead of those mandated by the permit (***R v Atlantic Recycling* [2024]** [27]-[28]).

Further reading

Enforcement and environmental offences

Criminal convictions are, generally, considered to be the most serious penalty which can be imposed by law in England and Wales. However, as Ogus and Abbot discuss, regulatory powers including the ability to suspend or revoke environmental permits may also operate as effective forms of sanction and censure. For discussion of the low usage of these more serious forms of penalty, consider reading:

Anthony Ogus and Carolyn Abbot, "Sanctions for Pollution: Do we have the right regime?" (2002) *14(3) Journal of Environmental Law 283*

12.2.3 Causing or knowingly permitting

Liability for a breach of **reg 12(1)(b)** requires the defendant to either have caused **or** knowingly permitted a restricted activity. Although, as discussed below, this means that a defendant may be found liable despite efforts to prevent the unauthorised activity (***Alphacell Ltd v Woodward* [1972]**), this does not mean that the offence stemming from **sub-s(b)** is one of strict liability. Both causing and *knowingly* permitting necessarily involve an element of fault.[11]

---

10 Department for Environment, Food and Rural Affairs, "Environmental permitting: Core guidance: For the Environmental Permitting(England and Wales) Regulations 2016 (SI 2016 No 1154)" (March 2020) <https://assets.publishing.service.gov.uk/media/5fb3a39dd3bf7f37d7e7270e/environmental-permitting-core-guidance.pdf

11 Vehicle Inspectorate v Nuttall [1999]; Riley and Others v Crown Prosecution Service [2016] where the High Court held that "knowingly permitting" did require fault in the context of an offence under the Animal Welfare Act 2006.

In ***Price v Cromack* [1975]**, the defendant was charged with an offence of causing the pollution of a stream under relevant environmental offences at that time. The defendant had permitted two lagoons to be built on his land to be used as part of an agreement that the land could be used as part of the disposal of animal waste by various means, including through existing sewers. A breach in the wall of one of these lagoons meant that waste was escaping into nearby land and subsequently into a local stream and this situation was exacerbated by a breach in the wall separating the two lagoons such that both were releasing the waste they stored. The question for the court was whether by allowing the construction of these lagoons, the defendant had "*caused*" the waste to pollute the stream.[12] In quashing the defendant's conviction, Lord Widgery (at 994) held that causing could not logically encompass the defendant who only "*stands by and watches the polluting matter cross his land into the stream*" even if he has contracted to permit the waste to be brought onto his land.

Drawing on ***Price***, the court in ***Attorney-General's Reference No 1 of 1994* [1995]** held that multiple defendants can each *cause* pollution, going on to explain:

> *"(1) It is question of fact in each case whether a defendant "caused" the polluting matter to enter controlled waters.*
>
> ...
>
> *(3) The word "causes" is to be given its plain commonsense meaning and is not to be refined by introducing concepts such as causa causans, effective cause, novus actus, proximate or principal cause.*
>
> *(4) The word "causes" involves some active participation in the operation or chain of operations resulting in the pollution of controlled waters.*
>
> *(5) "Mere tacit standing by and looking on" (per Lord Widgery C.J. in Price v. Cromack) is insufficient to amount to causing."*

Consequently, whilst a pure omission – simply "looking on" – could not amount to causing, where a defendant operates but fails to maintain a system, the act of operating the system is a positive act capable of amounting to a *causing* (***AG Reference No 1 of 1994*** at [370]).

In ***Mark Stone and Salhouse Norwich Ltd v Environment Agency* [2018]** the defendants were charged with knowingly permitting another party to use a site leased from the defendants as a waste storage facility without the proper permit under an earlier version of the permitting regulations. At appeal, the court at [50] discussed whether knowingly permitting required a positive act by the defendant or

---

12 As the defendant had not been charged with *knowingly permitting* the pollution to occur, it was not open to the Courts to consider this as an alternative way of committing the offence. To some extent, this means that the case is merely the application of Alphacell: see discussion in National Rivers Authority v Yorkshire Water Services Ltd [1995].

whether some lower mental requirement was sufficient, concluding that knowingly permitting required, at a minimum:

> "*(a) Knowledge that the regulated activity was occurring, and*
>
> *(b) The defendant doing nothing to prevent the activity occurring.*"

In some instances, the defendant may both have partially caused a breach of the regulations and knowingly permitted activities being carried out by others. Whether to charge the defendant with causing or knowingly permitting the position, or both will depend on the particular circumstances of such cases. Where the defendant has knowledge, or foresight, that the breach of the regulations would occur and failed to intervene but committed no positive act, however, they should only be charged with knowingly permitting the activity (***Empress Car Company (Abertillery) Ltd v National Rivers Authority*** (also reported as ***Environment Agency v Empress Car Co (Abertillery) Ltd)*** **[1998]**).

In the News

Health and safety offences and the environment

In addition to the specific environmental offences discussed in this chapter, operators of regulated facilities and other undertaking activities with a potential impact on the environment will also need to be cognisant of a wide range of other offences, such as workplace health and safety offences, which might arise due to their operations. For example, in ***Exolum Pipeline System Ltd v Health and Safety Executive*** **[2024]**, the Court of Appeal upheld the conviction of a fuel pipeline operator for **Health and Safety at Work Act 1974** offences relating to workers exposed to risk from a leaking high-pressure pipe. At the same time, the fine imposed on the operator was reduced from £2.3m to £1.5m. Consider reading:

Peter Craig, "Fire fined £2.3m after pipeline leak left workers at risk of 'flammable cloud'" (*Grimsby Live*, 27 March 2023)

12.2.4 Regulatory defences

Two defences to the regulatory offences discussed above are set out in **reg 40**. The defence under **reg 40(2)** is a narrow defence applicable to the discharge of polluted water from abandoned mines. The more widely applicable offence arises under **reg 40(1)** where the defendant acts in an emergency situation where the breach was carried out:

> *in order to avoid danger to human health in a case where—*

(a) *the person took all such steps as were reasonably practicable in the circumstances for minimising pollution, and*

(b) *particulars of the acts were furnished to the regulator as soon as reasonably practicable after they were done.*

12.3 Environmental Protection Act 1990 offences

In addition to the offences discussed above, a range of offences arise out of the **Environmental Protection Act 1990**. These include small scale offences, such as littering (**s87**) as well as more complex offences, such as failing to comply with a notice requiring the remediation of land which is contaminated (**s78M**). **Part 2** of the Act sets out offences in relation to controlled waste, which encompasses:

a. *Household waste, such as waste from a residential home, caravan or other domestic property (**s75(5)**).*

b. *Industrial waste, such as waste from a factory, mine, or site connected to public transport services* (**s75(6)**).

c. *Commercial waste, such as waste from sites used for business, whether for consumers or trade, other than that which is household or industrial waste* (**s75(7)**).

This definition of waste is broad in scope with some arguing that the general approach taken to defining waste (and how to distinguish it from non-waste, particularly in the case of useful industrial by-products)[13] is overly complex in nature and often fails to satisfy the need for legal certainty.[14]

12.3.1 Prohibition on unauthorised or harmful deposits, treatment or disposal of waste

An offence under **s33(1)** applies where a defendant:

- *Deposits or knowingly causes or knowingly permits the deposit of controlled waste on land, in the absence of suitable environmental permitting, or*

13 Whether material capable of being waste is, in fact waste or is instead non-waste which the defendant or another intends to put to use is a question of fact for the jury to determine: R v W [2010].

14 Martha Grekos and Satnam Choongh, "Finding a workable definition of waste: is it a waste of time?" (2006) Journal of Planning & Environment Law 463, in particular at 464, 479.

- *Submits or knowingly causes or knowingly permits the submission of controlled waste to a disposal or recovery facility not operating under an environmental permit, or*
- *Retains, treats or disposes of controlled waste in a manner likely to pollute or cause harm to human health.*

In the context of this offence, to *deposit* should be given its ordinary, everyday meaning of to "*put, place(d) or set down*" the waste in question (***Thames Water Utilities Ltd v Bromley Magistrates' Court* [2013]** at [25]) In ***Milton Keynes District Council v Fuller & McVeigh* [2011]** at [40]-[41] the High Court held that the defendants who had moved waste, dumped by others, from in front of the gate to their property had not deposited it for the purpose of the offence, although emphasising that on different facts a subsequent movement of controlled waste could amount to a deposit. Similar principles should be applied to other terminology, such as "*submit(ting), treat(s)* or *dispose(s)*", as well as to the need for a risk of harm to human health where acts which are harmful because of the risk they create are likely to be sufficient (***Leighton* [1997]**).

Reflective question

Thaisa, a sole trader, runs a white goods shop and offers home delivery to her customers. As part of the service which she provides, she also offers to take away old appliances which customers are replacing with new purchases as well as small amounts of rubbish where customers are decorating or carrying out DIY. Simon orders a new dishwasher from Thaisa's store and asks her to take away his existing dishwasher along with several old cans of paint which he has no further use for. Thaisa takes the old dishwasher and leaves it on a patch of wasteland on the edge of an industrial estate. She places the paint cans in the yard at the back of her business, however, places one of the cans upside down. Paint leaks from the can and runs into a stream on adjoining land. Consider Thaisa and/or Simon's liability.

As with the regulatory offences discussed above, a defendant may commit the offence with only a minimal amount of fault through causing or knowingly permitting a depositing, submitting or other prohibited act by another. Where the offence is committed through a defendant depositing, submitting or retaining, treating or disposing of waste themselves, the offence is one of *strict* liability.[15] It is not necessary for the prosecution to prove that the defendant knew no environmental permit applied, simply knowing that a deposit is to occur is sufficient for liability (***Shanks & McEwan (Teesside) Ltd v Environment Agency* [1999]**). Similarly, it is not necessary for the prosecution to prove that a defendant has both knowingly permitted *and* caused a disposal or has deposited and disposed of waste, for example, the

15 Although the defendant is able to establish a defence by demonstrating that they took reasonable precautions and exercised due diligence under s33(7).

different aspects of **s33** represent different ways of carrying out a single offence, rather than separate offences (***Leighton*** **[1997]**).

12.3.2 Breach of a duty of care in respect of waste

Under **s34(1)(a)-(aa)** a duty of care applies to *any person who imports, produces, carries, keeps, treats or disposes of controlled waste* to take all reasonable measures to prevent *another* person from breaching the requirements of **s33** or contravening any of the requirements of **reg 12**, discussed above. For example, in ***Trafalgar Leisure Limited*** **[2009]** the Court of Appeal suggested that failure by a business to lock a bin to prevent others from depositing waste into it could amount to a breach of this duty.[16] Although the legislation speaks of this as a duty of care, employing the language of tort, a breach of this duty is an offence under **s34(6)**.

Additionally, this duty of care also requires the defendant themselves to take reasonable steps to prevent waste escaping from their control or the control of another (whether or not such an escape occurs)[17] and only to transfer the waste to authorised persons or haulers accompanied by a written description to assist with that person's duty to themselves prevent waste escaping (**s34(1)(b)-(c)**). A defendant remains in control of waste on their property, even if they have engaged an independent contractor who also has control over the waste, such that a defendant is required to take reasonable steps to ensure that the waste is disposed of in accordance with the duty (***Mountpace Ltd v Haringey London Borough Council*** **[2012]**).

Further reading

Sentencing and environmental offences

As Parpworth and Thompson discuss, the sentencing of offenders convicted of offences under the **Environmental Protection Act 1990** demonstrates some of the complexity involved in cases which may vary from an honest but negligent defendant who briefly and minimally goes beyond a permit they hold to a defendant who wilfully and frequently engages in extensive "fly-tipping".

Consider reading: Neil Parpworth and Katherine Thompson, "Fly-tipping: a real environmental crime" (2009) *9 Journal of Planning & Environment Law 1133*

16 Although, in this case, the defendant's conviction was quashed on the basis that there was insufficient evidence of a such a failure at the close of the prosecution case.

17 Camden LBC v Mortgage Times Group Ltd [2007]

12.4 Nuisance

Two types of nuisance are relevant to the criminal law connected to the environment, although in drastically different ways. The **Environmental Protection Act 1990** identifies a range of *statutory nuisances* which can form the basis of a prosecution where a local authority has served a notice on the defendant (**s80**). Public nuisance was, prior to the **Police, Crime, Sentencing and Courts Act 2022**, a common law offence, however, it is now set out in statute.

12.4.1 Statutory nuisances

The various statutory nuisances which a local authority is under a duty to detect, investigate and prevent through enforcement actions include:

- *Keeping a premises in a state where it is prejudicial to health or a nuisance;*
- *Where smoke, fumes or gasses are escaping a property in a manner prejudicial to health or a nuisance;*
- *Where dust, steam, smells or odours from commercial activities are escaping a property in a manner prejudicial to health or a nuisance;*
- *Where waste or other materials are accumulated or left in a manner prejudicial to health or a nuisance;*
- *The keeping of animals or insects in a manner or place which is prejudicial to health or a nuisance; and,*
- *Where noise or artificial light is emitted from the premises in a manner which is prejudicial to health or a nuisance.*[18]

A local authority which detects a nuisance or is satisfied that a nuisance is likely to occur or reoccur is empowered to issue an *abatement notice* on the person responsible,[19] which may impose limitations, restrictions or prohibitions intended to prevent or limit the nuisance.

Failure to comply with an abatement notice without reasonable excuse constitutes an offence under the **Environmental Protection Act 1980**, **s80(4)**. What constitutes a reasonable excuse should take into account the purpose behind the ability of local authorities to issue abatement notices. In ***London Borough of Waltham Forest v Mitoo* [2016]**, the defendant failed to comply with an abatement notice by playing music loudly in the evening. The defendant argued that he had only

---

18 Environmental Protection Act 1990, s79. N.B. Exceptions apply to various categories of these statutory nuisances, such as light which is emitted from a bus station, see s79(5B)(e).

19 Or, if they are unknown, on the owner or occupier of the premises concerned: Environmental Protection Act 1990, s80(2).

done so to drown out other noise coming from building works nearby. The High Court rejected this argument, explaining at [14] that:

> *"[T]he existence of someone else's noise could not possibly be a good reason for Mr Mitoo to make yet more noise. Were his contention correct, it would mean that his neighbours would have to suffer not one, but two, types of noise. A statutory scheme intended to stem nuisance would then have perversely led to its multiplication."*

Those on whom an abatement notice are served are entitled to appeal. The appeal is heard by a magistrates' court and the appeal must be made within 21 days of the notice being served upon them.[20]

12.4.2 Public nuisance

The common law offence of public nuisance existed alongside the tort of public nuisance prior to the abolition of the common law offence by **s78 Police, Crime, Sentencing and Courts Act 2022** (**PCSCA 2022**). Both the offence and the tort were defined as a nuisance which *materially affects the reasonable comfort and convenience of life of a class of Her Majesty's subjects* with it being *sufficient to show that a representative cross-section of the class has been so affected* (**Attorney-General v PYA Quarries Ltd [1957]**). Public nuisance was distinguishable from the tort of private nuisance by being *"so widespread in its range or so indiscriminate in its effect that it would not be reasonable to expect one person to take proceedings on his own responsibility to put a stop to it'* (**PYA Quarries Ltd** at 191) such that the Attorney-General might bring the claim on behalf of those affected (***Rimmington* [2006]**).

In ***Rimmington*****,** the House of Lords held that introduction of the statutory nuisances identified in **s79 Environmental Protection Act 1990** and other offences stemming from that act, discussed above, meant that conduct which would previously have been charged as a common law offence, but which was now covered by those provisions, should be charged only under the statutory provisions. However, this did not amount to the abolition of the common law offence which could only be achieved through express provision by Parliament (***Rimmington*** at 274). **s78(6) PCSCA 2022** did, however, abolish the common law offence replacing it with an offence under **s78(1)** where:

- *A person does an act or fails to do an act required by law; and*
- *The act or omission;*
    - *Causes or creates a risk of serious harm to the public or a section thereof, or*
    - *Obstructs the public or a section thereof from exercising or enjoying a public right; and,*

20 Environmental Protection Act 1990, s80(3)

- *And the person intends or is reckless that their act or omission will have that effect.*

The *actus reus* requirements of the offence can be satisfied through either an act or an omission, provided that the defendant's conduct *either* creates a risk of serious harm or actually harms a section of the public. The leading authority on the offence is ***R v Smith and Others* [2024]** where the defendants were charged with the offence after carrying out a "Just Stop Oil" protest at Silverstone racing circuit. The defendants encroached onto the racing circuit during a Grand Prix Formula 1 race and sat down blocking half of the track. In upholding the defendants' convictions, the Court of Appeal pointed out that – unlike the previous common law offence – the new statutory offence did not require proof that the nuisance had harmed/risked harming/obstructed a *"significant"* section of the public (paras [42]-[43]). The court went on to explain at [49] that:

> *"As a matter of common sense, the greater the number of persons placed at risk, the easier it is likely to be to conclude that they can properly be regarded as "a section of the public". But, as counsel for the appellants realistically accepted, there is no minimum number. A "section of the public" is, in our view, simply a group of persons within a larger group or body of persons. It will be a question of fact in each case whether the smaller group can fairly be described as "a section of the public."*

Where the offence charged is that the defendant has caused or created a risk of serious harm, this is qualified by **s78(2)**. This defines serious harm as death, personal injury, disease, loss of property, damage of property, and serious distress, annoyance, inconvenience or loss of amenity. Where the offence charged is that the defendant has obstructed the exercise or enjoyment of a right, it is not necessary to establish that any harm, annoyance, distress or similar has been suffered, or has risked being suffered, serious or otherwise.[21]

The *mens rea* of the offence requires the defendant to, at a minimum, have been reckless as to causing harm, creating a risk of harm, or obstructing the exercise or enjoyment of a public right. In cases where the defendant's actions were intentional, the defendant's motivation for their actions should not be taken into account,[22] except to the extent that motivations might be relevant to the defence

21 See, for example, Trowland [2023]

22 Although there is limited analysis of this point in the context of the new criminal offence, comparable principles are expressed by the High Court in Jockey Club Racecourses v Kidby and Others [2023], where the defendant had already plead guilty to a s78 offence related to a previous nuisance.

of *reasonable* excuse available under **s78(3)**. Where argued, the defence of reasonable excuse must be established by the defendant on the balance of probabilities.[23]

Further reading

As the Law Commission note in their 2015 report, *Simplification of Criminal Law: Public Nuisance and Outraging Public Decency (Law Com No 358, 2015)*, which preceded the **Police, Crime, Sentencing and Courts Act 2022**, following the introduction of the statutory nuisances the law ended up in a "somewhat paradoxical" situation where environmentally damaging acts which had previously been prosecuted as public nuisance were charged as other offences and "various forms of misbehaviour in public rather than environmental nuisance" were charged as public nuisance (**para 3.20**). The Law Commission advocated retaining the use of public nuisance for so-called "environmental nuisance" alongside the way in which it has been employed to address "behavioural nuisance" suggesting (at **para 3.27**) that:

> "Arguably, it makes sense to keep public nuisance as the apex of the pyramid, reserving it for the most serious cases of deliberate or irresponsible misbehaviour. Most of the particular offences and procedures we have listed have limited penalties, and often involve a two-step process of first giving a notice and then waiting for non-compliance. This is not always adequate for the most serious and urgent cases."

The use of the offence created by **s78** has, to-date, primarily arisen in the context of *behavioural nuisances* – coincidentally, often by those motivated by concerns about climate change. However, it is unclear whether this reflects "how effective the regulatory scheme is", as the Law Commission might hope (see **para 3.28**), or other consequences of the abolition of the common law offence.

Consider Reading: Law Commission, "Simplification of Criminal Law: Public Nuisance and Outraging Public Decency" (Law Com No 358, 2015)

12.5 Evaluation and reform

As we have seen in this chapter, the law on environmental offences is diverse, incorporating a range of statutory offences, which enforce and underpin complex regulatory regimes. The context of these offences is important. With increasing social and political attention to the climate emergency and consequential reform to the

23 Explanatory Notes to the Police, Crime, Sentencing and Courts Act 2022, para 711.

regulatory regimes which governments use in an attempt to address these concerns; whilst there is limited scope for the use of domestic law to prosecute individuals for climate change,[24] the range of circumstances in which criminal law is turned to as an enforcement mechanism when regulations are breached has the potential to grow.

The number of "serious pollution incidents" has remained relatively static over the past decade, with the five-year average of incidents in England decreasing from 570 incidents in 2015 to 526 incidents in 2022, and the Environment Agency observing that nearly half of all serious incidents stem from facilities and activities that they did not regulate under the **Environmental Permitting (England and Wales) Regulations (SI 2016/1154)**.[25] The Environment Agency has brought over 5000 prosecutions for offences under the **2016 Regulations** or equivalent prior Regulations from 2007 or 2010.[26] In a recent report, the Agency's regulatory noted the significant cost of waste crime, estimating it to be £1 bn a year with 48% of all waste "perceived as being illegally managed".[27]

It has been suggested that the environmental offences discussed in this chapter are infrequently deployed by the regulators and that consequently:

> "[P]roblems [are] encountered both by the regulator, and those subject to the regulation, in predicting the outcome of each case, and in understanding the appliable standards."[28]

However, others have noted some positive benefits of alternative forms of enforcement, in particular enforcement undertakings. These are agreements between the Environment Agency and the would-be defendant which "[o]ften … include promises to remedy the harm causes as well as to compensate third parties" where "[i]n practice, this compensation often takes the form of a donation to a conservation

---

24 For discussion of the arguments for doing this, however, see, Mark Byrne, "Climate Crime: Can Responsibility for Climate Change Damage be Criminalised?" (2010) 4(3) Carbon & Climate Law Review 278

25 Environment Agency, "Review of activities regulated by the Environment Agency, 2022" (Environment Agency, 28 February 2024) <https://www.gov.uk/government/publications/review-of-activities-regulated-by-the-environment-agency-2022/review-of-activities-regulated-by-the-environment-agency-2022> accessed 17 January 2025

26 Environment Agency, "Environment Agency Prosecutions" (06 January 2025) https://www.data.gov.uk/dataset/6f06910a-8411-4117-9905-6284f1997c33/environment-agency-prosecutions accessed 17 January 2025

27 Environment Agency, "Environment Agency Chief Regulator's report 2023-2024" (17 January 2025) <https://www.gov.uk/government/publications/environment-agency-chief-regulators-report-2023-24/2e06554f-6fca-4e39-85cf-561a7b143a4a> accessed 17 January 2025

28 Emma Lees, *Interpreting Environmental Offences: The Need for Certainty* (Hart 2015) 1

or wildlife trust".[29] Nehme and Pedersen note, these alternatives to criminal prosecution can provide significant support to community projects, however, "the accountability attached to community benefits is weak" and this aspect of such measures is in need of reform.[30]

Activity

Suppose that you are a policy officer at the Department for Environment, Food and Rural Affairs. You have been asked by the Minister to prepare a new guidance document advising businesses on their obligations under environmental legislation and the various potential consequences for non-compliance. Prepare a one-page summary of the different offences under the **Environmental Permitting (England and Wales) Regulations (2016/1154)** and the **Environmental Protection Act 1990.**

Many of the environmental offences discussed in this chapter are likely to be committed by corporations, rather than individuals, which creates additional challenges surrounding prosecution and sentencing. As Malcolm notes "a company cannot be sent to prison or suffer a remedy in the same personal fashion as one of its directors" and therefore despite legislation also enabling directors to be prosecuted in their own right, questions remain over the effectiveness of the criminal law in preventing offending behaviour.[31] It has also been suggested that the strict liability imposed by some of the provisions discussed in this chapter "does not provide strong incentives for directors to proactively address environmental risks" due to the fact it is imposed on companies rather than individuals.[32]

The United Kingdom is not an outlier in employing a hybrid criminal and regulatory approach to activities which can carry a risk to the environment. Faure and Svatikova argue that the use of administrative proceedings in the Flemish region of Belgium, as well as in England and Wales, demonstrates that taking a hybrid approach is more practical in economic terms than approaching the problem through the use of criminal law alone – although they stress that this does not take account of the environmental effectiveness of hybrid methods of enforcement.[33]

29 Ole W Pedersen, "Revisting the Role of Negotiation and Trivialization in Environmental Law Enforcement" (2019) 46(1) Journal of Law and Society 29, 32

30 Marina Nehme and Ole W Pedersen, "Accountability and offsetting in environmental law enforcement" (2022) 49(1) Journal of Law and Society 93, 116

31 Rosalind Malcolm, "Prosecuting for environmental Crime: Does Crime Pay?" [2002] 14(4) Environmental Law and Management 300, 303

32 Ben Chester Cheong, "Bridging the accountability gap by enhancing UK corporate and personal liability for environmental harms" (2024) 45(11) Company Lawyer 363, 366

33 Miichael G Faure and Katarina Svatikova, "Criminal of Administrative Law to Protect the Environment? Evidence from Western Europe" (2012) 24(2) Journal

12.6 Summary

In this chapter, we have discussed a range of offences connected to the protection of the environment established through the **Environmental Permitting (England and Wales) Regulations** (**2016/1154**) and the **Environmental Protection Act 1990**. The key points to take away from this chapter are:

- The **Environmental Permitting (England and Wales) Regulations** (**2016/1154**) (**EPR 2016**) apply to a range of different facilities and activities which pose a risk to the environment, such as the processing or storage of waste.
- It is an offence under **EPR 2016, reg 12** to operate a facility in a regulated category or cause or knowingly permit a water discharge activity or a groundwater activity, except where authorised by an environmental permit.
- The offence under **EPR 2016, reg 12** can be one of *strict* liability where it is alleged that the defendant operated a regulated facility without an environmental permit themselves.
- Where it is alleged that a defendant *caused* a breach, this word should be given its ordinary meaning and could require some active participation in events by the defendant. *Knowingly permitting* a breach can be committed without a positive act by the defendant where the defendant knew the activity was occurring or would occur and they did nothing to prevent it.
- The **Environmental Protection Act 1990** (**EPA 1990**), **s33(1)(a)** created an offence in relation to controlled waste where the defendant deposits or *knowingly causes* or *knowingly permits* the deposit of controlled waste on land.
- It is also an offence under **EPA 1990, s33(1)** where a defendant disposes of controlled waste in a manner likely to pollute or cause harm to human health.
- A duty of care is established by **EPA 1990, s34** which applies to anyone *who imports, produces, carries, keeps, treats or disposes of controlled waste* requiring them to take reasonable steps to prevent the waste escaping from their control.
- The duty of care under **s34** also requires reasonable measures to be taken to prevent anyone else from committing an offence under **s33** or under the **EPR 2016, reg 12**.
- Environmental offences can also arise under what are termed *statutory nuisances* identified in **s79 EPA 1990**. These nuisances exists alongside the statutory offence of public nuisance created by **s78 Police, Crime, Sentencing and Courts Act 2022**.
- The offence under **s78** has primarily been used in the context of environmental protesting, however, it is possible it also holds a latent role in addressing serious environmental pollution not addressed by other statutes.

---

of Environmental Law 253, 285

- The complex interrelationship between the regulatory regimes created by the legislation discussed in this chapter and criminal law raise questions about the effectiveness of criminal and non-criminal penalties and sanctions in addressing polluting activities.

Further reading

Julie Adshead, "Doing Justice to the Environment" (2013) *77(3) Journal of Criminal Law 215*

David Bullock, "Public Nuisance and Climate Change: The Common Law's Solutions to the Plaintiff, Defendant and Causation Problems" (2022) *85(5) Modern Law Review 1136*

Michael G Faure and Katarina Svatikova, "Criminal or Administrative Law to Protect the Environment? Evidence from Western Europe" (2012) *24(2) Journal of Environmental Law 253*

Miranda Forstyth and Felicity Tepper, "Environmental Enforceable Undertakings: An Innovative Tool to Repair and Prevent Environmental Harm" (2024) *36(3) Journal of Environmental Law 385*

Ole W Pedersen, "Legislative Overreach, Adaption and Administrative Re-regulation in Environmental Law" (2022) *42(3) Oxford Journal of Legal Studies 818*.

CHAPTER 13

Defences: Fault

13.1 Introduction

In this chapter we look at defences relating to fault, i.e. a denial of the fault element. In **Chapter 14** we look at defences where there is justification, i.e. a potentially good lawful reason for the defendant's actions.

Overview of defences

In terms of defences, D can in terms of defences utilise:

(a) **Deny the *actus reus***, e.g. deny causation (see **Chapter 3**)

(b) **Deny the *mens rea*** – state a specific form of defence involving the absence of fault (see **Chapter 4**).

This chapter will cover absence of fault defences.

(c) **State a general defence** – this is often a denial the act itself was unlawful by virtue of a permissible legal excuse/justification.

(d) **State a specific defence**, i.e. specific to the offence e.g. in **Chapter 2** we saw **s5 Criminal Damage Act 1971** regarding lawful excuse**,** and in **Chapter 9** we saw **s2 (1) Theft Act 1968** regarding absence of dishonesty.

(e) State a partial defence, i.e. a defence which lowers the offence category. E.g. in **Chapter 4** we have seen how loss of self control and diminished responsibility can be pled by the defendant to lower the offence of murder to one of voluntary homicide.

The above categorisations above are not watertight. The defences often involve difficult underlying public policy decisions about not opening the floodgates of weak meretricious applications.

By the end of this chapter you can be expected to know and be able to evaluate the law on defences involving absence of fault specifically:

Automatism and insanity

These are clearly linked defences.

	Automatism	Insanity
Effect	1. Total destruction of voluntary control shown by medical evidence	1. Defect of reason
Cause	2. Caused by an external factor	2. Caused by an internal factor: a "disease of the mind"
Limit	3. D's condition must not be self-induced	3. D did not know the nature and quality of the act OR D did not know what he was doing was wrong
Burden of proof	Evidential: Defence raise the defence and must produce some evidence Legal: P must disprove the defence beyond reasonable doubt, no automatism, i.e. prove no automatism exists	Evidential: Court, prosecution or defence may raise the issue Legal: P – must prove beyond reasonable doubt D – must prove on a balance of probabilities

	Automatism	Insanity
D's liability	Acquittal	Special verdict – not guilty by reason of insanity and limited range of sentencing options

Intoxication

Intoxication is not strictly a defence. It involves rules about what evidence can be used of intoxication to rebut an accusation of culpable *mens rea.*

1)	What type of intoxication is involved?	Voluntary or involuntary
2)	Drunken *mens rea* is *mens rea*	
3)	What type of offence is involved?	Basic or specific intent

Mistake

As with intoxication, it is not a defence but an aspect of the *mens rea* of a crime. We will explore that mistakes need not be reasonable; that there is strong presumption favour of *mens rea* and when mistakes of civil law can negate the *mens rea.*

13.2 Automatism

13.2.1 Voluntary actions

1. When we reviewed the *actus reus* concept at **Chapter 3** we noted the D's actions or conduct would need to be shown to be voluntary.

   "No act is punishable if it is done involuntarily"

   *(**Bratty v A-G for Northern Ireland** **[1963]** per Lord Denning).*

2. Andrew Ashworth has helpfully labelled the automatism defence as synonymous with "authorship", i.e. if D is not the "author" of his own actions he should have a defence of denial of authorship.

For example, Derek is knocked over by a strong wind and bumps into Mia. The wind is described as an act of God which is a new intervening act. Similarly, where

Andreena crashes her car whilst driving, when she is attacked by a swarm of bees[1], this will also be an act of God.

The new intervening act may be the actions of a third party. For example, Dimitri is punched during a robbery and falls into a window, breaking it.

Alternatively the actions of a third party may be the new intervening act.

In the examples Derek, Andreena and Dimitri are is obviously not morally culpable and nor should they be legally culpable for the damage which ensues.

In terms of *actus reus*, they clearly did not "author" their actions. In terms of *mens rea*, they did not act intentionally or recklessly.

13.2.2 Definition of automatism

Bratty v Attorney-General of Northern Ireland **[1963]**

The facts were D was suffering from psychomotor epilepsy. D was charged with murder by strangulation of an 18-year-old girl. D stated he a "terrible feeling" and that "a sort of blackness" came over him. D was able to give some account of what happened.

D's defence was "rode three horses" (i.e., three arguments). Firstly, automatism by virtue of psychomotor epilepsy. Secondly, he was incapable of forming intent based on his mental state. Finally, he was guilty but insane due to a disease of the mind.

The trial judge refused to leave 1. (automatism) and 2. (intention) to the jury but left 3. (insanity) to the jury. The jury convicted.

The House of Lords dismissed the appeal stating epilepsy was a disease of the mind as it had an internal cause. They endorsed the judge as right to leave only defence 3 to the jury who rejected it.

In ***Bratty*** Lord Denning laid out the key principles:

1. **Total destruction of voluntary control usually shown by medical evidence (*Bratty* at 409):**

   "No act is punishable if it is done involuntarily...people ... prefer [the term] "automatism" [which] ***means an act which is done by the muscles without any control by the mind,*** *such as a spasm, a reflex action or a convulsion; or an act done by a person* ***who is not conscious of what he is doing,*** *such as an act done whilst suffering from concussion..."*

---

1 An example from Devlin J in Hill v Baxter.

Medical evidence (Bratty at 413-414)

"In order to displace the presumption of mental capacity, the defence must give sufficient evidence from which it may reasonably be inferred that the act was involuntary.

The evidence of the man himself will rarely be sufficient unless it is supported by medical evidence which points to the cause of the mental incapacity. It is not sufficient for a man to say, "I had a blackout": for blackout....is one of the first refuges of a guilty conscience and a popular excuse. The words of Devlin J in Hill v Baxter [1958] 1 QB 277 should be remembered:

> *"I do not doubt that there are genuine cases of automatism and the like, but I do not see how the layman can safely attempt without the help of some medical or scientific evidence to distinguish the genuine from the fraudulent.""*

2. **Caused by an external factor – Distinguishing external causes and internal causes (*Bratty* at 410)**

*"....[earlier cases] ... seem...to have assumed that other diseases such as epilepsy or cerebral tumour are not diseases of the mind, even when they are such as to manifest themselves in violence. I do not agree...It seems to me that **any mental disorder which has manifested itself in violence and is prone to recur is a disease of the mind**.*

***'[A]gain, if the involuntary act proceeds from a disease of the mind, it gives rise to a defence of insanity, but not to a defence of automatism.** Suppose a crime is committed by a man in a state of automatism or clouded consciousness due to a recurrent disease of the mind. Such an act is no doubt involuntary, but it does not give rise to an unqualified acquittal, for that would mean that he would be let at large to do it again. The only proper verdict is one which ensures that the person who suffers from the disease is kept secure in a hospital so as not to be a danger to himself or others. That is, a verdict of guilty but insane."*

3. **D's condition must not be self-induced**

13.2.3 Elements of automatism: What must be proved?

a) Total destruction of voluntary control usually shown by medical evidence

***Attorney General's Reference (No 2 of 1992)* [1994]**

The facts were D (a lorry driver) was travelling on a motorway. D stated the white lines and a straight featureless road hypnotised him into a trance like state. D was aware of the bright lights and was steering in a straight line.

D was charged with causing death (by careless driving in modern terminology).

D attempted to state a "defence" of automatism.

The trial judge allowed the "defence" of automatism to go before the jury and D was acquitted.

The Attorney-General referred the case to the Court of Appeal on a point of law.

The Court of Appeal stated the "*defence of automatism should not have been left to the jury*" and confirmed:

1. Automatism is only available for a total destruction of voluntary control
2. Automatism is NOT available for impaired, partial, or reduced control.

Per Lord Taylor CJ at 105:

> *"In our judgment, the "**proper evidential foundation" was not laid** in this case by... [the] evidence of "driving without awareness".*
>
> *As the authorities...show, the defence of **automatism requires** that there was a **total destruction of voluntary control on the [D's] part. Impaired, reduced, or partial control is not enough.***
>
> *[At trial it was] accepted that **someone "driving without awareness"...retains some control**. [Such a person]...would be able to steer the vehicle and usually to react and return to full awareness when confronted by significant stimuli."*

In ***Sandie Smith* [1982]** the facts were of post menstrual tension when charged with threats to kill did not amount to automatism. The Court of Appeal refused to allow the defence as it was not a total destruction of control by an external factor.

In ***Broome v Perkins* [1987]** D's car was driven erratically for five to six miles. D was charged with driving without due care. D stated a defence of hypoglycaemia (low blood sugar level due to excess insulin injected). The High Court stated this was not a total destruction of voluntary control and D exercising conscious control of the car and therefore should have been convicted.

b) Caused by an external factor

(i) This is an extremely problematic area of the law.

(ii) It is suggested students ignore what you know about medicine and instead focus on public policy![2]

(iii) The courts have described this area of the law a "quagmire" (***Gower* [2025]**).

(iv) The recent authority of ***Gower* [2025]** helpfully summarises the law by distinguishing external causes and internal causes.

External causes: something outside D, automatism

e.g.

• Anaesthetics	(***Quick* [1973]** & ***Sullivan* [1984]**)
• Concussion by a blow to the head	(***Sullivan* [1984]** & ***Burgess* [1991]**)
• Diabetes Where hypoglycaemia applies, i.e. low level of blood sugar caused by excess of insulin injected	(***Quick* [1973]**)
• Drugs ingested involuntarily	(***Quick* [1973]**)
• Hypnosis	(***Quick* [1973]**)
• Post traumatic stress disorder	(***T* [1990]**)
• Swarm of bees	(***Hill v Baxter* [1958]**)

Internal causes: something inside D, insanity

e.g.

• Arteriosclerotic	(***Hill v Baxter* [1958]**)
• Brain tumour	(***Bratty v Attorney General for Northern Ireland* [1963]**)
• Diabetes Where hyperglycaemia applies, i.e. high level of blood sugar caused by failure to take insulin	(***Bingham* [1991]** & ***Hennesy* [1989]**)
• Driving without awareness	(***AG Ref No 2 1992* [1994]**)
• Epilepsy	(***Sullivan* [1984])**
• Sleepwalking	(***Burgess* [1991]**)
• Stress, anxiety and depression	(***Hennesy* [1989]** & ***Gower* [2025]**)

2 See, Gower [2025]

4. Some examples from the case law

In ***Quick* [1973]**, the facts were D (a nurse) who was diabetic assaulted V (a patient). D was charged with ABH. D ran the defence of automatism stating the automatism arose from hypoglycaemia (low blood sugar level due to excess insulin injected). The trial judge directed that this was in fact insanity. The defendant entered a guilty plea and then appealed the judge's ruling. The Court of Appeal said the conviction was unsafe and the appeal was allowed. The requirements of automatism could have been made out and should have been left to the jury.

1. Total destruction of voluntary control
2. External factor
3. Not self-induced.

Per Lawton LJ (pp 922-923):

> *"A malfunctioning of the mind of transitory effect caused by the application to the body of some external factor such as violence, drugs, including anaesthetics, alcohol and hypnotic influences cannot fairly be said to be due to disease....*
>
> *In this case Quick's alleged mental condition, if it ever existed,* ***was not caused by his diabetes but by his use of the insulin prescribed by his doctor****.*
>
> *Such malfunctioning of the mind as there was,* ***was caused by an external factor*** *and not a bodily disorder in the nature of a disease which disturbed the working of his mind. It follows in our judgment that Quick was entitled to have his defence of automatism left to the jury."*

In **Sullivan [1984]**, the facts were D committed an assault whilst having an epileptic fit. D was charged with GBH. He ran the defence of automatism. The trial judge would not allow the defence to go to the jury D then changed his plea to guilty to ABH. D then appealed. The House of Lords held the defence was insanity and there was no defence of automatism because the epilepsy as a cause was internal.

Per Lord Diplock (at 173):

> *"My Lords, it is natural to feel reluctant to attach the label of insanity to a sufferer from psychomotor epilepsy of the kind to which the appellant was subject, even though the expression in the context of a special verdict of 'not guilty by reason of insanity' is a technical one which includes a purely temporary and intermittent suspension of the mental faculties of reason, memory and understanding resulting from the occurrence of an epileptic fit. But the label is contained in the current statute, it has appeared in this statute's predecessors ever since 1800. It does not lie within the power of the courts to alter it. Only Parliament can do that..."*

In ***Hennessy* [1989]**, D took a car without consent. D suffering from diabetes resulting in hyperglycaemic state (i.e. an internal excess of sugar due to the absence of insulin). The trial judge ruled this was not automatism as it was an internal cause. D then entered a guilty plea to the offence and appealed.

The Court of Appeal ruled this was an insanity case. The hyper state was a internal disease of the body which effects the working of the mind and insanity was the proper plea.

Per Lord Lane CJ (at 294ff):

> *"....hyperglycaemia, high blood sugar, caused by an inherent defect, and not corrected by insulin is a disease, and if, as the defendant was asserting here, it does cause a* ***malfunction of the mind****, then the case may fall within M'Naghten Rules. ...*
>
> *[c.f.] in Quick's case the fact that his condition was or may have been due to the injections of insulin, meant that* ***the malfunction was due to an external factor*** *and not to the disease. The drug it was that caused the hypoglycaemia, the low blood sugar..."*
>
> (**Confirmed stress anxiety or depression are not external causes: the impact of *Rabey* [1980]**): *"the ordinary stresses and disappointments of life which are the common lot of mankind do not constitute an external cause.*
>
> *"Stress, anxiety, and depression can no doubt be the result of the operation of external factors, but they are not ... in themselves separately or together external factors of the kind capable in law of causing or contributing to a state of automatism. They constitute a state of mind, which is prone to reoccur."*

In ***T* [1990]** D a 23-year-old was charged with robbery and assault. D had previously been raped and there was clear evidence she was suffering from post-traumatic stress disorder (PTSD) at time of the offences. The Court of Appeal held PTSD could amount to an external factor.

In ***Bingham* [1991]** D was arrested for shoplifting. D was diabetic. D's defence was automatism that whilst suffering from hypoglycaemia (low blood sugar level due to excess insulin injected) they were in an automatic state. The trial judge refused to leave this to the jury. The Court of Appeal, consistent with *Quick*, allowed the appeal and said evidence should have been left to the jury.

In ***Burgess* [1991]** D claimed to have carried out violent GBH assault hitting his girlfriend over the head with a video recorder and a bottle whilst sleepwalking. D claimed automatism. The trial judge rejected and said sleepwalking was an internal factor therefore only a plea of insanity was available. The Court of Appeal upheld the conviction. Sleepwalking is not automatism as there is an internal cause, namely a sleep disorder, which was a disease of the mind.

Per Lord Lane CJ (at 98):

> *"... we respectfully adopt what was said by Martin J and approved by a majority in the Supreme Court of Canada in* ***Rabey v The Queen [1980] 2 SCR 513, 519, 58:***
>
> > *"Any malfunctioning of the mind or mental disorder having its source primarily in some subjective condition or weakness internal to the accused (whether fully understood or not) may be a 'disease of the mind' if it prevents the accused from knowing what he is doing, but transient disturbances of consciousness due to certain specific external factors do not fall within the concept of disease of the mind..."*
>
> *...[W]e accept of course that sleep is a normal condition, but the evidence in the instant case indicates that sleepwalking, and particularly violence in sleep, is not normal."*

c) D's condition must not be self-induced

In ***Quick* [1973]** the Court of Appeal confirmed automatism is not applicable when self-induced (see above for the facts).

Lawton LJ at 922–3 stated:

> *"A self-induced incapacity will not excuse ... nor will one which could have been reasonably foreseen as a result of either doing, or omitting to do something, as, for example, taking alcohol against medical advice after using certain prescribed drugs, or failing to have regular meals while taking insulin ...*
>
> *Had the defence of automatism been left to the jury, a number of questions of fact would have had to be answered ...*
>
> > *-To what extent had he brought about his condition by not following his doctor's instructions about taking regular meals?*
> >
> > *-Did he know that he was getting into a hypoglycaemic episode? If yes,*
> >
> > *-Why did he not use the antidote of eating a lump of sugar as he had been advised to do?*
>
> *On the evidence which was before the jury Quick might have had difficulty in answering these questions in a manner which would have relieved him of responsibility for his act."*

In ***Bailey* [1983]** D, a diabetic, had not followed a food and insulin regime. D then hit V with an iron bar and was charged with GBH. The defence of automatism based on hypoglycaemia (low blood sugar level due to excess insulin injected) was rejected by the trial judge as self-induced.

The Court of Appeal confirmed the decision and dismissed the appeal. If D was at fault, then the defence is not available as there are policy grounds for not allowing the defence even though D was clearly in a state of automatism.

Per Griffiths LJ at 765:

> *"...In our judgment, selfinduced automatism, other than due to intoxication from alcohol or drugs, may provide a defence to crimes of basic intent. The question in each case will be whether the prosecution have proved the necessary element of recklessness. In cases of assault,* ***if [D] knows that his actions or inaction are likely to make him aggressive, unpredictable, or uncontrolled with the result that he may cause some injury to others, and he persists in the action or takes no remedial action when he knows it is required, it will be open to the jury to find that he was reckless.****"*

In ***Coley* [2013]** D smoked very large quantities of cannabis and blacked out. D believed he was a character in a video game. D used his keys; picked up a knife and then entered his neighbours house and killed V. D then sought to claim in the alternative either automatism or insanity. The trial judge found D was not able to rely on either.

The Court of Appeal upheld the conviction and both defences failed.

A) Automatism:	No defence
1. Total destruction of voluntary control?	NO destruction
2. Caused by an external factor	YES cannabis
3. D's condition must not be self-induced	NO it was clearly self-induced
B) Insanity	No defence
1. Defect of reason	YES
2. Caused by an internal factor a disease of the mind?	NO
This was temporary self-induced disturbance	
3. D did not know ...	YES

d) Burden of proof

Evidentially: Defendant raises the defence and must produce some evidence.

Legally: Prosecution must disprove the defence beyond the reasonable doubt defence of automatism is not applicable.

13.3 Insanity

13.3.1 Introduction

1. The law on insanity is outdated and desperately needs reform

"this quagmire of law seldom entered nowadays save by those in desperate need of some kind of a defence" (Lawton LJ in ***Quick* [1973]**).

2. Insanity can exist

(a) At the time of the crime	Insanity
(b) At the time of the trial	Fitness to plead

3. Who decides? The decision is for the jury

(a) At the time of the crime	Jury
(b) At the time of the trial	
Step 1 Fitness	Judge
Step 2 If unfit, finding of fact	Jury

4. English law remains governed by the common law in *M'Naghten's Case* (1843); [1843-60].

The facts were Daniel M'Naghten (D) shot Sir Robert Peel's secretary. The medical evidence was D had delusions as to right and wrong and no self-control. D was charged with murder. The Jury found D not guilty by reason of insanity.

The House of Lords using Lord Chief Justice Tindal's question set the law.

(a) Starting point: Presumption of sanity unless the contrary is proven.

(b) Three requirements: For insanity to be available:

(i) Defect of reason from a disease of the mind

(ii) Caused by an internal factor, i.e. a "disease of the mind"

(iii) D did not ... know the nature and quality of the act OR that the act was wrong.

Quote:

"... the jurors ought to be told in all cases that every man is to be ***presumed to be sane, and to possess a sufficient degree of reason to be responsible for his***

crimes, until the contrary be proved to their satisfaction*; and that to establish a defence on the ground of insanity, it must be clearly proved that, at the time of the committing of the act, the party accused was labouring under such a defect of reason, from disease of the mind, as not to know the nature and quality of the act he was doing; or, if he did know it, that he did not know he was doing what was wrong."*

5. The verdict is a "special verdict"

"not guilty by reason of insanity" (**Trial of Lunatics Act 1883, s2**).

13.3.2 Elements of insanity

a) Defect of reason

This must be a complete loss of the capacity to reason.

In ***Clarke* [1972]** D was charged with theft from a shop. D's defence was an absence of intention to permanently deprive. D stated they had in an absent-minded moment place the item in their bag. D suffered from depression. At trial, the judge thought insanity was shown and D entered a guilty plea to the offence. The Court of Appeal ruled the conviction should be quashed. What needed to be shown was:

1. D must show they were entirely deprived of the power of reasoning
2. Not just momentary failure due to absent mindedness; confusion and depression.

These were not defects of reason.

b) Caused by an internal factor – a "disease of the mind"

The defect of reason must be caused by an internal factor – a "***disease of the mind***".

In ***Kemp* [1957]** D suffering from arteriosclerosis or hardening of the arteries (a brain tumour) had blood congested in the brain causing a temporary loss of consciousness. D was charged with GBH on his wife using a hammer.

In the Court of Appeal the ruling was the defence would be insanity as this was a disease of the mind.

Per Devlin J at 407:

> *"**The law is not concerned with the brain but with the mind**, in the sense that **"mind" is ordinarily used, the mental faculties of reason, memory and understanding.***
>
> *If one read for "disease of the mind" "disease of the brain", it would follow that in many cases the plea of insanity would not be established because it could not be proved that the brain had been affected in any way, either by degeneration of the cells or in any other way...*
>
> *Hardening of the arteries is a disease which is shown on the evidence to be capable of affecting the mind in such a way as to cause a defect, temporarily or permanently, of its reasoning, understanding and so on, and so is in my judgement a disease of the mind which comes within the meaning of the Rules."*

In ***Bratty v Attorney-General of Northern Ireland* [1963]** epilepsy was held to be an internal fact – insanity (see above for the facts).

Per Lord Denning at 412:

> *"...what is a 'disease of the mind' within the M'Naghten Rules...is a **question for the judge**. The major mental diseases, which the doctors call psychoses, such as schizophrenia, are clearly diseases of the mind...."*

In ***Sullivan* [1984]** epilepsy was held to be internal and thus insanity was the correct plea (see above for the facts).

Lord Diplock:

> *"it matters not ...whether the impairment itself is permanent or is transient and intermittent, provided that it subsisted at the time of commission of the act."*

Here is a chronological summary of the outcomes

***Bratty v AG NI* [1963]**	Epilepsy	Internal: Insanity
***Quick* [1973]**	Hypoglycaemia	External: Automatism
***Sullivan* [1984]**	Epilepsy	Internal: Insanity
***Hennessy* [1989]**	Hyperglycaemia	Internal :Insanity
***T* [1990]**	PTSD	External: Automatism
***Bingham* [1991]**	Hypoglycaemia	External: Automatism
***Burgess* [1991]**	Sleepwalking	Internal: Insanity

c) D did not know the nature and quality of the act or that what he was doing was wrong

D did not know the nature and quality of the act

In ***Codere* (1917)** Lord Reading CJ stated: "*Nature and quality" means the* physical nature and quality:

> *"The Court is of opinion that in using the language "nature and quality" the judges were only dealing with the physical character of the act and were not intending to distinguish between the physical and moral aspects of the act. That is the law as it has been laid down by judges in, many directions to juries, and as the Court understands it to be at the present time."*

Example from Lord Denning:

> *"Throwing a baby onto a fire-thinking it was a log."*

Route 1 There is no *mens rea* as no intention

Route 2 There is insanity.

In ***Sullivan* [1984]** Lord Diplock stated the phrase "*not know the nature and quality of the act*" means for a jury direction "*He did not know what he was doing*"."

D did not know what he was doing was wrong

In ***Windle* [1952]** D killed V his wife by an overdose of aspirin. D showed knowledge of the law: "I suppose they will hang me for this." The Court of Appeal held D knew it was legally wrong and thus insanity was no defence. The court interpreted "*wrong*" as contrary to the criminal law.

Per Lord Goddard CJ at 832:

> ***"A man may be suffering from a defect of reason, but, if he knows that what he is doing is wrong - and by "wrong" is meant contrary to law - he is responsible**...[I]n the opinion of the court, there is no doubt that the word "wrong" in the M'Naghten Rules means contrary to law and does not have some vague meaning which may vary according to the opinion of different persons whether a particular act might not be justified."*

The Commonwealth jurisdictions overwhelmingly moved away from ***Windle* [1952]** e.g. see ***Johnson* [2007]** and commentary by David Ormerod. Other countries were reverting to an earlier authority ***Davis* (1881)**.

In the important recent case ***Keal* [2022]** Lord Burnett CJ clarified *"in order to establish the defence of insanity within the M'Naghten Rules on the ground of not knowing the act was "wrong", [D] must establish* ***both that***

*(a) [D] did not know that his act was unlawful (i.e. contrary to law); [**AND**]*

(b) [D] did not know that his act was "morally" wrong [i.e. contrary to the morals of ordinary people]."

This important authority thus limits D's ability to plead the defence. It has been confirmed in ***Usman* [2023]**.

13.3.3 Who evidentially raises the defence?

The defence can be raised by the defence; the prosecution; or the court.

13.3.4 Legal burden of proof

The legal burden of proof varies depending on who raised it.

If the prosecution raise it, they must prove beyond reasonable doubt.

If the defence raise it, they must prove on a balance of probabilities.

13.3.5 Fitness to plead stage 1: fitness hearing

This is held under **s4 Criminal Procedure (Insanity) Act 1964**.

a) Test *Pritchard* (1836)

A person is unfit to plead if they would not be able to:

(i) Comprehend the trial process

(ii) Put forward a defence

(iii) Challenge jurors

(iv) Give proper instructions

(v) Follow the evidence.

b) Burden of proof

1. The burden is upon the court to consider if D was capable of the Pritchard i) -v).
2. The standard of proof depends on who is asserting the lack of fitness:

If on defence	Balance of probabilities
If on prosecution	Beyond reasonable doubt

c) Procedure under s4

1. Two or more registered medical practitioners complete reports.
2. The judge rules whether the D is fit. The judge is not bound to accept medical evidence regarding fitness (e.g. regarding vascular dementia) and is entitled to make a decision based on the measures available which could encourage engagement (***Vinnell*** **[2024]**).
3. An order may be reversed if D is initially found unfit but prior to a finding of fact becomes fit. In this case D may then have a standard trial (***R (Hasani) v Crown Court at Blackfriars*** **[2006]**).

13.3.6 Fitness to plead stage 2: fact finding hearing

This is held under **s4A Criminal Procedure (Insanity) Act 1964**.

1. If D is ruled unfit by a judge, then the court appoints an advocate (this does not have to be the same as the instructed defence advocate) to represent D's interests.
2. A jury is then empanelled to make a finding of fact as to whether the act is proven (i.e. a fact-finding hearing relating to the *actus reus* elements of the offence).
3. Test for proof of the act: criminal standard beyond reasonable doubt.
4. The same rules of evidence apply:
    - Burden on the Crown
    - Standard beyond reasonable doubt
    - Hearsay inadmissible unless rendered admissible (***Chal*** **[2008]**)
    - Bad character inadmissible unless rendered admissible (***Creed*** **[2011]**).

N.B. Many people may be fit but require significant adaptations to the trial process to secure their participation. (Note **ECHR Art 6 Right to a fair trial** incorporates participation; intermediaries and special measures).

13.3.7 Consequences

The following consequences apply where the defence of insanity is proved or D is found to be unfit but to have committed the crime.

Criminal Procedure (Insanity) Act 1964, s5

Sentencing options:

- Hospital Order (with or without restriction)
- Supervision Order
- Absolute Discharge.

Exception for murder and any other offence for which the sentence is fixed by law where the court must make a hospital order with restriction.

13.4 Intoxication

13.4.1 Introduction

There is no defence of intoxication.

Intoxication offers merely the capacity for D to deny the *mens rea* of the offence.

The law is complex and inextricably linked to policy considerations.

The chronology of the key cases indicates how the principles emerge.

A recent helpful summary of some broad principles is given by ***Taj (Simon)* [2019], [2018]** which was heard by a five judge panel.

Sir Brian Leveson P:

> *"54. The following five themes emerge from a close reading of their Lordships' judgments in Majewski's case:*
>
> *(i) The principle that* ***self-induced intoxication does not amount to a defence*** *to criminal responsibility is a long-standing common law principle.*
>
> *(ii) The underlying* ***rationale of the principle is recklessness, namely that persons should be criminally responsible for their reckless conduct in taking drink or drugs and their actions flowing therefrom.***
>
> *(iii) The principle is founded in* ***pragmatism and policy, namely the needs of society to maintain order and to keep public and private violence under control****.*
>
> *(iv) It would bring the law into* ***contempt if the principle were otherwise and self-induced intoxication was a defence to criminal responsibility****.*
>
> *(v) Criminal behaviour as a result of drink and drugs is* ***one of the serious menaces facing society today****."*

Recent cases to reiterate core principles include ***Campeanu* [2020]**, ***Mohamadi* [2020]**, ***Aidid* [2021]**:

(i) Drunkenness may give rise to questions regarding intention.

(ii) Fundamentally juries must be sure D had intent having regard to the evidence.

(iii) Voluntary intoxication is evidence D may not have the required state of mind.

(iv) Directions to juries must be if necessary be carefully framed adapting the Crown Court Compendium Chapter 9.

However failure to give the ***Sheehan* (1974)** jury direction (see below) does not automatically render a conviction unsafe:

"9. A direction about the effect of intoxication by alcohol and/or drugs on D's state of mind will be necessary only if:

(1) D claims not to have formed the required state of mind (mens rea) because he/ she was intoxicated by such substances; and

(2) there is evidence that D may have consumed such substances in such a quantity that D may not have formed that state of mind."

13.4.2 Chronology of key cases

In ***Beard* [1920]** D was charged with rape and murder. Ds defence was:

"I was so drunk I did not know what I was doing."

The House of Lord upheld the conviction for murder on the facts and ruled:

1. *"Drunkenness is no defence unless D is so drunk, he was incapable of forming the intent to commit the crime.*
2. *Drunkenness can form evidence for a denial of mens rea defence to a crime of specific intent."*

Per Lord Birkenhead LC at p 499-500:

> *"...where a **specific intent** is an essential element in the offence, evidence of a state of drunkenness rendering [D] incapable of forming such an intent should be **taken into consideration** in order to determine whether he had in fact formed the intent necessary to constitute the particular crime. **If he was so***

drunk that he was incapable of forming the intent required he could not be convicted of a crime which was committed only if the intent was proved."

For basic intent: "*the cause of the punishment is the drunkenness which has led to the crime, rather than the crime itself.*"

3. *"Drunkenness cannot form evidence for a denial of mens rea of a defence to a crime of basic intent."*

In ***Morgan*** **[1976]** per Lord Simon of Glaisdale, at p216:

> "*By crimes of* **basic intent** *I mean those crimes whose* **definition expresses** *(or, more often, applies)* **a mens rea which does not go beyond the actus reus***.*
>
> "*The actus reus generally consists of an act and some consequence. The consequence may be closely connected with the act or remotely connected with it:* ***but with a crime of basic intent the mens rea does not extend beyond the act and its consequence,*** *however, remote, as defined in the actus reus."*

In ***Majewski*** **[1977]** there was a helpful reiteration and elucidation of ***Beard***. On the facts D had consumed alcohol and drugs. D, whilst under the influence, committed assaults. D was charged with ABH on a pub landlord and customers.

D's defence was to the effect, "Yes, I did it but I was intoxicated, so I had no *mens rea*".

The trial judge ruled intoxication was no defence to basic intent crimes and D was convicted.

The House of Lords upheld the conviction and dismissed the appeal. The reasons for the ruling have given certainty and clarity.

1. **Self-induced intoxication was no evidence for defence of absence of *mens rea* for offences requiring only a basic intent (i.e. recklessness)**

   e.g. Common assault/battery; ABH; and criminal damage

2. **Self-induced intoxication was evidence for a defence of absence of *mens rea* to offences requiring specific intent (i.e. intention)**

   e.g. Murder or **s18 OPA 1861**

3. **Justification: a legal fiction that self-induced intoxication is itself a reckless course of action: Lord Elwyn-Jones, i.e. a finding of "prior fault" replacing the correspondence principle**

Per Lord Elwyn-Jones LC (at 469-475):

> *"[1] ...the judges have evolved for the purpose of protecting the community a substantive rule of law that, in crimes of* **basic intent as distinct from crimes of specific intent, selfinduced intoxication provides no defence** *and is irrelevant to offences of basic intent...*
>
> *[2] ...Selfinduced alcoholic intoxication has been a factor in crimes of violence, like assault, throughout the history of crime in this country. But voluntary drug taking with the potential and actual dangers to others it may cause has added a new dimension to the old problem with which the courts have had to deal in their endeavour to maintain order and to keep public and private violence under control. To achieve this is the prime purpose of the criminal law*...
>
> *[3] ...***[I]f a man consciously and deliberately takes alcohol** *and drugs not on medical prescription, but in order to escape from reality, to go "on a trip", to become hallucinated, whatever the description may be* **and thereby disables** *himself* **from taking the care he might otherwise take** *and as a result by his subsequent actions causing injury to another - does our criminal law enable him to say that because he did not know what he was doing he lacked both intention and recklessness and accordingly is entitled to an acquittal? ...*
>
> *[4] ...If a man of his own volition takes a substance which causes him to cast off the restraints of reason and conscience, no wrong is done to him by holding him answerable criminally for any injury he may do while in that condition.* **His course of conduct in reducing himself by drugs and drink to that condition in my view supplies the evidence of mens rea, of guilty mind certainly sufficient for crimes of basic intent***. It is a reckless course of conduct and recklessness is enough to constitute the necessary mens rea [for basic intent crimes]...[T]he drunkenness is itself an intrinsic, an integral part of the crime, the other part being the evidence of the unlawful use of force against the victim. Together they add up to criminal recklessness.*
>
> *[5] On this I adopt the conclusion of Stroud in 1920, 36 LQR 273 that:*
>
>> *"...it would be contrary to all principle and authority to suppose that drunkenness (and what is true of drunkenness is equally true of intoxication by drugs) can be a defence for crime in general on the ground that a person cannot be convicted of a crime unless the mens was rea. By allowing himself to get drunk, and thereby putting himself in such a condition as to be no longer amenable to the law's commands, a man shows such regardlessness as amounts to mens rea for the purpose of all ordinary crimes.""*

Per Lord Salmon (at 482):

> *"A man who by voluntarily taking drink and drugs gets himself into an aggressive state in which he does not know what he is doing and then makes a vicious assault can hardly say with any plausibility that what he did was a pure accident*

which should render him immune from any criminal liability ... In strict logic this view cannot be justified. But this is the view that has been adopted by the common law of England which is founded on common sense and experience rather than strict logic."

In ***Heard* [2007]** D exposed his penis and rubbed it on the thigh of a police officer. D was very drunk and could not remember the incident. D was charged with sexual assault.

Ds defence was "intentional touching" meant the offence was a specific intent crime and he did not have specific intent.

The trial judge rejected this and stated the offence was one of basic intent.

The Court of Appeal dismissed the appeal and upheld the conviction.

1. Drunken intent is still an intent.
2. A specific intent offence is an offence where the intention went beyond the act itself such as to purposes or consequences.
3. A basic intent offence is an offence required proof only of the intention to do the *actus reus*.
4. The words "intentional touching" are thus read as a composite and thus the crime is one of basic intent and intoxication was no defence, i.e. volitional intention (which we mentioned at **Chapter 3** and **Chapter 6**).

Obiter the drunken dancers whose arm flails and touch a woman's breast would not be guilty as this was an accident.

David Ormerod in his commentary in (2007) Crim LR 654 was critical stating the case "may cause considerable confusion" and should this be extended to all offences? There are "several reasons why it is respectfully submitted this would be undesirable..." i) Lack of clarity; ii) Lack of certainty; iii) ***Majewski*** had been "knocked into pragmatic shape: it was an established, familiar and universally applied test".

13.4.3 Burden of proof

Evidential burden on defence: to provide some evidence of intoxication which can be put before the jury.

Legal burden on the prosecution: to prove beyond all reasonable doubt that despite such evidence, D still had the necessary *mens rea*.

13.4.4 Elements of intoxication: What must be proven?

a) Voluntary or involuntary intoxication

1. Voluntary consumption of alcohol or dangerous drugs

This is where D knowingly takes alcohol or drugs.

D can only rely on intoxication to deny the *mens rea* for crimes of specific intent.

Dangerous drugs are, those where there is common knowledge the taker "may become aggressive or do dangerous and unpredictable things" (***Bailey* [1983]**).

LSD ***Lipman* [1970]**

Alcohol

Intoxication for "Dutch courage" is not a defence.

In ***Attorney-General of Northern Ireland v Gallagher* [1963]** D was charged with murdering his wife. D killed whilst under the influence of whiskey. D stated his defence as insanity and intoxication. Clearly murder is a specific intent crime.

The House of Lords upheld the conviction stating D who becomes deliberately intoxicated, to enable them to commit the specific intent crime cannot raise the defence.

Drunkenness, which simply impairs moral sense, perception and self-control is no defence. Intoxication is only a defence to murder where D is so drunk, he did not know what he was doing and could not form the necessary intention.

Per Lord Denning at 382:

> "*My Lords, I think the law on this point should take a clear stand. If a man, whilst sane and sober, forms an intention to kill and makes preparation for it, knowing it is a wrong thing to do, and then gets himself drunk so as to give himself* **Dutch courage** *to do the killing, and whilst drunk* **carries out his intention, he cannot rely on this selfinduced drunkenness as a defence to a charge of murder***, nor even as reducing it to manslaughter...[T]he wickedness of his mind before he got drunk is enough to condemn him...*" [Because of prior intent]

2. Involuntary consumption

This is where D does not knowingly take alcohol or drugs. D can rely on intoxication (if proven) to deny the *mens rea* for any crime. In ***Hardie* [1984]** D was charged with arson whilst D was suffering from depression. D took Valium tablets which belonged to another. Valium is usually a sedative but this Valium did not calm D down. D in fact became aggressive and set fire to the flat. The trial judge rule that there was no defence of intoxication to argue. The Court of Appeal allowed the appeal. This was a form of involuntary intoxication:

1. Jury should have been directed to consider whether taking the Valium was reckless.
2. When D anticipated a sedative effect, D arguably then had no "*prior fault*".
3. This was involuntary intoxication and he could use it as a defence to the basic intent crime of criminal damage, on the basis it was a sedative and not conclusive proof of recklessness.

Per Parker LJ at 853:

> *"... the defence was that the Valium was taken for the purpose of calming the nerves only, ... and that [D] was told it would do him no harm. There was **no evidence that it was known to [D] or even generally known that the taking of Valium in the quantity taken would be liable to render a person aggressive or incapable** of appreciating risks to others or have other side effects such that its self-administration would itself have an element of recklessness.*
>
> *"... wholly different in kind from drugs which are liable to cause unpredictability or aggressiveness. It may well be that the taking of a sedative or soporific drug will, in certain circumstances, be no answer, for example in a case of reckless driving, but if the effect of a drug is merely **soporific or sedative** the taking of it, even in some excessive quantity, **cannot in the ordinary way raise a conclusive presumption against the admission of proof of intoxication** for the purpose of disproving mens rea in ordinary crimes, such as would be the case with alcoholic intoxication or incapacity or automatism resulting from the self-administration of dangerous drugs...the drug is, in our view, wholly different in kind from drugs which are liable to cause unpredictability or aggressiveness."*

In ***Allen* [1988]** D drank what he wrongly thought was a low alcohol wine. D was charged with buggery and what is now sexual assault. Ds defence was "I was so drunk I was not responsible for my actions". The trial judge did not leave the involuntary intoxication defence to the jury as the crime was a one of basic intent. The Court Appeal dismissing the appeal, upheld the convictions.

1. The consumption of alcohol was voluntary.
2. Alcohol consumption does not become involuntary if you don't know the alcohol's strength.
3. The prosecution must prove the *mens rea* of the crime.

OD Involuntary intoxication is probably confined to the cases where D:

(i) Did not know he was taking alcohol or an intoxicating drug at all, as where his drink, or his food is "laced" without his knowledge; or

(ii) Where he becomes intoxicated through taking drugs in accordance with a medical prescription.

Probably an evidential burden on D to show the drinking was involuntary.

3. Drunkenness removing inhibitions is not sufficient

In ***Kingston* [1995]** D had a history as a paedophile. A blackmailer spiked D's coffee. D was then led to the V (a drugged 15-year-old boy). D committed (what is now) a sexual assault on V. D's defence was that involuntary intoxication removed inhibitions for a specific intention crime. The trial judge ruled drugged intent was still intent. The House of Lords upheld the conviction.

1. The case was one of disinhibition.
2. The drug did not create a desire that had not previously existed.
3. The drug enabled an existing desire to be released and acted upon.
4. The spiking was only relevant to the culpability aspect of the sentence.
5. Where it was proved that the necessary intent was present when the act required to constitute the offence had been committed by [D] the defence of involuntary intoxication was not open to him as a means of securing his acquittal.

b) Drunken *mens rea* is *mens rea*

(i) D who lacks intent or recklessness is not guilty.

(ii) Drunken intent is intent. Drunkenness is no defence unless D is so drunk, he was incapable of forming the specific intent to commit the crime.

In ***Sheehan* (1974)** Geoffrey Lane LJ (at 312) gave the important jury direction:

> *"where drunkenness and its possible effect on the defendant's mens rea is an issue".*
>
> *"[1] [W]arn the [Jury] that the mere fact that the defendant's mind was affected by drink so that he acted in a way in which he would not have done had he been sober does not assist him at all, provided that the necessary intention was there. A drunken intent is nevertheless an intent.*

[2] [T]he jury should merely be instructed to have regard to all the evidence, including that relating to drink, to draw such inferences as they think proper from the evidence, and on that basis to ask themselves whether they feel sure that at the material time the defendant had the requisite intent."

NB Drunken recklessness is recklessness.

c) Specific intent and basic intent offences

Intoxication is evidence that can be used to deny the *mens rea* of a specific intent crime.

Specific intent

1. Specific intent *mens rea*

Intention.

2. Examples

Murder (***DPP v Beard* [1920]**)

GBH/Wounding with intent: **OPA 1861**, **s18** (***Davies* [1991]**)

Theft, **TA 1968**, **s1** (***DPP v Majewski* [1977]**)

Robbery, **TA 1968**, **s8** (***DPP v Majewski* [1977]**)

Burglary, **TA 1968**, **s9(1)(a)** (***Hutchins* [1988]**)

Attempt to commit a specific intent offence (***Clarkson* (1971)**)

Participation (see **Chapter 15**)

Criminal damage reckless as to endangering life (***Coley* [2013]**)

3. Impact

YES, intoxication is evidence for a defence to the extent of the absence of intention but the specific intent offence can be replaced by a lesser offence where reckless-ness will suffice.

e.g. 1. Murder to manslaughter

e.g. 2. **s18** to **s20**

e.g. 3. Theft no lesser offence so acquitted

e.g. 4. Attempt

Underlying assault such as **s20**, if assaulted. Otherwise acquittal.

e.g. 5. Criminal damage, reckless as to endangering life

- Simple criminal damage

4. Why?

Insufficient fault is proved.

Basic intent

Intoxication cannot be used as evidence to deny the *mens rea* of a basic intent offence.

1. Basic intent *mens rea*

Recklessness

2. Examples

Manslaughter (***DPP v Beard* [1920]**; ***Lipman* [1970]**)

Rape (***Heard* [2007]**; ***Grout* [2011]**)

Sexual assault (***Heard* [2007]**)

Causing GBH/Wounding: **s20 OPA 1861** (***Aitken* [1992]**)

ABH: **s47 OPA 1861** (***Bolton v Crawley* [1972]**)

Common assault and battery (***DPP v Majewski* [1977]**)

Simple criminal damage (reckless): **s1(1) Criminal Damage Act 1971** (***Caldwell* [1982]**)

Taking a motor vehicle without consent

3. Impact

Intoxication is not evidence for a defence to the extent of absence of recklessness.

4. Why?

The **prior fault doctrine** operates to attribute the *mens rea* from the earlier reckless intoxication. This breaches the correspondence principle.

13.5 Mistake

Mistakes can sometimes negate the *mens rea* of the offence.

There is no "defence" of mistake, merely application of mistakes to the elements of the offence.

13.5.1 Mistakes need not be reasonable

In ***Lamb* [1967]** D as a "joke" pointed a gun at V (his best friend) and pulled the trigger. The gun fired the killing V. D had checked chamber of the gun to ensure the chamber facing V was empty. D did not know pulling the trigger made the chamber rotate. D was charged with constructive manslaughter. D argued a simple defence of accident, namely an absence of *mens rea*, i.e. "I was mistaken in my belief that the pulling of the trigger would not discharge a bullet".

The trial judge said mistake was irrelevant as was the evidence of three experts who stated that this mistake was natural for ordinary people. The question: Was D's mistake obliged to be reasonable?

The Court of Appeal quashed the conviction stating:

1. *Mens rea* is an essential element of an offence.
2. The underlying assault required proof of intent
3. The prosecution were obliged to prove the intent to harm for the underlying assault.

> *"... it would, of course, have been fully open to a jury, if properly directed, to find the defendant guilty because they considered his view as to there being no danger was formed in a criminally negligent way. But he was entitled to a direction that the jury should take into account the fact that he had undisputedly formed that view and that there was expert evidence as to this being an understandable view."*

In ***Morgan* [1976]** Lord Hailsham stated:

> *"'mens rea' means 'guilty or criminal mind',*
>
> ...to insist that a belief must be reasonable to excuse it is to insist that either
>
> *[D] is to be found guilty of intending to do that which in truth he did not intend to do, <u>or</u> that his state of mind, though innocent of evil intent, can convict him if it be honest but not rational."*

Lord Hailsham indicated **mistake is tested subjectively.**

> "There is no requirement that the mistake be one that a reasonable person would have *made*."

However the more unreasonable the mistake the less likely a jury are to *accept* it. Statute can exclude this by providing a mistake must be a reasonable one, e.g. **s1 SOA 2003**.

13.5.2 Strong presumption favour of *mens rea*

***B* [2000]** D was charged with **s1(1) Indecency with Children Act 1960** by inciting a girl under 14 to commit an act of gross indecency. D accepted the touching. D stated a defence that they were mistakenly unaware V was under 14 and V had ostensibly consented.

The House of Lords held:

1. Offence was not strict liability.
2. D had a defence if D honestly but mistakenly believed V was over 14.
3. D's belief did not have to be based on reasonable grounds.

The reason was a mistake as to an element of the *actus reus* provides a defence unless there is a statutory provision making clear it cannot (e.g. Post **SOA 2003 G [2008]**). Lord Nichols: *"as a matter of principle the honest belief approach must be preferable [to objective route]."*

In ***K* [2002]** where D was charged with **s14 Sexual Offences Act 1956** indecent assault and stated he honestly believed V was a 16- (not 14-) year-old girl. The House of Lords confirmed D's honest belief she was over 16 was a defence. Therefore the prosecution must must prove the absence of the belief.

However the strong presumption can be rebutted by clear statutory wording.

13.5.3 Mistakes of the civil law can negate the *mens rea* of an offence

Maxim: Ignorance of the law is no defence.

a) Mistakes of criminal law

D cannot argue he did not know it was an offence to murder someone.

b) Mistakes of civil law

D can argue specifically under the **Theft Act 1968**, **s2(1)(a):**

> *if he appropriates the property in the belief that he has in law the right to deprive the other of it, on behalf of himself or of a third person.*

This is even if D is making a mistake as to civil law (e.g. a finders keepers argument).

It is a mistake of law relating to the *actus reus* which required a *mens rea* element.

13.6 Evaluation and reform

As noted at the beginning of this chapter, several of the "defences" discussed above are not strictly defences at all, but instead situations where – because of internal or external factors – the defendant does not possess the *mens rea*, or **fault**, necessary to commit the offence. Several of these defences are grounded in fundamental principles of criminal law, including the maxim that a guilty act does not make a defendant guilty unless their mind is guilty, which we encountered in **Chapter 4**. However, the availability of these defences and the limitations imposed on them is also shaped by policy considerations.

Such policy considerations include concerns over making defences available to undeserving defendants, particularly those who display "prior fault", even where this potentially oversimplifies the culpability involved in the defendant's prior actions.[3] Public safety is also a key concern, shaping both the availability and consequences of a defence of insanity; although some have expressed concerns about a lack of clarity and certainty on this point following the introduction of **s76 Criminal Justice and Immigration Act 2008**.[4]

13.6.1 Legal certainty and legal clarity

Legal certainty provides the law must be sufficiently available, certain and enable the individual to know the legal boundaries of their actions and potential consequences

3 Findlay Stark, "Prior Fault"' (2014) 73 Cambridge Law journal 8

4 Mark Dsouza, "Intoxication, psychoses, and self-defence: Evaluating Tajn [2018] EWCA Crim 1743" (2018) 9 Archbold Review 6

of breach[5]. Legal clarity provides that the law must be accessible, clear, intelligible, and predictable[6].

The piecemeal development of several of the defences discussed in this chapter has resulted in a lack of clarity surrounding their application. This is particularly noticeable when looking at the law on **automatism** and **intoxication** which, it has been said are "so complex, unprincipled and incoherent that it deserves to be reviewed with a view to reform".[7] A key example of this incoherence can be seen in situations where the defendant appears to have **self-induced** their mental state.

Although, generally, policy suggests that a defendant should not be able to avoid liability for **basic intent** offences where they recklessly cause their own intoxication or autonomy,[8] there is some uncertainty surrounding this approach in instances of **specific intent** offences. As we saw during this chapter, a defendant charged with a specific intent offence may demonstrate that they did not possess the necessary intention due to self-induced automatism or intoxication. However, individual cases such as ***McGhee* [2013]** appear to undermine this point,[9] with defendants being found liable for specific intent offences after self-inducing involuntary behaviour through alcohol or drugs.

13.6.2 Equality before the law: protected characteristics and socio-economic barriers

Equality provides that equality before the law (including disability, gender, gender identity, race, sexual orientation, and socio-economic) is relevant and impacts on the unequal power relationships in society has a significant impact on the system.

The complexities around **insanity** and **automatism**, including the distinctions between the two defences, raise significant issues for defendants living with health, including mental health, conditions. Commentators have pointed out the significant

---

5 Richard Buxton, "The Human Rights Act and the substantive criminal law" (2000) Criminal Law Review 331, 332
6 Rimmington; Goldstein [2005]; [2006] Lord Bingham
7 Ronnie Mackay, "R v Coley; R v McGhee; R v Harris: insanity – distinction between voluntary intoxication and disease of the mind caused by voluntary intoxication" (2013) Criminal Law Review 923, 929
8 Findlay Stark, '"Prior fault"' (2014) 73 Cambridge Law journal 8
9 JJ Child and Alan Reed, "Automatism is Never a Defence" (2014) 65 Northern Ireland Legal Quarterly 167, 179

degree of stigma associated with the insanity defence and the oversimplification of the mental capacity of those living with mental health conditions which it entails.[10]

13.6.3 Fair warning; fair labelling and sufficient breadth principles

a) Fair warning

Fair labelling is an area where many of the defences discussed in this chapter can be subject to some critique. Given that **automatism** and **insanity** can both stem from a medical condition outside of the defendant's control, the distinction between internally and externally caused mental states has been described as "problematic, and at times capricious, in that it fails to make an appropriate classificatory division between physical and mental disorders" as well as failing to recognise situations where internal and external factors overlap.[11] The label attached to those found not guilty by reason of insanity, as well as being potentially stigmatising, appears inappropriate to some of the situations in which it is applied.

b) Fair labelling

Fair labelling involves labelling criminal offences at a macro scale to indicate categorisation, indicative punishment scales and specialist ancillary orders[12]. Fair labelling involved labelling at a micro scale – it helps with categorising the wrongdoing with a public label which has a communicative value to wider society[13].

The total exoneration of those in self-defence, duress, necessity and ACR circumstances seems to fairly draw the line in law and morality.

c) Sufficient breadth

There appears to be sufficient breadth to the defences.

d) Practicality, cost, and expense

1) Practicality – the law remains complex and could be easily clarified by codification.

10 Justice, "Mental health and fair trial" (2017) <https://files.justice.org.uk/wp-content/uploads/2017/11/06170615/JUSTICE-Mental-Health-and-Fair-Trial-Report-2.pdf> para 5,12
11 JJ Child and Alan Reed, "Automatism is Never a Defence" (2014) 65 Northern Ireland Legal Quarterly 167, 169
12 James Chalmers and Fiona Leverick, "Fair Labelling in Criminal Law" (2008) 71 Modern Law Review 217, 221-222
13 James Chalmers and Fiona Leverick, "Fair Labelling in Criminal Law" (2008) 71 Modern Law Review 217, 221-222

2) Avoid undue cost and expense

The standard self-defence does not appear to have issues.

The householder needs clarification.

There is a large body of case law regarding duress.

13.6.4 Human rights: autonomy and welfare principles

In ***Usman* [2023]**, the defendant argued that the continued application of the rules established in ***M'Naghten* (1843)** constituted a breach of his rights under **ECHR, Arts 2–3, 5–6** and **14**, in part because medical knowledge around mental health had developed so significantly since the 19th century. The Court of Appeal rejected these arguments and the judgment suggests that the current judicial perspective on this issue is that reform is a matter for Parliament.

13.6.5 International comparators and reform: practicality principle and politics

The Law Commission, Intoxication and Criminal Liability (Cm 7526, 2009)

The Law Commission's 2013 *Criminal Liability: Insanity and Automatism* discussion paper described the distinctions drawn between insanity and automatism as "crude" and suggested that they produced "arbitrary classifications".[14] The Commission proposed significant reforms, including abolishing both defences and the introduction of a new special verdict of "not criminally responsibly by reason of recognised medical condition" where a defendant lacked capacity to:

> "(i) rationally to form a judgment about the relevant conduct or circumstances;
>
> (ii) to understand the wrongfulness of what he or she is charged with having done; or
>
> (iii) to control his or her physical acts in relation to the relevant conduct or circumstances as a result of a qualifying recognised medical condition."[15]

---

14 The Law Commission, *Criminal Liability: Inanity and Automatism* (Discussion Paper, 2013) 105

15 The Law Commission, *Criminal Liability: Inanity and Automatism* (Discussion Paper, 2013) 193

Although the Law Commission's proposals for reform of the law on insanity were received positively by some legal commentators, they have not resulted in significant reform to date. As noted above, ***Usman*** **[2023]** suggests that Parliament's inaction in response to the report may inhibit significant reform of insanity through case law.

Several of the defences we have explored in this chapter are approached differently, depending on whether the crime the defendant is charged with is one of basic or specific intent. As cases such as ***Heard*** **[2007]** demonstrate, this is further complicated by uncertainty around the categorisation of offences as ones of basic or specific intent: as Loughnan and Gless note, in New South Wales, Australia this uncertainty has been addressed through legislation and codification of which offences fall into each category.[16]

Scotland provides another interesting point of comparison to England and Wales, having seen significant reform and discussion around various defences in recent years. As Chalmers discusses, Scots law takes a markedly different approach to insanity, enabling the defence even where a defendant knows that what he is doing is "legally" wrong, provided that the defendant does not know that what he is doing is "morally" wrong.[17]

In the News

Automatism and "sexsomnia"

The distinction between internal and external factors has been particularly challenging to apply in the context of sleepwalking. Although discussed in Bratty ***v Attorney-General for Northern Ireland*** **[1963]** in the context of automatism, sleepwalking arising from an internal factor (e.g. a medical condition) was considered a form of insanity in ***Burgess*** **[1991]**. However, recently, there have been concerns regarding the availability of sleepwalking based automatism defences in cases of sexual offences:

Shanti Das, '"Guilty men have got away with it": fears over rise of "sexsomnia" defence in rape cases' *The Guardian* (London, 14 April 2024)

<https://www.theguardian.com/society/2024/apr/14/fears-sexsomnia-defence-in-cases#:~:text=In%20about%20a%20third%20of,to%20a%20not%2Dguilty%20verdict> accessed 06 April 2025

16 Arlie Loughnan and Sabine Gless, "Understanding the Law on Intoxicated Offending: Principle, Pragmatism and Legal Culture" (2016) 3 Journal of International and Comparative Law 345, 354-355

17 James Chalmers, "Insanity and automatism: notes from over the border and across the boundary" (2014) 65 Northern Ireland Legal Quarterly 205, 209.

13.7 Summary

This chapter has introduced a range of ways in which a defendant can avoid liability due to an absence of fault. The key points to take away from this chapter are:

- **Automatism** provides a defence where an external factor causes the defendant to act involuntarily, and the defendant is not at fault. **Automatism** is distinct from **insanity**, which focuses on a defect of reasoning caused by a disease of the mind (i.e. an internal factor).
- Whilst **insanity** is an issue in many cases involving defendants living with mental health conditions, whether a condition constitutes a "disease of the mind" depends upon whether it impacts "mental faculties of reason, memory and understanding" which includes other health conditions, as well as mental health ones.
- In order to be found **not guilty by reason of insanity**, a defendant must either not appreciate the physical character of what they are doing **or** not appreciate that what they are doing is wrong. Defendants who are found not guilty for this reason may be subject to a Hospital Order.
- A defendant who is **voluntarily intoxicated** cannot rely on their intoxication to disprove crimes of **basic intent**. If charged with a crime of **specific intent**, they may be not guilty if their intoxication means that they did not possess the necessary *mens rea*, although they may be guilty of an alternative lesser offence.
- A defendant's mistaken but **honest belief** can be relevant to their *mens rea*, dependent upon the offence. Although an intoxicated belief will generally not demonstrate an absence of fault.
- The law on **insanity**, **automatism** and **intoxication** is frequently critiqued, including by bodies such as The Law Commission, with proposals as to specific and more widespread reform.

Further reading

Andrew Ashworth, "Ignorance of the Criminal Law, and Duties to Avoid it" (2011) *74 Modern Law Review 1*

John Child, "Drink, drugs and law reform: a review of Law Commission Report No 314" (2009) *Criminal Law Review 488*

Arlie Loughnan and Nicola Wake, "Of Blurred Boundaries and Prior Fault: Insanity, Automatism and Intoxication" in Alan Reed et al (eds) *General Defences in Criminal Law* (Routledge 2014)

James Mason, "The Willed Trance: Volition, Voluntariness and Hypnotised Defendants" (2020) *85 Journal of Criminal Law 26*

John Rumbold and Martin Wasik, "Special feature on automatism" (2015) *53 Medicine, Science and the Law 147*

CHAPTER 14

Defences: Justification

14.1 Introduction

In **Chapter 13** we looked at defences relating to fault. In this chapter we look at defences relating to justification. This is usually a justification external to the harm and fault elements, but which bears on the moral rectitude to punish.

Aims of this chapter

By the end of this chapter you can be expected to know and be able to evaluate the law on defences involving justification

We cover four groups of defences involving justifications under **Chapter 14**. Each of them is in effect the of the defendant stating**:**

"I was justified because…"

Defence	Defendant stating
• **Self defence**	"I needed to defend myself and used proportionate force'
• **Duress**	"I had no choice they would kill or seriously injure me or my family"
• **By threats**	Clear threats compelling action: "I was compelled by threats to so act..."
• **By circumstances**	Clear circumstances compelling action: "I was compelled by circumstances to so act..."
• **Necessity**	"This was a necessary action and my action was the least worst of the available options" This significantly overlaps with the defence of duress by circumstances.

- **Infancy/Age of criminal responsibility (ACR)**

  Autonomy impaired by lack of capacity:

  "I lacked capacity as I was under the age of 10."

14.2 Self defence

14.2.1 Availability

1. Self-defence is normally seen as a defence of justification.
2. It is available in relation to any crime committed by force.
3. It is the most commonly used defence.
4. It most often arises in relation to **Chapter 7** Offences against the person.
5. When a crime has the term "unlawful" as an element this is normally seen as an element of the *actus reus*.
6. Self-defence is a denial that the force was "unlawful".
7. A crime which includes proof that D was not acting in self-defence (or indeed has some other defence) is thus unlawful.

14.2.2 Procedure and burden

1. Procedurally the evidential burden is on the defence to raise sufficient evidence to leave the issue to the jury.
2. Once the evidential burden is satisfied legally, the prosecution must then prove beyond reasonable doubt that there was no such self-defence. (***Lobell* [1957]**; confirmed in ***Wheeler* [1967]** at 830 and ***Abraham* [1973]** at 1273).
3. If there is *prima facie* evidence of the self-defence it should be left to the jury.

   Even as in this case where the primary defence was alibi; the secondary implication was self-defence. Both issues should have been left to the jury (***Bonnick* (1978)**).
4. Even where the defence state "accident" (i.e. a denial of *mens rea*) and self defence issues overlap both should be left to the jury (***Dickens* [2005]**).

14.2.3 What is the test for self-defence?

In ***Gladstone Williams* [1987]** Lord Lane CJ helpfully summarised that self-defence is "the exercise of any necessary and reasonable force to protect himself".

The case of ***Owino* [1996]** at 132-133 makes it clear there is a two-step test:

Step 1 Necessity (subjectively assessed)

> *"The jury have to decide whether [D] honestly believed that the circumstances were such as required him to use force to defend himself from an attack or a threatened attack. In this respect D must be judged in accordance with his honest belief, even though that belief may have been mistaken."*

Step 2 Proportionality (objectively assessed)

> *"The jury must then determine whether the force [D] used was reasonable in the circumstances as he believed them to be..."*

Step 3 Public policy

> In recent times it is clear a step 3 has been added. In the context of self-defencing involving a householder, a mentally disordered or intoxicated person, one must additionally examine whether there is a public policy limitation on the defence.

14.2.4 When can force be used?

It is clear from the case law, force can be used in four circumstances:

a) *Defending one's own person*

b) *Defending other people*

c) *Defending one's own property and defending property belonging to another*

d) *Prevention of crime and lawful arrest.*

(**Criminal Law Act 1967**, **s3(1)**).

a) Defending one's own person

An individual can use necessary proportionate force to defend themselves from an attack by another.

b) Defending other people

An individual can use necessary proportionate force to defend other people from an attack by a third party, e.g. in ***Rose* (1884) 15 Cox CC 540** D was acquitted of Murder on grounds of self-defence. D having shot dead his father who had launched a murderous attack on his mother. The court ruled the principle of the common law that self-defence extends to D who uses reasonable force to protect others from physical attack.

In ***Duffy* [1967]** the court confirmed *obiter* there is no **"***need for a special/familial relationship to exist to*" enable D to defend a third party being attacked. Thus the scope was extended to include people beyond those who are closely related.

More recently ***Hichens* [2011]** D was living with V. V's ex-boyfriend was due to come to the door. On previous occasions V's ex-boyfriend had been abusive to V. D then slapped V possibly. D contended he slapped V in self-defence of V from attack by the ex-boyfriend. D stated he had wanted to shock V to "come to her senses". At trial D was convicted and that conviction was upheld by the Court of Appeal but they noted *obiter* there may be rare occasions where D could act in defence of V against a third party to prevent a crime being committed by the third party. However, on the facts, the slap was far too remote from the third-party threat and could not be made out.

c) Defending one's own property and defending property belonging to another

An individual can use necessary proportionate force to defend one's own property or another's property from an attack by another, e.g. in the historic case of ***Hussey* (1925)** D's tenant shot V, his landlord. D stated self-defence of property. The trial judge did not mention defence of property. The appeal was allowed and Lord Hewart CJ said:

> *"[Approved] Archbold's Criminal Pleading, Evidence and Practice, 26th ed. p. 887,*
>
> *"In defence of a man's house,* ***the owner or his family may kill a trespasser who would forcibly dispossess him of it****, in the same manner as he might, by law, kill in self-defence a man who attacks him personally; with this distinction,*

> *however, that in defending his home **he need not retreat**, as in other cases of self-defence, for that would be giving up his house to his adversary."*

Note this level of force would probably now far exceed that which was reasonable and would be governed by **s76 CJIA 2008** (see below).

d) Prevention of crime and lawful arrest – s3(1) Criminal Law Act 1967

3.—Use of force in making arrest, etc.

*(1) A person **may use such force as is reasonable** in the circumstances **in the prevention of crime**, or in effecting or assisting in the lawful arrest of offenders or suspected offenders or of persons unlawfully at large.*

*(2) Subsection (1) above shall **replace the rules of the common law on the question when force used for a purpose mentioned in the subsection is justified by that purpose.***

1. **This statutory public law defence co-exists with the private common law defence of self defence. This was confirmed in *McInnes* [1971]** and ***Attorney-General of Northern Ireland's Reference (No 1 of 1975)* [1976].**
2. **Terms**

Private defence	Common Law defences known as the private defence
Public defence	**CLA 1967**, **s3** known as the public defence

3. **Impact**

D escapes both civil and criminal liability because his actions cease to be unlawful.

e.g. ***Williams (Demario)* [2020]**; in this case D was robbed of a silver chain by V. D chased V. D eventually caught V and fatally stabbed V. The Court of Appeal held D was not defending his property, nor was D preventing the commission of a robbery. The reality was D was engaged in an act of retaliation or revenge.

4. **Self defence and the European Convention on Human Rights**

Art 2 ECHR – right to life

1. *Everyone's right to life shall be protected by law. No one shall be deprived of his life intentionally save in the execution of a sentence of a court following his conviction of a crime for which this penalty is provided by law.*
2. *Deprivation of life shall not be regarded as inflicted in contravention of this Article when it results from the use of force which is no more than absolutely necessary:*

(a) in defence of any person from unlawful violence;

(b) in order to effect a lawful arrest or to prevent the escape of a person lawfully detained;

(c) in action lawfully taken for the purpose of quelling a riot or insurrection.

Permitted use of force – Art 2(2) ECHR)

***Da Silva v UK* (2016)** (Grand Chamber of the ECtHR)

H Subjective, honest reasonable belief will satisfy the requirements of **Art 2**

Noting good objective reasons remain evidentially relevant.

5. Prevention of crime read strictly

The nexus between action and prevention of immediate crime e.g. Extinction Rebellion and Just Stop Oil will struggle to utilise **ECHR Art 10** and **Art 11** (see ***Jones (Margaret)* [2006]**; ***R (DPP) v Stratford Magistrates' Court* [2017]**; ***Ziegler* [2022]**; ***Brown (James Hugh)* [2022]**).

14.2.5 Requirements

14.2.5.1 Necessary force: subjective test

1. The anticipated attack must be specific and imminent ***Devlin v Armstrong* [1971]**.

2. Factual mistakes

In ***Gladstone Williams* [1987]** D punched V. D thought V was a committing an unlawful assault on a third party (a youth). V was in fact a witness to the third party committing a robbery. V was lawfully trying to detain the third party as an act of self-defence/lawful arrest.

D's defence was they had made a mistake as to factual necessity of his actions. D was charged with ABH and was convicted at trial. The Court of Appeal quashed the conviction.

1. Following ***Morgan* [1976]** (see **Chapter 13**) D's mistaken belief in the necessity to use the force provided it is genuine is a defence.

2. The trial judge should have directed the jury to consider the facts as D believed them to be, however unreasonable D's belief:

Per Lord Lane CJ, at 415, stated:

"The reasonableness or unreasonableness of [D's] belief [re Necessity] is material to the question of whether the belief was held by [D] at all.

If the ***belief*** *was in fact held, its* ***unreasonableness, so far as guilt or innocence is concerned, is neither here nor there. It is irrelevant****. Were it otherwise, [D] would be convicted because he was negligent in failing to recognise that [V] was not consenting or that a crime was not being committed and so on. In other words the jury should be directed*

> *[i.] the* ***prosecution have the burden or duty of proving the unlawfulness of the defendant s actions;***
>
> *[ii.]* ***if [D] may have been labouring under a mistake as to the facts, he must be judged according to his mistaken view of the facts;***
>
> *[iii.]* ***that is so whether the mistake was, on an objective view, a reasonable mistake or not.***

In summary, what needs to be shown is that [D] believed that he or she was responding to an unjust threat, whether or not in fact there was an unjust threat."

Example – *Beckford* [1988]

D (a police officer) was sent to arrest V. D was told V was armed with a gun and dangerous. D shot V dead. The prosecution case was D had shot V when V was unarmed. The defence case was V had fired at D and D had shot V in self defence.

The trial judge's direction was self-defence exists if D "*reasonably believed*" he was in danger of death or serious injury and had then used necessary and proportionate force.

The question on appeal was whether D must have reasonably (objectively) believed he was in danger or would it be sufficient if D mistakenly (subjectively) believed he was in danger?

The Privy Council allowed the appeal, stating D was entitled to his defence of self-defence if he used such force as **he** thought was reasonable in the circumstances. D would be "*judged on the facts as he perceived them to be*". This was even if his belief was not reasonable.

Lord Griffiths at 145, following **Morgan [1976]** (see **Chapter 13**):

> *"There may be a fear that the abandonment of the objective standard demanded by the existence of reasonable grounds for belief will result in the success of too many spurious claims of self-defence ...[this is not so]'*
>
> ***"'the test to be applied for self-defence is that a person may use such force as is reasonable in the circumstances as he honestly believes them to be in the defence of himself or another'."***

You may ask: why is this so generous? The reality is the jury would need adequate evidence and to believe D's account before they find in his favour.

***Oatridge* (1992)** confirmed juries must be directed on mistaken belief.

This is now confirmed in **s76(4) Criminal Justice and Immigration Act 2008** (**CJIA**), (D is entitled to rely on mistaken but genuine belief):

If D claims to have held a particular belief as regards the existence of any circumstances—

*(a) the reasonableness or otherwise of that belief is relevant to the question whether D genuinely held **it; but***

(b) if it is determined that D did genuinely hold it, D is entitled to rely on it for the purposes of subsection (3), whether or not—

(i) it was mistaken, or

(ii) (if it was mistaken) the mistake was a reasonable one to have made.

Pre-emptive protection is permissible (see below linked issue of no duty to retreat)

Beckford [1988] *– for the facts see above. Lord Griffiths p 144:*

> *"a man about to be attacked does not have to wait for his assailant to strike the first blow or fire the first shot; circumstances may justify a pre-emptive strike."*

No duty to retreat

s76(6A) CJIA confirms:

In deciding the question mentioned in subsection (3), a possibility that D could have retreated is to be considered (so far as relevant) as a factor to be taken into account, rather than as giving rise to a duty to retreat.

This confirmed ***Hussey*** at 161 per Lord Hewart CJ:

> *"in defending his home he need not retreat, as in other cases of self-defence, for that would be giving up his house to his adversary."*

***Julien* [1969]** at 843 Widgery LJ stated:

> *"**It is not,** as we understand it, **the law that a person threatened must take to his heels and run...but what is necessary is that he should demonstrate by his actions that he does not want to fight**. He must demonstrate that he is prepared to temporise and disengage and perhaps to make some physical*

> *withdrawal; and that that is necessary as a feature of the justification of self-defence is true, in our opinion, whether the charge is a homicide charge or something less serious."*

***McInnes* [1971]** also confirms D is entitled to stand his ground. Edmund Davies LJ p 1607:

> *"We prefer the view expressed by the Full Court of [South] Australia [in Howe [1958] SASR 95] that* a failure to retreat is only an element in the consideration upon which the reasonableness of [Ds] conduct is to be judged."

In ***Keane and McGrath* [2010]** Hughes LJ stated:

> *"[D] must act on the instant at any rate in a large number of cases. If he does so and does no more than seems honestly and instinctively to be necessary, that is itself strong evidence that it was reasonable. It is strong evidence, not conclusive evidence."*

Turning the tables

Self-defence could arise if D was the original aggressor. But self-defence would only arise where the original V's response is so out of proportionate that the "roles are reversed" or the "tables had been turned".

14.2.5.2 Proportionate force: objective test

s76 Criminal Justice and Immigration Act 2008

s76 permits reasonable force for purposes of self-defence etc.

The law on reasonable force is governed by a particularly badly drafted piece of legislation which consolidates numerous common law authorities and adds the householder.

Below, in addition to the statute, commentary is integrated.

s76(1) *Was the degree of force reasonable?*

(a) an issue arises as to whether a person charged with the offence ("D") is entitled to rely on a defence within subsection (2), and

(b) the question arises whether the ***degree of force*** *used by D against a person ("V")* ***was reasonable in the circumstances.***

Commentary

s76 *is dealing with self-defence and confirms specifically the proportionate/reasonable force aspect of the defence.*

s76(2) *The defences are—*

(a) the common law defence of self-defence;

(aa) the common law defence of defence of property; and

(b) the defences provided by section 3(1) of the Criminal Law Act 1967 (c. 58) … (use of force in prevention of crime or making arrest).

s76(3) *(Proportionality determined by circumstances as D believed them to be)*

The question whether ***the degree of force*** *used by D was reasonable in the circumstances is to be decided* ***by reference to the circumstances as D believed them to be****, and subsections (4) to (8) also apply in connection with deciding that question.*

s76(3) *confirms the proportionality issue relates to the circumstances as D believed them to be*

s76(4) *(D is entitled to rely on mistaken but genuine belief)* – See above under **Stage 1 Necessity**

s76(5) *(Impact of mistakes attributable to voluntary intoxication)* – See below **under Stage 3 Policy**

s76(5A) *(Householder case – any level of force as long as not grossly disproportionate)* – See below under **Stage 3 Policy**

s76(6) *(Standard Case – any level of force as long as it is reasonable in the circumstances as D believed them to be)*

In a case other than a householder case*, the degree of force used by D is not to be regarded as* ***having been reasonable*** *in the circumstances as D believed them to be if it was disproportionate in those circumstances.*

COMMENTARY: Standard cases – any level of force as long as it is reasonable in the circumstances as D believed them to be (reasonable synonymous with proportionality)

s76(6A) *(No duty to retreat)*

(See above)

s76(7) *(Margin of appreciation – No expectation for D to weigh to a nicety; honest* and instinctive actions are accepted)

(7) In deciding the question mentioned in subsection (3) the ***following considerations*** *are to be taken into account (so far as relevant in the circumstances of the case)—*

(a) that a person acting for ***a legitimate purpose may not be able to weigh to a nicety the exact measure of any necessary action****; and*

(b) that ***evidence of a person's having only done what the person honestly and instinctively thought was necessary for a legitimate purpose constitutes strong evidence that only reasonable action*** *was taken by that person for that purpose.*

This confirms there no need to weigh to nicety. Honest and instinctive decision making is allowed. It confirmed ***Palmer*** **[1971]** at 831-832 per Lord Morris:

> *"If there is some relatively minor attack, it would not be common sense to permit some action of retaliation which was wholly out of proportion to the necessities of the situation.*
>
> *If an attack is serious so that it puts someone in immediate peril, then immediate defensive action may be necessary.*
>
> *"If the moment is one of crisis for someone in imminent danger, he may have to avert the danger by some instant reaction...*
>
> *"If there has been attack so that defence is reasonably necessary, it will be recognised that* ***a person defending himself cannot weigh to a nicety the exact measure of his necessary defensive action****. If a jury thought that in a moment of unexpected anguish a person attacked had* ***only done what he honestly and instinctively thought was necessary, that would be most potent evidence that only reasonable defensive action had been taken.***
>
> *"A Jury will be told that the defence of self-defence, where the evidence makes its raising possible, will fail only if the prosecution shows beyond doubt that what [D] did was not by way of self-defence."*

s76(8) *(Not prevent other matters, i.e. open the common law)*

(8) [Subsections (6A) and (7) are] ***not to be read as preventing other matters from being taken into account where they are relevant*** *to deciding the question mentioned in subsection (3).*

s76(8A) *Miscellaneous*

*(8A) For the purposes of this section "****a householder case****" is a case where—*

(a) the defence concerned is the ***common law defence of self-defence,***

(b) *the force concerned is* ***force used by D while in or partly in a building****, or part of a building, that* ***is a dwelling*** *or is forces accommodation (or is both),*

(c) ***D is not a trespasser*** *at the time the force is used, and*

(d) *at that time* ***D believed V to be in, or entering, the building or part as a trespasser****.*

(8B) Where—

(a) *a part of a building is a dwelling where D dwells,*

(b) *another part of the building is a place of work for D or another person who dwells in the first part, and*

(c) *that other part is internally accessible from the first part, that other part, and any internal means of access between the two parts, are each treated for the purposes of subsection (8A) as a part of a building that is a dwelling.*

(8C) Where—

(a) *a part of a building is forces accommodation that is living or sleeping accommodation for D,*

(b) *another part of the building is a place of work for D or another person for whom the first part is living or sleeping accommodation, and*

(c) *that other part is internally accessible from the first part, that other part, and any internal means of access between the two parts, are each treated for the purposes of subsection (8A) as a part of a building that is forces accommodation.*

(8D) Subsections (4) and (5) apply for the purposes of subsection (8A)(d) as they apply for the purposes of subsection (3).

(8E) The fact that a person derives title from a trespasser, or has the permission of a trespasser, does not prevent the person from being a trespasser for the purposes of subsection (8A).

(8F) In subsections (8A) to (8C)—

"building" includes a vehicle or vessel, and

"forces accommodation" means service living accommodation for the purposes of Part 3 of the Armed Forces Act 2006 by virtue of section 96(1)(a) or (b) of that Act.

s76(9) *Purpose to clarify the operation of the existing defences*

(9) This section, except so far as making different provision for householder cases, ***is intended to clarify the operation of the existing defences*** *mentioned in sub-section (2).*

COMMENTARY: If this is clarification then my goodness help us. The common law was clear.

The provision is widely seen as unnecessary political manoeuvring to be seen to do something when nothing needed doing.

***Keane and McGrath* [2010]** confirmed (**s76 CJIA 2008**) *"did not alter the law as it had stood for many years. It was not an exhaustive statement of the law of self-defence, but it did state the basic principles".*

76(10) *Definitions*

(10) In this section—

(a) "legitimate purpose" means—

- *(i) the purpose of self-defence under the common law,*
- *(ia) the purpose of defence of property under the common law, or*
- *(ii) the prevention of crime or effecting or assisting in the lawful arrest of persons mentioned in the provisions referred to in subsection (2)(b);*

(b) references to self-defence include acting in defence of another person; and

(c) references to the degree of force used are to the type and amount of force used.

No partial defence of excessive force exists

The case of ***Clegg* [1995]** confirmed no partial defence of self-defence exists.

On the facts D was a soldier working in Northern Ireland at a checkpoint. D asked the driver of a car to stop. The driver drove the car through the checkpoint away from D. D fired his gun and several shots hit V (who was the passenger in the car). The fourth shot hit and killed V.

The question on appeal was: *"Where a soldier or police officer in the course of his duty kills a person by firing a shot with the intention of killing or seriously wounding that person and the firing is in self-defence…or in the prevention of crime, but constitutes force, which is excessive and unreasonable in the circumstances, is he guilty of manslaughter and not murder?"*

The House of Lords upheld the conviction for murder noting:

1. Self-defence is a total defence which results in acquittal if D is found to have used necessary and proportionate force.
2. No distinction of self-defence and prevention of crime.
3. No exception for army or police officers.
4. No partial defence. Killing by using disproportionate force is murder.

There was no threat to D or his colleagues. This confirmed ***R v McInnes*** **[1971]**.

However do note D could alternatively seek to use a partial defence, for example:

1. Loss of self-control? or 2. Diminished Responsibility? See ***Martin (Anthony)*** **[2001]**.

Core principles

There is an unnecessary complexity of structure brought in by the statute, so let's shake down to the core principles

(1)	Necessary force	Subjective test	Did D subjectively need to defend himself?
(2)	Proportionate force	Objective test	Was the forced used proportionate?
(3)	Policy exceptions		Is there a specific policy exception?
(a)	The householder		See below
(b)	The mentally disordered person		See below
(c)	Intoxication		See below

14.2.5.3 Policy exceptions

The Householder

CJIA 2008, s76(5A)

(Householder case – *any level of force as long as not grossly disproportionate*)

> "In a householder case, the degree of force used by D is *not to be regarded as having been reasonable in the circumstances* as D believed them to be if it was *grossly disproportionate* in those circumstances."

N.B. This only applies to self-defence in the narrow sense of defence of the person (i.e. not defence of property).

COMMENTARY

1. *Collins* [2016]

On the facts the deceased was Mr Collins (V) who was in the course of burgling D's house. D found V (burglar) committing a burglary and placed V in a headlock. D's wife phoned the police. D could be heard to say hurry up or else he would break V's neck. The police attend. V is badly injured and later dies.

The prosecution do review but do not prosecute on the basis of the evidential test namely that there would not be a realistic prospect of conviction based on the householder defence of self-defence under **s76(5A) CJIA 2008**.

Mr Collins wife brings a claim based on **ECHR Art 2** stating **s76(5A)** was not compatible and using **s3 Human Rights Act 1998**, the domestic provision needs to be construed compatabily with the **ECHR Art 2**. The High Court in an important judgment ruled that the judicial review failed. The commentary of the High Court was:

"i. s.76 (5A) properly construed allowed the jury to convict if the force was unreasonable. This was so even where the force was not 'grossly disproportionate'

ii. The plain words of the s.76 (5A) Criminal Justice and Immigration Act 2008 read in the context of

-their statutory setting,

-legislative purpose, and

-the common law on self-defence,

meant that in householder cases, the force used in self-defence was not unreasonable simply because it was disproportionate, only if it was grossly disproportionate.

iii. It was open to a jury to conclude that the force used by a householder in self-defence was objectively disproportionate but nonetheless reasonable given what the householder believed the circumstances to be.

iv. Section 76 (5A) was compatible with ECHR art.2(1); the existence of the defence did not deter offences against the person in householder cases.

The judgment Blackstone's Criminal Practice 2015 (Reproduced in 2025 Edition).

"The fundamental test still remains that in s. 76(1)(b), i.e. ***whether the force used was 'reasonable in the circumstances'.***

The new provision merely affects the interpretation of '(un)reasonable in the circumstances' so that force is not by law automatically unreasonable in householder cases simply because it is disproportionate, provided it is not grossly disproportionate."

2. *Ray* [2017]

In this case D was at home with a third party (TP). TP's ex-partner V attends the home as D's threatening violence. D tried to make V leave. D then stabbed V to death. D was charged with murder. D's defence was self-defence and utitlised **s76(5A)**. At trial D was found guilty of murder.

The judge's direction was to:

"*i. Consider whether the force was grossly disproportionate?*

ii. If it was not grossly disproportionate: Was the force used reasonable?"

The Court of Appeal dismissed D's appeal on the facts but gave useful guidance on directing the jury.

Lord Thomas CJ construed the Act as follows:

"*Para 25. In determining the question of whether the degree of force used is reasonable …*

[Step 1] ***[Whether the degree of force was grossly disproportionate?***

> *IF YES the degree of force was* **not reasonable** *and the defence of self-defence is not made out.*
>
> *IF NO I.E. the degree of force was not grossly disproportionate GO TO STEP 2*

*[Step 2] [W]****hether that degree of force was reasonable taking into account all the circumstances of the case as D believed them to be?***

> ***The use of disproportionate force which is short of grossly disproportionate is not, on the wording of the section, of itself necessarily the use of reasonable force.***
>
> *The jury are in such a case, where [D] is a householder, entitled to form the view, taking into account all the other circumstances (as [D] believed them to be), that the degree of force used was either reasonable or not reasonable.*

Para 29.[The provision] is ***narrow and not of the wide-ranging effect ...we accordingly reject the contention that provided the degree of force used by a householder is not grossly disproportionate then it is necessarily reasonable."***

Para 33-28:

"It would often be helpful to spell out the circumstances which the jury should consider in determining whether the degree of force was reasonable, such as

- *the* ***shock*** *of encountering the intruder,*
- *the* ***time of day,***
- *the* ***presence of others****,*
- *the* ***desire to protect the house and its occupants (particularly children),***
- *the* ***picking up of an object that would lawfully be to hand in the home****; and*
- *the* ***intruder's conduct.****"*

Unfortunately this is a complex area of the law and arguably requires further resolution by the Appellate Courts or Parliament.

We can state confidently:

1. **Grossly disproportionate force is never reasonable**, e.g. shooting an unarmed burglar dead with a gun.
2. **Reasonable force is reasonable**, e.g. shooting dead a burglar armed with a gun where necessary and reasonable force used.

There is potentially a gap **namely three force which is not reasonable but not grossly disproportionate**, e.g. shooting a burglar armed with a baseball bat dead where not reasonable but not grossly disproportionate. ***Ray*** is useful but arguably departs from the statutory purpose.

In ***Gill*** **[2023]** police with a search warrant broke in through D's front door. Police identified themselves 24 seconds after entry by shouting "police". Two seconds thereafter D stabbed V police officer in the arm. D entered not guilty pleas to **s18 OPA 1861**. D stated necessary (albeit mistaken) proportionate force was used as he thought this was a robbery by other drug dealers (he admitted drug dealing). The Court of Appeal said the judge was wrong to not allow **s76 (5A)** to be engaged. The judge was reading words to the statute which did not exist. A re-trial was ordered at which D was found guilty of unlawful wounding.

3. Tresspass: *Cheeseman* [2019]

D was a solider in barracks. D whilst drunk heard V in Ds room destroying some of his property. D stabbed V. D was charged with attempted murder. D ran the defence of self-defence by a householder under **s76(5A)**. The short question was: Whether the room was a dwelling and V a trespasser? The trial judge ruled the defence was not available as V was not a trespasser. The Court of Appeal stated the defence could apply if D believed V was a trespasser. On the merits, although V provoked D there was clearly no reasonable force and **s76(5)** applied

4. Removal of trespassers from land

An occupier can use reasonable force to remove a trespasser from the occupiers of land: ***Day (Edina)* [2015]**.

Now it appears removing a trespasser from a car is more problematic, e.g. ***Burns* [2010]**; and ***Francis* [2011]**.

The mentally disordered person

A second policy issue is the mentally disordered person. A mentally disordered person cannot "condition" the level of force to be reasonable as the test is objective.

A notorious example is ***Martin (Anthony)* [2001]**. On the facts D was being burgled by two males at his isolated farmhouse. D shot one of the male burglars 1 (V1) dead. D shot the other burglar (V2) causing injury. D had been repeatedly burgled.

D was charged with the murder of V1.

The Court of Appeal substituted the conviction for murder with a conviction for manslaughter.

1) Diminished responsibility: new evidence

D had new evidence of a psychiatric condition that he would have perceived the circumstances as being a greater threat was not admissible. This diminished D's responsibility and thus he was convicted of voluntary manslaughter by way of diminished responsibility.

2) Self defence

The jury should consider whether D's actions were reasonable actions of self-defence on the facts D believed them to be.

3) Reasonable person not reasonable person with D's mental condition

Rejected the conditioning proposed to consider how a reasonable person with D's mental condition would have reacted.

In ***Oye* [2013]**, **[2014]** D was being dealt with by the police. D punched V's (police officers). D believed he was being attacked by evil spirts.

The Court of Appeal ruled again, *"Insanity could not render unreasonable force reasonable"***.** D who was insane could not rely on delusions to render the use of force reasonable.

Thus an "insane" person could not set the standards of reasonableness as to the degree of force used by reference to his own insanity; the position still required objective assessment.

Intoxication

There is no defence of mistake as to necessity or the level of force where the mistake is attributable to intoxication that was voluntarily induced.

s76(5) CJIA 2008:

But subsection (4)(b) ***does not enable D to rely on any mistaken belief attributable to intoxication that was voluntarily induced.***

This confirms ***O'Grady*** **[1987]** at 999 where the Court of Appeal precluded D from using self-defence, when voluntarily intoxicated and using excessive force.

Per Lord Lane CJ:

> *"We have come to the conclusion that* ***where the jury are satisfied that [D] was mistaken in his belief that any force or the force which he in fact used was necessary to defend himself and are further satisfied that the mistake was caused by voluntarily induced intoxication, the defence must fail.***
>
> *"We do not consider that any distinction should be drawn on this aspect of the matter between offences involving what is called specific intent, such as murder, and offences of so-called basic intent, such as manslaughter.*
>
> *"Quite apart from the problem of directing a jury in a case, such as the present where manslaughter is an alternative verdict to murder, the question of mistake can and ought to be considered separately from the question of intent.*
>
> *"A sober man who mistakenly believes he is in danger of immediate death at the hands of an attacker is entitled to be acquitted of both murder and manslaughter if his reaction in killing his supposed assailant was a reasonable one. What his intent may have been seems to us to be irrelevant to the problem of self-defence."*

In ***O'Connor*** **[1991]**, similarly where D killed friend in belief that he was under attack. The court ruled *obiter "where [D] because of self-induced intoxication formed a mistaken belief that he was using force to defend himself a plea of self-defence failed"*.

Similarly in ***Hatton* [2006]** D and V met at a nightclub and returned to D's flat. D then killed V. D stated he mistaken believed V was attacking him with a stick as a weapon. The trial judge ruled D was not able to rely on a drunken mistake. The Court of Appeal dismissed the appeal confirming that in *"self-defence D could not rely on the fact he made a drunken mistake of fact".*

In the most recent authority ***Taj (Simon)* [2019]** the unusual facts were D had long term alcohol and drug issues. D had been drinking in the preceding days causing paranoia. D saw V's van which had broken down on the Embankment in London. D stopped to offer V help. D became convinced V was a terrorist as there were electric wires. D called the police who attended and realised V was an electrician and after a false attempt to restart the van told V to call the AA or equivalent for support. D remained convinced V was a terrorist and saw V on the phone thinking he was receiving instructions to detonate a bomb. D attacked V with a tyre lever.

D was charged with attempted murder and ran a defence of self-defence based on **CJIA 2008 s76(4)** reliance based on a genuine belief even if the belief is not reasonable. Note **s76(5)** mistaken belief not attributable to intoxication which was voluntarily induced.

The Court of Appeal ruled **s76(5)** excluded D's mistaken belief. D could not rely on the defence due to his voluntary intoxication. In all events the level of force was not reasonable.

14.3 Duress

14.3.1 Duress by threats

Examples:

- A orders D (bank manager) at gun point to open the bank vault.

  If D fails to do so, A states he will shoot D dead.
- A orders D to steal from a shop.

  If D fails to do so, A states he will chop D's legs off.
- A orders D to stab V.

  If D fails to do so, A will break D's son's arm.

These are situations where:

1) D is compelled by the threat of death or GBH; and

2) D has no reasonable opportunity to avoid the threat being carried out; and
3) in the circumstances a reasonable person would so act and there is no policy exception.

Example of how limited the defence is: in ***Cole*** **[1994]** D was convicted of committing two robberies at building societies. D stated he was in debt to money lenders, which necessitated the criminal behaviour. D stated A had threatened him, his girlfriend and child with violence if not repaid. The Court of Appeal dismissed the appeal against conviction. D could not rely on duress by threats since threateners had not nominated the crime and immediate peril was lacking. Duress is rigidly limited by policy concerns.

14.3.2 Duress by circumstances

Examples:

- D escapes from prison because it is on fire (this could also be self-defence/necessity).
- D drives in excess of the speed limit because he is being chased by an angry mob.
- D who does not hold full driving licence, takes control of the car to convey A, the driver, who has suffered a heart attack to a nearby hospital.

These are situations where:

1) D is compelled by the circumstances; and
2) D has no reasonable opportunity to avoid the threat being carried out; and
3) in the circumstances a reasonable person would so act and there is no policy exception.

An example is ***Willer*** **(1986)** where D had driven recklessly whilst he was trying to escape from a gang of youths. This was not duress by threats because the youths did not say: "*Drive Recklessly or else.*" The Court of Appeal stated in the circumstances D was allowed to use duress of circumstances as a defence.

14.3.3 Common factors in duress by threats and duress by circumstances

1) D receives a threat of death or serious injury (death/GBH or other serious injury) to D or D's family; and
2) D had no reasonable opportunity to avoid the threats or circumstances; and
3) the reasonable person would so act and there is no policy exception.

The leading authority is now ***Hasan* [2005]**.

a) D receives a threat of death or serious injury (death/GBH or other serious injury) to D or Ds family

i. Confined to death or serious injury

Provisional view that duress should be regarded as confined to threats of death or serious injury and that a threat of false imprisonment would not of itself suffice (***Dao* [2012]** (*obiter*)).

ii. Covers threats to kill/GBH/rape

Threats to kill or do GBH	(***Hudson and Taylor* [1971]**, see facts below)
Threats to rape	(***Hammond* [2013]**)

iii. Is not

- **Is not threats to property**

  "....as a result of experience and human valuation, the law draws [a line] between threats to property and threats to the person..'

  The defence is available where there is a '[well grounded] fear, produced by threats of death or GBH...as overbears [D's] wish not to perform the act."

(***DPP for Northern Ireland v Lynch* [1975]** per Lord Simon at p932).

- **Is not threats to reveal D's homosexuality**

***Valderrama-Vega* [1985]**

iv. To whom?

The limitation seems to be to D, D's immediate family or those for whom D is responsible.

a) D is available where threats are made to D's wife and immediate family; and

(***Hurley and Murray* [1967]** and ***Ortiz* (1986)**).

b) Those for whom D is responsible

***Hasan* [2005]** per Lord Bingham.

b) D had no reasonable opportunity to avoid the threats or circumstances

Example:

1) Threat

Bank manager who is told he or his children will be killed if he does not provide bank robbers money.

2) Reasonable opportunity to avoid?

Bank manager has no reasonable opportunity to avoid

c.f. Threat will be carried out in four days' time.

D has the opportunity to contact the police and would be unlikely to succeed with the d of duress.

3) Reasonable person test

Reasonable person would so do.

The older case of ***Hudson and Taylor* [1971]** is now disapproved of. In that case, A's threatened to fillet witnesses (two young women) if they gave evidence contrary to A's positionality. Therefore D's (the women) commit perjury and lie on oath.

At their trial, the trial judge states D's have no defence because the threats were not sufficiently immediate.

The Court of Appeal stated the defence of duress to the perjury was available because:

> *"threat was operating on their minds at the time".*

Per Lord Widgery LJ at 207:

> *"In the present case [of perjury] the threats ... were likely to be no less compelling, because their execution could not be effected in the court room, if they could be carried out in the streets of Salford the same night.*
>
> *"In the opinion of this court it is always open to the Crown to prove that D failed to avail himself of some opportunity which was* ***reasonably open*** *to him to render the threat ineffective, and that on this being established the threat in question can no longer be relied on by the defence. In deciding whether such an opportunity was reasonably open to the accused* ***[objective test]*** *the jury should have regard to his age and circumstances* ***[subjective test]****, and to any risks to him which may be involved in the course of action relied on."*

This is somewhat bizarre given that in the circumstances they were in a court of law where protection could be availed. It is submitted the case was wrongly decided.

In the crucial case of ***Hasan* [2005]** Lord Bingham was very critical of ***Hudson*** stating:

> *"[27] [Hudson had] the unfortunate effect of weakening the requirement that execution of a threat must be reasonably believed to be imminent and immediate if it is to support a plea of duress ...*

> *"I can understand that the Court of Appeal [in Hudson] had sympathy with the predicament of the young [D's] but I cannot, consistently with principle, accept that a witness testifying in the Crown Court at Manchester has no opportunity to avoid complying with a threat incapable of execution then or there.*
>
> *"[28] [It should] be made clear to juries that if the retribution threatened against D or his family or a person for whom he reasonably feels responsible is not such as he reasonably expects to follow immediately or almost immediately on his failure to comply with the threat, there may be little if any room for doubt that he could have taken evasive action, whether by going to the police or in some other way, to avoid committing the crime with which he is charged."*

In ***Abdul-Hussain and others* [1999]** the facts were D's were Shia Muslims fleeing from Saddam Hussein's regime in Iraq under which they claimed they faced various forms of persecution. They had escaped to Sudan but were on the point of being returned to Iraq, where they feared they would be killed. They therefore hijacked an aircraft. D's hijacked a plane from Sudan to Jordan using imitation weapons. D's forced the plane to fly to the UK.

D's stated a defence of duress of circumstances. The trial judge refused to leave the defence of duress to the jury on the basis there was insufficient evidence that the threat of death or GBH had been sufficiently immediate at the time the offences were committed.

The Court of Appeal allowed the appeal noting the key issue was whether the threat was operating on the minds of D's and whether the threat was immediate was a relevant factor in deciding whether the defendants' response was proportionate; duress was not restricted to where the defendants' criminal act was a spontaneous response to the threat. The court requested legislation to define duress with precision.

Rose LJ:

> *"Imminent peril of death or serious injury to D, or those to whom he has responsibility, is an essential element of both types of duress...*
>
> *"The peril must operate on the mind of the defendant at the time when he commits the otherwise criminal act...*
>
> *"But the execution of the threat need not be immediately in prospect...if Anne Frank had stolen a car to escape from Amsterdam and been charged with theft, the tenets of English law would not, in our judgment, have denied her a defence of duress of circumstances, on the ground that she should have waited for the Gestapo's knock on the door."*

c) The reasonable person would so act and there is no policy exception

If the reasonable person would so act, and there is no policy exception, then the defence of duress can be made.

For example in ***Hegarty* [1994]** the Court of Appeal upheld D's conviction for robbery was following TJ's refusal to admit evidence from two medical witnesses to the effect that D suffered from a "*grossly elevated neurotic state*":

> "*...as [the] test predicated a 'sober person of reasonable firmness' there was* ***no scope for attributing to that hypothetical person as one of the characteristics of the defendant*** *a pre-existing mental condition of being 'emotionally unstable' or in a* ***'grossly elevated neurotic state'****.*"

In ***Bowen* (1996)** D was charged with obtaining goods on credit by deception. D's defence was two men had threatened to attack his family home with petrol bombs if he did not comply.

The trial judge's duress direction from ***Graham*** was followed but, regarding characteristics of D to be attributed to the reasonable person, refused to accede to D's argument that a low IQ of 69 was a characteristic that could be said to have affected his ability to withstand the threats or inhibit him approaching the police.

The Court of Appeal, in dismissing the appeal, stated:

Do take account:

- Age and sex of the D can be taken into account, and his physical health or disability might be taken into account.

Do not take account:

- Pliability, timidity or vulnerability (short of recognised psychiatric impairment) would **not of themselves amount to characteristics**.

Per Stuart-Smith LJ at 163-166:

> "*(1) It seems clear that* ***age and sex are****, and* ***physical health or disability may be, relevant characteristics****...the mere fact that the* ***accused is more pliable, vulnerable, timid or susceptible to threats than a normal person*** *are* ***not characteristics with which it is legitimate to invest the reasonable/ordinary person for the purpose of considering the objective test****......*
>
> "*(2) ...[D] may be in a category of persons who the jury may think less able to resist pressure than people not within that category. Obvious examples are age, where a young person may well not be so robust as a mature one; possibly sex, though many women would doubtless consider they had as much moral courage to resist pressure as men; pregnancy, where there is added fear for the unborn child; serious physical disability, which may inhibit self-protection; recognised mental illness or psychiatric condition, such as post-traumatic stress*

disorder leading to learned helplessness....psychiatric evidence may be admissible to show that the accused is suffering from mental illness, mental impairment or recognised psychiatric condition provided persons generally suffering from such condition may be more susceptible to pressure and threats and thus to assist the jury in deciding whether a reasonable person suffering from such a condition might have been impelled to act as the defendant did. It is ***not admissible*** *simply to show that in the doctor's opinion an accused, who is not suffering from such illness or condition, is* ***especially timid, suggestible or vulnerable to pressure and threats****. Nor is medical opinion admissible to bolster or support the credibility of the accused."*

14.3.4 Directions

a) The direction in duress by threats cases

The *leading case of* ***Graham*** **[1982]** *at* ***300*** states the direction for the jury is two fold:

> *"[1] Subjective*
>
> *'Was [D], or may [D] have been, impelled to act as he did because, as a result of what he reasonably believed [the threatener] had said or done, he had good cause to fear that if he did not so act [the threatener] would kill him or ... cause him serious physical injury? '*
>
> *[2] Objective*
>
> *'If so, have the prosecution made the jury sure that a sober person of reasonable firmness, sharing the characteristics of [D], would not have responded to whatever he reasonably believed [the threatener] said or did by taking part [in the offence].'*
>
> *The fact that a defendant's will to resist has been eroded by the voluntary consumption of drink or drugs or both is not relevant to this test."*

Flatt **[1996]** confirmed Limb [2] where D a drug addict was convicted of possession of a prohibited drug with intent to supply. D had stated he had been forced to look after the consignment of drugs by a drug dealer to whom he owed money and who had threatened to shoot members of D's family if he did not co-*operate*.

b) The direction in duress by circumstances cases

The direction to the jury in duress by circumstances cases is similar.

For example in ***Martin*** **[1989]** the facts were D *was* driving whilst under a disqualified charge. D stated his suicidal wife threatened to kill herself unless he drove their lazy son to work, "If that boy is late for work once more, I will kill myself". D ran the defence of duress of circumstance, i.e. "I had to do it."

The Court of Appeal stated the trial judge should have allowed the jury to hear the evidence per Simon Brown J at 653-654:

> *"...the defence is available only if, from an objective standpoint, the accused can be said to be acting* ***reasonably and proportionately*** *in order to avoid a threat of death or serious injury...the jury...should be directed to determine... two questions."*

The court stated the jury direction was:

> *"[1] Subjective*
>
> *'Was [D], or may he have been, impelled to act as he did because as a result of what he reasonably believed to be the situation he had good cause to fear that otherwise death or serious physical injury would result'*
>
> *[2] Objective*
>
> *'if so, would a sober person of reasonable firmness, sharing the characteristics of the [D], have responded to that situation by acting as the [D] acted?"*

14.3.5 Policy exceptions

a) Self-induced duress

For very obvious reasons the courts are keen to restrict the ambit of the defence. Therefore if the duress is self induced the court will not allow the defence to run.

In ***Fitzpatrick* [1977]** on the facts D had voluntarily joined the IRA and tried to raise a defence of duress to a charge of robbery. At trial, the judge withdrew the defence of duress from the jury. On appeal to the Northern Ireland Court of Appeal that court held that on public policy the defence could not be made available to those who voluntarily joined violent criminal associations, and then found themselves forced to commit offences by their fellow criminals.

Per Lowry LCJ:

> *"(1): In criminal law, therefore, the defence of duress does not derive from the wrongful conduct of the other party to a contract or of a victim who has himself provoked the criminal act of the [D], but enures for the benefit of a person who has been compelled by the coercion of a third party to commit a crime against society and against an innocent victim. Accordingly,* ***it is reasonable to expect that the accused, if he is to benefit from this defence, should himself be morally innocent****...If a person behaves immorally by, for example, committing himself to an unlawful conspiracy, he ought not to be able to take advantage*

> *of the pressure exercised on him by his fellow criminals in order to put on when it suits him the breastplate of righteousness.......*
>
> *"(2):A practical consideration is that,* ***if some such limit on the defendant's duress does not exist, it would be only too easy for every member of an unlawful conspiracy and for every member of a gang except the leader to obtain an immunity denied to ordinary citizens****. Indeed, the better organised the conspiracy and the more brutal its internal discipline, the surer would be the defence of duress for its members. It can hardly be supposed that the common law tolerates such an absurdity."*

In ***Sharp* [1987]** on the facts D voluntarily joined a gang. The gang committed a series of armed robberies. D's defence was duress including to one of the robberies which had resulted in constructive act manslaughter.

CAH: Quashed because D did not know it was of a violent nature.

Lord Lane CJ said (at 861):

> *"... where a person has voluntarily, and with knowledge of its nature, joined a criminal organisation or gang which he knew might bring pressure on him to commit an offence and was an active member when he was put under such pressure, he cannot avail himself of the defence of duress."*

Similarly in ***Shepard* (1987)** D was a member of a shoplifting gang. D's defence was D only took part in a burglary because of threats of violence to D and family. The Court of Appeal quashed the conviction as duress was wrongly withdrawn.

Per Mustill J at 51 cited approvingly of Kenneth Jones J, the trial judge in ***Sharpe*** who stated:

> *"It is not merely a matter of joining in a criminal enterprise****; it is a matter of joining in a criminal enterprise of such a nature that the defendant appreciated the nature of the enterprise itself and the attitudes of those in charge of it****, so that when he was in fact subjected to compulsion he could fairly be said by a jury to have voluntarily exposed himself and submitted himself to such compulsion.*
>
> *"... the concerted shoplifting enterprise did not involve violence to the victim either in anticipation or in the way it was actually put into effect. The members of the jury have had to ask themselves whether the appellant could be said to have taken the risk of P's violence simply by joining a shoplifting gang."*

Also in ***Heath* (1999)** the principle extended to D's not in a criminal organisation voluntarily exposing themselves to the risk of being subjected to threats.

In that case D was charged with possession of a Class B drug with intent to supply and sought to rely on the defence of duress. There was evidence that D was a heroin user who had run up a debt of £1,500 with his supplier. Supplier threatened if he did not pay off his debt he would do GBH to D's girlfriend. He was forced to collect a consignment of shampoo (actually cannabis).

The Court of Appeal agreed with the trial judge's decision to refuse to leave the defence of duress to the jury on the basis D had voluntarily exposed himself to the risk of such threats was upheld. ***Sharp*** was extended to a situation where D knew that becoming indebted to a drug dealer he might put himself at risk of being threatened with violence if he did not carry out certain offences in order to clear his debt.

In ***Hasan* [2005]** D convicted of aggravated burglary. D's defence was he had participated in the burglary only because S (who was a violent gangster) had threatened to harm him and his family if he did not. The trial judge directed the jury that, if he had voluntarily put himself in the position in which he knew he was likely to be subjected to threats, then he could not rely on the defence of duress.

The House of Lords ruled:

1. Defence of duress would not be available if, as a result of D's voluntary association with others engaged in criminal activity, he foresaw or ought to have foreseen the risk of being subjected to any compulsion by threats of violence.
2. There was no need to show that D foresaw what kind of crime he would be compelled to commit.
3. Approved the direction that D could rely on duress if he had been facing, or had reasonably believed he was facing, a threat of death or serious injury to himself or his family.

The correct direction on this issue, as restated by Lord Bingham, would now be as follows:

> *"If a person voluntarily becomes or remains associated with others engaged in criminal activity in a situation where he knows or ought reasonably to know that he may be the subject of compulsion by them or their associates, he cannot rely on the defence of duress to excuse any act which he is thereafter compelled to do by them."*

An example is ***Ali (Israr)* [2008]** stated associating with persons from whom threats of violence could reasonably be foreseen was sufficient to amount to self-induced duress and thus render D ineligible form running the defence.

b) Murder

- Duress and necessity recognise that D is having to make choices between competing evils.

Dudley and Stephens (1884) on the facts D's, TP and a cabin boy, were cast adrift in a boat following a shipwreck. D & S agreed that as the cabin boy was already weak and looked likely to die soon, they would kill him and live off his flesh and blood for as long as they could. Dudley carried out the killing and both were charged with murder following their rescue.

At trial the defence was necessity – otherwise D's would die. At common law there was no defence of necessity.

The High Court ruled they could be guilty of murder but the death penalty was commuted to six months hard labour.

Per Lord Coleridge CJ at 287-288:

"[1] ***What if, out of perceived duress of circumstances, D intentionally kills P to save D's life?***

'... it is enough in a Christian country to remind ourselves of the Great Example whom we profess to follow. It is not needful to point out the ***awful danger of admitting the principle which has been contended for****.*

Who is to be the judge of this sort of necessity?

By what measure is the comparative value of lives to be measured*? [Not value one above another]*

Is it to be strength, or intellect, or what*? It is plain that the principle leaves to him who is to profit by it to determine the necessity which will justify him in deliberately taking another's life to save his own. In this case the weakest, the youngest, the most unresisting, was chosen.*

[2] ***What if, out of perceived duress of circumstances, D intentionally kills P to save D's life?***

Was it more necessary to kill him than one of the grown men? The answer must be "No"...*It must not be supposed that in refusing to admit temptation to be an excuse for crime it is forgotten how terrible the temptation was; how awful the suffering; how hard in such trials to keep the judgment straight and the conduct pure.*

We are often compelled to set up standards we cannot reach ourselves, and to lay down rules which we could not ourselves satisfy*. But* ***a man has no right to declare temptation to be an excuse,*** *though he might himself have yielded to it, nor allow compassion for the criminal to change or weaken in any manner the legal definition of the crime."*

Examples

E.g.1 Motorist driving on a mountain road sees a huge boulder rolling towards his car in which four small children lie. He deliberately swerves his car to one side, knowing that he will hit and kill an elderly man standing at the roadside.

Eg. 2 Pilot flying to crash into a Summer Fair (100's) or a School field (1).

A: It will not avail him, when charged with murder, to say that he acted to save five lives at the cost of one.

In ***Howe* [1987]** D with another was convicted of murder. D had stated the defence of duress: they believed they would themselves be killed if they did not carry out the killing. The trial judge ruled that duress could be raised as a defence only in respect of the first count, in which they were charged as accessories to murder.

The House of Lord dismissed appeal.

1. Duress could not be a defence to murder, whether the defendant is charged as a principal or accessory.
2. Upheld the decision of the Court of Appeal in ***Graham*** (see above) was correct.

Per Lord Hailsham LC at 432:

> *"To permit a D to kill an innocent person because of threats made to his own life would involve overruling"* (**Dudley & Stephens**).
>
> *"I do not at all accept in relation to...murder that it is either good morals, good policy or good law to suggest... that the ordinary man of reasonable fortitude is not to be supposed to be capable of heroism if he is asked to take an innocent life rather than sacrifice his own. Doubtless in actual practice many will succumb to temptation, as they did in Dudley and Stephens. But many will not, and **I do not believe that as a "concession to human frailty"** the former should be exempt from liability to criminal sanctions if they do. I have known in my own lifetime of too many acts of heroism by ordinary human beings of no more than ordinary fortitude to regard a law as either **"just or humane" which withdraws the protection of the criminal law from the innocent victim and casts the cloak of its protection upon the coward and the poltroon in the name of a "concession to human frailty"**."*

c) Attempted murder

In ***Gotts* [1992]** D attempted to stab his mother to death because father said he would have shot him if he did not. The House of Lords confirmed duress was *"no defence to murder or to attempted murder"*.

Per Lord Jauncey:

> *"(1) Is there logic in affording the defence to one who intends to kill but fails and denying it to one who mistakenly kills intending only to injure? If I may give two examples:*

(1a) A stabs B in the chest intending to kill him and leaves him for dead. By good luck B is found whilst still alive and rushed to hospital where surgical skill saves his life.

(1b) C stabs D intending only to injure him and inflicts a near identical wound. Unfortunately D is not found until it is too late to save his life.

I see no justification of logic or morality for affording a defence of duress to A who intended to kill when it is denied to C who did not so intend.

(2a) E plants in a passenger aircraft a bomb timed to go off in midflight. Owing to bungling it explodes while the aircraft is still on the ground with the result that some 200 passengers suffer physical and mental injuries of which many are permanently disabling, but no one is killed.

(2b) F plants a bomb in a light aircraft intending to injure the pilot before it takes off but in fact it goes off in midair killing the pilot who is the sole occupant of the airline.

"It would in my view be both offensive to common sense and decency that E, if he established duress, should be acquitted and walk free without a stain on his character notwithstanding the appalling results which he has achieved, whereas F who never intended to kill should, if convicted in the absence of the defence, be sentenced to life imprisonment as a murderer."

14.4 Necessity

Examples

(i) A and B are roped climbers – A loses his footing and is pulling B to his certain death. C, a nearby marksman fires his gun at the rope severing it. A falls to his death. B is saved.

(ii) S a surgeon, performs an abortion operation on W, a 12-year-old girl, who is 30 weeks pregnant. The medical evidence is that to W will die if she gives birth.

14.4.1 Any residual defence of necessity at common law?

D may not himself be threatened with death or grievous bodily harm, but he is faced with a choice between breaking the law to prevent harm to others, or observing the law and risking such harm.

There may be scope for a defence where D's will to resist is not overborne as such, but he simply chooses a course of action that involves the lesser of two evils.

There may be scope for a defence where D is acting to prevent a harm falling some way short of an immediate threat of death or grievous bodily harm.

14.4.2 D kills X in order to save Y

In ***Re A (Children) (conjoined twins: surgical separation)* [2000]**

The facts were the twins Jodie and Mary were conjoined. It was known that if J was separated from M the likelihood was J would survive and have a good future but M would die.

However if the twins were not separated both twins would die within six months. Sadly M lacked organs to pump blood and J's organs could pump blood for one but not two. The parents objected to the operation.

The question set: was it lawful for surgeons to operate to separate conjoined twins J & M?

The Court of Appeal ordered the operation to separate the twins would not be unlawful.

Whilst the doctors would have intent to kill Mary, the operation would be lawful because of the necessity to preserve Jodie.

Robert Walker LJ, saw the case as one where the principles of necessity should apply so as to absolve the surgeons performing the operation from liability. He observed:

> *"In the absence of Parliamentary intervention the law as to the* ***defence of necessity is going to have to develop on a case-by-case basis****, as Rose LJ said in Abdul-Hussain [1999] Crim LR 570.*
>
> *"I would extend it, if it needs to be extended, to cover this case. It is a case of doctors owing conflicting legal (and not merely social or moral) duties. It is a case where the test of proportionality is met, since it is a matter of life and death, and on the evidence [M] is bound to die soon in any event. It is not a case of evaluating the relative worth of two human lives, but of undertaking surgery without which neither life will have the bodily integrity (or wholeness) which is its due. It should not be regarded as a further step down a slippery slope because the case of conjoined twins presents an unique problem."*

Brooke LJ concluded there were three preconditions for the application of the doctrine of necessity:

"(i) the act is needed to ***avoid inevitable and irreparable evil****;*

(ii) **no more** *should be done* ***than is reasonably necessary for the purpose to be achieved;***

(iii) *the* ***evil inflicted must not be disproportionate to the evil avoided****."*

In his view, given that the interests of [J] had to be preferred to the conflicting interests of [M], all three of these requirements were satisfied on the given facts.

"If a sacrificial operation on conjoined twins were to be permitted in circumstances like these...[I have] no room for concern felt [that] people would be too ready to avail themselves of exceptions to the law which they might suppose to apply to their cases....such an operation is, and is always likely to be, an exceptionally rare event..."

Ward LJ accepted that **surgeons** performing an operation to separate the twins would cause the death of M and would do so with the **necessary intent to support a charge of murder**. Regarding the availability of a defence that would absolve the surgeons of any liability he accepted that it would be unfair for the law to put medical practitioners in an impossible situation:

> *"What are the doctors to do if the law imposes upon them a duty which they cannot perform without being in breach of [M]'s right to life if at the same time the respecting of her right puts them in breach of the equally serious duty of respecting [J]'s right to life? A resort to a sanctity of life argument does not enable both rights to receive the equal protection the doctrine is supposed to provide each of them equally. In those circumstances it seems to me that* ***the law must allow an escape through choosing the lesser of the two evils****. The law cannot say, "heads I win, tails you lose"... the conclusion has to be that the carrying out of the operation will be justified as the lesser evil and no unlawful act would be committed."*

He concludes by suggesting that the answer lies in "*seeing the surgeons as intervening to protect J from M*". For these purposes M's action did not have to be characterised as unlawful, in the sense that she might be seen as an "unjust aggressor".

E.g. He drew the analogy with a "*..six-year-old boy indiscriminately shooting all and sundry in the school playground.*" His actions would not be unlawful, given his age, but Ward LJ was of the view that:

> *"....****in law killing that six-year-old boy in self-defence of others would be fully justified and the killing would not be unlawful****. I can see no difference in essence between that resort to legitimate self-defence and the doctors coming to [J's] defence and removing the threat of fatal harm to her presented by [M's] draining her lifeblood. The availability of such a plea of quasi self-defence, modified to meet the quite exceptional circumstances nature has inflicted on the twins, makes intervention by the doctors lawful."*

14.4.3 Limitations on the availability of necessity as a defence

In ***Bourne* [1939]** D was a gynaecologist who performed late abortions on young women who had been a V of rape, in a public hospital with agreement of parents. The Court of Appeal said the person was not guilty under **s58 OAPA 1861** of *"unlawfully procuring a miscarriage"*. Because D did not act *"unlawfully"*, he *"acted in good faith"* in the exercise of his clinical judgement & not unlawful.

In ***F v West Berkshire Health Authority* [1990]** the House of Lords ruled the *"necessity"* of carrying out an operation to *"sterilise a woman"* who did not have the mental capacity to consent to such an operation.

In ***Buckoke v Greater London Council* [1971]** Lord Denning MR famously stated:

> *"Whilst a driver of an emergency vehicle would not be able to plead a defence of necessity if he drove through a red light whilst answering an emergency call, such a person ought to be congratulated rather than prosecuted."*

In ***Howe* [1987]** Lord Griffiths said that it was *"inconceivable"* that a hijacked woman motorist forced to act as a getaway driver, or a witness forced to give misleading information to the police concerning a robbery or murder, would be prosecuted.

Examples of duress of circumstances/necessity

In ***Conway* [1989]** D had driven recklessly to protect his passenger from what he honestly believed to be an assassination attempt.

The Court of Appeal quashed the conviction for reckless driving as it had been caused by fear of attack from thugs (honest mistake – plain clothes police officers).

In ***Backshall* [1998]** D had been convicted of driving without due care and attention whilst trying to escape from a pedestrian he believed was about to attack him.

The Court of Appeal knew D should have been permitted to put the defence of duress of circumstances before the jury, given the apparent threat of death or GBH created by the circumstances.

In ***Bell* [1992]** D drove his car to **escape from pursuers** threatening violence despite the fact that he was over the blood alcohol limit. The Court of Appeal stated D should have been permitted to put the defence of duress of circumstances before the jury, given the apparent threat of death or GBH created by the circumstances.

In ***Pommell* [1995]** the police found D in bed with a gun. D explained that he "took it off a geezer who was going to do some people some damage with it". D was convicted of unlawful possession of the gun.

The trial judge had ruled that the defence of duress of circumstances was not available in the circumstances of the case. The Court of Appeal stated if true, D's account could enable him to use the defence of duress of circumstances and quashed his conviction.

In ***Rodger* [1998]** the case concerned jail break where D stated to the effect, "I had to do it, I would have committed suicide". The Court of Appeal stated he had no defence of duress for having your own suicidal tendencies. The causative feature giving rise to the plea must be "*something extraneous*" to D, i.e. not D's own suicidal tendencies.

Sir Patrick Russell at 145:

> *"If allowed it could amount a* ***licence to commit crime*** *dependant on the personal characteristics and vulnerability of the of the offence. As a matter of policy that is undesirable and in our view it is not the law and should not be the law."*

14.5 Age of criminal responsibility (ACR)

14.5.1 Pre-1998

1.1 Children under 10: irrebuttable presumed incapable of criminal responsibility (*doli incapax*) (**s50 Children and Young Persons Act 1933**).

1.2. Children between 10–14 (i.e. 10, 11, 12, 13) there existed a rebuttable presumption the child was incapable of criminal responsibility unless the presumption is rebutted by the prosecution proving the child had "mischievous discretion", i.e. knew the act was "seriously wrong" not just naughty or mischievous (***JM v Runeckles* (1984)**).

1.3 The latter still applies to the trial of offences committed before 30/09/1998 by children aged between 10-14. This is very important, for example in the prosecution of historical sex abuse cases. ***PF* [2017]**.

14.5.2 Post-1998

2.1 Children under 10: Irrebuttable presumed incapable of criminal responsibility (*doli incapax*) (**s50 Children and Young Persons Act 1933**).

2.2 Children 10 +: Children over the age of 10 are capable of committing a criminal offence ([the] rebuttable presumption of criminal law that a child aged ten or over is incapable of committing an offence is hereby abolished) **s34 Crime and Disorder Act 1998**; technical argumentation was laid to rest and purposive interpretation ***JTB* [2009]**.

14.5.3 Generally

- Different processes in the police station; court (The Youth Court); sentencing; and detention.
- Very interesting, important complex area of the law.
- Age very important to subjective elements of offences e.g. regarding *mens rea*; loss of self control; diminished responsibility; duress; and self defence.

14.6 Evaluation and reform

14.6.1 Legal certainty and legal clarity

The law on self-defence was at common law certain and clear. The new statutory provision which was politically motivated is not well defined but only the householder defence appears problematic. The courts in ***Collins*** and ***Ray*** appear to have polished the edges to make it **ECHR Art 2** compliant.

Duress is such a rare defence but it appears to be certain and relatively clear and accord with sensible policy reasons for being very restrictive.

14.6.2 Equality before the law: protected characteristics and socio-economic barriers

There does not appear to be any equality barriers to the law. The law legitimately differentiates those who are defending themselves, compelled to act or under the age of capacity.

14.6.3 Fair warning; fair labelling and sufficient breadth principles

a) Fair warning

The defences do appear to give fair warning to the community of the consequences. The householder defence could be clarified by a Supreme Court Judgment or

Parliament revisiting the threshold perhaps placing it back in statute as "reasonable". Duress policy decisions accord with common sense and warning.

There is an argument that necessity would be better framed by statute.

b) Fair labelling

The total exoneration of those who have a good claim to self-defence, duress, necessity and ACR circumstances seems to fairly draw the line in law and morality.

c) Sufficient breadth

There appears to be sufficient breadth to the defences.

d) Practicality, cost, and expense

1) Practicality – the law could easily and helpfully be codified
2) Avoid undue cost and expense

The standard self-defence does not appear to have issues.

The householder defence needs clarification and perhaps statutory reform.

There is a large body of case law regarding duress but, in reality, it is a very rarely used defence because:

i. cases where duress clearly exists are not prosecuted; and
ii. it is such a restrictive defence that the chance of using it is very limited.

14.6.4 Human rights: autonomy and welfare principles

The position for purposes of **ECHR Article 7** legal certainty seems to be relatively certain on all matters except the householder defence.

The position on **Article 2** right to life is clearly laid out by the European Court of Human Rights and English law seems to accord.

14.6.5 International comparators and reform: practicality principle and politics

a) Comparators

None cited

b) *Law Commission Consultation Paper 177 on Duress*

Would allow duress as a partial defence to first degree murder.

The conditions would be:

i. Threat of death or serious violence

ii. Directed at D/D immediate family or person proximate

iii. Good reason and causation, i.e. threat caused action

iv. No available escape to take evasive action against the threat

v. Not available where self-induced by voluntary membership

vi Test is reasonable person of ordinary courage might have acted as D did.

In the News

The householder who kills in self defence

Please read these two articles:

1. Audrey Gillan, "Life for farmer who shot burlgar" *The Guardian* (London, 20 April 2000)

   <https://www.theguardian.com/uk/2000/apr/20/tonymartin.ukcrime3> accessed 06 April 2025

2. Kevin Rawlinson, "Householders can use 'disproportionate' level of force against intruders" *The Guardian* (London, 15 January 2016)

   <https://www.theguardian.com/law/2016/jan/15/high-court-rejects-challenge-to-householder-defence-law> accessed 06 April 2025

These both relate to householders who kill an invader.

The law has difficult policy decisions to make.

Arguably English law values sanctity of life as more important than the sanctity of private property.

However there is widespread public concern according to the media that those who have a home invasion should be able to use more force then standard self defence.

Utilising the law described above in relation to self defence, how would you advise the householder in these cases? When is it necessary to use force? What is a proportionate level of force?

14.7 Summary

Students should now be more confident on the four key themes:

- **Self defence**

  Knowing is availability and limits.

- **Duress**

  Knowing how clear threats/circumstances can operate to compel behaviours but also how restrictive the defence is.

- **Necessity**

  Knowing how rarely the defence is used and the obvious policy limitations.

- **Infancy/age of criminal responsibility (ACR)**

  Knowing autonomy is impaired by lack of capacity and thus those under the age of 10 are exempt from standard rules.

Further reading

LK Bleasdale-Hill, "Our Home is Our Haven and Refuge—A Place Where We Have Every Right to Feel Safe": Justifying the Use of Up to "Grossly Disproportionate Force" in a Place of Residence' (2015) *Criminal Law Review 407*.

Mark Dsouza, "Understanding the 'Householder Defence': Proportionality and Reasonableness in Defensive Force" (2016) *75 Cambridge Law Journal 192*.

Catherine Elliott, "Interpreting the Contours of Self-Defence Within the Boundaries of the Rule of Law, the Common Law and Human Rights" (2015) *79 Journal of Criminal Law 339*.

Fiona Leverick, "Is English Self-Defence Law Incompatible with Article 2 of the ECHR?" (2002) *Criminal Law Review 347*.

Mark P Thomas, "Defenceless Castles: The Use of Grossly Disproportionate Force by Householders in Light of R (Collins) v Secretary of State for Justice" (2015) *80 Journal of Criminal Law 407*.

CHAPTER 15

Participation

15.1 Introduction

Crimes often have more than one participant. For example, in order to effect a robbery it would be practically useful to have four or more people. You could have one person leading the theft aspect; person two and three holding the victim or "blocking" and person four person acting as "look out". The participation of all four would be important even though they all played different roles in the "enterprise".

The criminal offences throughout this book are premised on charging one defendant (P) for an offence. The reality is particular crimes will often have more than one defendant present and participating to effect the "successful" completion of the crime. Common examples include:

- homicide offences (such as murder or manslaughter);
- non-fatal offences against the person (such as causing grievous bodily harm with intent); and

- theft-related offences (particularly robbery and burglary).

Where more than one person is party to a completed crime, the terminology used to describe this has varied but the term "joint enterprise" served as a useful shorthand to indicate more than one person has "joined" the "enterprise" of committing the crime. In the modern era one of us, writing elsewhere,[1] has submitted "joint participation" more accurately explains the law (see ***Bastian v The King* [2024]**, ***PC* [Bahamas]**).[2]

Since 2016, ***Jogee***; ***Ruddock v R* [2016]**[3] (from now on ***Jogee***) is the leading common law source. The Supreme Court Judgment of ***Jogee*** is a fundamental statement and realignment of the guiding principles. This chapter will use the terminology of principals and accessories and will be advanced as general principles applicable to all criminal offences.

Aims of this chapter

By the end of this chapter you can be expected to know and be able to evaluate the law on participation in criminal offences.

The chapter will focus on each aspect of the accessory's (A) liability.

Actus reus

- Proof of a completed base *actus reus* of the primary offence
- Proof of as mode of participation

Mens rea

- Proof of as knowledge of the primary type of criminal offence(s)
- Proof of as intention to assist or encourage P's *actus reus* and *mens rea*

Other issues

- Overwhelming Supervening Event (OSE)
- Withdrawal

---

1 See Alan Birbeck, "Participation" in Mark Lucraft (General Editor) *Archbold Criminal Practice* (2025 edn), Ch 18 Participation

2 Joint Participation term approved by the Criminal Law Week 2024 Issue 31; Page 1; Senior Circuit Judge Philip Katz KC endorses the new approach of this author in Archbold 2025 onwards namely it the preferred use of the term Joint Participation rather than outdated terms Joint Enterprise or Parasitic Accessorial Liability. See also David Ormerod commentary on Lewis [2010]; Rudi Fortson KC [2025]

3 Jogee; Ruddock v R. [2016] SC & PC

15.2 Procedure re: Principals (P) and Accessories (A)

The rules of criminal evidence, criminal law and criminal process proceed on the basis that the responsibility for a crime can be either as the **principal** – the person who is the primary cause of the *actus reus* (this includes joint principals); or the **accessory** – the person who is a secondary cause of the *actus reus*.

15.2.1 Statute

s8 Accessories and Abettors Act 1861

8. Whosoever shall aid, abet, counsel, or procure the commission of any indictable offence, whether the same be an offence at common law or by virtue of any Act passed or to be passed, shall be liable to be tried, indicted and punished as a principal offender. (For the magistrates there is the equivalent provision in **s44 Magistrates' Courts Act 1980**).

15.2.2 Indictment

There is no requirement that the indictment specifies who is the principal and who is the accessory.

Terminology Alert!

Indictment: this is effectively the "charge sheet" in Crown Court proceedings stating what specific charges must be proven.

This is a significant practical advantage to the prosecution to not require specificity as long as there is a basis of liability proven either as principal, joint principal, or accessory.

This is a significant practical disadvantage to the defence as "reading a verdict" is problematic where a jury do not reason a verdict other than through a "route to verdict".

If convicted, principals and accessories are liable to the same maximum sentence. However, the individual's sentence will of course vary depending on the level of harm caused, their role and their culpability.

Where the prosecution are unable to say whether D was the principal or accessory, it is legitimate to advance the case in the alternative, i.e. D is either principal or accessory provided the directions are clearly made (***Giannetto* [1997]**; ***Tirnaveanu* [2007]**.

In ***Smith (James Alexander)* [2023]** it was confirmed that "*[s]ometimes it is not possible to determine exactly whose hand performed the vital act, but this does not matter providing that if the is proved that each defendant either did it himself or intentionally assisted or encouraged it*".

15.2.3 Terminology

a) Principal [P]

The principal (P singular) is the main party who is the most immediate cause of the *actus reus*/conduct of the offence, e.g. the person stabbing is the principal, i.e. the "stabber".

Throughout this chapter we will refer to them as P (singular).

b) Joint principals [Ps]

Where there is more than one person making a direct contribution to the *actus reus* of the offence there can be joint principals, e.g. two persons stabbing the victim, i.e. the "joint stabbers".

Throughout this chapter we will refer to them as Ps (plural).

c) Accessories [A or As]

Accessories are the secondary party who assist(s) or encourage(s) P's *actus reus, e.g. person 1 stabs the victim [P]; person 2 acts as the lookout [A].*

Throughout this chapter we will refer to the secondary party as A (singular); and As (plural) where there is more than one.

15.2.4 Liability as an accessory applies to all offences unless excluded by statute

Liability applies to all criminal offences, unless specifically excluded by a statute, allow for more than one person to be charged and indicted. E.g. **s73 Sexual Offences Act 2003**, protection of children.

15.3 AR: Proof of the completed base *actus reus* of the primary offence

If there is no base *actus reus* for the primary offence there can be no liability as a principal or as a secondary party for the completed offence.

Please note this does not rule out inchoate liability (see **Chapter 16**) such as attempt etc (***Assistant Recorder of Kingston-upon-Hull, ex p. Morgan*** [1969]; ***Loukes*** **[1996]**.

15.4 AR: Proof of accessories completed mode of participation

15.4.1 Traditional modes of participation: aid, abet, counsel, or procure

The traditional modes of participation arise from **s8 Accessories and Abettors Act 1861**. There are four words used: aid, abet, counsel or procure.

These courts have stated the words should be given their ordinary meaning, if possible. The courts believe that as four words are used there is a distinction between their meeting: ***Attorney-General's Reference (No.1 of 1975)*** **[1975]**. This could be open to the criticism that there are four words but their meaning is opaque and overlaps.

There is no need for the act of assistance or encouragement to be contemporaneous: ***Stringer (Ian Bryan) and Stringer (Ian)*** **[2011]**.

a) Aid and abet

An aider and abettor may be present giving active assistance to the principal; he may be some distance away. There is some commentary that the aiding was the action and abetting was the mental element: ***Ferguson v Weaving*** **[1951]**. However this is not clear. The dictionary is helpful in that aid is "a helper, an assistant" and abet is to: "1.Urge on to do something...; 2. Support, uphold; 3. Encourage or countenance ...by active assistance."[4]

b) Counsel

Counsel appears to mean to "*advise*" or "*solicit*": ***Calhaem*** **[1985]**. Again the dictionary is helpful in stating that counsel is to "recommend (a plan, suggestion)."[5]

4 Angus Stevenson (ed), *Shorter Oxford English Dictionary* (6th edn, OUP 2007)
5 Angus Stevenson (ed), *Shorter Oxford English Dictionary* (6th edn, OUP 2007)

c) Procure

Procure is said to mean to "produce by endeavour" i.e. you take steps to produce the event: ***Attorney-General's Reference (No.1 of 1975)* [1975]**.

There must be a causal relationship between the procurer and the person who is the most direct cause of the *actus reus*. The dictionary states that procure is the "act of procuring something; the action by which something is attained" and that procuratory is the "authorisation of one person to act for another".[6]

d) Problematic terminology

It is submitted all of these traditional modes/terms are problematic. They are old fashioned. Their meaning is opaque and they are not legally certain or clear. However the statute remains in force.

15.4.2 Modern Modes of Participation: Assisted or Encouraged (A & E)

Jogee (para 86) in part justified the change of the common law approach to participation based on a recent statute, namely **s44 Serious Crime Act 2007**.

s44 provides:

> *(1) A person commits an offence if—*
>
> *(a) he does an* ***act capable of encouraging or assisting the commission of an offence; and***
>
> *(b)* ***he intends to encourage or assist its commission.***

N.B. We will explore this section in **Inchoate offences**.

Jogee therefore helpfully re-frames the modern modes of participation away from the archaic terms ("aid, abet, counsel, and procure") and towards the new terminology ("encourage or assist").

It is submitted this is a better frame for communication of the same substance as the older terms, without losing the depth of meaning.

The terms are clearer, i.e. assisting is to "give help or support";[7] e.g. I assist by blocking, holding, supplying.

---

6 Angus Stevenson (ed), *Shorter Oxford English Dictionary* (6th edn, OUP 2007)
7 Angus Stevenson (ed), *Shorter Oxford English Dictionary* (6th edn, OUP 2007)

Encouraging is to "urge, incite, recommend, advise";[8] e.g. I encourage by requesting, cajoling, shouting etc.

15.4.3 Omissions: Presence v Participation

Presence

An accessory does not have to be present at the scene of the crime.

However an accessory frequently is present at the scene. Voluntary presence of A at the scene of a crime is evidence for a jury to consider.

e.g. In ***Wilcox v Jeffery* [1951]** it was held that a journalist encouraged an illegal working arrangement where they knowingly attended a jazz concert. Other authorities include ***Coney* (1882)**; ***Allan* [1965]**; ***Clarkson* (1971)**; and ***Bauer v DPP* [2013]**.

Jogee (para 11) notes:

> *"Both association and presence are likely to be very relevant evidence on the question whether assistance or encouragement was provided. Numbers often matter.*
>
> ***"Most people are bolder when supported or fortified by others than they are when alone**. And something done by a group is often a good deal more effective than the same thing done by an individual alone.*
>
> *"A great many crimes, especially of actual threatened violence, are, whether planned or spontaneous, in fact encouraged or assisted by supporters present with the principal lending force to what he does. Nevertheless, neither association nor presence is necessarily proof of assistance or encouragement; it depends on the facts: see **Coney (1882) 8 QBD 534, 540, 558**."*

Jogee (para 12) goes on:

> *"In many cases that would be impossible to prove.*
>
> *"There might, for example, have been many supporters encouraging P so that the encouragement of a single one of them could not be shown to have made a difference. The encouragement might have been given but ignored, yet the counselled offence committed.*
>
> *Conversely, there may be cases where anything said or done by A has faded to the point of mere background or has been spent of all possible force by some overwhelming intervening occurrence by the time the offence was committed. Ultimately it is a question of fact and degree whether A's conduct was so distanced in time, place, or circumstances from the conduct of P that it would not be realistic to regard P's offence as encouraged or assisted by it."*

---

8 Angus Stevenson (ed), *Shorter Oxford English Dictionary* (6th edn, OUP 2007)

Therefore presence alone is not sufficient for liability.

Participation

Some form participation in the act is crucial: ***National Coal Board v Gamble* [1959]**.

No need to find a measurable contribution

A defence argument was A needed to make a measurable contribution towards the primary offence. This has been rejected in recent case law. ***Jogee*** (para 12) is clear that once encouragement or assistance is proved to have been given there is no need to find a "*measurable contribution*" by an accessory to the commission of the crime by a principal: ***Rowe* [2022]** and ***Hussain (Mohammed Saddam)* [2023]**.

15.5 MR: proof of accessories knowledge of the primary type of criminal offence(s)

15.5.1 A must have knowledge of the primary type of criminal offence(s)

A must have knowledge of the primary type of criminal offence(s) e.g.:

P A builder sold a house for £250 over the maximum permitted by a statutory regulation.

A Solicitors acting in the conveyancing had no knowledge of relevant fact.

The court quashed A's convictions on the basis they had no knowledge of the facts which made the situation criminal stating:

> "*Before a person can be convicted of aiding and abetting the commission of an offence, he must at least know the essential matters which constitute that offence.*"

(***Johnson v Youden* [1950]**)

15.5.2 A is not required to know the precise offence contemplated by P just the type of offence

"*A may intentionally assist or encourage P to commit one of a range of offences...*

> *If so, A does not have to "know" (or intend) in advance the specific form which the crime will take. It is enough that the offence committed by P is* ***within the range of possible offences which A intentionally assisted or encouraged him to commit."***

(***Jogee*** (para 14) confirming ***Maxwell*** **[1978]**)

15.5.3 Knowledge/contemplation of the same "type" of crime

A must have contemplated the same type of crime committed by P, e.g. where A supplied P with cutting equipment used to break into a bank.

A thought it would be used for some illegal purpose but did not know what.

The court held for A to be found guilty more than mere suspicion was required.

(***Bainbridge*** **[1960]** at 133–4).

15.5.4 A Issuing to P a "blank cheque"

e.g. P bombed public house in Northern Ireland. A was the driver of the car. A argued he did not know the precise type of offence which was to be committed. It was held it was obvious the attack was terrorist in nature but not clear if bombing, shooting or other offence was to take place.

Jogee (para 15) confirms ***Maxwell*** **[1978]** that where:

> *"A did not know the precise form of attack that they were intending to carry out (which was in fact an explosion), ... it was held to be enough that he knew that they were intending to carry out a violent attack on the inn and that he intended to assist them to do so."*

e.g. Lowry CJ in ***Maxwell***, at 1374:

> *"[A's] guilt springs from the fact that he* ***contemplates*** *the commission of one (or more) of a number of crimes by [P] and he intentionally lends his assistance in order that such a crime will be committed ...the relevant crime must be within the contemplation of [A] and only exceptionally would evidence be found to support the allegation that [A] had given [P] a completely blank cheque. [A] must ... have contemplated the bombing [of the public house] as not the only possibility but one of the most obvious possibilities among the jobs which [Ps] were likely to be undertaking."*

Endorsed by Lord Scarman in ***Maxwell***, at 1363:

> *"[A] may have in contemplation only one offence, or several; and the several that he contemplates he may see as alternatives. [A] who leaves it to [P] to choose is liable, provided always the choice is made from the range of offences from which [A] contemplates the choice will be made."*

15.6 MR: proof of accessories intention to assist or encourage P's *actus reus* and *mens rea*

Jogee states the second *mens rea* requirement as:

> *"the mental element in assisting or encouraging is an intention to assist or encourage the commission of the crime."*

Jogee states at [10]:

> *"If the crime requires a particular intent,*
>
> *[A] must intend to assist or encourage [P] to act with such intent.*
>
> *"[A's] intention to assist [P] to commit the offence, and to act with whatever mental element is required of [P], will often be co-extensive on the facts with an intention by [A] that that offence be committed.*
>
> *"Where that is so, it will be seen that many of the cases discuss [A's] mental element simply in terms of intention to commit the offence.*
>
> *"But there can be cases where [A] gives intentional assistance or encouragement to [P] to commit an offence and to act with the mental element required of him, but without [A] having a positive intent that the particular offence will be committed.*
>
> *"That may be so, for example, where at the time that encouragement is given it remains uncertain what [P] might do; an arms supplier might be such a case."*

This confirms ***National Coal Board v Gamble* [1959]**.

Weapons

See [90]–[94] of ***Jogee***. It is not necessary for A to know that P carried weapons or a particular type of weapon in order for them to be convicted of murder, provided the prosecution prove that A was a joint participant to cause at least really serious harm and that they had the requisite intent.

Change of target

The fact that the main target of a joint participation attack is clearly identified does not mean that the joint participations scope cannot also include a conditional intention to attack anyone who gets in the way:

> *"... There is no such legal principle. It is a matter for the jury to say whether that intention is proved or not. That is a question which, of course, has to be considered by carefully evaluating the evidence on which the prosecution relies."* ***BHV* [2022]**.

The organised gun fight scenario

In the circumstances of A firing a gun at P and then P firing back at A but killing V (who can be a member of As gang).

A could be guilty of encouraging or assisting P's primary offence of murder by the intention to encourage the said offence ***Gnango* [2012]**.

The original case has many potential interpretations as the judgments diverge on routes to liability. It is submitted A's indirect intention is foreseeing as a virtual certainty the encouragement of P to fire at A would be sufficient to found liability.

A would thus be an accessory to the killing by P of the innocent V bystander (shot by a bullet intended for A).

Similarly ***Morgan* [2021]** made clear that persons engaging in a "gun fight" intending to kill or inflict really serious injury, could be guilty of the murder of those who die, regardless of whichever gang/group they were a member of provided the ***Jogee*** requirements were made out.

This deterrent message has been confirmed in ***Seed (Issa)* [2024]**. Where A, A2 and V drove to the scene of a "gun fight" between their gang and a rival gang. During the gunfight, unidentified members of the other gang (P) fired and V was killed by their bullet. A1 and A2 were convicted of the murder of V. The court stated re-reading ***Gnango*** in light of ***Jogee***. Firstly causation of death was made out. Secondly A1 and A2 were assisting or encouraging P. Thirdly, they had knowledge of the primary type of offence. Finally there was proof of A's intention to assist or encourage P's *actus reus* and *mens rea*. This could properly be inferred where two or more persons engage in, or assist or encourage, shooting at each other, each knowing that it was a virtual certainty that the other(s) would be armed and would either open or return fire, and each intended to kill or to cause really serious injury. There was no defence to say it was a member of my own gang killed and nor could there be any question of self-defence on the part of someone whose intention in such a situation was to shoot to kill (or to cause serious injury) and to be shot at in return.

The organised knife fight scenario

A recent case clarified the position if there was an organised or spontaneous knife fight between rival gangs. ***ARU; AOC; BHL* [2024]** distinguished itself from ***Gnango*** and ***Seed***.

The facts were three Ds were charged with Count 1 murder and Count 2 manslaughter (in the alternative). The case was prosecuted having reviewed ***Gnango* [2011], [2012]** namely on the basis of a "*common intention*" by the rival gangs.

The Court of Appeal ruled there was no case to answer on Count 1 murder on the basis.

1. Cases in which opposing sides engage in violence with a common purpose of the kind required to fix all participants with liability will be rare.
2. The circumstances are rare where there is an organised gun shootout where death is a virtual certainty (see above ***Gnango*** and ***Seed***).
3. The court indicated it would require very clear evidence of agreement to stab to apply the ***Gnango*** reasoning.
4. As ***Seed* [2024]**; emphasised:
    a. knowledge of the other parties possession of weapons and their intention to use them had to be virtual certainty;
    b. reciprocity must be demonstrated.
5. The sadly more common place stabbings where two rival groups fight (either in pre-planned or unplanned incident of violence) and fatal violence occurs should not proceed on the basis of "common intention" but the standard principles of participation liability.

15.7 Overwhelming Supervening Acts (OSA)

15.7.1 Overwhelming supervening acts

Jogee recognised there may be rare cases in which there is said to be an "*overwhelming supervening act*" ***Jogee*** para [97] states:

> "*It is possible for death to be caused by some overwhelming supervening act [OSA] by [P] which nobody in [A's] shoes could have contemplated might happen and is of such a character as to relegate his acts to history; in that case [A] will bear no criminal responsibility for the death.*"

There appears to be some similarity in this test to new intervening acts breaking the chain of causation. You will remember that the case law is restrictive in that area and only allows for exceptional unforeseeable actions to break the chain of causation.

Jogee para [98] also indicated a move away from the old term of "*fundamental departure/fundamentally different act*":

> "*If that crime is murder, then the question is whether he intended to assist the intentional infliction of grievous bodily harm at least, which question will often, as set out above, be answered by asking simply whether he himself intended grievous bodily harm at least.*
>
> "*Very often he may intend to assist in violence using whatever weapon may come to hand. In other cases, he may think that P has an iron bar whereas he turns out to have a knife, but the difference may not at all affect his intention to assist, if necessary, in the causing of grievous bodily harm at least.*
>
> "*…knowledge or ignorance that weapons generally, or a particular weapon, is carried by P will be evidence going to what the intention of A was and may be irresistible evidence one way or the other, but it is evidence and no more.*"

The focus appears to move to the evidential value of A knowing P was carrying a weapon as evidence of whether A intended to assist or encourage P's *actus reus* and *mens rea*.

15.7.2 Early OSA judgments

The subsequent caselaw is clear that an OSA will be exceptionally rare. The majority of the cases focus on A being unaware P had a weapon.

- ***Brown (Cleon Edwin)* [2017]** (at [29]–[30])

  The judge correctly focused on the joint participation and then A's intention.

- ***Ibrar* [2017]**

  P's use of a knife was not an OSA which A could not have contemplated and no direction on "*fundamental departure*" was required.

  The jury must focus on joint participation and intent.

- ***Tas* [2018]**

  The fact A was unaware P had a weapon does not mean A is not liable.

  The question appears to be: whether the OSA had so distanced A in time, place or circumstance as to be an OSA?

- ***Harper* [2019]**

  The presence or absence of the knife was not an OSA.

- ***Lanning and Camille* [2021]**

  What matters was A's intention to assist or encourage.

The leading authority is now ***Grant (Tony Lee)* [2021]**; which states at para [34] the question is:

> *"Whether [A's] conduct may have been 'so distanced in time, place or circumstances from the conduct of [P] that it would not be realistic to regard Ps offence as [having been] encouraged or assisted by it[?]"*

The court is clear, other than in exceptional circumstances, "*which are not readily easy to envisage, there will be no need to direct the jury on the concept of OSA simply because the fatal injuries were inflicted using an entirely different kind of weapon or method of killing than that originally contemplated*".

The case law for the OSA appears to indicate the actions of A would need to be "*spent of force*" and whilst knowledge of carrying the weapon may be evidence of intention it is no more than evidence. Similarly, lack of knowledge of the weapon appears to be evidence of lack of intention but no more than evidence.

15.8 Withdrawal and incapacity

A may be able to escape liability for assisting or encouraging an offence if he makes an effective withdrawal before the offence is actually committed.

15.8.1 Effective withdrawal from planned offending

In order to make an effective withdrawal it is submitted the following factors will be relevant considerations:

(a) How much assistance has already been provided?

(b) How proximate in time to the offence was the withdrawal?

(c) How clearly communicated was the withdrawal?

(a) How much assistance has already been provided?

The greater the assistance provided the more difficult it will be for D to state they have withdrawn. ***Bryce* [2004]** appears to note if assistance was provided a further act that amounted to a countermanding of the earlier assistance and a withdrawal from the common purpose; repentance alone would not suffice.

(b) How proximate in time to the offence was the withdrawal?

The greater the proximity to the offence the more difficult it is to evidence withdrawal

Sufficient notice:

- ***Grundy* [1977]** – Two weeks was sufficient to leave to the jury.
- ***Whitefield* (1984)** – Giving notice and playing no active role.

Insufficient notice:

- ***Becerra* (1975)** – A leaving the scene of the burglary with the words "Let's go" was not sufficient.

Roskill LJ at 219:

> *"... if [he] wanted to withdraw at that stage, he would have to 'countermand', to use the word that is used in some of the cases or 'repent' to use another word so used, in some manner vastly different and vastly more effective than merely to say 'Come on, let's go' and go out through the window."*

- ***Rook* (1993)**

e.g. A had agreed with Ps to murder the wife of one of the Ps. A did not turn up on the day.

V was murdered. A had assisted and encouraged the crime with intention.

D not given sufficient withdrawal

See also ***Baker* [1994]**.

(c) How clearly communicated was the withdrawal?

In ***Whitehouse* [1941]** Sloan JA noted the importance of timely communication:

> *".... where practicable and reasonable there must be timely communication of the intention to abandon the common purpose from those who wish to dissociate from the contemplated crime to those who desire to continue in it. What is 'timely communication' must be determined by the facts of each case."*

The quote was approved in ***Becerra and Cooper* (1975)** and ***Grundy* [1977] Crim** and applied in ***Whitefield* (1984)**.

The recent Irish case ***Twomey* [2024]** is a helpful summary of core principles.

The test for withdrawal being: is it reasonably possible that:

"(1) A demonstrated clearly, by words or actions, to P that they were withdrawing from the offending before the offence was committed.

If YES-A has withdrawn

If NO- consider (2) and (3) below namely taking proportionate steps to fully withdraw

(2) Did A take steps to undo the effect of their previous involvement or to prevent the crime?

(3) Did As steps for those purposes amount to everything that was reasonable and proportionate, having regard to the nature and extent of As previous involvement?

(4) Were As steps taken in a timely fashion, in the sense that A acted at a time when it was reasonably possible that they may be able either to undo the effect of their prior involvement or to prevent the crime?"

The case notes that the evidential burden is on A to adduce evidence and then it appears the legal burden reverts to the prosecution to prove beyond reasonable doubt no such withdrawal occurred.

15.8.2 Withdrawal from spontaneous violence?

It appears to be very difficult to withdraw from spontaneous violence. *e.g.* ***Mitchell* [1993]** which stated, where the violence is spontaneous, the issue is not withdrawal but whether P had gone beyond the scope of the joint venture. This was confirmed in ***O'Flaherty, Ryan and Toussaint* [2004]**. Where there is evidence of withdrawal, the evidence should be left to the jury to decide whether it amounts to an effective withdrawal in the particular circumstances. See also ***Mitchell* [2008]**; ***Campbell* [2009]**; ***Rajakumar* [2013]**.

15.8.3 P's incapacity does not impact as potential liabilty

A may be liable as an A even if P is legal incapable e.g.

- P incapable by age.

***Eldershaw* (1828)** (boy under 14 abetting rape).

Michael **(1840)**:

- P incapable by gender: ***Ram*** **(1893)** (woman abetting rape);
- P incapable by mental disorder/legal insanity: ***Tyler*** **(1838)**; or
- P incapable by lacking *mens rea*: ***Stringer*** **(1992)** (letter dictated by boss typed by secretary).

15.8.4 Victims: Protection by statute

A person for whose protection an act has been passed cannot be convicted as an accessory to a crime against themselves:

- ***Tyrrell*** **[1894]**: V female was under 16 could not be guilty under what is now **s26 Sexual Offences Act 2003**.
- ***Whitehouse*** **[1977]**: V female daughter under 16 could not assist and encourage incest by P (her father).

15.9 Freestanding liability

15.9.1 P has no *actus reus*: A cannot be convicted

Where P has no *actus reus* A cannot be convicted

e.g. ***Thornton v Mitchell*** **[1940]**

P Bus Driver relied on A when reversing.

A The bus Conductor was negligent whilst directing P. Two pedestrians injured one died.

Charged with driving without due care.

CA found:

P Not guilty as had driven with due care.

A Could not be an accessory as P was not driving without due care.

N.B. The *actus reus* of gross negligence manslaughter could have been made out with A as the principal.

15.9.2 P is not identified: A can be convicted

Where P cannot be identified A can nevertheless be convicted

e.g. ***Grogan* [2021]**

P not identified as the person stabbing V.

Numerous possible Ps including A.

A could not be proved to be the stabber.

Prosecution could prove the crime based on A being an accessory.

15.9.3 P is acquitted: A can be convicted

Where P is acquitted A can nevertheless be convicted in the following situations:

1. Admissibility of evidence against A not against P: see ***Humphreys and Turner* [1965]**.
2. P insufficient evidence. A sufficient: ***Davis* [1977]**. See also ***Burton* (1875)**.
3. P acquitted at an earlier trial, no bar to A's subsequent conviction: ***Hui Chi-Ming* [1992]**. The same applies if P is acquitted in the same trial: ***Hughes* (1860)**.

15.9.4 P has no *mens rea* or a total defence: A can be convicted

Where P has no *mens rea* or a total defence A can nevertheless be convicted.

In ***Bourne* (1952)** A (the appellant) was convicted of aiding and abetting his wife to commit buggery with a dog in circumstances where the wife, if charged, would have been entitled to an acquittal on the basis of duress.

> *"There is no doubt that [A] was properly indicted for being a principal in the second degree to the commission of the crime of buggery. That is all that it is necessary to show. The evidence was, and the jury by their verdict have shown they accepted it, that [A] caused his wife [P] to have connection with a dog, and if he caused his wife to have connection with a dog, he is guilty, whether you call him an aider and abettor or an accessory, as a principal in the second degree. For that reason, this appeal fails and is dismissed."*

Similar applies in ***Cogan and Leak* [1976]**. Other examples include: ***Millward* [1994]**; ***Pickford* [1995]**; ***DPP v K and B* [1997]**; ***Watkins* [2010]**.

15.9.5 P has lesser *mens rea* than A: A can be convicted of the greater offence

Where P has a lesser *mens rea* than A, A can still be convicted of the greater offence.

e.g.		No death	Death
P	did not have intention to do GBH	Guilty **s20**	Guilty manslaughter
A	did have intention to do GBH	Guilty **s18**	Guilty murder

In ***Howe* [1987]** it was held that where a person has been killed and that result is the result intended by another participant, the mere fact that the actual killer may be convicted only of the reduced charge of manslaughter for some reason special to himself, does not result in a compulsory reduction for the other participant (***Richards* [1974]** overruled).

See also ***Dang* [2014]**.

15.9.6 A has lesser *mens rea* than P: A can be convicted of the lesser offence

Where A has lesser *mens rea* than P, A can be convicted of the lesser offence.

***Gilmour* [2000]**, Sir Robert Carswell CJ (at 414) gave the useful example:

> *"Suppose [P] and [A] agree that [P] will post a specific incendiary device to V, [A] contemplating only superficial injuries to V when he opens it but [P] foreseeing and hoping that the injuries will be serious or fatal.*
>
> *If V is killed as a result,*
>
> *[P] will clearly be guilty of murder,*
>
> *[A] is clearly not guilty of murder as an accessory* ***but***
>
> *should be guilty of manslaughter because the act done by [P] is precisely what was envisaged.*
>
> *The fact that [P] happens also to have the mens rea of murder is irrelevant because it does not change the nature of the act that he does or the manner in which he does it."*

***Jogee* [2016], [2017]**

Note if A does not have intention to kill or do GBH but does have intention to commit ABH, A could be guilty of constructive act manslaughter:

"[96] If a person is a party to a violent attack on another, ***without*** *an intent to assist in the causing of death or really serious harm, but the violence escalates and results in death, he will be not guilty of murder but guilty of manslaughter.*

"So if A participates by encouragement or assistance in any other unlawful act which all sober and reasonable people would realise carried the risk of some harm (not necessarily serious) to another, and death in fact results ... [that too will be manslaughter]."

15.10 Evaluation and reform

15.10.1 Legal certainty and legal clarity

Legal certainty provides the law must be sufficiently available, certain and enable the individual to know the legal boundaries of their actions and potential consequences of breach[9]. Legal clarity provides that the law must be accessible, clear, intelligible, and predictable[10]. In a participation liability case the jury is the tribunal of fact governed by the directions on the law given by the judge. The research shows juries need clear and cogent guidance[11]. It is axiomatic, clear law is needed to give clear guidance. Therefore lets review each of the elements.

1. AR: Proof of a base actus reus of the primary offence

No change: this appears principled, certain and clear.

2. AR: Proof of as completed mode of participation

The new terminology of assisting and encouraging is very helpful for certainty and clarity. The terms are modern and clearer. Unfortunately however, the statute exists and the exact roles of the terms aid, abet, counsel and procure have not been removed.

3. MR: Proof of as knowledge of the primary type of criminal offence(s)

There is no change and this remains a relatively certain and clear provision.

---

9 Richard Buxton, "The Human Rights Act and the substantive criminal law" (2000) Criminal Law Review 331, 332

10 Rimmington; Goldstein [2005]; [2006]

11 Alan Travis, "The verdict on juries: fair, effective and efficient" *The Guardian* (London, 17 February 2010) <https://www.theguardian.com/uk/2010/feb/17/juries-fairness-research> accessed 06 April 2025, Cheryl Thomas, "Are juries fair?" (Ministry of Justice Research Series 1/10, February 2010) <https://www.ucl.ac.uk/judicial-institute/sites/judicial-institute/files/are_juries_fair.pdf> accessed 06 April 2025, Cheryl Thomas, "Ethnicity and the fairness of jury trials in England and Wales 2006-2014" [2017] Crim Law Review 860

4. MR: Proof of as intention to assist or encourage P's actus reus and mens rea

This is the significant change. This law in ***Jogee*** appears to positively ensure A's *mens rea* (intention to assist or encourage) is of comparable equivalence to P's (intention to kill or do GBH).

The requirement of intention to assist or encourage P's *actus reus* and P's *mens rea* appears difficult to prove.

5. Overwhelming supervening acts (OSA)

This narrows down what was the old fundamentally different act argument regarding weapons to the new overwhelming supervening acts as rare exceptional breaks. It seems logical but the case law is evolving and the practitioner community appears to be pushing against the logic of ***Jogee***'s focus on *actus reus* and *mens rea*. The Judiciary are robustly pushing back to ensure the focus is on elements 1–4 above.

6. Withdrawal

There is no significant change. The doctrine appears certain and clear and broadly consistent with the approach to the justification defence of duress.

7. Lack of theoretical underpinnings

A final important critique is that lack of theoretical underpinnings may undermine the efficacy of the case. There are a number of theories one could use to justify censure and sanction for joint crimes where the principal (P) and accessory (A) should be held liable. Firstly, Causative Theory (AKA Derivative theory). This theory appears consistent with post-2016 ***Jogee***. The theory is A has in part "caused" the crime, as liability is derivative from the P's actions. This gives rise to restrictive liability and focuses on the individual's actions and the individual's intent.

Secondly, Harm Theory which is consistent with pre-2016 cases. This notes assisting a crime is harmful to society and regardless of the causative link. This would give rise to extensive liability and may have some deterrent effects.

15.10.2 Equality before the law: protected characteristics and socio-economic barriers

Equality provides that equality before the law (including disability, gender, gender identity, race, sexual orientation, and socio economic) is relevant and impacts on the unequal power relationships in society and has a significant impact on the system.

There are strong arguments that participation is an are of the law which does have an adverse impact on equality. Why?

1. There is a disproportionate impact on BME communities.[12]
2. A disproportionate number of those serving sentences for joint enterprise charges were BME, and Muslim[13].
3. There are over 11 times as many black/black-British prisoners in the sample who are serving time under joint enterprise compared to the proportion of black/black-British people in the general population.[14]
4. The media expressed repeated and significant concerns about so called "Joint Enterprise" liability.[15,16,17]
5. A recent *Crown Prosecution Service Joint Enterprise Pilot 2023: Data Analysis* published in September 2023[18] reviews the statistics. It notes the dominance of men, gang related (although not universally); London centred; frequently with two defendants charges; the majority under the age of 24; male; low levels of disability. The notable disproportionate nature of an in population % of 4.04 of black persons but in the CPS caseload 30.15%. In the media there are numerous reports of concerns[19].

---

12 William Wilson and David Ormerod, "Simply Harsh to Fairly Simple: Joint Enterprise Reform" [2015] Crim LR 3

13 William Wilson and David Ormerod, "Simply Harsh to Fairly Simple: Joint Enterprise Reform" [2015] Crim LR 3

14 Ben Crewe et al, "Joint Enterprise: The Implications of an Unfair and Unclear Law" [2015] Criminal Law Review 252

15 Simon Hattenstone, "Most people prosecuted under joint enterprise from minority ethni background" *The Guardian* (London, 30 September 2023) <https://www.theguardian.com/law/2023/sep/30/most-people-prosecuted-under-joint-enterprise-from-minority-ethnic-background> accessed 06 April 2025

16 Simon Hattenstone, "Join enterprise prosecutions to be monitored for racial bias" *The Guardian* (London, 16 Febuary 2023) <https://www.theguardian.com/law/2023/feb/16/joint-enterprise-prosecutions-to-be-monitored-for-racial-bias> accessed 06 April 2025

17 Zoe Williams, "The UK should be ashamed of 'joint enterprise' convictions. America has put us on notice" *The Guardian* (London, 15 November 2022) <https://www.theguardian.com/commentisfree/2022/nov/15/uk-joint-enterprise-convictions-injustice-supreme-court-racially-biased> accessed 06 April 2025

18 Crown Prosecution Service, "Join Enterprise Pilot 2023: Data Analysis" (CPS, 29 September2023) <https://www.cps.gov.uk/publication/crown-prosecution-service-joint-enterprise-pilot-2023-data-analysis> accessed 06 April 2025

19 Simon Hattenstone, "Most people prosecuted under joint enterprise from minority ethni background" *The Guardian* (London, 30 September 2023) <https://www.theguardian.com/law/2023/sep/30/most-people-prosecuted-under-joint-enterprise-from-minority-ethnic-background> accessed 06 April 2025

6. Post ***Jogee*** *there remains significant issues about equality before the law. It is obvious but there remains a question of how much of a role the substantive law can have in preventing criminal behaviour. It may be that the battleground is now wrongly focused on the "net" of the substantive law and should be re-focused on the social welfare opportunities including support for young persons' education, health and association (e.g. youth groups) rather more than on law reform?*

15.10.3 Fair warning; fair labelling and sufficient breadth principles

Fair warning

The law should give fair warning to the community of the consequences. There is a strong argument many of the young people caught up in so called "gang crime" or "organised crime groups" have little insight in relation to the likely consequences. The Crown Prosecution Service have responded with guidance on charging which is helpful to lawyers but perhaps not to the general public.[20] Public awareness regarding weapons amnesties appears on the increase, but an education campaign may assist to support young people to avoid gangs/organised crime groups through constructive activity.

Fair labelling

Fair labelling involves labelling criminal offences at a macro scale to indicate categorisation, indicative punishment scales and specialist ancillary orders[21]. Fair labelling involved labelling at a micro scale – it helps with categorising the wrongdoing with a public label which has a communicative value to wider society[22].

How good at fair labelling is the new law? This is an area where the ***Jogee*** impact can be argued to be significant. There is much notice that juries are more frequently directed to consider where the primary offence is murder, the secondary participant may be only aware of the prospect of assault and thus liable for manslaughter. Thus fair labelling at a micro scale, i.e. labelling the offender's conduct appears to be fairer.

---

20 Crown Prosecution Service, "Secondary Liability: charging decisions on principals and accessories" (CPS, 4 July 2024) <https://www.cps.gov.uk/legal-guidance/secondary-liability-charging-decisions-principals-and-accessories>accessed 06 April 2025

21 James Chalmers and Fiona Leverick, "Fair Labelling in Criminal Law" (2008) 71 Modern Law Review 217, 221-222

22 James Chalmers and Fiona Leverick, "Fair Labelling in Criminal Law" (2008) 71 Modern Law Review 217, 221-222

Sufficient breadth

There appears to be sufficient breadth to capture offending, but whether it remains too broad is open to question. Notably the organisation "Joint Enterprise Not Guilty by Association" has pointed out the ***Jogee*** decision has not made a difference to the many unsuccessful appeals for 1985–2016 cases and there are strong criticisms of the law still to be made.[23] Powerful criticism of the law persists in the media.[24]

15.10.4 Human rights: autonomy and welfare principles

The position for purposes of **Art 7 ECHR** legal certainty seems to have improved (see above **Legal Certainty**). The position in terms of equality (**Art 14 ECHR**) does not seem to have changed (see above **Equality**). Autonomy is respected by increasing the mental element of the accessory. Societal welfare through deterrent law could be argued to be diminished by a change of the theoretical underpinnings. There is an argument the old law (pre ***Jogee***) did offer more by way of deterrence but it is submitted that argument is weak given the limited impact deterrence has on criminal behaviour.

15.10.5 International comparators and reform: practicality principle and politics

Comparators

Miller* [2016]** has not followed ***Jogee. Their approach is consistent with the 1985–2016 approach, i.e. A is liable if A foresaw P might intentionally kill or do GBH. The principles are settled and they state they would only change position if Parliament changed. Similarly ***Cham Kam Shing* [2016]** has not followed ***Jogee***. It maintains the distinction between joint enterprise and other forms of secondary liability

Also New Zealand's **s66(2) Crimes Act 1961** was upheld by the Supreme Court of New Zealand in ***Burke v The King* [2024]** where the law was consistent with the case law preceding **Jogee**.

Law Commission

There are significant advantages to the Law Commission review. It would focus on legal certainty; clarity; equality; labelling; human rights; and comparators. It would

23 See, jointenterprise.co/JengbaLinks.html accessed on 09 April 2025

24 Janet Cunliffe, "My blind son was jailed for being at the scene of a murder. Hald this tide of joint enterprise convictions" *The Guardian* (London, 11 August 2022) <https://www.theguardian.com/commentisfree/2022/aug/11/boys-lives-ruined-joint-enterprise-law> accessed 06 April 2025

be free from the constraints of fact-based litigation. It could review the whole law and engage in full consultation.

Law Commission, Participating in Crime (Law Com No 305, 2007)[25]

Clause 1 of the Bill

"1.48 Under clause 1 of the Bill, [A] would be liable for a principal offence committed by [P] if [A]

- *assisted or encouraged [P] to perpetrate the conduct element of the principal offence and*
- *intended that the conduct element should be perpetrated.*

This would have the effect of narrowing the scope of secondary liability in cases where [A] and [P] are not parties to a joint criminal venture.

1.49 For the purposes of clause 1, [A] 'intends' only if he or she acts in order that the conduct element of the principal offence is perpetrated. In our use and understanding of the word 'intention', we adopt the common law meaning. This means that if [A] foresaw as a virtual certainty [P] engaging in the conduct element of the offence, that would be evidence from which the jury or magistrates could (but would not have to) find that [A] intended the perpetration of the conduct element."[26]

Clause 2 of the Bill

" 1.50 Clause 2 would govern [As] liability where [A] and [P] have formed a joint criminal venture. This will cover both agreed offences and collateral offences committed by [P] in the course of the joint criminal venture.

1.51 In relation to clause 2, [A] would be liable for any offence committed by [P] provided that its commission fell within the scope of the joint venture. A joint criminal venture is formed when the parties agree to commit an offence or when they share with each other a common intention to commit an offence. [A] would be liable for any offence (agreed or collateral) that he or she foresaw might be committed as a possible result of the venture. The mere fact that [A] was not present when the offence was committed or that he or she would rather that it was not committed would not in itself preclude a jury finding that the offence fell within the scope of the joint venture."

---

25 Law Commission, *Participating in Crime* (Law Com No 305, 2007) <https://cloud-platform-e218f50a4812967ba1215eaecede923f.s3.amazonaws.com/uploads/sites/30/2015/03/lc305_Participating_in_Crime_report.pdf> accessed 06 April 2025

26 Law Commission, *Participating in Crime* (Law Com No 305, 2007) <https://cloud-platform-e218f50a4812967ba1215eaecede923f.s3.amazonaws.com/uploads/sites/30/2015/03/lc305_Participating_in_Crime_report.pdf> accessed 06 April 2025 (bullet points added)

Private Members Significant Contribution Bill

Joint Enterprise (Significant Contribution) Bill 2023[27] was proposed by some MPs. It was designed as a Bill to amend **s8 Accessories and Abettors Act 1861**, to provide that only a person who directly commits, or who makes a significant contribution to the commission of an offence may be held criminally liable. The 2019–2024 Parliament dissolved before it had a chance for fuller debate.

Practicality, cost, and expense

1) Practicality: the Law must be sufficiently practical and enforceable to achieve its goals. The law remains complex.
2) Avoid undue cost and expense: the law remains costly and expensive in terms of appeals. Although notably the volume of fresh post-2016 appeals appears less. However problems exist that in terms of trials there are fewer pleas; longer trials; and judicial directions were complex and technical which can lead to more appeals[28]. It was noted 17% of all homicide trials involve joint enterprise and between 2005–2013, 1853 prosecutions for murder included four or more defendants (up to 20% of homicide trials per annum). Between 2005–2013, 4590 homicide trials with two or more defendants (up to 44% of all homicide trials per annum).[29]
3) Notably the findings of one report indicate ***Jogee*** has led to more charges[30].
4) There may also be some links to social media disputes between groups.

---

27 Joint Enterprise (Significant Contribution) Bill HC Bill (2023-2024) 27 <https://bills.parliament.uk/bills/3550> acceded 06 April 2025

28 Maeve McClenaghan et al, "Joint Enterprise: An investigation into the legal doctrine of jjoint enterprise in criminal convictions" (Bureau of Investigative Journalism 2014) <http://embed.documentcloud.org/documents/1100186-joint-enterprise-investigation/?embed=1> accessed 06 April 2025; discussed in William Wilson and David Ormerod, "Simply Harsh to Fairly Simple: Joint Enterprise Reform" [2015] Crim LR 3

29 Maeve McClenaghan et al, "Joint Enterprise: An investigation into the legal doctrine of jjoint enterprise in criminal convictions" (Bureau of Investigative Journalism 2014) <http://embed.documentcloud.org/documents/1100186-joint-enterprise-investigation/?embed=1> accessed 06 April 2025; discussed in William Wilson and David Ormerod, "Simply Harsh to Fairly Simple: Joint Enterprise Reform" [2015] Crim LR 3

30 Haroon Siddique, "Joint enterprise ruling has not led to fewer homicide charges, report finds" *The Guardian* (London 27 April 2022) <https://www.theguardian.com/law/2022/apr/27/joint-enterprise-ruling-has-not-led-to-fewer-homicide-charges-report-finds> accessed 06 April 2025

In the News

Jogee and gangs

Please read these three articles

1. Owen Bowcott, "Ameen Jogee jailed for manslaughter in joint enterprise test case" *The Guardian* (London, 12 September 2016) <https://www.theguardian.com/law/2016/sep/12/ameen-jogee-jailed-manslaughter-police-officer-joint-enterprise-test-case> accessed 06 April 2025
2. Janet Cunliffe, "My blind son was jailed for being at the scene of a murder. Hald this tide of joint enterprise convictions" *The Guardian* (London, 11 August 2022) <https://www.theguardian.com/commentisfree/2022/aug/11/boys-lives-ruined-joint-enterprise-law> accessed 06 April 2025
3. Haroon Siddique, "Labour urged to reform joint enterprise law to stop 'systemic injustice'" *The Guardian* (London, 28 July 2024) <https://www.theguardian.com/law/article/2024/jul/28/labour-urged-to-reform-joint-enterprise-law-to-stop-systemic-injustice> accessed 06 April 2025

Firstly, it is obvious that on a harm level there is a human tragedy for those who are deceased and those impacted by their death. There is also a significant societal harm and cost when young men are then incarcerated for life.

Secondly, it is obvious that attributing fault to participants as we have noted before is problematic. A jury is not omnipotent and cannot and does not know all the facts or easily establish "Who did what?"; "What did they intend?". Each trial by its nature is an imperfect exercise in history.

Thirdly, the age of the defendants is often young and it may be difficult for them to articulate their defence personally or due to peer pressure.

Do you think ***Jogee*** should have been guilty of murder or manslaughter?

How do we as a society ensure a proper balance between liability for active participants and lesser or no liability for those less involved or not involved?

Would the **Joint Enterprise (Significant Contribution) Bill 2024** reform proposals that A must have made a significant contribution have improved the law and given juries greater clarity?

15.11 Summary

In this chapter:

- **Procedure**: Regarding principals (P) and accessories (A), we focused on the process of charging; the distinction between principals (P) and accessories (A).
- **AR: Proof of a base actus reus of the primary offence**: The starting point for liability is a completed *actus reus* of the primary offence.
- **AR: Proof of as completed mode of participation**: We reviewed the modes of participation including the traditional modes: aid, abet, counsel or procure and post ***Jogee*** the arguably much more helpful terminology "encouraging or assisting the commission of an offence". We noted mere presence is insufficient and participation in some mode is required.
- **MR: Proof of as knowledge of the primary type of criminal offence(s)**: We noted the proof of knowledge of the primary type of criminal offence(s) was required. However knowledge by A of the precise offence of P is not required. This is the so called "blank cheque" approach and the logic of liability on that basis.
- **MR: Proof of as intention to assist or encourage P's actus reus and mens rea**: The proof of A's intention to assist or encourage the commission of the crime.
- **Overwhelming Supervening Acts (OSA)**: We looked at the rarity of the OSA. The OSA appears to be something nobody in As position could have contemplated. Post ***Jogee*** the weapons used is now of less significance. The significance attaches to the AR and MR elements noted above, particularly intention to assist or encourage.
- **Withdrawal**: The clear public policy reasons for the difficulties of **withdrawing** from an enterprise of planned offending including:
  - a) How much assistance has already been provided?
  - b) How proximate in time to the offence was the withdrawal?
  - c) How clearly communicated was the withdrawal? We also noted the near impossibility of withdrawal from spontaneous violence.
- **Innocent agents and victims**: Innocent agents and victims are protected.
- **Freestanding liability**: Who can be liable where the parties' positions differ?
  1. P has no *actus reus*: A cannot be convicted.
  2. P is not identified: A can be convicted.
  3. P is acquitted: A can be convicted.
  4. P has no *mens rea* or a total defence: A can be convicted.

5. P has lesser *mens rea* than A: A can be convicted of the greater offence.
6. A has lesser *mens rea* than P: A can be convicted of the lesser offence.

- **Evaluation framework**: We utilised the evaluation framework to review particular problems with certainty, clarity, equality and the potential need for statutory reform.

Further reading

Dennis Baker, "Prosecuting Complicity: The CPS Legal Guidance on Secondary Liability" (2018) *82(4) Journal of Criminal Law 338.*

Matthew Dyson, "Principals without Distinction" [2018] *Crim LR 296.*

David Ormerod, and Karl Laird, "Jogee: Not the End of a Legal Saga But the Start of One?" [2016] *Crim LR 539.*

William Wilson and David Ormerod, "Simply Harsh to Fairly Simple: Joint Enterprise Reform" [2015] *Crim LR 3.*

CHAPTER 16

Inchoate liability

16.1 Introduction

Inchoate means not fully formed, partial, or incomplete. In criminal law, inchoate offences are offences where the offender has set out on the path to committing an offence but has not yet completed the offence in full. This includes forms of liability you may have heard of, such as attempt, as well as more complex forms of liability such as assisting or encouraging the commission of an offence.

This chapter begins by discussing liability for attempting an offence under **s1(1) Criminal Attempts Act 1981** (**CAA 1981**) where a defendant takes steps towards the commission of an indictable offence. Throughout this chapter, you will see that inchoate offences such as attempt cannot be viewed in isolation. In order to fully apply the law on attempt, it is important that you have a good knowledge of the offence(s) which are being attempted, so that you can determine where attempt becomes the commission of the "full" offence. The chapter then considers conspiracy, primarily an offence under **s1 Criminal Law Act 1977** (**CLA 1977**).

In **Chapter 15**, we saw how defendants may sometimes be liable for participation in crimes, even where they are not the principal offender. Under **ss44–46 Serious Crimes Act 2007** (**SCA 2007**) a defendant can be liable for encouraging or assisting an offence, without it being necessary for the principal to have gone on to commit the offence. Towards the end of this chapter, we will consider the significance of **SCA 2007** and potential future reforms to the law on inchoate liability.

Aims of this chapter

By the end of this chapter, you will:

- Be able to explain the distinction between different forms of inchoate liability and be able to identify which are applicable in a range of practical scenarios.
- Understand how to apply the law on attempt, conspiracy and other forms of inchoate liability in a problem scenario, with reference to relevant case law.
- Be able to critically evaluate key aspects of the law on inchoate liability and identify the significance of proposed reforms to the law.

16.2 Attempts

As we have seen in other chapters, a defendant is only liable for an offence where they satisfy all of the *actus reus* and *mens rea* requirements for the offence. This means that where a defendant has undertaken some, but not all, of the requirements of an offence, they will not be liable under that offence. Attempt addresses this situation and enables those who have tried to commit criminal offences but not yet completed the actual offence, to be punished. The offence is set out in **s1(1) CAA 1981** which states that:

> *If, with intent to commit an offence to which this section applies, a person does an act which is **more than merely preparatory** to the commission of the offence, he is guilty of attempting to commit the offence.*

Generally, it is only an offence to attempt an offence which is triable on indictment. Summary offences, as well as the offences of conspiracy, attempting to aid and abet, etc. and attempting to assist after an offence are typically incapable of forming a **s1 CAA 1981** attempt offence (**s1(4) CAA 1981**).

However, other legislation can create offences of attempting to commit a summary offence, which are governed by the same principles as the attempts discussed here (**s3 CAA 1981**). An example of this can be seen with the offence created by **s136 Licencing Act 2003** which criminalises carrying out *or attempting to carry out* a licensable activity.[1] Conversely, some offences are committed as soon as they

1 See, generally, Colin Manchester, "Unauthorised provision of alcohol and entertainment" [2005] Criminal Law Review 548, 549

are attempted and are therefore incapable of constituting an inchoate offence. An example of this with the offence of intending to pervert the course of justice (***Williams (Kevin John)* (1991)**).

Inchoate liability is more complex where a defendant intends to commit acts beyond England and Wales. Generally, a defendant can only be liable for an attempt where the attempted offence is a crime in English law (**s1(4) CAA 1981**). However, **s1A CAA 1981** also creates liability where a person attempts to commit theft, fraud and several other dishonesty related offences in other jurisdictions, even where succeeding would only be an offence in the other jurisdiction and not England and Wales.

16.2.1 An act that is more than preparatory

Firstly, the *actus reus* of the offence requires the commission of an act by the defendant. As committing a criminal act would amount to an offence, not an attempt, it is clear that there is no requirement that the act by the defendant be illegal. Nor need the act be inherently immoral: any act will do. However, an omission will not suffice – the defendant must positively act.

Secondly, the act must be "more than merely preparatory" for the commission of the offence. In an often cited passage from ***Gullefer* (1990)** the Court of Appeal explained that:

> *"It seems to us that the words of the Act of 1981 seek to steer a midway course. They do not provide, as they might have done, that [...] the defendant must have reached a point from which it was impossible for him to retreat before the actus reus of an attempt is proved. On the other hand the words give perhaps as clear a guidance as is possible in the circumstances on the point of time at which [...] [a] "series of acts" begin. It begins when the merely preparatory acts come to an end and the defendant embarks upon the crime proper. When that is will depend of course upon the facts in any particular case."*

In ***MS* [2021]** the Court of Appeal returned to this passage when addressing a case of attempted child abduction. The defendant, the child's mother, was arrested attempting to take the child out of the country in defiance of a court order. Although the defendant was not yet at the point of taking the child out of the country, having been arrested some distance from the port they intended to depart from, the court held that, on the facts of the case, the defendant had embarked upon the offence.

s4(3) CAA 1981 explains that where the judge determines there is sufficient evidence to demonstrate the defendant has gone beyond mere preparation, it is then a question for the tribunal of fact to determine whether the defendant did attempt the offence. Given the multitude of ways a defendant might go about attempting an offence, whether they have embarked upon the offence itself is often answered through reference to "*common sense*" (***DPP v Moore* [2010]**). However, some examples of this distinction in practice can be seen in cases such as:

- ***MH* [2004]** where the defendant was guilty of attempting to rape his former wife after attacking her and removing her clothes whilst making statements to the effect that he wanted to have sex with her, without the prosecution needing to prove that the defendant attempted penetration.
- ***Jones* (1990)** where the defendant got into the complainant's car and pointed a loaded shotgun at him. The defendant was guilty, despite there being several further steps (including pulling the trigger) before he would have committed the intended offence.

Where it has been held that the defendant has gone beyond mere preparation, which can be compared with cases such as:

- ***Geddes* [1996]** where the defendant was found trespassing in a school lavatory with a knife, rope and masking tape. The defendant had not gone beyond mere preparation and was not guilty of attempted false imprisonment.
- ***Campbell* (1991)** where the defendant was arrested with an imitation gun and a threatening note outside of a post office. The defendant was not guilty as the acts leading up to entering the post office and making the threat were likely only mere preparation ahead of the beginning of the offence.

Activity

Suppose that you are a Crown Prosecutor. You have been asked to look at the following cases and determine whether there is sufficient evidence of a defendant going beyond mere preparation to justify charging them with attempt. What charges would you decide have sufficient evidence and are within the public interest to bring?

- A defendant was arrested with a cricket bat whilst driving to the house of their former employer, who had recently dismissed them.
- A defendant was found with a fake cheque for £15,000 and a completed deposit form in the lobby of their bank.
- A defendant was arrested with a handgun waiting outside the property of a well-known politician.
- A defendant was captured by the police after breaking the window of a jewellery store. Due to the arrival of the police, the defendant ran away before entering the store or reaching inside the window.

16.2.2 Intent to commit the substantive offence

The *mens rea* of attempt is an intention to commit the substantive offence itself. Where a substantive offence may be committed intentionally or recklessly, the defendant must demonstrate an intent in order for an attempt to occur. For example, with the offence of criminal damage contrary to **s1 Criminal Damage Act 1971** – which may be committed intentionally or recklessly – a defendant would need to intend to destroy or damage property to be liable for attempted criminal damage. Similarly, foresight alone will not categorically demonstrate that something was the defendant's intent (***Pearman* [1984]**).

As we discussed in **Chapter 4**, establishing intent is a significant burden on the prosecution. In some instances, the requirement to prove intent in order to establish an attempt offence will be a higher standard to reach than the substantive offence. For example, some offences under the **Proceeds of Crime Act 2002** can be committed where a defendant has knowledge or suspicion that property is the proceeds of crime, however, to attempt such an offence would require more than suspicion (***Pace and Rogers* [2014]**). Similarly, attempted murder requires proof of intention to kill, whilst murder can be committed either with an intention to kill or an intention to cause grievous bodily harm.

Further reading

The approach taken in ***Pace and Rogers* [2014]** is arguably necessary to prevent defendants from committing attempt offences without in any way intending the offence. However, it poses a challenge to the approach taken in ***Khan* (1990)** which held that the defendant may be attempting an offence when they are merely reckless to surrounding circumstances, provided that they intend the offence generally. For further discussion of the conflict between these two judgments, see:

J J Child and Adrian Hunt, "Pace and Rogers and the Mens Rea of Criminal Attempt: Khan on the Scrapheap?" (2014) *78 Journal of Criminal Law 220*

16.2.3 Impossible attempts

Where a defendant attempts to commit an offence which is physically impossible – for example, attempting to speed in a vehicle with a top speed below the speed limit – there is nothing to prevent the defendant being liable for an attempt. **s1(2) CAA 1981** states that:

> *A person may be guilty of attempting to commit an offence to which this section applies even though the facts are such that the commission of the offence is impossible.*

In ***Shivpuri* [1987]** the defendant was arrested whilst in possession of a suitcase which contained what the defendant thought to be heroin, which he was attempting to bring into the country. In fact, the suitcase contained an unprohibited vegetable material. Despite the offence of harbouring a controlled substance being impossible, the House of Lords held that the defendant's mistake as to the fact of what he was carrying did not prevent him being liable for attempting to harbour a controlled drug.

16.3 Conspiracy

In many situations, a defendant may intend to commit an offence jointly with others, who either assist or encourage the commission of the offence or who intend to be involved directly in the commission of the offence as well. In the latter case, all of the defendants may be liable for conspiracy. The main form of conspiracy to be aware of is statutory conspiracy contrary to **s1 CLA 1977** which applies in situations where there is:

- *An agreement between two or more people*
- *To a course of conduct by one or more of them*
- *Which necessarily amounts to a criminal offence*
- *With the parties intending to reach the agreement*
- *Intending the agreement to be carried out and the offence to be committed.*

16.3.1 Agreement between two or more people

The Law Commission's report on *Conspiracy and Attempts* describes "the essence of a conspiracy [being] a meeting of two or more minds".[2] Agreement may be demonstrated informally by words or by actions and the courts have repeatedly resisted requiring anything akin to a contractual agreement to have taken place (***Austin* [2015]**). However, it is necessary for the defendant and at least one other to have gone beyond negotiating with one another or considering their position; the parties must have reached a decision and agreed to commit the offence.

In ***Scott* (1979)** the defendant was charged with conspiracy to supply controlled drugs. The defendant agreed to deposit cheques that she received from two men. At a later stage, the defendant realised that these cheques were to be the proceeds of drug dealing and decided to deposit these should she receive them. The defendant successfully appealed her conviction for conspiracy to supply controlled drugs,

2 Law Commission, *Conspiracy and Attempts* (Law Com No 318, HC 41 2009) Para 7.11

on the basis that at no stage had she communicated her intent to deposit the cheques and so there was no meeting of minds between her and the other parties.

Under **s2(2) CLA 1977** a conspiracy does not arise where the only people with whom the defendant agrees are:

- *Their spouse or civil partner* (**s2(2)(a)**)
- *People below the age of criminal responsibility* (**s2(2)(b)**)
- *The intended victims* (**s2(2)(c)**).

However, these do not apply in cases where there are three or more conspirators and the defendant and at least one other does not fall under one of the exceptions. For example, where a defendant is charged with conspiracy involving her husband and others, the exception would not apply (***Chrastny* (1992)**).

The wording of **s2 CLA 1977** is specific. Although society has seen shifts in attitudes towards and rights for unmarried couples in recent decades, unmarried couples are not able to argue that they are in a relationship akin to marriage for the purposes of **s2(2)(a)** (***Suski* [2016]**). Similarly, the person to which drugs are supplied does not fall within the definition of victim, it is therefore possible for a defendant to be charged with conspiracy in relation to the supply of drugs to himself (as in ***Drew* [2000]**).

Terminology Alert!

"Closed", "Chain" and "Wheel" conspiracies

The most basic form of conspiracy involves an agreement between only two defendants, sometimes called a "closed" conspiracy (e.g. ***Horne* [2020]**).

In cases involving more than two defendants, it may be that the defendants are a collective, with each reaching an agreement with the entire group. However, there are more complex conspiracies where conspirators do not always have direct connections with everyone involved in the conspiracy.

> *"What are referred to as 'chain' conspiracies and 'wheel' conspiracies are different in structure. In a chain conspiracy, A agrees with B, B with C and C with D. In a wheel conspiracy: A at the hub recruits B, C & D. In each it is necessary that the defendants must be shown to be a party to the common design and aware that they are part of a common design to which they are attaching themselves."* (**Johnson and Others [2020]** at [27]).

16.3.2 To a course of conduct by one or more of the conspirators

Those involved in a conspiracy must agree that one or more of them will carry out a course of conduct. This course of conduct may be specific, with agreement that an act will be carried out in a particular way against identifiable victims, or it may be more general, involving agreement to carry out actions without a targeted victim (e.g. ***Ali (Abdulla Ahmed)*** **[2011]**).

The wording of **s1 CLA 1977** requires the act to be carried out by one of the parties to the conspiracy. An agreement that entails a third party carrying out an offence will not amount to a conspiracy, even if there is an agreement to encourage the offence. In ***Kenning and Others*** **[2008]**, the defendants were charged with conspiracy to aid and abet the production of cannabis by selling equipment which could be used in cannabis production. Their conviction was overturned by the Court of Appeal in part because the agreed course of conduct did not involve any of the conspirators growing cannabis themselves.

The agreement may be that the course of conduct will only be carried out if certain circumstances arise and still amount to an offence (***Reed*** **[1982]**). Similarly, an agreement to a course of conduct which may result in one offence or another, dependent upon circumstances and the way the agreement is put into effect, will still constitute a conspiracy (***AG Reference No 4 of 2003*** **[2004]**).

16.3.3 That will amount to a criminal offence

It is not necessary for the conspirators to be aware that their agreed course of conduct constitutes a criminal offence. However, it is necessary that the agreement, if carried out, would inevitably amount to at least one criminal offence. An agreed course of conduct which laid the groundwork for offences by third parties, without any substantive offences being committed, would not amount to a conspiracy (***Kenning and Others*** **[2008]**).

Under **s1(1)(b) CLA 1977** where the agreed course of conduct is impossible –defendants who agree to murder a man they do not know is already dead, for example – the fact that the agreement cannot be carried out does not prevent a conspiracy. Where a course of conduct would involve a criminal offence, if the facts making it impossible were different, a conspiracy may exist.

16.3.4 Intent to reach the agreement

The *mens rea* of conspiracy requires the defendant to have intended to reach the agreement with the other conspirators. In ***Hedgcock*** **[2007]** the defendant discussed carrying out highly unpleasant sexual and violent acts. The Court of Appeal held that there was insufficient evidence that the defendant intended to reach a "*real*" agreement. Instead, it was probable that the discussions, which contained several false statements by Hedgecock, was a fantasy discussed for the purpose of sexual gratification.

The defendant's motivations are not relevant when determining whether they intended the agreement to be reached. In ***Yip Chiu-Cheung* [1995]** one of the conspirators was, in fact, an undercover police officer who had entered into the agreement to further his objective of exposing the criminal enterprise. This did not prevent the undercover officer from being a co-conspirator.

16.3.5 Intent that the agreement will be carried out and the offence committed

It is also necessary for the defendant to intend for the agreement to be put into effect and the offence to be carried out. In ***McPhillips* [1989]** the defendant agreed with others to plant a bomb but, unbeknownst to his accomplices, intended to give a warning so that the bomb did not kill anyone. The defendant was guilty of conspiring to cause an explosion contrary to the **Explosive Substances Act 1883** but not guilty of conspiracy to commit murder.

Reflective question

Henry and Thomas discuss a plan for Thomas to kill Henry's husband, Carl, when out drinking one evening. The next day, Thomas orders a weapon on the internet thinking the plan will go ahead the following day. Henry, however, raised the suggestion in jest and did not plan for the murder to actually happen. Consider Thomas and Henry's liability for conspiracy to commit murder.

It is not necessary for a defendant to intend to play an active role in whatever is agreed or for the defendant to have a stake in the offence succeeding (***Siracusa* (1990)**). In ***Anderson* (1985)**, the House of Lords gives a pertinent example of this issue:

> *"The proprietor of a car hire firm **agrees for a substantial payment to make available a hire car to a gang for use in a robbery** and to make false entries in his books relating to the hiring to which he can point if the number of the car is traced back to him in connection with the robbery. **Being fully aware of the circumstances of the robbery in which the car is proposed to be used he is plainly a party to the conspiracy to rob**. Making his car available for use in the robbery is as much a part of the relevant agreed course of conduct as the robbery itself. Yet, once he has been paid, **it will be a matter of complete indifference to him whether the robbery is in fact committed or not**. In these days of highly organised crime the most serious statutory conspiracies will frequently involve an elaborate and complex agreed course of conduct in*

which many will consent to play necessary but subordinate roles, not involving them in any direct participation in the commission of the offence or offences at the centre of the conspiracy. ***Parliament cannot have intended that such parties should escape conviction of conspiracy on the basis that it cannot be proved against them that they intended that the relevant offence or offences should be committed.****"*[3]

In order to demonstrate that a defendant intended the offence to be committed, it is also necessary to demonstrate that the defendant had knowledge of any circumstances that are required for the commission of the substantive offence (**s1(2) CLA 1977**). It is not sufficient that a defendant is reckless, negligent or suspicious that those circumstances exist, only actual knowledge will suffice (***Saik* [2006]**).

Where, for example, a defendant is charged with conspiracy to convert criminal property – where the substantive offence is committed if the defendant has knowledge or suspicion that the property is criminal property – the defendant would need actual knowledge that the property was criminal property for a conspiracy to arise (***Pace* [2014]**).

This applies even in cases involving substantive offences of strict liability. For example, it is an offence to wear or carry an emblem which reasonably suggests support for a prescribed terrorist organisation under **s13 Terrorism Act 2000** even where the defendant has no knowledge this suggestion is being made (***Pwr v DPP* [2020]**). However, a defendant could not conspire to commit this offence without knowledge that the emblem would cause a reasonable suspicion of support.

Further reading

Conspiracy and withdrawal

The offence of conspiracy occurs at the point at which an agreement is reached with the necessary intent. A defendant who then withdraws their agreement before the commission of the offence is still guilty of the original conspiracy, although they would not be liable for any courses of action which were only agreed among the remaining conspirators after they had withdrawn. For a critique of this position and argument that the law should incentivise conspirators to withdraw, consider reading:

Claire de Than and Jesse Elvin, "Towards a Rational Reconstruction of the Law on Secondary Participation and Inchoate Offences: Conspiracy" in Alan Reed and Michael Bohlander (eds) *Participation in Crime: Domestic and Comparative Perspectives* (Routledge 2013)

3 Anderson (1985) 81 Cr App R 253, 258-259 (emphasis added)

16.3.6 Common law conspiracy

Prior to the **CLA 1977** conspiracy was an offence at common law. The common law offence was abolished, other than where preserved by **s5(2)–(3).** The only remaining common law conspiracy offences are:

- Conspiracy to defraud
- Conspiracy to corrupt public morals or outrange public decency.

Conspiracy to defraud at common law is distinct from offences under the **Fraud Act 2006.** It captures situations where the conspirators agree dishonestly to injure the economic rights of the victim, with no need for this to arise from a deception, or situations where the conspirators agree to mislead the victim intending them to act contrary to their duty. (***Evans and Others* [2014]**). In both cases, evidence of dishonesty beyond mere secretive and deceptive behaviour will be necessary for actions to amount to a conspiracy to defraud (***Goldshield* [2009]**).

Conspiracy to corrupt public morals or outrage public decency has a long established history dating back to 19th century case law (see ***Hamilton* [2007]**). It appears that the corruption of public morals need not amount to a criminal offence in itself. In ***Knuller v DPP* [1973]** a magazine providing a dating column for homosexual men was deemed capable of constituting a conspiracy to corrupt or outrage, although this specific example would be highly unlikely to amount to an offence today.

16.4 Assisting or encouraging

The offences of assisting or encouraging the commission of an offence are a further form of inchoate secondary liability. These forms of liability were introduced by the **Serious Crime Act 2007** in response to the belief that the relationship between participatory and inchoate offences was beset with "uncertainty and incoherence".[4] In particular, the earlier law did not create liability where a defendant assisted a principal offender who "did not go on" to commit the offence.[5]

The government of the day introduced these offences as part of the **SCA 2007** on the basis that these forms of liability were "particularly important in relation to organised crime where the relationships between those involved in offences are more complex and key players often go to great lengths to distance themselves from the actual commission of offences they have encouraged or assisted".[6] However, the offences themselves are not limited to situations involving organised crime.

---

4 Law Commission, *Participating in Crime* (Law Com No 305, Cm 7084 2007) para 1.12

5 Law Commission, *Participating in Crime* (Law Com No 305, Cm 7084 2007) para 1.41

6 Home Office, *New Powers Against Organised and Financial Crime* (Cm 6875, 2006) 24

16.4.1 Intentionally encouraging or assisting an offence

The offence of intentionally encouraging or assisting an offence provides a framework for all three of the offences discussed in this section. It is set out in **s44 SCA 2007** and requires:

- *An Act*
- *Which is capable of encouraging or assisting the commission of an offence*
- *Intent by the defendant to encourage or assist the commission of the offence.*

Although **s44** speaks specifically of a defendant committing *an act*, a defendant may be liable for a failure to act where they are under a duty to do so (**s65(2)(b)**) or where the defendant's actions are a broader course of conduct (**s67**).

There is limited guidance on the meaning of assistance or encouragement, and it has been commented that the wording of the legislation is broad in scope (***Mustafa* [2019]**). **SCA 2007** explains that encouragement can take the form of threats or other forms of pressure on the would-be principal offender (**s65(1)**) as well as encouragement or assistance which is welcomed by the principal. Similarly, the act makes clear that assistance can take the form of "steps to reduce the possibility of criminal proceedings" (**s65(2)(1)**).

However, the examples given by the legislation are not exclusive and whether an act can assist or encourage will depend upon an analysis of the facts of a given case. In ***Sadique* [2013]** the defendant had been involved in the supply of chemicals which could be used to "cut" controlled drugs. As the "*chemicals were capable of misuse by others to commit offences of supplying or being concerned in the supply*" of drugs, the defendant's actions in distributing the chemicals could constitute an offence, subject to *mens rea* requirements. The fact that the chemicals could also be used for other purposes did not prevent the defendant's actions being capable of assisting or encouraging an offence.[7]

In the News

Encouraging or assisting self-harm

Under provisions in **s184 Online Harms Act 2023** it is a specific offence to assist or encourage self-harm through electronic or digital communication. These provisions recently came into force in Scotland, using the approach already in force in England and Wales:

PA Media, "Up to five years in prison for self-harm threats under new Scots law" *STV News* (31 January 2024)

7 Omar Sadique v R [2013]

The defendant's act needs not actually encourage or assist an offence (**s49(1)**) and there is no need for the principal offender to be aware of the defendant's assistance or encouragement. Case law on the sentencing of those convicted of assistance and encouragement offences acknowledges that there are different degrees of assistance or encouragement which may be given (***Wood* [2019]**), although the extent of the defendant's assistance or encouragement does not affect whether they are guilty of the offence.

The *mens rea* of **s44** requires the defendant to have intended to encourage or assist the commission of an offence. This intent can be inferred where the defendant intends to assist or encourage *the doing of an act which would amount to the commission of that offence* (**s47(2)**). However, foresight that an act would assist or encourage an offence is not sufficient, an intent to assist or encourage must be demonstrated (**s44(2)**). The defendant need not know or intend that what they assist or encourage is a criminal offence, although they must believe or be reckless regarding any fault or circumstances required for the commission of the substantive offence (**s47(5)**).

Further reading

Sentencing assistance and encouragement of an offence

The sentencing of offenders convicted of encouragement or assistance offences is set out in **s58 SCA 2007**. The maximum sentence is the same as the maximum for the offence which has been assisted or encouraged by the defendant's act and judges use the same sentencing guidelines as that offence. A number of cases have been required to explore the implications of this approach in unusual circumstances, such as where the defendant was a practicing barrister or serving police officer at the time they encouraged the principal offender. Consider reading:

***R v Reeve (Kerry)* [2018]**

***R v Henry Hendron* [2024]**

16.4.2 Encouraging or assisting an offence in the belief it will be committed

Encouraging or assisting an offence in the belief it will be committed is set out in **s45 SCA 2007** and replicates the same *actus reus* requirements as the **s44** offence requiring *(1) an act which (2) is capable of assisting or encouraging the commission of an offence.*

The distinction between the two offences is found in the *mens rea*. Whilst the **s44** offence requires an intention to assist or encourage, **s45** instead requires the defendant to believe both (1) that the offence will be committed and (2) that their actions will encourage or assist this. A defendant who believes only that the offence may be committed or that their actions may encourage or assist will not be guilty of a **s45** offence (***Watling* [2012]**), although liability could arise under **s44** or **s46**.

Where an offence is ongoing, the defendant may be liable to encouraging or assisting it in the belief that it will continue to be committed. In ***Scott v DPP* [2022]** the defendant made numerous phone calls and texts to a prisoner at HMP Bristol who was in possession of an unauthorised mobile phone. The defendant was guilty on the basis that their actions encouraged the continuation of an ongoing offence. It would not be an offence to encourage an offence which had already taken place, such as where a defendant speaks approvingly of an offence which has concluded, unless this encouraged the assistance of further offences.

Further reading

Belief and recklessness

The different forms of *mens rea* used in the offences of assisting and encouraging within the **Serious Crime Act 2007** has been critiqued in academic commentary. Consider reading:

J J Child, "Exploring the Mens Rea Requirements of the Serious Crime Act 2007 Assisting and Encouraging Offences" (2012) *76(3) Journal of Criminal Law 220*

16.4.3 Encouraging or assisting offences believing one or more will be committed

Whilst **ss44–45** require the defendant to have assisted or encouraged the commission of a specific offence, **s46** addresses situations where the defendant's act has encouraged or assisted the commission of a range of different offences. It is important to note that this assistance or encouragement should stem from a single act or a course of conduct. A defendant who has committed several unrelated acts of assistance or encouragement would more likely be charged with multiple **ss44–46** offences.

The *actus reus* of the offence is broadly similar to **ss44–45** although with the requirement that the act assist or encourage *one or more of a number of offences* (**s46(1)**). As an example, in the first major appeal addressing **s46**, one defendant had made a Facebook group called "Smash down in Northwick Town" during the time of widespread rioting in 2011 and was convicted on the basis that this was capable of encouraging riot, burglary and/or criminal damage (***Blackshaw* [2011]**). The charge sheet should specify the number of offences (**s46(3)**) and failure to mention an offence within the charge sheet prevents a defendant from being convicted on the basis that they assisted or encouraged that specific offence (***Sadique* [2011]**).

The *mens rea* of **s46** is broadly similar with that of **s45**, focusing on a belief that one of a number of offences *will* be committed (***Atkinson* [2020]**). A defendant does not need to have a specific belief as to which of many offences will be committed, provided be believes that at least one of them will.[8] In ***Rowlands* [2019]** the defendant supplied drug dealers with a substance which could be used to "cut" cocaine and other controlled substances. This was capable of assisting the commission of offences related to the supply of drugs, despite the defendant not knowing which specific controlled drugs these were.

16.4.4 The defence of acting reasonably

A statutory defence exists under **s50 SCA 2007** to offences under **ss44–46** where a defendant acts reasonably in light of circumstances they know or reasonably believe to be true. The defendant's actions must be objectively reasonable, which **s50(3)** is to be assessed taking into account:

> *"(a) the seriousness of the anticipated offence (or, in the case of an offence under section 46, the offences specified in the indictment;*
>
> *(b) any purpose for which [the defendant] claims to have been acting;*
>
> *(c) any authority by which he claims to have been acting.*

Recently, **s50A SCA 2007** was inserted by the **National Security Act 2023** creating a comparable provision which applies to UK defence and intelligence forces in limited situations involving acts or offences outside of England and Wales.

16.5 Evaluation and reform

Looking at the different offences discussed in this chapter, as well as the participation offences discussed in **Chapter 15**, reveals the complexity of the law involving inchoate crimes committed by multiple defendants. The operation of the law in this area is made even more complex by practical considerations, such as whether there is sufficient evidence to charge defendants with the substantive offence where this

8 Indeed, where a defendant does have a specific belief, a **s46** charge would likely be inappropriate: Omar Sadique v R [2013].

has been committed.[9] In addition to offences of conspiracy, an offence under the **Criminal Law Act 1977**, and attempts, under the **Criminal Attempts Act 1981**, the law on inchoate liability was amended significantly by the creation of offences in **ss44–46 Serious Crime Act 2007**.

However, **SCA 2007** offences, in particular, have been criticised for being "some of the most convoluted offences in decades" demonstrating "excessive complexity" and liability which is "too broad and creates an unwarranted incoherence".[10] One particular point of confusion has been the relationship between the different offences, in particular the relationship of **s46** to the offences under **ss44–45**. In ***Sadique* [2013]**, the Court of Appeal went to lengths to stress:

> *"As we have already explained, the 2007 Act created three distinct offences. It is not open to the court to set one or other of them aside and the legislation must be interpreted to give effect to the creation by statute of the three offences. It may well be that the common law offence of inciting someone else to commit an offence was less complex. It may equally be that the purpose of the legislation could have been achieved in less tortuous fashion. Nevertheless these three distinct offences were created by the 2007 Act, with none taking priority over the other two. S.46 creates the offence of encouraging or assisting the commission of one or more offences. Its specific ingredients and the subsequent legislative provisions underline that an indictment charging a s.46 offence of encouraging one or more offences is permissible."*[11]

As Storey notes, few **SCA 2007** cases have raised appeals on substantive law, with most addressing sentencing considerations.[12] However, more broadly, the gradual development of the law on inchoate offences over many years, through a combination of case law and statutory reform, means that some aspects of the law discussed in this chapter, as well as the law on participation discussed in **Chapter 15**, are inconsistent. For example, the defence of acting reasonably which applies to offences of assisting or encouraging under **SCA 2007** does not apply to the offence of conspiracy under **CLA 1977**. The Law Commission have pointed out that this discrepancy is undesirable and have advocated that the decision in ***Yip Chiu-Cheung* [1995]** be overturned by legislation, to enable those acting reasonably to prevent crime to claim a defence to conspiracy charges.[13]

---

9 See, Law Commission, *Conspiracy and Attempts* (Law Com No 318, HC 41 2009) Para 164

10 David Ormerod and Rudi Fortson, 'Serious Crime Act 2007: the Part 2 offences' [2009] Criminal Law Review 389, 389

11 Omar Sadique v R [2013]

12 Tony Storey. 'Encouraging the Continuation of a Pre-Existing Offence Under the Serious Crime Act 2007: Scott v DPP [2022] EWHC 91; [2022] 1 WLR 2231, Divisional Court' (2022) 86(6) Journal of Criminal Law 496

13 Law Commission, *Participating in Crime* (Law Com No 305, Cm 7084 2007) Para 5.22

Arguments also exist about the labelling of offenders who commit inchoate offences,[14] particularly those of assistance and encouragement, and whether there is sufficient differentiation between different forms of encouragement or assistance within "sentencing tariffs or label[s]".[15] The complexity of the **ss44–46** provisions appears to further complicate these arguments. The different forms of *mens rea* within and across the offences may make it challenging for a jury to determine whether a specific offence has been committed,[16] impacting which labels can be applied to offenders who assist or encourage.[17]

The uncertainty this discussion demonstrates makes the law open to criticism on the basis that it undermines a defendant's right to legal certainty under **Art 7 ECHR**. In ***Sadique* [2011]** the defendant unsuccessfully argued that **s46** was "*too vague and uncertain*". However, the court's decision that **s46** was not vague or uncertain may be criticised, given that the interpretation of **s46** in ***Sadique* [2011]** was considered flawed by the same court in ***Sadique* [2013]**.

In 2013, the Justice Committee looked at the introduction of **SCA 2007** offences of assisting and encouraging and whether this had achieved the government's objective of making the law sufficient, as well as practical and clear, in scope. Submissions to the work of the committee "suggested the need for a complete repeal and replacement" of the new offences.[18] The committee note the original proposals put forward by the Law Commission, arguably significantly less complex than the eventual legislation, which were:

> Law Commission (2007) *Draft Participating in Crime Bill*:
>
> "(1) Where a person (P) has committed an offence, another person (D) is also guilty of the offence if—
>
> (a) *D did an act with the intention that one or more of a number of other acts would be done by another person,*
>
> (b) *P's criminal act was one of those acts,*
>
> (c) *D's behaviour assisted or encouraged P to do his criminal act, and*
>
> (d) *subsection (2) or (3) is satisfied.*

---

14 See, generally, James Chalmers and Fiona Laverick, 'Fair Labelling in Criminal Law' (2008) 71 Modern Law Review 217

15 Dennis J Baker, 'Complicity, Proportionality and the Serious Crime Act' (2011) 14(3) New Criminal Law Review 403, 404

16 Justice Committee, *Post-legislative scrutiny of Part 2 (Encouraging or assisting crime) of the Serious Crime Act 2007* (HC 639 2013) 8

17 Dennis J Baker, 'Complicity, Proportionality and the Serious Crime Act' (2011) 14(3) New Criminal Law Review 403, 419

18 Justice Committee, *Post-legislative scrutiny of Part 2 (Encouraging or assisting crime) of the Serious Crime Act 2007* (HC 639 2013) 9

> (2) *This subsection is satisfied if D believed that a person doing the act would commit the offence.*
>
> (3) *This subsection is satisfied if D's state of mind was such that had he done the act he would have committed the offence.*[19]

Whilst these proposals were amended as the legislation which became **SCA 2007** passed through Parliament, they continue to offer a modified approach to the issue of inchoate secondary liability. Although there have been some welcome clarifications in recent years, including ***Rowlands* [2019]** and ***Atkinson* [2020]**, it is clear that further developments to the law in this area are needed to give sufficient certainty and clarity on inchoate liability.

16.6 Summary

This chapter has explored situations where a defendant may be liable without a substantive offence actually taking place. The key points to take away from this chapter are:

- Where a defendant has taken steps which are "more than merely preparatory" for the commission of a substantive offence, they may be liable for attempt under **s1 Criminal Attempts Act 1981**.
- In situations involving more than one defendant, where there is an agreement that an offence will be committed by at least one defendant, all those who are involved in the agreement may be liable for conspiracy, an offence under **s1 Criminal Law Act 1977**.
- Whilst the offence of attempt will require some action on the part of the defendant(s) towards the commission of the offence; this can be distinguished from conspiracy which is committed at the point at which an agreement is reached with the intention that it be carried out.
- Where a defendant encourages or assists another to commit an offence, they may be liable to an offence under **Part 2 Serious Crime Act 2007**. Unlike participatory liability, discussed in **Chapter 14**, liability under **SCA 2007** does not require the principal to have committed the substantive offence.
- Liability for assisting and encouraging can arise where the defendant intends to assist or encourage a specific offence (**s44**), assists or encourages an offence believing it will be committed (**s45**) or assists or encourages one of several offences believing at least one will be committed (**s46**).
- The offences under **ss44–46 SCA 2007**, in particular, have been criticised for being unclear and many have proposed that they be significantly reformed.

---

19 Law Commission, *Participating in Crime* (Law Com No 305, Cm 7084 2007) 157

Further reading

J J Child, "Defense of a Basic Voluntary Act Requirement in Criminal Law from Philosophies of Action" (2020) *23(4) New Criminal Law Review 437*

Hannah Wishart, "Criminal culpability, criminal attempts and the erosion of choice theory" (2013) *77(1) Journal of Criminal Law 78*

J J Child, "Exploring the Mens Rea Requirements of the Serious Crime Act 2007 Assisting and Encouraging Offences" (2012) *76(3) Journal of Criminal Law 220*

David Ormerod and Rudi Fortson, "Serious Crime Act 2007: the Part 2 offences" [2009] *Criminal Law Review 389*

Christopher M. V. Clarkson, "Conduct Requirement in Attempts" (2009) *29(1) Oxford Journal of Legal Studies 25.*

Index